THE VARIED SOCIOLOGY OF PAUL F. LAZARSFELD

PAUL F. LAZARSFELD

1962

THE VARIED SOCIOLOGY

OF

PAUL F. LAZARSFELD

Writings Collected and Edited by
PATRICIA L. KENDALL

COLUMBIA UNIVERSITY PRESS
New York   1982

Library of Congress Cataloging in Publication Data

Lazarsfeld, Paul Felix.
The varied sociology of Paul F. Lazarsfeld.

"Selected Bibliography of the works of Paul F.
Lazarsfeld": p.
Bibliography: p.
Includes indexes.
1. Sociology.   2. Sociology—Methodology.
3. Sociology—Statistical methods.   4. Social
sciences—Research.   I. Kendall, Patricia L.
II. Title.

HM24.L364	301	81-24205
ISBN 0-231-05122-0 (cloth)		AACR2
ISBN 0-231-05123-9 (paper)		

Columbia University Press
New York *and* Guildford, Surrey

Copyright © 1982 Columbia University Press
All rights reserved
Printed in the United States of America

Contents

Foreword

This collection presents examples of the diverse topics which occupied the attention of Paul F. Lazarsfeld during his half-century of teaching, research, and writing. I have selected articles that, first, illustrate the scope of Lazarsfeld's concerns, although they do not exhaust them. A second principle has also guided the selection: to make available articles that originally appeared in books or journals of only limited circulation. Some articles, therefore, of obvious importance in Lazarsfeld's work, were omitted since they are readily available in other sources. But even within these boundaries, the process of selection has been difficult. The initial selections would have resulted in a book of some 900 pages, clearly a practical and financial impossibility. Choices had to be made: to retain one relatively long article I had to sacrifice several others that were shorter.

I decided to divide the book into three sections which best characterize Lazarsfeld's chief interests: (1) articles with a historical orientation; (2) articles dealing with methodological problems; and (3) articles concerned with applications of qualitative and quantitative methods. The lines between these categories are not always distinct; in some cases, articles that were placed in one section might reasonably have been placed in another. But these groupings nevertheless represent distinct foci of Lazarsfeld's thought, and help one organize his papers for republication. References in the articles to works in progress, "recent" research, or academic affiliation have not been updated; similarly, the term Negro has been retained throughout.

Historical Orientation

Those not thoroughly familiar with Lazarsfeld's work may be surprised at the extent to which a historical interest permeated his writings. We include here three articles in which this historical element is especially pronounced.

The first article, "An Episode in the History of Social Research," is the most clear-cut piece of autobiography that Lazarsfeld ever wrote. While there are autobiographical allusions in several of his articles, this, in his own words, was a memoir. First published in 1968, it was one of a series of chapters in a book on the intellectual migration from Europe to America between 1930 and 1960; the editors of the volume were two historians. In his contribution, Lazarsfeld traces the intellectual influences to which he was exposed from his late adolescence through his experiences as a student at the University of Vienna during the post–World War I period. He then outlines his career, first as an instructor in a *Gymnasium* in Vienna, then as an assistant to the psychologists Karl and Charlotte Bühler in the university. Under their sponsorship, he created a research bureau, the first of several that he would eventually found. His activities in that institute brought him to the attention of the Rockefeller Foundation, which invited him to come to the United States for two years of study and travel. Lazarsfeld then traces his odyssey from the University of Newark to Princeton to Columbia, culminating in 1945 with the recommendation of an external university committee that the Bureau of Applied Social Research receive some support from the Columbia administration.

The second article in this section, "The Obligations of the 1950 Pollster to the 1984 Historian," treats history in a forward-looking manner. As its title suggests, it is concerned with the research that must be done in the present to satisfy the needs of historians writing in the future. Lazarsfeld supports his argument by citing historians and others whose hypotheses about past situations might have been bolstered had research findings regarding contemporary attitudes been available.

Two aspects of this article are worthy of particular mention. One concerns the selection of 1984 as the reference point for the future. Lazarsfeld makes quite clear that in part he had in mind the Orwellian notion that, in a dictatorship, history is continually revised in the light of present political considerations.

Second, although no polling organization responded directly to Lazarsfeld's challenge of 1950, research begun during the late 1960s and early 1970s started to provide the kind of data he had in mind. For example, in 1967 the Department of Labor embarked on a large-scale longitudinal study of occupational and educational histories which is continuing to this day. Almost simultaneously the National Opinion Research Center of the University of Chicago began an annual social survey which covered a wide variety of factual and attitudinal issues: educational and occupational histories of parents and self, work satisfaction, fears about the encroachment of government on individual liberties, attitudes on controversial issues such as abortion, experiences and fears of becoming a victim of crime, and much more. The data from these surveys are available to anyone willing to pay the costs of the computer tapes on which the information is stored.

Moreover, as early as 1946, Elmo Roper, then president of a prominent polling organization, established the Roper Center in Williamstown, Massachusetts, a repository for survey data collected by many academic and commercial institutions. It is likely that at least some of the information stored in the center during the thirty-five years of its existence would be relevant to the needs oulined by Lazarsfeld in his article.

The third article in this section is quite different from the first two. Unlike the personal recollections of the memoir and the forward looking challenge to pollsters of the 1950s, "Notes on the History of Quantification in Sociology" is, as its title suggests, a straightforward and well-documented history of the development of quantitative methods—in Germany, France, Belgium, and Great Britain—beginning in the eighteenth century. This paper is unique in one important respect: unlike most of Lazarsfeld's writing, it is based on extensive use of archival data. The style of this article is that of orthodox history.[1]

The Logic of Methods (Methodology)

The papers in this second section deal with the logic of different sociological methods. The first article, "Problems in Methodology," was written in response to an invitation extended by the committee planning the program for the 1957 meetings of the American Sociological Association. In it Lazarsfeld considers the "major themes" which occupied methodologists of the mid-1950s. These include the location of topics, the clarification of terms, the explication of research techniques, and so forth. He then moves on to two methodological problems in which he was particularly interested. The first is the formation of concepts; here Lazarsfeld traces the various stages involved in the development of sociological concepts. He then considers problems of multivariate analysis. Under this heading he spells out the logic of conditional relationships and contextual analysis, providing examples to illustrate his exposition. The article ends with a consideration of the kinds of multivariate analysis made possible by panel techniques.

Lazarsfeld is most often identified as a pioneer in the field of quantitative analysis. His well-known "elaboration paradigm," described in the second of the methodological papers, made its debut in an oral presentation at the 1946 meetings of the American Sociological Association. "The Interpretation of Statistical Relations as a Research Operation" is the written version of that talk.[2] In this article he shows how the nature of the relationship between two variables can be clarified by the introduction of a third. This form of multivariate analysis was subsequently developed further by several of Lazarsfeld's former students.[3]

The final article in this section, "On the Relation Between Individual and Collective Properties" (with Herbert Menzel), deals with a methodological issue which has become prominent in the last few decades. Increasingly, the units of analysis in social research are collectives (hospitals, union locals, colleges, and so on) rather than individuals. It therefore has become important to consider the characteristics of such collectives. Lazarsfeld and his collaborator turn their attention to this issue. They analyze the main properties that refer to collectives and then the corresponding properties that refer to individual members of these collectives.

**Application of
Qualitative and Quantitative Methods**

Just as Lazarsfeld's historical interests will be unfamiliar to many readers not thoroughly acquainted with his work, so will his concern with qualitative data and qualitative analysis. I therefore decided to include one major paper dealing with these themes as a further antidote to the stereotyped views of his work.

This article, "Some Functions of Qualitative Analysis in Social Research" (with Allen Barton), was published in 1955. Although it appeared in a German journal, it was written in English and was made available (for a time) as a reprint of the Bureau of Applied Social Research. To arrive at the several functions of qualitative data, Lazarsfeld and his coauthor examined more than 100 studies based on qualitative data and codified the uses to which these data were put. These uses range from "the construction of descriptive systems" to "suggested relationships" to "matrix formulations" to "support of theory." So far as can be ascertained, systematic analysis of the functions of qualitative data has not advanced measurably beyond those areas during the past quarter-century.

In the second article, "The Use of Panels in Social Research," Lazarsfeld spells out the kinds of questions which can be answered most effectively by the so-called panel techniques.[4] Although panel studies had been carried out prior to the publication of this article,[5] the unique features of the method had not been fully appreciated. Lazarsfeld's contribution here was preliminary systematization of the technique.[6]

The final article in the collection, "Friendship As Social Process: A Substantive and Methodological Analysis," represents one of the most fruitful collaborations between Lazarsfeld and Robert K. Merton. For this reason, if for no other, it is appropriate to include it in this volume.[7] The article has three parts. In the first, Merton draws on a study of residents in two housing projects which he and his collaborators were engaged in analyzing. As the title of the article suggests, he is concerned with the processes involved in the formation, maintenance, and dissolution of friendships among residents. In the second part of the article, Lazarsfeld undertakes a formalization of the processes which Merton had suggested. He indicates, through hypothetical figures from a hypothetical panel study, the findings that would have supported Merton's speculations. In the final section, Merton articulates the several contributions that the formal analysis made to the substantive theorizing.

It should be noted that all three articles in this final section might have been placed in the section on methodology. (The last even has the word "methodological" in its title.) To have done this, however, would have resulted in a large, seemingly undifferentiated grouping of papers, and there are in fact significant differences in emphasis. It seemed useful to distinguish among papers which deal with the *application* of particular methods, included here, and those which analyze the *logic* of methods, placed in the second section.[8]

As was indicated at the outset, the three parts into which this volume is divided, and the papers included in them, do not exhaust the areas in which Lazarsfeld was interested and in which he worked. Two fields which do not find a place here are applied sociology and mathematical sociology, more particularly latent structure analysis and the algebra of dichotomies.

Lazarsfeld's concern with applied social research reaches back as far as work in the Vienna Institute and was as recent as his last publications.[9] In between, he exercised his prerogative as president of the American Sociological Association to organize the program of the 1962 meetings around the theme of "the uses of sociology"; out of this grew a lengthy volume with that title.

The basic outlines of latent structure analysis were worked out by Lazarsfeld in 1946, and were refined over the next 20 years.[10] His interest in the algebra of dichotomies developed probably as a result of his work in latent structure analysis.[11] He became increasingly preoccupied with it and turned to it whenever he had a spare moment. Thus, the outsides of folders, the backs of letters—whatever writing surface was available— were filled with matrixes of probabilities. In his more reflective moments, Lazarsfeld said that, when he retired, he would spend his time with his p_{123}s and his $\bar{p}_{12}$s. It is a pity that that time never came.

New York   Patricia L. Kendall
September 1981

Acknowledgments

I am indebted to several people who helped me assemble this book.

First of all, I owe a special debt of gratitude to John Moore, director of Columbia University Press, who suggested that the press would be interested in publishing a selection of Lazarsfeld's papers. I do not think he had any idea, when he made this suggestion, that it would take as long as it has to submit a final manuscript. Putting all the pieces together involved the making and remaking of numerous decisions, and this was a lengthy process. Throughout I have been helped by his patience.

As he has at critical points in the past, Robert K. Merton, University Professor Emeritus and Special Service Professor at Columbia University, came to my assistance when I needed it most. He helped me select from the many articles that might have been included. Moreover, he suggested an organizing principle for the collection.

I am also indebted to Bernard Bailyn, Adams University Professor at Harvard University, and to Professor David Caplovitz of the Graduate School of the City University of New York. They made useful editorial suggestions regarding the foreword that I had drafted. As a result of their help, it is now a smoother and more informative piece.

Thomas Gorman undertook the construction of the indexes with enthusiasm happily guided by intelligence. As a result, they will help the reader trace continuities in that part of Lazarsfeld's work represented in this volume.

Finally, I am indebted to Kathleen McCarthy who led me step by step through the intricacies involved in producing a book for Columbia University Press. Although I must have seemed to her a very slow learner, I think that, in the end, I finally caught on.

Introduction

JAMES S. COLEMAN

Paul Lazarsfeld was one of those rare sociologists who shaped the direction of the discipline for the succeeding generation. It is this that gives the key to the fascination that Lazarfeld's life and work holds for many sociologists, for they know, or are at least dimly aware, that had it not been for Lazarsfeld, they might have been pursuing quite different directions in sociology, and pursuing them in a different manner. Here, too, is the key to the hostility that some sociologists felt toward him (in particular, those sociologists engaged in scholarly, nonempirical, social philosophy in the European tradition). They saw a discipline being captured, taken away from them, moved in directions they neither liked nor had the skills to pursue.

Because of the strength of Lazarsfeld's personality, it is difficult for those who practiced sociology contemporaneously with Lazarsfeld to view his work apart from his person. It is useful to remind ourselves of the ways in which Lazarsfeld changed the direction of sociology. There are six specific ways that seem to me most important: the transformation of opinion polling into survey research; the initiation of survey panel methods; the initiation of systematic audience, mass communications, and market research; the initiation of survey methods in the study of political sociology; the development of modern mathematical sociology; and the invention of university-based organizations for large-scale applied social research.

1. Lazarsfeld was of major importance in transforming public opinion polling methods into survey analysis, that is, into the analytical use

1

of sample surveys to draw inferences about causal relations that affect the actions of individuals. It is difficult to imagine sociology without such analysis (which has been extensively developed in recent years through the extra power that computers provide), but before Lazarsfeld and a few others carried out the transformation, this methodological tool central to empirical research in sociology was nonexistent. Here the impact of Lazarsfeld resides as much in the examples he provides in papers which make substantive contributions to audience research, voting behavior, and other areas as in formal methodological papers. Still, one methodological paper was of particular importance. This is a paper he wrote with Patricia Kendall in 1950 that attempted to codify the new directions that he had been taking, showing analytical methods for identifying spurious relations and intervening variables.[1] This work has been carried considerably further and integrated into the main body of statistical analyses, first by Herbert Simon and H. M. Blalock and subsequently by others.[2]

2. He pioneered in the use of survey panel methods, that is, the further transformation of public opinion polling beyond cross-sectional surveys into panels involving two or more interviews of the same sample, or "panel". The introduction of panels allowed Lazarsfeld to pose a central question, which is even now not satisfactorily answered: How can panel data be used to draw inferences about the effects of various attitudes and actions on one another? The problems that Lazarsfeld posed, both in panel analysis generally and in his well-known "sixteenfold table" problem (which asks about the "mutual effects"—as Lazarsfeld termed it—of two attributes on each other), are among the most enduring in sociological methodology. The problems have spawned literally hundreds of publications, ranging from those in which the term "cross-lagged correlations" appears somewhere in the title to Leo Goodman's use of log-linear models to address the causal problems posed by panel data.[3] A considerable part of my own methodological work has been directed to this class of problems posed by Lazarsfeld.[4]

3. One of the principal initiators of audience research and mass communications research generally, Lazarsfeld was a major force in shaping the fledgling market research industry. And because he was one of the few persons in an academic center to carry out audience and market research (and because, being at Columbia, he was in New York), he populated this infant industry with persons who had worked under him at the Columbia University Bureau of Applied Social Research—some who obtained the Ph.D. others who never did. I should remark in passing that there are many in sociology who ignore or disdain work in market research. They so so at the peril of missing new ideas. Ever since the development of the La-

zarsfeld-Stanton program analyzer and the panel-analysis problem, the field of market research has been the source of both prototypical problems and innovations of technique. In the thirties and forties, it was comparable to policy research today. Business then, and government now, brought problems that helped invigorate the discipline. Market research has since largely left the academy, with a loss to both it and the academy, and it seems probable that policy research will do so as well, spawning as before a new industry, but at a loss to both the social sciences and policy research.[5]

4. First with the 1940 "Sandusky Study," to use Lazarsfeld's shoptalk title,[6] and then with the 1948 "Elmira Study,"[7] Lazarsfeld initiated the methods that have come to dominate the empirical analysis of voting behavior, both in sociology and in political science. For those who carry out studies of the determinants of voting behavior today as a matter of course, it may seem natural that such work be pervasive in political sociology. But until Lazarsfeld's voting studies, such an assumption could hardly be made. Work in political behavior was based on analyses of election outcomes and of different results in different voting districts. It was Lazarsfeld who opened up this area of behavior to sample surveys.

5. Lazarsfeld was one of the "founders" of modern mathematical sociology. Although there have been attempts to apply mathematics to sociology since its inception, only in the 1950s did there come to be extensive growth and development, leading this mode of work to become an established part of the discipline. Lazarsfeld was of major importance to this development in a variety of ways: through his own work on latent structure analysis, through his teaching, through a lecture series at Columbia that resulted in 1953 in *Mathematical Thinking in the Social Sciences,* through the Behavioral Models Project at the Columbia University Bureau of Applied Social Research (in which Duncan Luce, Howard Raiffa, Theodore Anderson, Gerald Thompson, Lee Wiggins, and others took sustained part), and in still other ways. At that time, there were several attempts to use mathematics seriously for the study of social behavior. One was by Stuart Dodd, at the University of Washington. Another was by Nicolas Rashevsky, a biophysicist at the University of Chicago. There were others. But of all those then struggling to make headway, Lazarsfeld more than any other made a contribution that has grown and become an intrinsic part of sociological investigation. A major reason, I suspect, was that Lazarsfeld's empirical concerns were as strong as his methodological or formal concerns. His interest was in solving substantive problems, and his use of mathematics was continually guided by this interest.

6. By bringing into being the Columbia University Bureau of Applied Social Research (and before that, similar organizations in Vienna

and at the University of Newark), Lazarsfeld created the prototype of the university-based organization for large-scale social research, a prototype that has been the model for many other research centers, both in the United States and abroad. Such organizations have evolved since Lazarsfeld's model, and it is unclear what future evolution will bring. But Lazarsfeld early conceived the notion of a university social research organization that would carry out projects financed by foundations, business firms, labor unions, and government, and the idea has grown and has been transmuted into the university organizations for policy research, which execute projects largely financed by government.

These ways of transforming the discipline constitute largely methodological and technical innovations rather than substantive ones. My claim in the first paragraph, that Paul Lazarsfeld was instrumental in changing the direction of sociology, may thus seem too strong. Still, the first four of these innovations, and to a lesser extent the fifth and sixth, all contribute to a substantive change of the first order. This is a change in empirical social research, from the study of fixed social structures to the study of individual action.

Lazarsfeld throughout his career asserted that his first interest was in what he called "the empirical analysis of action"—the study of *individual* action—and sample surveys (including panels) became the principal tool. Lazarsfeld's methodological and technical innovations enabled an increasingly large body of sociologists to engage in the empirical study of action.

In the era prior to Lazarsfeld's influence, empirical social research had largely taken the community as the focus of analysis. Lazarsfeld's colleague at Columbia, Robert S. Lynd, pioneered this work with his *Middletown* studies. From the Chicago school, Lloyd Warner and A. B. Hollingshead exemplified it as well with their studies of stratification in American communities (the Yankee City series and *Elmtown's Youth*). There were, in addition, on the borderline between anthropology and sociology, other community studies, such as West's *Plainville, U.S.A.* Some of this research even used sampling methods and systematic interviews for data collection. But the unit being characterized was always the community—not the individuals within it. In some cases, the goal was a description of the stratification system of the community. In others, it was a description of the structure of power and decision making. But always the data from individuals served only as indicators of some aspects of community.

Some of Lazarsfeld's work used a local community as the setting, in keeping with this tradition of research. Before he came to the United States, it was Marienthal; after he came, it was Sandusky, Ohio, and Elmira, New York, for voting studies and Decatur, Illinois, for the study of opinion leadership. But with the sole exception of the Marienthal study, in which the community truly was the unit of analysis, all these studies used the community merely as the setting or context for the empirical analysis of individual action.

Lazarsfeld was interested in why people voted as they did, why they bought what they bought, why they used particular mass media. Most of his methodological work was aimed at answering this kind of question. What he called "reason analysis" was his attempt to dissect expressed motives, as exhibited in his classic paper "The Art of Asking Why,"[8] by using the actor's own explanation of his action. His focus on market research, or "buying decisions," and political sociology, or the study of "voting decisions," showed his intentions clearly. He tried, in the study of attitudes and in the development of latent structure analysis, to model mathematically what goes on inside the individual to make him act as he does. But above all, he led survey research in the direction of analyzing individual action in a social context. Panel analysis was an extension of this.

These same tools in the hands of other, subsequent researchers have led to different questions, but questions of the same *form*: What factors lead to occupational mobility of an individual? What are the determinants of drug use? What factors affect achievement in school or attainment of a high level of education? Answering these questions involves the empirical analysis of individual action. The "outcomes" of interest are at the individual level, not at the level of a collectivity such as a community. This, of course, is not the only direction that sociologists have taken since the 1940s, but it has constituted a major one in empirical sociology.

How did Lazarsfeld come to pursue this direction? How did

this change in direction happen when it did and why has it shown such continuing vitality? Was it the result of nothing more than the strong personalities of Lazarsfeld and other leaders? And why did this change transform the discipline of *sociology*, rather than becoming merely an interesting branch of social psychology?

The Marienthal study certainly exemplified the kind of empirical research that did not analyze individual actions but used them only as indicators of the community's state. Moreover, Lazarsfeld came from Europe, where the scholarly tradition was stronger than the empirical one and where sociological theory emphasized social units above and beyond the individual. Even though Lazarsfeld came from a different European tradition— a social psychological tradition transmitted through the Bühlers' laboratory—he had more intellectual contact with the German scholarly work in sociological theory than did his American contemporaries.

I believe that the transformation in Lazarsfeld's work (for it was a transformation, as a comparison between Marienthal and all his American work shows) arose through a contrast he experienced when he immigrated to America. He was suddenly exposed to a society where closed communities, once like Marienthal, had been pried open by the mass media, resulting in a vast amorphous society in which products seemed to be sold, attitudes seemed to be formed, and individual actions seemed to be shaped, no longer by *interpersonal* communication, but by communication from the mass media to atomistic individuals. One of the most enduring substantive contributions of Lazarsfeld to sociology was to show that the process is not so simple, that interpersonal communication *does* play an important part, that there are opinion leaders and followers, that there is a two-step flow of communication.

In such a society, where the old structures were no longer so binding, encompassing, and powerful, the focus of interest *must* be on individual action. It cannot any longer be the community, treated as an inviolate unit, as a single actor. This does not mean, of course, that social structure is no longer important but only that it cannot be treated as fixed, and sociological analysis cannot be confined to fixed social units but must include both individuals and social structure. I will not argue that the methods used by

Lazarsfeld are the best or even debate whether they are adequate to the task. But I will argue that this substantive direction, the analysis of individual action in a social context, is a mutation in the discipline which occurred more through Paul Lazarsfeld's work than the work of any other.

The change in the discipline followed a similar change in society itself, a change from closed communities like Marienthal to the individualistic society that we know today, characterized by social and geographic mobility. The studies of social stratification in communities of New England and Illinois carried out by Warner and Hollingshead were truly sociological, studies in which the community was the unit of analysis. But what made them anachronistic shortly after their publication was the radical change in American society that began just before the Second World War and accelerated after it and the similar change in European society some years later. Stratification systems of communities lost their compelling quality, both because greatly increased segmentation of life roles allowed escape from an oppressive environment, and because, first in the United States and then elsewhere in the West, emigration from the community became such an easy and attractive alternative. The society changed from one in which the relevant units of analysis were geographic communities to one in which they were no longer so. It may be that the reason neither the American critics of Lazarsfeld's "abstracted empiricism" nor the European critics of Lazarsfeld's "American sociology" could recognize this change in society and reflect it in their work is that neither experienced the abrupt change of setting that Lazarsfeld did. In 1931 he was observing the closed community of Marienthal, a community with many links to its feudal origins; in 1933 he was in New York, the center of the mass communications industry that, more than ever before, was helping to transform life throughout America. The critics may not have liked Lazarsfeld's way of studying this more amorphous social structure; but it was certainly more appropriate than their methods that assumed the fixity of structures that were dissolving—and they had no alternatives to offer.[9]

The power of the social changes that broke apart fixed communities and made individual action an appropriate focus of analysis is part of the reason behind the transformation of *sociology* as a discipline. But in part the change was also a result of the intense dialogue that developed in the Columbia Sociology Department between Lazarsfeld's ideas and Robert Merton's ideas. Merton's were unarguably in the mainstream of contemporaneous sociology, and their encounter with Lazarsfeld's helped focus attention on the directions of work taking place at Columbia. Confronted by the Lazarsfeld–Merton combination and the social changes themselves, the discipline was inevitably led to concentrate on the empirical analysis of individual action.

The essays in this book constitute a tiny fraction of Paul Lazarsfeld's total output as a sociologist. Yet they exhibit the elements that were important in the change of direction that he imposed on the discipline. Some are among the more reflective and introspective of Lazarsfeld's papers. Thus they help give insight into the views that Lazarsfeld himself had about what he was doing. Some provide keys to particular aspects of the directions in which Lazarsfeld helped take the discipline. Altogether, they constitute an important part of the record of a major change in the character and direction of sociologists' empirical study of society.

The book is divided into three parts: Historical Notes on Social Research, The Logic of Method, and Qualitative and Quantitative Analysis. The first part provides a view of the history of social research and helps us see just how Lazarsfeld shaped the direction of social research (although this is not the intention of the papers contained in it). The second part shows Lazarsfeld's contributions to the more philosophical aspects of methodology. The last part contains papers that actually played some role in that redirection of the discipline. They present differing facets of his work, not showing all the elements of change he imposed in the discipline but providing a good insight into the way this change was accomplished.

PART ONE
Historical Notes on Social Research

[1]

An Episode in the History
of Social Research:
A Memoir

Autobiographies deserve to be written under any one of three conditions: if the author is a man of great achievement (Einstein, Churchill); if, owing to his position, he has been in contact with many important people or important events (a foreign correspondent); or if by external circumstances he can be considered a "case" representing a situation or development of interest.

In this last sense biographies have long been a tool of social research. Critical situations, like extreme poverty, culture conflicts, and concentration camps, have been studied through the medium of personal documents. In general the source of the material and the analyst who tries to draw conclusions from them are separate: the witness and the expert play distinct roles. The present essay is an effort to combine their two functions. I define myself as an expert witness.

But witness of what? I have been involved in two developments: the expansion of social research institutes in American universities and the development of a research style which prevails in many of them. Both of these elements have their roots in my previous European experience. My task in this paper becomes therefore to analyze as clearly as possible the steps, the social and psychological mechanisms, by which the European part of my professional biography came into play after I moved to this country, thirty-six years ago.

From Donald Fleming and Bernard Bailyn, eds., *The Intellectual Migration: Europe and America 1930–1960* (Cambridge: Harvard University Press, 1968). Copyright©1968 Perspectives in American History. Reprinted by permission.

The general theme of this essay is rather easily stated. When my academic career began, the social sciences in Europe were dominated by philosophical and speculative minds. But interest in more concrete work was visible—symbolized, for instance, by the fact that Ferdinand Toennies, the permanent president of the German Sociological Society, instituted in that organization a section on sociography. Without any formal alignment my research interests developed in this empirical direction. At the same time in the United States behaviorism and operationalism dominated the intellectual climate; and yet here too a minority interest began to make itself felt, exemplified, for example, in the publication by the Social Science Research Council of two monographs on the use of personal documents, and the intense interest in intervening variables and attitudes.[1]

In this situation I became a connecting cog. A European "positivist" was a curiosity welcomed by men aware of the subtler trends in the American social sciences. While in Europe the development of social science was arrested with the coming of Hitler, in America the evolving trends broadened, became diversified and refined, and required new institutional forms. My experiences and interests permitted me to play a role in this development. Obviously most of the things I did would have come about anyhow. Still, intellectual transportation needs carriers, and it was my good luck that I was one of them.

The present essay tries to account for my experiences by a procedure applicable, I believe, to any descriptive material, personal or collective. If I were forced to devise an academic title for the pages that follow I would call them a contribution to the study of innovation in higher education. I have included documentary material to enable the reader to form his own judgment of certain questions and to illustrate the available historical sources. At the same time I have tried to organize such material around a number of general ideas—integrating constructs—which I hope will be of interest to students of innovation. This relieves me of the problem of assessing the merit of the innovation and puts the weight on the mode of analysis.

On a recent occasion I urged my colleagues to study the work of social scientists from the point of view of "the decisions lying behind the final product; there is no reason why some of this exegesis should not be written by the authors themselves. We shy away too much from intellectual autobiographies."[2] I am indebted to the editors for providing me with the opportunity for such an exercise.

Calendar of External Events

In the general character of life in Vienna after the First World War, three elements proved to be decisive for the story that follows: the political climate, interest in what was then called "psychology," and concern with what today is described as efforts at "explication."

I was active in the Socialist Student Movement, which was increasingly on the defensive before the growing nationalistic wave. We were concerned with why our propaganda was unsuccessful, and wanted to conduct psychological studies to explain it. I remember a formula I created at the time: a fighting revolution requires economics (Marx); a victorious revolution requires engineers (Russia); a defeated revolution calls for psychology (Vienna).

No sociology was taught at the university except for some lectures by a social philosopher, Othmar Spann.[3] My social reference group was the movement around Alfred Adler, whose opposition to Freud had a strong sociological tinge. He had a considerable following among teachers, and was influential in the educational reform movement sponsored by the socialist municipality of Vienna.

Education in a broad sense was of great concern. As a schoolboy—well before entering the university at the age of eighteen— I tried to combine the ideas of the German youth movement with socialist propaganda among my colleagues.[4] Once I became a student I adhered to the rules of the earlier years: now I was "too old" to be a *révolté* and so I became an amateur "educator." I took jobs as counselor in socialist children's camps and as a tutor in high schools for working-class youngsters. All this was part of an effort to promote the spirit of socialism.[5]

Intellectually, the main influence was a group of writers famous in science and the philosophy of science: Ernst Mach,

Henri Poincaré, and Einstein. I was impressed by the idea that mere "clarification" was a road to discovery. Euclid's theorem on parallels was not truth but an axiom; it made no sense to say that an event on the moon and another on earth occurred simultaneously. All the ideas which later became known as "explications" held a great fascination for me, and this interest often merged into the conviction that "knowing how things are done" was an educational goal of high priority. When, as a student, I worked in the field of labor education, I often lectured on "how to read a newspaper"; what is a news service, how does one take into account the sources of news, what should one watch for in different countries? One of the Alfred Adler's main collaborators edited a series of small pamphlets applying his ideas to various substantive areas; I wrote my contributions under the title "Behind the Schools' Backdrops." The main idea was that much anxiety could be avoided if families understood how schools are organized, how report cards come about, how teachers differ from each other in their perceptions of their students, etc.[6] At that time I had virtually no contact with the "Wiener Kreis" although its main leaders had already settled in Vienna. The obvious similarity of what I have just described with their teachings is probably more due to a common background than to direct influence.

Attending the university was a matter of course in a middle-class family, even one of limited means. The natural field of study for someone actively participating in political events was a doctorate in *Staatswissenschaft,* a modified law degree with a strong admixture of economics and political theory. But for me mathematics was a second pole of attraction, and for several years I took courses in both fields. It was almost accidental that I ended with a doctorate in applied mathematics. Immediately after the degree, I began teaching mathematics and physics in a *Gymnasium.*

While I was still a student, my interest in social science took a new turn with the arrival of two famous psychologists at the University of Vienna. There had been no real psychology there until Charlotte and Karl Bühler were appointed in 1923 to build up a new department. Karl Bühler was a leading academic figure who, as a younger man, had contributed to a major revolution in experimental psychology through his work on the psychology of thinking. His wife, Charlotte, considerably younger than he, was made associate professor, and was, in fact, the administrator of the department. (I will hereafter use the correct European term, institute.) I participated in their early seminars and, after a while, was asked to give a course in statistics.

Slowly, my work as assistant at the university expanded, and I also taught courses in social and applied psychology. I received a small remuneration, by no means sufficient to give up my position in the *Gymnasium*. Still, my desire to shift entirely to the Psychological Institute increased, and around 1927 I got the idea that I would create a division of social psychology at the institute. This would permit work on paid contracts, and from such sources I would get a small but adequate salary, in keeping with the generally low standard of living. The idea was realized in the form of an independent Research Center (*Wirtschafts-psychologische Forschungsstelle,* a term connoting broadly the application of psychology to social and economic problems), of which Karl Bühler was the president. From then on, I directed the applied studies of this center, and at the same time gave my courses at the university institute and supervised dissertations. A number of students worked at the Research Center, and quite a few dissertations were based on data collected there.[7]

Charlotte Bühler divided her work between child and adolescent psychology. My own activities were closely connected with hers in the latter field. She had organized a series of monographs on adolescent psychology, and I was commissioned to write one on youth and occupation. The volume, *Jugend und Beruf,* appeared in 1931. It contained a number of papers by other members of the institute as well as some of my own. A large part of the book was devoted to a ninety-page monograph in which I summarized all the literature then available on occupational choices among young people. At the same time, I published papers on statistical topics, and—in various magazines of the Socialist Party—on topics in industrial and political sociology. My statistical lectures were published as a "Manual for Teachers and Psychologists." It was probably the first European textbook on educational statistics, and was used widely in various universities.[8]

Around 1930, I began to organize a study of Marienthal, a village south of Vienna whose population was almost entirely unemployed.[9] My two main collaborators were Hans Zeisel, now professor at the University of Chicago, and Marie Jahoda, now professor at Sussex University in England. (The latter subsequently did important reports on unemployed youth for the League of Nations and the International Labor Office.) The Marienthal study brought me to the attention of the Paris representative of the Rockefeller Foundation, and in 1932 I obtained a traveling fellowship to the United States, where I arrived in September 1933.[10]

During the first year of my fellowship in America, I participated in various studies and visited the few university centers where social research was taught. In February 1934, the Conservative Party in Austria overthrew the constitution, outlawed the Socialist Party, and established an Italian-type fascism. My position in the secondary school system was cancelled and most members of my family in Vienna were imprisoned, but my vague position as assistant at the university was nominally unaffected. This gave the sympathetic officers of the Rockefeller Foundation the pretext for extending my fellowship another year, nominally obeying the rule that it was necessary for a Fellow to have an assured position to which he could return.

At the end of the fellowship, in the fall of 1935, I decided to stay in this country. With the help of Robert Lynd, Professor of Sociology at Columbia, I obtained a position in New Jersey as a supervisor of student relief work for the National Youth Administration, whose headquarters were at the University of Newark. In the fall of 1936, a Research Center was established at that university, with me as director. This center was patterned along the lines of its Viennese predecessor, and will be discussed in connection with it.

In 1937, the Rockefeller Foundation established at Princeton University a major research project on the effect of radio on the American society. I was appointed director of this new "Office of Radio Research," which, in 1939, was transferred to Columbia University. For one year I was a lecturer there, and in 1940 I became a permanent member of the Department of Sociology, as associate professor. The Office of Radio Research, later trans-

formed into the Bureau of Applied Social Research, had a tenuous existence in the beginning, but in 1945 it was incorporated
into the university structure. I have remained at Columbia, working at the Bureau and in the Department of Sociology, ever since.

A Research Style and Its Probable Roots

To describe the origin of the new research style, I shall use
two sources: publications which appeared in German while I
was still in Austria, and papers I wrote immediately after coming
to the United States in order to explain the Viennese work to
a new audience. In a way, I am extending this latter effort here,
adding interpretation. I am organizing my remarks around three
factors which seem to me significant: an ideological component,
an intellectual "press," and certain personal characteristics.

1. *The ideological component.* The political motivation is
most noticeable in the emphasis on *social stratification,* which
permeated the main Austrian publications. *Jugend und Beruf*
stressed that the then flourishing literature on adolescent psychology really dealt only with middle-class adolescents; it urged
separate attention to the problems of working-class youths, who
at that time started work at the age of fourteen. The whole
monograph was organized around a sharp distinction between
the two groups.[11]

The discussion of a "proletarian youth" was tied up with a
sociopsychological reinterpretation of the notion of "exploitation." The idea was that working-class youths, by going to work
at the age of fourteen, were deprived of the energizing experience
of middle-class adolescence. Because of this, the working-class
man never fully developed an effective scope and could, therefore, be kept in an inferior position. This theme reappeared in
the Marienthal study: the effect of unemployment was to reduce
the "effective scope" of working-class men. The frequently cited
paper by Genevieve Knupfer, "Portrait of the Underdog,"
comes from a Columbia doctoral dissertation of 1947, which was
the first work to assemble stratification data taken from public
opinion surveys. Here the emphasis was on the low level of
aspiration and the narrow "life space" prevailing in low income

groups.[12] The line of argument was practically identical to that which now forms the ideological basis of New York's "Mobilization for Youth." And one could make an interesting comparison between my early book and the contribution of Herbert Gans in the recent *Uses of Sociology* volume,[13] although I am sure that there is no direct continuity. An important difference is that Gans stresses community action, while in the original case emphasis was placed on a delay in the beginning of manual work and changes in the educational system.

This attention to stratification and the social significance of working-class adolescence had a visible Marxist tinge. One other trace of this influence is not as explicit, but is easily documented. In *Jugend und Beruf* there was special pride in showing the effect of objective factors upon individual reactions. Various tables indicate that the occupational structure of German cities, as well as fluctuation of the business cycle, are reflected in the occupational plans of young people of working-class background. I also reported findings to the effect that the religious background of the family is related to the occupational plans of middle-class youths.[14]

In this early work there was another emphasis which we would today attribute to Durkheim, although I am quite sure that at the time I did not know of his existence. In the introduction to *Marienthal* I stressed that we wanted to study "the unemployed *village* and not the unemployed men." In another sentence it was stated that, because of this, we did not introduce personality tests, with no further explanation of what was meant by the phrase. But the implication was clear that the social structure has dominance over individual variations.

Another trace of the political climate can be found in the emphasis on decision making. The Austro-Marxist position put all hope on the winning of elections rather than on the Communist belief in violence, and therefore there was great interest in how people voted. From this origin a rather curious and important functional displacement occurred. At that time, the University of Vienna was dogmatically conservative, and it would have been unwise for staff members to undertake the unbiased study of people's voting decisions. As a conscious substitute, I turned to the question of how young people develop their occupational plans. A series of detailed case studies was collected with the help of a group of students. But then I was faced with the well-known difficulty of analysis.

For many months, I did not know how to proceed, until finally, in a rather strange way, I found a solution. Among the students working with me was a young woman who came to the attention of one of the earliest American market research experts. He needed some interviews in Austria at the time, and because of the training of this student (she subsequently was my main collaborator in the field work for the Marienthal study), he asked her to do some of the interviews on why people bought various kinds of soaps. Market research was then completely unknown in Austria, and she told me about this commission as a kind of curiosity. I immediately linked it up with my problem of occupational choice. Obviously, my difficulty was that such choices extended over a long period of time, with many ramifications and feedbacks. If I wanted to combine statistical analysis with descriptions of entire choice processes, I had better, for the time being, concentrate on more manageable material. For the methodological goal I had in mind, consumer choices would be much more suitable.

Such is the origin of my Vienna market research studies: the result of the methodological equivalence of socialist voting and the buying of soap.[15]

Still, I had learned enough from the case studies on occupational choice to make one more political point in *Jugend und Beruf*. The implications for a planned society were quite clear: most young people have no decided occupational plans and therefore would not mind being guided—as a matter of fact might like to be guided—to an occupational choice; it should, consequently, be easy to fill the occupational quotas established through a central economic plan.

2. *The intellectual climate.* I have mentioned some of the episodes that directed me toward empirical studies. Given this inclination, it is relevant to clarify the specific shape it took in the European climate in which I did my early professional work, for it is this force which will help to explain the role I was destined to play in the United States.

The Bühlers, in the newly created Psychological Institute at the University of Vienna, had begun to concentrate on the integration of approaches, an effort best exemplified by the important book of Karl Bühler, *Die Krise der Psychologie*. He had become prominent as an introspectionist, and he was also well acquainted with the tradition of cultural philosophy, and especially the thought of Wilhelm Dilthey, as a result of his broad philosophical training; in addition, during a trip to the United States he had come into contact with American behaviorism. His book is an effort to analyze these three sources of psychological knowledge: introspection; interpretation of cultural products such as art, folklore, biographies, and diaries; and the observation of behavior. But the key to Bühler's thought throughout was the need to transcend any one approach or any one immediate body of information to reach a broad conceptual integration.

It is difficult for me to say now whether I was genuinely influenced by this ecumenical spirit, but I certainly never missed the chance to show that even "trivial" studies, if properly interpreted and integrated, could lead to *important* findings, "important" implying a higher level of generalization. Thus, I once summarized a number of our consumer studies by carving out the notion of the proletarian consumer. He is

> less psychologically mobile, less active, more inhibited in his behavior. The radius of stores he considers for possible purchases is smaller. He buys more often at the same store. His food habits are more rigid and less subject to seasonal variations. As part of this reduction in effective scope the interest in other than the most essential details is lost; requirements in regard to quality, appearance and other features of merchandise are the less specific and frequent the more we deal with consumers from low social strata.

One of the studies that contributed to the notion of the proletarian consumer dealt with preferences for sweet and bitter chocolate; low-income people preferred the former (and quite generally prefer sweet smells, loud colors, and many other strong sense experiences). And yet this study also shows that one can quite easily miss an important point. The president of the sponsoring concern joined the Board of the Vienna Research Center and at the first meeting gave a fine testimonial of how this study

had increased the sales of his chocolate division. In fact, however, the study had not yet been delivered, and all I could conclude was that he wanted to be helpful with this white lie. I know
now what had really happened: I failed to discover the Haw-
thorne Effect; the chocolate division got so involved in our study
that they simply became active and sold more.

Altogether, the consumer purchase became a special case of
a problem which had great sanctity in the European humanistic
tradition: *Handlung*, action.[16] Bühler himself had written a fundamental paper on language as a special form of action,[17] and
it was in these terms that I reported on the nature of the Austrian
market studies soon after I came to this country.[18] In "The
Psychological Aspect of Market Research" (1934) I included in
a half-dozen pages on "the structure of the act of purchasing"
diagrams and new terms ("Accent on Motivation") intermingled
with, if I may say so, interesting examples on the purchase of
sweaters and soaps. The general idea was that "the action of a
purchase is markedly articulated and that different phases and
elements can be distinguished in it." The trend toward deducing
a "theoretical outlook" from specific data may be exemplified
by the following quotation:

> The "time of deliberation," the "anticipated features of the purchase,"
> "the relation to previous purchases" are only examples of what we could
> call the psychological "coordinates" of a purchase. It seems to us that
> one of the outstanding contributions of the psychologist to the problem
> of market survey is the careful, general study of the structure of the
> purchase, in order to prepare us to find in a special study what could
> possibly be characteristic for the investigated commodity.

It would have been unacceptable just to report that *X* percent
of people did or thought this or that about some topic. The task
was to combine diverse findings into a small number of "integrating constructs." At the same time, it was imperative to explicate as clearly as possible the procedures by which such
greater depth was achieved.[19] In a paper written in 1933 summarizing the Austrian experience, the following four rules were
singled out and amply exemplified:

a. For any phenomenon one should have objective observations as
   well as introspective reports.

b. Case studies should be properly combined with statistical information.
c. Contemporary information should be supplemented by information on earlier phases of whatever is being studied.
d. One should combine "natural and experimental data." By "experimental," I meant mainly questionnaires and solicited reports, while by "natural," I meant what is now called "unobtrusive measures"—data deriving from daily life without interference from the investigator.

Mere description was not enough. In order to get "behind" it a variety of data had to be collected on any issue under investigation—just as the true position of a distant object can be found only by looking at it from different sides and directions. It is unlikely that I was entirely aware of the rules underlying the Viennese research tradition as it developed. But its structure was close enough to the surface so that I could articulate it fairly easily when I had leisure to reflect on our work here in this country.

The efforts to develop a theory of integrating constructs, their logical nature, and how they are arrived at were part of a need to legitimize empirical work. At that time, I was not familiar with various papers by Toennies in which he tried to introduce the idea of sociography into the tradition of German sociologists. It would be interesting today to compare these two developments in more detail. Some critics today oppose survey research as restrictive and one-sided, pointing to the Columbia tradition as an evil influence.[20] It is useful to point out that, from its beginning, this tradition stressed the importance of a diversified approach. Legitimization, like woman's work, seems never to be done.

3. *The personal equation.* The personal element cannot be avoided. What made me so convinced that a combination of "insight" and quantification was crucial for the social sciences? In the introduction to *Marienthal* I made such a combination appear almost a moral duty. Thus, I had expressed dissatisfaction with unemployment statistics, as well as with casual descriptions of the life of the unemployed in newspapers and belles lettres. Then I stated:

> Our idea was to find procedures which would combine the use of numerical data with the immersion [*sich einleben*] in the situation. To this end the

following is necessary: we had to gain such close contact with the population of Marienthal, so that we could learn the smallest details of their daily life; at the same time we had to perceive each day so that it was possible to reconstruct it objectively; finally, for the whole a structure had to be developed so that all the details could be seen as expressions of a minimum number of basic facts.

It is worth noting the formulation of these sentences—they imply an imperative to carry out this methodological mission. Like all missionaries, we did not feel a need to justify further what the voices ordered us to do. Still the position was pervasive. In an appendix to the Marienthal book on the history of sociography, Hans Zeisel includes a six-page review of the "American Survey." He pointed out that the Chicago studies "for some strange reason did not pursue the statistical analysis of their material." From his reading, he could find only a few examples of the quantification of complex patterns. His review ends with the following remarks, which echo the program just mentioned before:

American sociography has not achieved a synthesis between statistics and a full description of concrete observations. In work of impressive conceptualization—for instance, in *The Polish Peasant*—statistics are completely missing; inversely, the statistical surveys are often of a regrettable routine nature.

I cannot trace this urge to quantify complex experiences and behavior patterns to any outside influences prevailing at the time. Under such conditions, the historian is forced to look for idiosyncratic elements; and they are abundantly available. I remember my excitement when, around 1925, I saw in the window of a bookstore a scatter-diagram in one of the first German monographs on correlation analysis. A few years later, the German sociologist Andreas Walter showed me an ecological map he had just brought back from a visit to Chicago—and I had the same reaction. Most consequential was the following episode. At the age of about twenty-four I listened to a leader of the Young Socialist Workers Movement, who read from questionnaires he had distributed. He used individual quotations to describe the misery of factory life. Immediately I asked myself why he did not make counts; he was surprised at the idea, and turned the questionnaires over to me. I did a statistical analysis, which later formed the base of one of my first papers. I also gave a report in one of the first Bühler seminars, which brought me to their attention.[21]

My subsequent work for Mrs. Bühler reinforced this whole tendency. Her major studies in child psychology took a middle position between the American Gesell, and the Swiss Piaget. The latter made his famous semi-experimental observations on a few children only, drawing from them the far-reaching developmental theories; Gesell made minute statistical observations without drawing any generalizations. Mrs. Bühler's fame was based on a theory of phases, which she "underpinned" with statistical observations. At one point her position influenced me in a way which had rather far-reaching consequences. For my *Jugend und Beruf,* I coordinated a large amount of data from various sources into a rather coherent system of concepts. She was pleased, and also accepted my position on the need to distinguish between middle-class and working-class adolescents. But she objected strenuously to the tone in which my section on proletarian youth was written. I was, indeed, full of compassion, talking about exploitation by the bourgeois society, and the hortative style of this section was quite different from the rest of the manuscript. I could not deny this fact, and finally rewrote it. None of the argument was omitted, but the whole tone became descriptive and naturalistic, instead of critical. I have no doubt that this episode affected my subsequent writings and is a contributing factor to the debate on the role of sociology that was later led by C. Wright Mills.

The Organization of Social Research

Today, the main features of a research bureau are well-known. There is a division of labor in the essential work: writing and pretesting questionnaires, analyzing tables, and drafting reports. Coordinating and guiding this work is an administrative as well as an intellectual challenge. A bureau director is probably a new kind of professional for whom recently the name "managerial scholar" has been created. The nature of the work requires a more hierarchical relation among the participant professionals than is habitual in an academic department.

In the context of this memoir, the question is how we hit upon this type of organization in the late 1920s. In part it was due, I believe, to the fact that I and many of my collaborators had team experience in the Socialist Party and in the youth movement; in my case, I would guess that this style of work was partly a psychological substitute for political activities. But the example of Charlotte Bühler certainly also played a role. She had a Prussian ability to organize the work activities of many people at many places. Some felt exploited by her, but I always appreciated her good training and help.

The problem of financing such institutes is also well-known today. The money has to be begged from public institutions and private industry. This was much more difficult forty years ago, because there were then no foundations, no tax deductions, and, all in all, the idea of research was not widely accepted. One depended on a few individuals and was in a perpetual financial crisis. I created a board for the Center which consisted of representatives from all political and industrial groups in Vienna.[22]

While today all this seems rather obvious, at the time it was watched with some surprise. This can be seen from a document which is interesting in a number of respects. The leading journal of sociology at the time was edited in Cologne by Leopold von Wiese. In 1934, in its last issue before it was halted by the Hitler government, von Wiese wrote a rather extensive review of *Marienthal*. He, like other professors of sociology and economics, used the long German Easter vacations to take students on short field trips to factories or villages (a monograph of von Wiese's, called *The Village*, resulted from such a trip). In his review he stressed, with approval, the difference between this tradition and our more organized enterprise.

My own efforts are forced to be of a merely deductive nature; we can only assume that the students who live for a few days with the local population get stimulation and some instructions which, I hope, will be useful later on when they do more extended work. The Vienna enterprise had a different structure where more advanced and theoretically better-trained observers could devote themselves to their task for a longer period of time (the participation of medical doctors was helpful) so that scien-

tifically valuable results were achieved, which went well beyond the mere
purpose of training students.

Von Wiese suspected that funds available to the Bühlers
through their American connections made this broader system
possible. Actually that played only a very small role. The respondents were paid for their time by the donation of second-
hand clothes we had collected in Vienna. The supervision and
the analysis were done by colleagues most of whom contributed
their time. We had a small subsidy for expenses from the central
trade union council.

Von Wiese raised two methodological objections. He disapproved of using the term "psychological" for work which he
considered essentially sociological; he was not aware of the
Vienna university structure, to which I have alluded above. And
on our basic position, expressed in the introduction to *Marienthal,* he commented as follows:

> I consider it too great a concession to statisticians that the authors propose
> "to reject all impressions for which they cannot find quantitative evi-
> dence." Fortunately they were not too strict in the application of this
> principle.

Von Wiese's complex reaction seems to me a particularly clear
indication that German sociology was beginning to take a new
turn at the time when it was, for all practical purposes, sup-
pressed by political events.

The Vienna Center was a sequence of improvisations, and the
basic elements of a research organization developed only slowly.
In spite of a number of external formalities it never fused into
a stable organization. It was only when I came to the University
of Newark that the different components, all concurrently in my
mind, could be integrated into some kind of an institutional plan.
Even so, the beginning in America was chaotic.

In the summer of 1935, I was obliged to return to Vienna to
exchange my student permit for an immigration visa. In October,
a few weeks after my arrival, I received word from Robert Lynd
that the New Jersey Relief Administration had collected ten
thousand questionnaires from youngsters between fourteen and

twenty-five as a project of the National Youth Administration, and needed someone to analyze the material. They had turned to Frank Kingdon, who had just been made president of the University of Newark, a small institution which he was expected to develop into a place of higher learning for underprivileged students of Essex County, New Jersey.[23] Kingdon had the intelligent idea that someone paid by the NYA to analyze the questions could, at the same time, teach some research courses at his university. Lynd had recommended me for the job, and I gratefully accepted it.

Kingdon and I got along well with each other from the start. At the first talk, I suggested that the plan should be extended, and the NYA project should be made the beginning of a "Research Center of the University of Newark," which I proposed to create at the same time. Obviously, the university could not contribute financially, except indirectly in the form of working space. It was up to me to keep the center alive by contracts, though Kingdon was later able to help by assigning relief money for the large number of unemployed students for whom I could invent work.

After a few months the situation was formalized. On June 19, 1936, Kingdon wrote me, in the name of the trustees, an official letter of appointment. In it he said,

> It is understood that we are offering you the position of Acting Director of the Research Center of the University of Newark for a twelve-month period beginning May 21, 1936, and continuing until May 21, 1937.
>
> It is understood that the basic salary for this position is $4,800, but that the University is obligated to pay you only one-half of this sum, the remaining part of your salary to be derived from other sources. It is understood that your salary will be paid in equal monthly installments of $200.
>
> It is also understood that a portion of this half-time that is to be made available to the University of Newark may be assigned to teaching. It is further understood that the University will not ask you to teach in excess of eight hours.

I suppose that this is the first document proposing a split appointment for a bureau director. Unfortunately, even today it is assumed in many universities that the director is partly responsible for his own salary.[24]

There were many unemployed students, and I had continuously to think of work topics to occupy them. With the help of my market contacts, I obtained the circulation figures for some twenty magazines in the hundred largest cities of the United States. By combining this with census data and various economic information, we wrote a paper characterizing the cities in terms of their magazine profile. This was published later on in one of the first issues of the newly created *Public Opinion Quarterly* (1937).[25] At the same time, I began to build up contacts with other agencies. The superintendent of schools for Essex County subsidized a study of local school problems, from which we published several small statistical monographs. The WPA started a large project on technological unemployment, with headquarters in Philadelphia, and I prevailed upon them to let me study the glass manufacturing town of Millville, New Jersey, which had become almost totally unemployed as a consequence of the introduction of glass-blowing machinery and the transfer of the main company to Ohio. Though this study was never completed because of the discontinuance of funds, it made it possible for me in 1935–36 to build up the first elements of a staff. And the Horkheimer Institute came to my help by locating some of their work at the Newark Center and paying for supervision. The best-known result of this collaborative effort is the book by Mirra Komarovsky, *The Unemployed Man and His Family* (1940).

In the spring of 1937, I wrote an official report to the Newark trustees in which I attempted to explain the whole idea of such a center, to show that it would be of value to the university, and to prove that it was financially viable. The aims of the field studies of the Research Center of the University of Newark, I wrote, were:

to give research training to students
to develop new methods of research
to publish finished studies
to help the City of Newark to a better understanding of its social and
    economic problems
to act as a consulting service to social and business agencies in the city
to give students the opportunity for gainful employment

to accumulate funds for the perpetuation and enlargement of the Center's
activities
to make the University, as a whole, better known locally and nationally.

Its utility, I argued, could be justified in a variety of ways. Salaries up to the amount of $1,500 were paid every month to students and graduates of the university; this did not include relief money and could therefore be said to be exclusively due to the existence of the center. About a thousand newspaper articles contained references to its work. "The Center and hence the University of Newark is represented through its Director on a variety of regional and national committees." I then listed ten studies in progress. Into this catalogue I put everything with which I was myself associated, including a number of articles I had published and commercial studies that I, as a personal consultant, was connected with.[26]

By 1936 the Newark Center had become known as something of a curiosity. One day Everett Hughes and Robert Park came to look at it, an honor which I did not fully appreciate at the time. George Lundberg (Bennington) and John Jenkins (Cornell) sent me students for training, among them Edward Suchman, who stayed with me until he joined Samuel Stouffer in the War Department. But the main indicator of a growing public interest is the fact that by the spring of 1937 I was considered a possible choice for director of the first major research project on mass communication, which the Rockefeller Foundation was about to sponsor.[27]

Throughout the entire course of this institutional development, research methodology was a characteristic feature. Partly, of course, this resulted from my own interest in "explications," mentioned above, but I am convinced that there is an intrinsic relation between research organization and methodology. In my presidential address to the American Sociological Association I expressed this point in a way which was perhaps a little exaggerated but which contains, I believe, the essential truth. Supervising even a small research staff makes one acutely aware of the differences between various elements of research operation and of the need to integrate them into a final product. Some assistants are best at detailed interviews, others are gifted in the handling of statistical tables, still others are especially good at searching for possible contributions from existing literature. The different roles must be made explicit; each has to know what is expected of him and how his task is related to the work of the others. Staff instruction therefore quickly turns into methodological explication. The point is perhaps akin to the kind of sociology of knowledge that Marxists employ when they argue that new tools of production are often reflected in new ways of intellectual analysis.

All of this still leaves open the question of how it happened that an organizational form developed in Vienna was relatively easily accepted and diffused in this country. For an interpretation I have to turn back to the two years of my fellowship, 1933 to 1935.

Atlantic Transfer—Directional Cues

The impact of European intellectuals on the United States can be studied in a variety of ways. One approach is to examine a certain field before and after the arrival of specific individuals. Another is to trace the contacts which the immigrant had and the references that Americans made to him either in their own publications or in communications solicited especially for that purpose. A third approach to the transfer phenomenon is to examine how the immigrant himself saw the situation. What was his strategy and experience? Since most of the men with whom this volume deals are no longer living, it seems incumbent upon the few survivors to provide some information on how such a sequence of events looks from within.

The idea of an "expert witness" described above is especially useful in this third approach. He reports his concrete experiences and at the same time tries to conceptualize them, to discuss episodes within coherent patterns. But the reader should be reminded that in this case the other participants may be considered expert witnesses too.[28] Historians could unearth additional documents, interview the other participants, and come to conclusions quite different from mine. There are no final verdicts here, only an interpretation of what might be called "strategy":

the moves which the actor made more or less consciously and intentionally; the general motivations that guided his reactions and choices; and the character of the total situation, even if the actor was not aware of what this was at the time. Perhaps the term "latent strategy" will serve best.[29]

The beginning of such analysis is found in what might be called *directional cues*. What did the person know about the country to which he came before his arrival? Where did he turn first? What antecedent experience guided his first moves?

I can summarize my experience along three lines, which at first were quite distinct but which ultimately converged: the continuation of my interest in research on unemployment; my interest in finding out more about American research techniques; and my desire to help the Vienna Research Center by establishing contacts for it with relevant organizations in this country.

The Marienthal study had received some attention in the United States through two channels. A visiting American psychologist had seen some of the material in Vienna and, on his return, wrote an article in the *Nation* called "When Man Eats Dog." At the International Psychological Congress in 1932, held in Germany, Mrs. Bühler arranged for me to be on the program; I reported on the first findings, and a number of prominent Americans, including Gordon Allport, Otto Klineberg, and Goodwin Watson, visited me to obtain more details. These were also some of the first people I saw when I came to the States.[30]

At the time my fellowship began, the Federal Emergency Relief Administration (FERA) had just established its first research unit. The Rockefeller Foundation arranged for me to work there as a volunteer. To do so, I moved to Washington and while there met several sociologists working as government consultants. They belonged to the then insurgent group of empiricists who soon thereafter created the Sociological Research Association as a spearhead for their position in the American Sociological Society. These men worked mainly with broad census-type data. Because of the following episode, I acquired something of a reputation in this group as a different kind of technician. The FERA was about to publish a monograph showing a marked correlation between unemployment and education. I suggested that the result might be the spurious effect of age, an idea which today would be commonplace. A cross-tabulation was made and indeed it turned out that the role of age was more important: poorly educated people were older and had a higher unemployment rate. This impressed the FERA research staff. When I spent some time in Chicago in the spring of 1934, they established a small tabulating unit for me so that I could help there on the multivariate analysis of their unemployment surveys.

During this early period I spent some time at the few places in which empirical social research was taught. I went to the University of Rochester to become acquainted with Luther Fry, who had written the first book on techniques of social research. I took over one of his classes for several weeks and organized a study of how people decide which movies to attend.[31]

At this time I did not think of myself at all as a sociologist. I went to no national or regional conventions of sociologists, although my fellowship would have provided the necessary funds. As a matter of fact I had only a vague notion of the state of sociology in the United States. I visited Chicago for a few weeks, but primarily to work with Arthur Kornhauser, a prominent applied psychologist. I have no recollection of any memorable meetings there, except for a respectful lunch with L. L. Thurstone. I am sure that I did not meet Samuel Stouffer during the first year. My strongest memory of the visit is an investigation of the University of Chicago faculty that the state legislature held at the time; and I recall being much impressed by Robert Hutchins.

My main sociological contact at this time was with Robert S. Lynd. Because of *Middletown* he was one of the first people I looked up. He was extremely generous with his time and advice. The important role he played in the first ten years of my professional life in the United States will become abundantly clear in the remainder of this essay.[32]

Throughout this period, my main concern was with the Research Center in Vienna. I had left it in precarious financial condition. The situation deteriorated after the putsch of the Dollfuss government which considered the center's activities and personnel subversive, probably with reason. My great hope was to get American research organizations or commercial firms interested in subsidizing some of the work in Vienna. I therefore spent a good part of my time with people who worked in the field of market research. I never succeeded in mobilizing help for Vienna, but my efforts had important consequences for me personally. It all began when some of the psychologists I met told me that I would be especially interested in a new development.

Around 1930, a group of prominent American psychologists, including E. L. Thorndike and J. M. Cattell, created a nonprofit organization called the Psychological Corporation (PSC). Their plan was, on the one hand, to promote the use of applied psychology among businessmen and, on the other hand, to provide academic psychologists with research opportunities and, I suppose, additional income. When I heard about this I immediately got in touch with the research director of the PSC and volunteered my time.

At the time, American market research was based mainly on rather simple nose-counting. Nonetheless, I expected the PSC, because of the academic status of its founders, to take about the same research position as our Viennese group. But in fact I did not find this to be the case. The PSC had to fight for its existence, and its research activities consisted of simple consumer surveys, in competition with other commercial agencies. I considered it almost a mission to help the PSC do pioneering rather than routine work. Toward this end I proposed a number of projects, always along the line of why people did this or that, but nothing came of these efforts. The PSC's director, who combined radical behaviorism with the desire to have the organization make money, objected that my questionnaires were too long. I used to counter with the anecdote of a woman who wanted to buy a dog; she was shocked to learn that the smaller the dog the more expensive it was, and finally asked what she would have to pay for no dog at all. Understandably, after a while my relations with the Psychological Corporation diminished to the vanishing point.[33]

Such were the main directional cues which guided my first activities. They were accompanied by a number of personal contacts, which were an important part of the process of transfer I am trying to describe. These can only be understood in terms of mutual interaction. Indeed, it will be necessary to shift back and forth between what I think were prevailing tendencies in

this country and certain patterns of conduct I had brought with
me.

Atlantic Transfer—Latent Strategies

A number of younger psychologists were consultants to the
Psychological Corporation, and together we formed a sort of
Young Turk movement. The member of this group I saw most
often at that time was Rensis Likert, then an assistant professor
at New York University. He became interested in the Viennese
type of complex market studies, and I cherish an English translation of a tea study which Likert made for his students. Finally,
Likert became an ardent advocate of the exclusive use of unstructured interviews, which we in Vienna combined with statistical data.[34]

Another encounter was with an applied psychologist from
Cornell, John Jenkins. He became interested in the complex
kinds of cross-tabulations we incorporated in our studies. In
Vienna I had worked up a mimeographed manual for my students, under the title "How to Get Along with Figures" (*Umgang mit Zahlen*; the title was taken from a famous eighteenth-
century book by Adolf von Knigge: *Über den Umgang mit
Menschen*).[35] Jenkins made an English translation for his students. I spent the summer of 1934 with him in Ithaca, and we
discussed the idea of a "new look" in applied psychology. He
later created a department specializing in this field at the University of Maryland.

Simultaneously, the small fraternity of commercial market research experts got interested in my work. Largely through the
efforts of Percival White, who wrote an early textbook on market
research, I was invited to talk at meetings and to participate in
committees of the recently created American Marketing Association. The Association was about to publish an official textbook, *The Techniques of Marketing Research*, and commissioned me to write four chapters. One of these, on interpretation,
contained references to depth psychology and is generally considered the beginning of "motivation research." The book was

widely used in business schools and helped me later on when I needed cooperation for our radio research work.

It was at that time that the first political questions were included in commercial market studies. Around 1935 polling had become an independent commercial activity, with results of interest to sociologists as well as to psychologists. While the former were quite hospitable, the latter were not, because the enterprise partook too much of the low academic status held by "applied psychology."[36] My sociological acquaintances listened with interest to my adventures in the market research world.

By the end of my first fellowship year, I had developed a network of personal and institutional contacts woven around a rather narrow range of professional activities. It had grown from an effort to help the Vienna Center, to which I intended to return. But the political events in Austria slowly nurtured the idea that I remain in the United States. I began to look at people with a view to possibilities of work here in the fall of 1937. Only a position connected with a university was conceivable. But the fact that I had a foot in both the commercial and the academic camps made for a certain amount of maneuverability, of which the following is a typical example.

At the University of Pittsburgh there was a research center which had been created by a man well-known in educational research: W. W. Charters. I spent two months at this Retail Research Institute which, by the time of my visit, was under the direction of David Craig. With him, I organized a number of studies on topics such as "How Pittsburgh Women Decide Where to Buy Their Dresses," or, "How Pittsburgh Drivers Choose Their Gasoline."[37] (The first study once made me a house guest of a local Pittsburgh tycoon, Edgar Kaufman, and the second brought me into repeated contact with Paul Mellon.) At that time a large trade association of the major retail stores was established in Washington; its president consulted me as to who should be research director, and appointed Craig upon my suggestion. Toward the end of my fellowship, Craig resigned from Pittsburgh and moved to Washington. Before leaving, he arranged for me to get a temporary appointment at his institute. The necessary meeting of the trustees had not yet taken place, but Craig wrote me a letter on official stationery, which was sufficient for me to obtain an immigration visa from the American consul in Vienna.

I subsume all these mechanisms of the transfer process under the broad notion of *latent strategy*. It would obviously be wrong to restrict it to a conscious manipulation. All of it has, rather, the character of an underlying vigilance which connects accidental situations to a latent goal. But not even this is enough of an explanation. One has to add a kind of "libidinal" element which makes all these things pleasurable within their own right. I was almost obsessed with the idea that I wanted to be connected with as many studies as possible, and used every occasion to add another one. So I soon obtained funds to study the adjustment of our immediate group, the nine European Rockefeller fellows; the questionnaires I used on that occasion thirty years ago are still available, and might be of some historical interest.[38]

Latent strategies and directional cues involve the interactions that always prevail between dispositions and situations. Latent strategies lead to selective perception of the environment, and they also become crystallized, more precise, more self-conscious as they meet success in an extending sequence of episodes. But what makes for a relatively high proportion of successes? Here I must take recourse to a term like "structural fit." Both the environment and the life style of the immigrant are patterned in a certain way. The elements of these two patterns may complement each other, and to some degree they did in my case. Thus in the first part of this paper I gave examples of my quantitative interests, controlled by strong conceptual training, fitting well into some nascent trends in the American community. Let me give two more examples of such structural fit. The first shows the protective role of a personal idiosyncrasy; the second shows the usefulness of a tangential approach to conventional rewards.

In a letter to Vienna, of which I happen to have a copy, I reported during my first fellowship year that "I find it more interesting to meet with what you might call second-string people; whenever I come to a new place, I pay a respect visit to the big shots and then stay with the people who accept me and make me feel comfortable."[39] Without my knowing it, that helped me escape a certain uneasiness regarding foreigners, which, in my opinion, was quite prevalent at the time; foreigners were rare, and it is understandable that people had ambivalent feelings about them. In 1935, when Lynd began to help me look for a job, he seems to have written one correspondent that I do not look very Jewish; I have the answer from the other man, who writes Lynd that he has heard nice things about me, but he wants to correct Lynd on one point: "Lazarsfeld shows clearly the marks of his race." In 1936, Hadley Cantril wrote Lynd that they were looking for a research director who would have my kind of training but not be so peculiarly "scattered." That the word reflected an image of foreignness would appear from his praise, somewhat later, of the first radio issue of the *Journal of Applied Psychology*:[40] "The two I especially liked," he wrote, "were those of Herr Director himself for they beautifully illustrate the trends one can discover if statistics are intelligently used." So, even at the moment when he approved of what I wanted to do, the notion of foreignness crept in.

When I appointed T. W. Adorno, newly arrived from Germany, to the radio project I repeatedly had to explain that he did not yet know his way around. I shall come back to this later; but for now let me note that my own reaction was characteristic. I have a memorandum of March 7, 1938, addressed to Cantril and Frank Stanton, the two directors of the project, in which I report on my first week of experience with Adorno. I wrote:

> He looks exactly as you would imagine a very absent-minded German professor, and he behaves so foreign that I feel like a member of the Mayflower Society. When you start to talk with him, however, he has an enormous amount of interesting ideas. As every newcomer, he tries to reform everything, but if you listen to him, most of what he says makes sense.

As late as 1941, when I was appointed to Columbia, Samuel Stouffer had to fight this ghost. He wrote, in a letter to the appointment committee that is one of the most thoughtful documents of support I have read in twenty-eight years on the receiving end of such mail, that

> In spite of the fact that he has lived in this country for seven years or more, he has a distinctly foreign appearance and speaks with a strong

accent. This prejudices some people against him, and I think some are further prejudiced because they feel that there is occasional arrogance in his manner. Actually, Paul is one of the most modest of men, but he does have a rather heavy Germanic way of presenting a topic which tends to make some people feel that there is not as much in the topic as the difficulty in following him would suggest. I think such critics would be occasionally right, but I can testify from experience that there is plenty of pure gold in them thar hills.

Obviously Stouffer felt uneasy about bringing up the topic, and so at the end caricatures himself as a kind of hillbilly.

I offer these examples as a way of characterizing the atmosphere of the period, an atmosphere notably different from the present in which foreign-born intellectuals are a dime a dozen in academic and professional life.[41] But, even so, I was not seriously hampered, because it never occurred to me to aspire to a major university job. I took it for granted that I would have to make some move similar to the creation of the Vienna Research Center if I wanted to find a place for myself in the United States.

This leads to the second illustration of the notion of structural fit. At about the time I arrived in the United States, the problem of how to introduce empirical social research into the university structure had become visible. It was obvious that a new type of research center was necessary, though none had successfully developed.[42] One reason for this was the lack of people whose experience and career needs equipped them to create and direct such centers. Missing from the scene, in other words, were *institution men*.[43]

I have always been interested in the type of men who played major roles in academic innovations. At various times I have tried to show that such innovations can often be traced to people who belong to two worlds but who were not safe in either of them. The best historical examples are Wilhelm von Humboldt who, as a hanger-on at Weimar, belonged to the lower Prussian aristocracy and created the University of Berlin in 1807. Another is Guillaume Budé, who was a hanger-on among the French humanists but who had access to the Court of Francis I and spent his life developing the Collège de France in opposition to the antihumanistic Sorbonne (1515 to 1550).

The institution man is a special case of a well-known sociological notion: the marginal man who is part of two different cultures. He lives under cross-pressures that move him in a number of directions. According to his gifts and external circumstances he may become a revolutionary, a surrealist, a criminal. In some cases his marginality may become the driving force for institutional efforts; the institution he creates shelters him and at the same time helps him crystallize his own identity. In my case there was a general convergence toward institutional innovation. Under the adverse economic circumstances in Austria and the strong current of incipient anti-Semitism, a regular academic career would have been almost impossible. When I came to the United States, I was neither individually known, like some of the immigrant physicists, nor connected with a visible movement, like the psychoanalysts and Gestalt psychologists. (The status of a Rockefeller Fellow helped in the beginning; but after a while I did experience the proverbial transition from a distinguished foreigner to an undesirable alien). On the positive side I did belong, marginally, to a number of areas between which bridges were bound to be built; social science and mathematics, academic and applied interests, European and American outlooks. It seems plausible that such a configuration would lead to a career detoured through an institutional innovation rather than routed directly toward individual mobility.

The form this took was the role of a bureau director, a role I have already touched on and will try to develop in the two sections that follow. One of the points I will come back to repeatedly is the need in this role to take reasonable risks, to try deviant innovations without coming into too much conflict with prevailing norms. And in this connection it seems fitting to end this section with the note of the risk I took in coming here. It will be remembered that I went to Vienna to apply for an immigration visa based on the promise of an appointment at the Retail Research Institute at the University of Pittsburgh. The day after I got my visa I received a cable from Craig telling me that he was leaving Pittsburgh because he had taken the job of research director of the Retail Federation; my appointment would have to be delayed until a successor could confirm it. In some way, then, my visa was of dubious legality, and, more important, I had no job waiting for me in the States.

I had intended to inform the Rockefeller Foundation of my

decision to move to Pittsburgh. Their regulations required return to the home base at the completion of the fellowship, but in view of the Austrian situation I could rather safely count on their understanding. Now having no guaranteed job, however, I doubted very much that an American foundation would also cooperate on a move which went against governmental regulations. Either a job or an affidavit of support by an American citizen was required.

I remember, of course, every detail of the few days and nights during which I had to make up my mind. I still had one month of fellowship money left; traditionally, the European fellows spent their last month traveling in Europe, as a kind of decompression procedure. I finally decided not to inform anyone, and used this last $150 to buy a third-class ticket on a slow American boat. I thus arrived in New York as the classic immigrant, penniless. A few weeks later, I began the work which led to the establishment of the University of Newark Research Center.

The Rockefeller-Princeton Radio Project

I spent most of the academic year 1936–37 on the tasks of raising money, supervising studies, and training staff at Newark.

Sometime during the spring I heard that the Rockefeller Foundation was prepared to set up a large project to study the effect of radio on American society. The reviewing officer was John Marshall, who was trained as a medieval historian. A project director was looked for, and the job was offered to a number of senior people. I was interested in such an appointment, but had no way to present my candidacy. I had had some previous experience in radio research. In 1930–31, our Vienna Center had done a large-scale survey of listener tastes for the Austrian radio.[44] One of my junior colleagues in the department of psychology, Herta Herzog, had written her dissertation under my supervision replicating an earlier English study. Persons of varied background had been asked to read a story over the radio, and questionnaires distributed to the listening public had made it possible to discover what social and other characteristics the audience could derive from voice and diction.[45]

During my fellowship years, I had visited the research departments of the major radio networks, and had established friendly relations with Frank Stanton, then a junior staff member of the Columbia Broadcasting System. I knew that he was somehow in touch with the Rockefeller plans, but I was not well enough acquainted with him to ask for his help. The main academic proponent for the idea was said to be Hadley Cantril, who, a few years earlier, had published a book with Gordon Allport on the psychology of radio. I had known Cantril in the first period of my fellowship during visits to Harvard, and was very much impressed by him. However, we had seen little of each other, and in any case it would have been embarrassing for me to approach him directly.

As was so often the case during that period, my main avenue of communicaton was Robert S. Lynd. Cantril wrote to him asking whether he had a suggestion for the directorship; he indicated that it should be someone of my training, at the same time mentioning that he had reservations about me personally. Lynd tried to dispel Cantril's doubts, and recommended me.

In July 1937, I went for six weeks to Europe to visit my parents and to attend to a number of other personal matters. While sitting in a mountain village I received a cable from Cantril offering me the directorship at the rather fabulous salary of $7,000, "two years or possibly four, headquarters Princeton." I cabled back that I was very much interested, but that I wanted to raise a number of questions, which I would do immediately by following mail. I wrote Cantril a two-and-a-half page single-spaced letter dated August 8, 1937, which crossed with one of his to me of about equal length, dated August 9, 1937. Cantril's letter urged me to take the directorship and explained the project.

> Princeton University, more particularly the School of Public and International Affairs, was given a grant of $33,500 a year for a period of two years—or a total grant of 67,000 dollars. This was to carry out a project which Stanton and I designed to investigate certain problems in radio research.

The sum mentioned was large indeed. The substantive purpose of the project was described as follows:

> Our idea was to try to determine eventually the role of radio in the lives of different types of listeners, the value of radio to people psychologically,

and the various reasons why they like it. The Rockefeller Foundation, through John Marshall, felt it was a new type of project getting at some of the "why" questions so long neglected.

The letter stressed that the formulation of purpose was intentionally vague, so that it would be possible to carry out varied research under its charter. One can see in the preceding quotation a considerable affinity to the Vienna tradition; indeed, Cantril and his teacher Allport had always been attentive to the work of Mrs. Bühler. Another element in the description was an emphasis on methods.

> We had thought that this would require two years of preliminary work on methods—that is, methods which we hoped to work out that would eventually enable us or others to get the final answers to the sort of questions that interested us.

The hope for a "final answer" was typical of the optimistic mood of the period. Now, after thirty years of further research in mass communication, most of us feel that we are still just about at the beginning. Cantril's letter included the expectation that the project would be continued for another period of two years, and on this point at least his confidence was justified by later events.

From my point of view the content of the project was not the main issue. I had created the Newark Research Center, and my problem was how the new proposal would affect it. So I first explained to Cantril what this center was about.

> I invented the Newark Research Center for two reasons. I wanted to direct a rather great variety of studies, so that I was sure that from year to year my methodological experience could increase—and that is, as you know, my main interest in research. And I tried to build up groups of younger students to be educated just in this kind of research procedures I tried to develop. Now as to the first point I think that your project would do splendidly. Radio is a topic around which actually any kind of research methods can be tried out and can be applied satisfactorily.

I quote this rather lengthy statement because it provides a check on the retrospective report I made in the preceding section: the formulation I made at the time hardly differs from my present point of view. Following this background information I raised two questions with Cantril. The first was:

> Would it be possible to set up at least part of your project in such a way that it could be used as a sort of training institution?

The second question goes to the heart of what I described as the attitude of the institution man. I told Cantril that it made me apprehensive to contemplate the Newark Center's collapse, which in all probability would come about if I took a leave of absence to direct the new project. Here is how I explained my feeling:

> I try to identify whatever I do with an institution which might after some time acquire the dignity which I myself, for reasons of destiny and maybe of personality, can hardly aspire to.

The remainder of my letter argues for the solution I proposed: the Rockefeller Project should be handled as an additional undertaking of the Newark Center. Considering the budget of this single study was more than three times the total budget of the center, it is not surprising that Cantril found my proposal rather absurd. He answered me with a letter that was friendly, complimentary, and persuasive. But on the crucial issue it was quite firm.

> Your suggestion about a tie-up with the Newark Research Center is, I fear, out. I'm sorry that you didn't get the money there, but it is one of these somewhat absurd American grants to an "institution" and it would be impossible to have the work carried on elsewhere.

On my return from Austria I immediately got in touch with Cantril to negotiate the institutional aspect. It is also characteristic of the institution man that I was not too impressed by the inviolability of rules. I do not recall the details of this meeting; but I can reconstruct it: Cantril and Stanton needed a director, and they probably realized that it would be too anxiety-provoking for me to give up the Newark Center as a base. In any case, Cantril was finally willing to change his mind. I have a copy of the letter I wrote to Lynd on September 9, 1937, at his summer residence explaining this development. Reading that four-page

single-spaced letter over today I am amused by the Machiavel-
lianism that I seem to have attributed to myself, at least by
implication. In all likelihood, Cantril did not feel it worthwhile
to bother much, once he had reassured himself that the interests
of the project and Princeton would be properly taken care of.
The substantive parts of the understanding, which marks the
turning point for the rest of my story, I reported to Lynd at
length. Cantril agreed, I wrote Lynd,

> that the actual headquarters of the project would be at the Newark Re-
> search Center and that I would be expected to come down to Princeton
> only for incidental meetings. In addition to my presence in Newark, he
> agreed that any amount of project money that would be allocated for
> research in an urban area could be spent from Newark, which means that
> I could appoint a number of people here for special studies. In practical
> terms, the whole arrangement therefore means that the Research Center
> has a huge new job.

The concern to have all my personal activities funnelled into
an identifiable institution merits a brief digression. I later tried
to persuade my associate directors to adopt this policy generally.
In a memorandum to Cantril and Stanton, written on February
8, 1938, I urged them to identify their "other" activities with
the Princeton Office of Radio Research:

> I feel that all of us should, as much as possible, use our prior activities
> or activities outside the project to feed the project itself. . . . I use just
> everything on which I have worked for the past years and call it radio
> now. . . . Frank is a very good investment from the standpoint of the
> project because of all the material and connections he may put at our
> disposal. I am quite confident that Had's previous and present work could
> be utilized in the same way if he would agree with my philosophy ex-
> pressed here. He and his students would still get all the credit here for
> the work. It will be published in the frame of the project instead of in a
> magazine.

Given the multiple involvements of my then associate directors,
one of whom became the president of a highly endowed research
foundation and the other the president of the Columbia Broadcasting System, my suggestion was met with little enthusiasm.
Nothing further was heard of it.[46]

In the fall of 1937, then, the symbiosis between Princeton and

Newark universities was created. The link was formalized by my appointment as Research Associate at Princeton University. The liberal formulation of the Rockefeller program permitted me to do any kind of specific study as long as I gave it some nominal connection with radio problems, and as a result a slow shift in the whole situation took place. Increasingly the Princeton Office of Radio Research became the main frame for my activities and Newark only the place of its physical location. I still had only a small staff, accidentally assembled, and I therefore had to write many of the early papers myself. In order to conceal this fact I invented a pseudonym, Elias Smith, under which three or four of the early project studies appeared. By now it should not be surprising that I considered it more important to publicize the institution than to lengthen my personal list of publications.[47]

By the spring of 1938, it had become clear to everyone concerned (although perhaps last to me) that the Office of Radio Research had become my main base of operations and that it had acquired an institutional life of its own. We accepted outside grants and made elaborate arrangements with various research agencies to obtain data for secondary analysis. This increasing functional autonomy of the Office was paralleled by a decline of the University of Newark, which soon thereafter collapsed. Sometime in the summer of 1938—and it is perhaps revealing that I can remember none of the details—Kingdon felt that he could use our space to better purpose and asked us to move. By then Edward Suchman had become the manager of our operations. It never occurred to us to move to Princeton; so many of our research contacts had been established in New York City. Suchman was commissioned to find appropriate space in New York, and in the fall of 1938 the Princeton Office of Radio Research moved to 14 Union Square where we rented a few rooms.

The Office of Radio Research—
Work and Policies

A detailed description of the activities of the Princeton Office of Radio Research would go far beyond the purpose of the present essay. Instead, I shall list a number of events and observations which influenced my subsequent work in this country. In the next section matters elucidating European-American research relations will be discussed.

1. Cantril and Stanton, my associate directors, met with me regularly every few weeks to plan and review current work. They allowed me full freedom of decision and provided many valuable contacts, and I kept them informed about everything through a steady flow of memoranda. Copies of many of these notes are preserved and others should be found in their files; it might be worthwhile some day to analyze these documents to obtain a picture of the ways an early bureau director kept things going. I tried in every way I could to foresee and to forestall possible difficulties and created the slogan that it is more important for a director to worry than to work. In addition, I was aware that, as a recent immigrant, much of the authority I had derived from the good will of my two associates, both of whom had much deeper roots in the American scene.

Cantril was correctly strict about budgetary arrangements, since the university held him accountable. I did not make life easy for him, because I often exceeded the Princeton budget, sure that I would cover the deficit with additional income from some other source. By and large, this worked out all right, but it might be appropriate here to point out one weakness in the image of the managerial scholar I had developed. As long as I handled situations myself I was somehow always able to balance the budget, though often I came in by the skin of my teeth. But in situations where I could not go on juggling or raising additional funds, the matter became more complicated. For instance, after I left Vienna for my American fellowship, many financial difficulties seem to have emerged. I received numerous letters, especially from the Bühlers, cursing me for the financial embarrassments I had created for them. Many of the concrete references in these letters I cannot understand today; but there can be little doubt that I had left behind a rather chaotic situation, even if the sums involved seem rather small by today's standards. In financial matters the doctrine of "reasonable risks" may involve special problems.[48]

2. While the budget of the project seemed very large at the time, it soon turned out that it did not permit the collection of

much primary materials. The original plan, as formulated by Cantril and Stanton, assumed that much time would be given to laboratory experiments, but perhaps because of my training, experiments played a small role once I became director. Almost by necessity much of the early work was based on what I later called *secondary analysis*. From Gallup we obtained polls in which he had asked comparative questions on newspaper reading and radio listening, and we analyzed them further. One of our main sources was program ratings which at the time were only used to compare the drawing power of various programs; we reanalyzed this material with special emphasis on social differences, using then as we do now the letters A, B, C to describe the socioeconomic status of respondents.[49]

The secondary analysis of program ratings formed a bridge to my long-standing concern with social stratification. In a memorandum to my associate directors (February 8, 1938), I developed a number of themes which kept recurring in much of our subsequent work.

> In a report by the Cooperative Analysis of Broadcasting I find consistently that the different economic groups show different tendencies in listening. Listening rises from A to C and goes down with the D group. [Here tables were inserted.]

It may seem odd today that these differences were then a surprise. In good Viennese fashion I immediately offered some tentative explanations.

> Probably the decline in listening from the C to A group is due to more education and more money for other kinds of entertainment in the higher groups. It might also be that in the C group the family spirit is more developed. The decline of listening from C to D might be due to bad housing conditions which drive people out of the home; there are still many ways in which this influence can work—for instance, by family discord or gang formation.

It interests me today that I was then aware of the continuity in my own work.

> Systematic comparison might yield very important results. I am speaking from a concrete experience in another field. When I wrote my book on

> Adolescents and Occupation I did nothing for months but collect figures
> on vocational choices all over Germany and Austria; they looked quite
> silly by themselves but gave marvelous leads when compared and the
> circumstances of their collection considered.

This first "concordance" had been written ten years earlier but
in this memo I still found some of the results "marvelous." And
it all led to an administrative policy for which I requested the
support of my associates.

> I am deeply convinced that current business research still contains a great
> wealth of information which has important social implications. Therefore
> I am so concerned with having sources continually comb the agencies for
> such results, which, of course, we shall have to examine very carefully.

The emphasis on this type of material ultimately had considerable influence on my own publications. The Austrian phase of
my research required a diversity of techniques applied to rather
small samples. Now I was faced with the task of making sense
of data from large samples, with relatively little information
about each respondent. This led to my concern with multivariate
analysis.[50]

My interest in methods of qualitative research also broadened.
For a long time I had felt that in this area too methodological
explications were needed and possible. In the introduction to
Komarovsky's study of unemployed families I had written:

> The present study . . . endeavored to contribute a more careful analysis
> of those non-quantitative procedures which very often are left to the
> laziness of "common sense." An assumption is often made that only
> quantitative procedures can be communicated, whereas all other proce-
> dures (insight, understanding) must be left to the inspiration of the student
> and the exigencies of the problem at hand. The non-quantitative methods
> cannot be formulated as explicitly as an arithmetic computation. But these
> procedures, now clothed in ambiguous terms, still remain to be described
> and standardized.

But not much happened until Cantril introduced an important
type of procedure into the activities of the project. He suggested
that a small number of open-ended interviews be conducted with
listeners who were fans of typical radio programs. His suggestion
was taken up by Herta Herzog, who was a staff member for the

first few years. The first and most widely quoted result of this approach was her discussion of the then popular Professor Quiz program.[51] She later made a similar study of listeners to daytime serials, in collaboration with T. W. Adorno, which appeared in the journal of the Horkheimer group which at that time was published in the United States.[52]

The largely qualitative nature of these first two studies was carried over into two subsequent enterprises where a tie-up with small-scale statistics was worked out. One was *The Invasion from Mars*,[53] and the other was the study of the Kate Smith War Bond Drive, a study that was supervised by Robert Merton and formed the basis of his book, *Mass Persuasion* (1947). The two studies just mentioned are examples of what was later dubbed "Firehouse Research." In both cases I had phoned Stanton the morning after the event and he provided money from his CBS research budget for immediate preliminary work. Today the bureaucratization of research applications makes such improvisations difficult. I find this regrettable and wish that emergency research funds that could be quickly mobilized as the situation demands were available.

3. Sometime during this period, Harold Lasswell created his well-known formula for research on mass communications: to investigate who says what to whom, with what effect. Content analysis and audience research deal with the second and the third elements in this formula. The study of effects, the fourth item, was continuously on my mind, and led to panel studies, to be discussed below. The neglect of the "who" by the Princeton project is conspicuous: we never made systematic studies of the kind that today would be called organizational research. I was certainly not oblivious to the problem. The study of the popular music industry referred to below was one early effort; at one point I also commissioned a summary of such available studies as Leo Rosten's analysis of Washington correspondents. This summary was carried out by Alexander George, who later became a distinguished research member of the Rand Corporation.

George's survey was to be part of a large compendium on communications research. Another section was to deal with content analysis and later appeared as a book under the authorship of Bernard Berelson.[54] Joseph Klapper's dissertation on the effects of mass media, later developed into a well-known book, was initially also a part of this enterprise.[55] Still another section on institutions resulted in a number of special studies, most notably a dissertation on unions in the communications industry.

Sometime around 1939 or 1940 our publication policy had become fairly well known, and a number of people offered me studies they had undertaken on their own. One of these approaches came from the professor of government at Harvard, Carl Friedrich. He had done a descriptive analysis of the relations between Congress, the Federal Communications Commission, and the radio industry. His study was subsequently published in the *Political Science Quarterly*, and I consider it a very fine example of institutional analysis, showing a perception of an important problem and providing significant factual information. I declined to include this study as one of our publications. My argument was that the evidence was too anecdotal and did not conform to the quantitative traditions of our project. I want to take this occasion to express my regret to Professor Friedrich. Today I suspect that I then had a more complex motivation characteristic of someone responsible for a new and struggling institution. The next point will provide the necessary background.

4. Communications research was, at the time, a new enterprise, and I gave speeches about it to rather high-level audiences such as the National Association of Broadcasters and the Association of American Newspaper Editors. On such occasions I faced a very difficult problem: the relation with the industry. In one of those speeches, later published in *The Journalism Quarterly*, I formulated the issue as follows:

> Those of us social scientists who are especially interested in communications research depend upon the industry for much of our data. Actually most publishers and broadcasters have been very generous and cooperative in this recent period during which communications research has developed as a kind of joint enterprise between industries and universities. But we academic people always have a certain sense of tightrope walking; at what point will they shut us off from the indispensable sources of funds and data?[56]

I finally thought of a compromise formula. In a speech, "The Role of Criticism in the Management of Mass Media," I started out by saying that the mass media were overly sensitive to the criticism of intellectuals, while the latter were too strict in their overall indictment; there ought to be a way of making criticism more useful and manageable for those who offer it and for those who receive it. An effective way to achieve this might be to make the development of critical talents an accepted part of the training and daily work of anyone connected with the mass media.

Not only should the problems of criticism be thoroughly discussed at conferences such as this, but they also should be the subject-matter of systematic courses and training programs. Students and researchers should come to think of criticism as something being systematically studied; they should be persuaded to undertake critical examinations of the mass media and to produce material amenable to criticism. If the whole area were institutionalized in this way, then there would be less emotionalism connected with it.

I made essentially four suggestions with journalism schools in mind. First, crusading is a traditional and accepted function for the journalist; there should be more careful study of which crusades succeed, which fail, and why; in addition, the question of crusading over the radio should be considered. My second point was that managers of the mass media should attempt to understand better why criticism of their activities is bound to be part of the liberal creed.

The liberals feel betrayed. They hoped that the increased time and money which they fought for would be channelized in directions and activities which interested them; instead it was drained off by the mass media. The situation of the liberals is much like that of the high school boy who, after weeks of saving, accumulates enough money to buy a bracelet for a girl, and who then learns that the girl has gone out with another boy to show off her nice new trinket. You can very well understand why the liberals are angry, and perhaps you can almost sympathize with them.

As a third point I suggested more attention to the critical help which the mass media can give each other. I pointed out that most newspapers had book critics but little discussion of radio programs was available. In this connection, I also cited the close relationship between audience research and literary criticism. Finally, as the fourth point, I suggested that some kind of periodic reporting of the content of mass media should be made available, so that all criticism would have a factual base.

> This country is rightfully proud of its many statistical services. But our social bookkeeping lags woefully when it comes to cultural matters. Social research is probably not yet ready to give us monthly information on how many people are happy or unhappy. But nothing would be easier than to set up a service based on sound sampling techniques which would periodically report the content of newspapers, magazines, and radio programs. It is just a matter of developing the appropriate motivation and providing the appropriate machinery.

In all of the work of the Princeton Office I tried to relate the research to public controversies, but usually thought of our office as serving a mediating function. Thus, for example, we served as a channel for a project of the progressive chairman of the Federal Communications Commission, Clifford Durr. He had commissioned Charles Siepmann to develop ideas on how the FCC could better work for higher broadcasting standards. This assignment resulted in two documents, the FCC's "blue book" promulgating stricter licensing standards, and Siepmann's *Radio: Second Chance*. To both publications the industry reacted with violent antagonism, and I prevailed upon John Marshall of the Rockefeller Foundation to provide a special budget so that I could organize a two-day conference among the industry, the FCC, and prominent scholars in the research field to discuss the issues.[57] Nothing much came of it, but I think this was purely because the beginning of the Second World War and the approaching involvement of the United States eclipsed interest in this kind of topic.

Just before the war, the FCC opened hearings on the question of whether newspapers should be permitted to own radio stations. We received funds to set up punched cards providing, for every station, data on ownership and on the way news programs were handled. These funds were provided by a committee including all radio stations owned by newspapers. This was, at the time, an important source of income for us, but I made it a condition of our work that the FCC would have complete access to our data. In retrospect, I consider it likely that the radio-newspaper committee accepted this neutrality because it was

known that the newspapers owning radio stations were careful
not to use them as a monopolistic device against competing
newspapers which did not own stations; they were amply re-
warded by the increase of advertising revenue, which did not
fall under the scrutiny of the FCC.

5. After one year of existence—in the fall of 1938—the project
was in a peculiar position. On the one hand my all-eggs-in-one-
basket policy had resulted in the collection of a great deal of
material and an enthusiastic work atmosphere within a small but
promising young staff. On the other hand, the "image" of the
office was not good. No central theme was visible, and we began
hearing rumors that important people questioned whether we
knew where we were going.

Clearly, something had to be done. There was indeed no major
study to which I could point; somehow I had to make acceptable
my policy of research improvisation guided by available material
and personal interests and contacts. It occurred to me that I
might persuade a journal to let me serve as guest editor for an
issue on radio research; by writing a general introduction I might
be able to pull together the various studies into something that
would look systematic. I remember vividly that both Cantril and
Stanton told me that this was against the American tradition,
that no editor would allow himself to be displaced by a guest
editor. (It would be useful to check whether this was, indeed,
the case at that time; today, certainly, guest editors are not at
all rare.) I was not discouraged—partly because in Europe guest
editors for scientific journals were well known.[58] Shopping
around, I was told that the editor of the *Journal of Applied
Psychology* might be amenable to such an arrangement. He was,
and the norm that supposedly existed was broken. In February
1939 the first radio research issue under my guest editorship
appeared.[59]

The issue well reflected the situation in which the project
found itself after a year. In an introduction I tried to lay out the
new field of radio research. From a policy point of view I had
three tasks. First, I had to make it convincing that this newcomer
was just as good as the older members of the family of applied
psychology; this I defined as "a sum total of techniques used
by psychologists when they are called upon to collaborate with

agencies empowered to perform specific social initiation.'' It was not difficult to show that, in this sense, radio research was a reasonable parallel to industrial or educational psychology. Second, I wanted to show that something new was developing. This was a movement from descriptive studies to more strictly interpretative work. I chose the following formulation:

> We should not be surprised if a discipline of ''action research'' should evolve one day, bringing out more clearly the great methodological similarity of many studies which now are not connected because they are done under different headings, such as criminology, market research, or accident prevention.

I have since preferred the phrase ''empirical study of action'' because the term ''action research'' acquired a different meaning.[60] And finally, as always, I tried to place the new activity in a broader context:

> The operation of radio certainly bears the imprint of the present social system and is, in turn, bound to have certain effects upon social institutions. . . . The study of radio could even serve as a way to a better understanding of some basic issues in our society. . . . Such problems call for study by sociologists, economists, anthropologists, and have at the same time their psychological side.

My prediction that the new field would partly belong to other social sciences, including sociology, certainly came true.

The contents of the issue reflect my efforts to make the improvisations of the first year appear coherent. The issue was divided into five sections: (1) index problems; (2) program research; (3) questionnaire techniques; (4) research in different fields of activities; (5) reports of other surveys, including a bibliography of ''current radio research in universities.'' In section two I included a number of studies done by other people. One of them was by Charles Osgood, then at Dartmouth, on the separation of appeal and brand name in testing spot-advertising. Another, by Cantril, dealt with the role of familiarity in the selection and enjoyment of radio programs. This was a well-designed experiment in which several radio stations participated; it was clearly a carryover from the pre-1937 plan for the project.

Section four exemplifies the way we used material from seemingly unrelated spheres. From the Komarovsky-Newark cases we culled some of the examples to show the importance of radio for unemployed people, and since Suchman's family owned a taxicab company, we presented an effort to see whether the recent introduction of taxi radios increased accidents. Gerhard Wiebe wrote on ratings of popular songs, and the venerable Elias Smith had two papers on index construction. Papers which later became closely identified with my work were "Interchangeability of Indices" and one on repeated interviews.

As a holding operation the issue was a success. The second year of the project brought up new problems and led, in turn, to the final phase of my story. First, however, there is another, special aspect of our activities to explain.

The Office of Radio Research— Culture Contacts

In the first years of the project I was still concerned with establishing connections between American and European research approaches. In the spirit of the present volume some of these early efforts to merge the research traditions may be worth recording.

1. Soon after the Princeton project began, I arranged a dinner meeting with several psychoanalysts to obtain from them ideas on what we should pay attention to in our program. The meeting was held on December 16, 1957, and, according to a somewhat defective record, at least the following people participated: Karen Horney, Harry Stack Sullivan, John Dollard, and Erich Fromm. Along with the invitation, I distributed a two-page, single-spaced list of questions I wanted to raise. Among these were the following: Can Freudian theory elucidate the entertainment value of radio and account for some especially successful programs? Can the method of free association be used in our study of radio listening? In developing types of radio listeners, will we have to go back to early childhood experiences? Would a psychoanalytic developmental theory clarify the role of radio at different ages? The list of questions ended with the following

paragraph:

> I am sure that in many of the cases you treated, radio was somewhat
> connected with the troubles of your patients. It would be very helpful for
> us if you could try to remember examples of this kind and tell about them
> in our meeting. We feel that you might have observed situations and
> incidents which are quite beyond the reach of our usual experimental
> methods.

I had a preliminary session with Fromm, at which I gave him
the necessary information for the initial statement he made at
the meeting; a six-page summary of his statement has survived.

I had no special involvement with psychoanalysis. The episode
was part of a general concern with combining humanistic and
quantitative approaches. Since that time, the convergence of
social research with psychoanalytical case studies has become
more familiar. In the 1937, however, our enterprise was probably
quite novel. It would be necessary to study the minutes in more
detail to decide whether the meeting really led to interesting
ideas.

2. A historical orientation was another concern of this kind.
When I submitted my first progress report to the Rockefeller
Foundation in 1939 I pointed out that efforts to assess the effects
of radio on American society fifteen years after this new medium
had appeared seemed a rather hazardous enterprise. To stress
the point I suggested the parallel of a professor who, in 1500,
might have been asked to assess the effect of printing on medieval society. After much careful empirical study, he might
have argued cogently that printing had not had much effect:

> For one, printing would be so expensive that it could not compete with
> the copying done by monks in a monastery. Furthermore, hardly anyone
> knew how to read, so what is the advantage of being able to provide larger
> numbers of copies? Then, too, religion was the only problem which really
> mattered in 1500, but the question of religion is for the pulpit, or for the
> private thought of individuals; it is not a topic which can be conveyed in
> print. And so for all these reasons, it is quite clear that printing will not
> have any effect on society, and that settles the matter in 1500.

For many years I used to lecture on mass media of communication in modern society. One of these talks is preserved be-

cause it finally became a Borah Foundation lecture, presented in Moscow, Idaho, in 1954; it has a rather extensive section on "historical retrospect." There was one idea which I used to reiterate.[61]

At the time of the American Revolution, there was a very simple two-sided relationship. On the one side were the citizens; on the other was the government. Anyone who had political theories or an interest in political activities was either an actual or potential publisher, so that the publisher shared common interests with other citizens. The citizen and the publisher together fought for their freedom to criticize the government. In the last century, however, the situation has become vastly more complicated. The simple two-sided relationship has been superseded by a complex three-cornered structure. The citizens still represent one corner, the government still represents another, but now there is also the communications industry. This leads to complicated and sometimes surprising alliances. *Occasionally the citizen forms an alliance with the industry against the government; occasionally with the government against the industry; occasionally he finds himself faced with an alliance between the government and industry.* Many questions about the mass media can be answered if this development from a two-sided to a three-cornered relationship is kept in mind; confusion results if the historical trend is lost from sight. [Italics provided now.][62]

The idea of latent strategy is again pertinent. This type of historical analysis seemed to me helpful for the policy problems discussed above. By stressing that controversial topics are eternal but at the same time variable in their implications, I could keep the Bureau maneuvering between the intellectual and political purist and an industry from which I wanted cooperation without having to "sell out." At the same time my historical interest was quite genuine and remained a characteristic feature of my activities. While the debate about mass culture was particularly acute, I sponsored Leo Lowenthal's work on the history of criticism of the mass media.[63] A few years later, when I was president of the American Association for Public Opinion Research, my address dealt with "The Historian and the Pollster," a theme which has remained a topic of discussion.[64] And from time to time I have published essays on such topics as the history of quantification, of concept formation, and of the empirical study of action.[65]

3. Still another convergence with the humanities was in the

field of music; this deserves more detailed discussion. I had always been interested in music, and when I became director of the Princeton project I immediately set up a special music division. The first two studies set the stage for the general program. To begin with, we started an institutional study of the popular music industry which, until then, had received little serious attention. At the same time, we initiated a survey to trace the effect of the New York City transmitter, WNYC, one of the first radio stations to broadcast large amounts of classical music. This was prior to the popularity of records, and interest in serious music was still quite rare; we wanted to know whether WNYC contributed to diffusion of such interests.[66]

But I had more general plans for this division. I had known about the work of T. W. Adorno on the sociology of music. He is now a major figure in German sociology, and represents one side in a continuing debate between two positions, often distinguished as critical and positivistic sociology.[67] I was aware of these controversial features of Adorno's work, but was intrigued by his writings on the "contradictory" role of music in our society.[68] I considered it a challenge to see whether I could induce Adorno to try to link his ideas with empirical research. In addition, I felt gratitude to the Frankfurt group led by Max Horkheimer, of which he was a member; they had helped support the work of the Newark Center, and I knew they wanted Adorno in this country. I therefore invited him to become part-time director of the music division of our project. To provide an expert on empirical data I appointed at the same time a former student of Stanton's, Gerhard Wiebe, who was a fine jazz musician, with a Ph.D. in psychology. Together, he and Adorno, I hoped, would develop a convergence of European theory and American empiricism.

The actual course of events was quite different from these expectations. Cooperation between the two men became difficult, and Adorno came to symbolize a more general problem. In a number of memos written in the spring of 1938 to my associate directors I explained the brilliance and importance of Adorno's ideas. This seemed to me necessary since his interviews with people in the radio industry had led to complaints of biased questions and distorted replies. This was the result,

I explained, of misunderstandings common in encounters of this sort. To straighten out the situation, I asked Adorno to summarize his ideas in a memorandum which I planned to circulate among various experts to secure a broader basis of support for his work. In June 1938 he delivered a memorandum of 160 single-spaced pages, entitled "Music in Radio." But it seemed to me that the distribution of this text would only have made the situation more difficult, for in English his writing had the same tantalizing attraction and elusiveness that it had in German. The notion of "fetish" played—as could be expected from a neo-Marxist—a central role. He proposed to use it

> wherever any human activity or any product of that activity becomes alienated from men so that they can no longer, so to speak, recognize themselves in it. Then they venerate it as something whose value is utterly divorced from the human activity which comprises it and from the function which it actually exercises upon other human activities. In any case (for instance, in the case of stars who have become fetishes) this is very close to the concept of suggestion by which people venerate something without quite knowing why . . . and without being immediately related to it. The scope of fetishes is larger, however, than that of suggestion and propaganda. In present day society, people are ready to throw the effects upon commodities because the commodity value is the fundamental value they acknowledge, even in cases where that value is not impressed upon them by any special propaganda for suggestion.

Critical theory scorns the use of definitions; but certainly Adorno was able to give vivid examples which helped to convey what he had in mind, as can be seen from another paragraph:

> But the musical fetish-making goes far beyond the limits of the so-called "stars" which, on the surface, seem to be responsible for the features mentioned here. The fetish actually takes possession of practically every musical category in radio. Music in radio is thought of in terms of private property. As an illustration let us cite the cult of famous musical instruments, either Stradivarius violins (even though the average listener is definitely unable to make any distinction between a Strad and another ordinary good violin); or the piano once played by famous people like Chopin or Richard Wagner; or, last but not least, certain elements of the composition which are overemphasized by radio technique and which, at the same time, seem to represent music as a commodity.

From the project's point of view the main problem was to see whether the phenomenon of fetishism could be described by a direct approach to a sample of listeners. (The same issue exists when Durkheim's structural notion of anomie is to be paralleled by the distribution of an individual characteristic now often called anomia.) Adorno and I agreed that he would establish a more discriminating typology; then a questionnaire might lead to a quantitative distribution of different types of music listeners. But no indicators for such a typology were developed because the direction he gave could hardly be translated into empirical terms. Thus, for instance, one of the types was described as follows:

> Sometimes music has the effect of freeing hidden sexual desires. This seems to be the case particularly with women who regard music as a sort of image of their male partner, to which they yield without ever identifying themselves with the music. It is this sort of attitude which is indicated by weeping. The amateur's weeping when he listens to music (the musician will practically never weep) is one of the foremost tasks of the analysis of the emotional side of music.

I wrote Adorno a detailed criticism of his memorandum, and we finally agreed that he would write a much briefer document which could then be discussed at a meeting with several experts. This meeting took place sometime during the winter of 1938/ 1939, but it was not profitable. John Marshall was present and probably felt that my efforts to bring Adorno's type of critical research into the communications field were a failure. The renewal of the Rockefeller grant in the fall of 1939 provided no budget for continuation of the music project.

I never regretted having invited Adorno to join the project. Soon after he left, the Horkheimer group devoted an issue of their journal to the problem of modern mass communication, and to this I contributed an essay in which I tried to explain the "critical approach" sympathetically to an American audience, and illustrated ways in which this basic position can lead to new research ideas.[69] I even tried to spell out "the operations into which critical communications research could be broken down." I used comparisons to highlight the main idea: the consumer movements fight misleading advertising and some economists deplore its wastefulness; but the critical approach thinks that any kind of promotion prevents people from developing their own standards of judgment. I ended the paper with the following sentences:

> [The] Office of Radio Research has cooperated in this issue because it was felt that only a very catholic conception of the task of research can lead to valuable results. . . . The writer, whose interests and occupational duties are in the field of administrative research, wanted to express his conviction that there is here a type of approach which, if it were included in the general stream of communications research, could contribute much in terms of challenging problems and new concepts useful in the interpretation of known, and in the search for new, data.

The defeat of this hope in the Princeton project has left a troublesome question in my mind. After the war Adorno was an active member of the Berkeley group that produced *The Authoritarian Personality*. Their basic concept of the fascistic character was developed by Adorno and was certainly no less speculative than what he wrote for us; nevertheless, his colleagues in California were able to convert his idea into the famous F-scale. I have an uneasy feeling that my duties in the various divisions of the Princeton project may have prevented me from devoting the necessary time and attention to achieve the purpose for which I engaged Adorno originally. As it was, the only product we were able to publish was a paper of his on the radio symphony; he himself later published an abbreviated version of the memorandum mentioned above.[70]

I take some comfort from the fact that not all contacts with German experts on esthetic matters misfired. Rudolf Arnheim had written sensitive essays on movies as a form of art. I commissioned him to analyze the scripts of about fifty daytime serials, which he did brilliantly. One of his observations has often been quoted since: the so-called soap operas, which consisted of continuing stories in which families found themselves in trouble which they succeeded in resolving only to encounter new troubles, were broadcast during the day and were listened to mainly by housewives. Arnheim noticed, and developed the implications of the fact, that the troubles were always caused by men and the solutions provided by women. I remember the collaboration with him as enlightening for me and useful for the project.[71]

When the office moved to Columbia and my permanent appointment there became conceivable, the university became my main reference group and the concern with culture contacts began to weaken. It is quite likely that in many other respects the American component in my marginal position became increasingly stronger. But obviously my concern with the relation between the two social science traditions never subsided. In 1959 I was the rapporteur on methodology for the Stresa Convention of the International Sociological Association. The main theme of my report was how to avoid misunderstandings between European and American sociologists.

From Princeton to Columbia

In several respects the second academic year of the Princeton Office of Radio Research (1938/1939) was similar to the first, but a certain amount of consolidation became visible. The papers of this period were published in a second issue of the *Journal of Applied Psychology*, entitled "Progress in Radio Research."[72] In the introduction I wrote as guest editor, I stated:

> At least three major trends in radio research have become noticeable. Studies on the effect of radio are moving into the foreground; material collected for commercial purposes is ever more frequently available for scientific analysis; and related areas such as reading research are developing so fast that the discipline of general communications research seems in the making.

The reference to the study of printed mass media deserves some comment. Circulation figures of magazines seem small compared to the size of radio audiences, but each copy of a magazine is read by several people; such readership figures are comparable to the audience rating. From our point of view, this opened a new area of secondary analysis: studying the structure of magazine "audiences" and drawing conclusions from a comparison with the distribution of radio listeners.[73]

Two activities moved into the foreground. One was what later became known as the Lazarsfeld-Stanton Program Analyzer. I had always been interested in popular music, and while still in

Vienna devised a technique by which one could relate the musical structure of a song to the emotional reactions of listeners. Now at the Princeton project I was able to extend the idea to all kinds of radio programs and finally to films. Stanton greatly improved the technical aspects of the device. We published a number of technical studies of this program analyzer but it was too expensive a procedure to use ourselves.[74] It was doubtful that we could patent it, but two commercial groups, CBS and the McCann-Erikson advertising company, paid us a fee for the right to use the device in their own research departments. Since then program analyzers have found a variety of commercial applications. I hope that one day the whole idea will become again an object of academic inquiry.

While the critical importance of the program analyzer faded after a time, panel studies became increasingly central in our activities. In going over the early files of the Princeton project, I was surprised to see how soon after our start we began to experiment with repeated interviews to study the effect of radio. Though I can find now no full reports on the subject,[75] there are memoranda to the staff and to the associate directors from 1938 indicating that we spent much of our project money on small pilot studies tracing the effect of various local campaigns in New Jersey.

Administratively, the main innovation in the later part of the Princeton period was a series of Rockefeller fellowships which John Marshall established for graduate students who wanted to specialize in communications research; we integrated the work of these fellows into our general program, and I was charged with supervising their work. The policy was to assign them to concrete media activities, such as a public affairs program emanating from the University of Chicago or a radio station serving a largely rural population and managed by the State University of Iowa. A number of these specialized studies were published by the Federal Educational Radio Commission. It might be worthwhile to trace the origin and demise of that commission as part of the history of early efforts in educational radio and television.

Toward the spring of 1939, the problem of renewal of the Rockefeller grant became urgent. John Marshall, who had followed our work closely, was in favor of it. He appointed a review committee that included Charles Siepmann, Harold Lasswell, Robert Lynd, and Lyman Bryson. They gave a favorable verdict,[76] but for people less directly informed about details, the lack of a central theme after two years seems to have made a poor impression. During a trip to Iowa I received a wire from John Marshall that the foundation officers required more solid evidence of achievement before they would approve our application.

The problem for us was to review the available material and to select a theme around which a good part of it could be organized. For a variety of reasons, a comparison between radio and printed media seemed the most promising choice. This is how *Radio and the Printed Page* (1940) was born, a book that appears to have played a considerable role in consolidating the field of communications research. It was a gruelling task to assemble the manuscript in a short period of time; we worked day and night literally, in relays, to accomplish it. I mobilized all conceivable resources, and I remember with special gratitude the help of Lloyd Free who volunteered to see us through this crisis. We had data from a Gallup poll on preferences for news reports, but they were not properly analyzed, and I therefore induced Samuel Stouffer to come to New York to supervise this part of the work. On his own initiative he added a clever analysis of newspaper circulation figures to trace the probable effect of radio; the two sections he contributed to the book are now properly included in his collected papers.[77]

We submitted the report on the morning of the deadline, which, if I remember correctly, was July 1, 1939. John Marshall was satisfied and considered it an appropriate basis on which to propose continuation of our project officially to the foundation.[78]

Meanwhile, internal difficulties had developed between Cantril and me. During the negotiations with the Rockefeller Foundation for a renewal of the grant, it became clear that an administrative decision had to be made. Either the project would stay at Princeton with Cantril as the main figure but with a new director, or, if I were to remain, the project would have to look for another institutional base. The foundation naturally turned to Stanton as a third insider to arbitrate the situation; from the outcome I gather that Stanton put his weight on my side. Lynd prevailed on President Dodds of Princeton to release the project. In the fall of 1939, the Office of Radio Research was turned over to Columbia University, and at the same time I was appointed a lecturer there.[79] The foundation gave us a temporary grant to prepare a proposal for a three-year continuation to begin March 1940.

The crucial part of the proposal we then wrote—from the point of view of further developments—was the following passage:

> It is proposed, by utilizing the panel technique developed in the first two years of the project, to locate those individuals who do change their habits in response to a continuous sequence of broadcasts; and then to study in detail the circumstances surrounding the listening and subsequent changes in these individuals. The plan involves the selection of two basically comparable but contrasting panels of some 200 persons each, and the interviewing of them six or eight times at intervals throughout the course of a continuous program sequence to which they listen.

I originally proposed that we carry out our test on "a program of the Department of Agriculture, since its innovations made major changes in American behavior and, it so happens, this Department has developed the most extensive use of the radio in support of its policies." I do not remember how this proposal was altered so that the November 1940 election became the focus of the first panel study. But such a change was carried out, and the result was *The People's Choice*.[80] The third edition of the book (1968) contains an extensive introduction that traces the impact of this first elaborate election study on subsequent political analysis both here and abroad.[81]

As far as work and administration were concerned, the move to Columbia made very little difference. We were located in a condemned building, the former site of the medical school on 59th Street and Amsterdam Avenue—a neighborhood then called Hell's Kitchen. (It is now part of the Lincoln Center area.) The financial core was the Rockefeller grant which had been renewed for three years. It was supplemented by a large number of commercial contracts. Often the fees were paid in checks made out to me personally, which were then redistributed as staff salaries. I was still rather uninformed about Internal Revenue regulations and in retrospect consider myself lucky not to have gotten into trouble handling funds in this way. The office had a supervisory board consisting of four Columbia professors and Frank Stanton. Somewhere along the line the organization acquired its present name, the Bureau of Applied Social Research.[82]

At about this time the United States prepared for and finally entered the war. In our little world this had two consequences. Stouffer had become research director for the United States Army and used the Bureau and its personnel for a variety of services. The fees provided by these assignments were turned over to the Bureau and were an important financial help. (We had a similar arrangement with the Office of War Information.) Robert Merton worked for a short while with Stouffer in Washington but returned to New York and channeled his work through the Bureau. He has remained an associate director and has played a crucial role in its subsequent development.[83] In our wartime work we concentrated on the testing of films and radio programs devised to maintain the morale of various sectors of the civilian and military populations. The main record of this effort is reported in the third volume of *The American Soldier*, which records, among a great many other things, the contribution to the war effort of the program analyzer, thinly disguised, on the advice of the editor of the volume, Carl Hovland, as the polygraph.[84]

By 1944 the need for a firmer organization became obvious. Columbia had a Council for Research in the Social Sciences, and for two years we received from them a subsidy of $5,000; they probably also assumed some financial supervision. My memory of the administrative details of this transitional period is as hazy as were the actual arrangements. Finally the Columbia Council, which up until then just dispensed small grants for faculty projects, commissioned its chairman, the economist Frederick Mills, to study the research efforts of the various departments in the Faculty of Political Science. A questionnaire was sent out; apparently only the Department of Sociology reported any form of organized activities. So Mills recommended to the Council in

August 1944 that

a special committee of the Council be created to supervise the Office of Applied Social Research and other agencies of the same sort that may operate under the auspices of the Council. This supervising committee should give particular attention during the present academic year to an evaluation of the work of the Office of Applied Social Research, and to means by which the work of this office might be more effectively related to other Columbia research activities.

The committee thus appointed was clearly aware that something new was taking place; but its positive recommendations were more in the nature of acquiescence than of leadership. In October 1944 it made a number of recommendations of which the following two were most pertinent to the Bureau's existence:

Emphasis will be on research and training for research. Conducting work under contracts with commercial or other organizations will not be considered inconsistent with this condition provided the research emphasis be maintained.

Accounts of research agencies operating under the supervision of the Committee on the Administration of Social Research Agencies should be established and administered by the Bursar, under the general provisions proposed by the Committee on Patents and the Committee on Industrial Research.

The great innovation was the decision that contract work would be permitted. Today, when 50 percent of Columbia's operating budget comes from contracts, this does not seem like a major revolution, but it marks, I believe, a real turning point in the history of American universities. Even so, the committee missed the main point we were trying to make. We did not—using a saying by Anatole France—look for freedom to sleep under the bridges of the Seine; we wanted Columbia to accept the positive duty of integrating into its general instructional program training in empirical social research.[85] We protested the committee's failure to respond to this possibility, and, as a result, the Council appointed a special committee to decide on the role of the Bureau within the structure of the university. The chairman of this crucial committee was Elliot Cheatham, Professor of Legal Ethics in the School of Law;[86] one of its members was Arthur MacMahon. The group met frequently between December 1944 and May 1945, and finally recommended the status which the Bureau has today, "a research unit of the Graduate Faculty of Political Science of Columbia University," with space on the campus and about 10 percent of its operating budget provided by the university. A large amount of correspondence and memoranda resulting from the work of the Cheatham Committee has fortunately been preserved, and I hope one day to analyze these documents in detail. I note, in reviewing the files quickly, a detailed fifteen-page memorandum written to Cheatham on his request that describes the operation of a social research center in terms that are quite literally applicable to the Bureau as it is today and to the whole range of similar institutions that have sprung up since then throughout the country. An initial letter of mine to Cheatham telescopes all the issues we faced at the time:

> It has almost become a commonplace that sociology is, at this moment, in a difficult stage of transition. The student in the field realizes that empirical research has become an integral part of sociology, but the universities have not yet developed budgetary and personnel provisions for such work. What one might call an institutional lag between the needs of the discipline and the administrative institution appears in practically all universities. The administrative problems with which your Committee is concerned at this moment can best be understood as deriving from the anomaly of having a division of the University which is essentially self-supporting.

I then conjured up a different way in which this problem could have been solved:

> I could have spent all my energies in promoting the idea that the University administration should provide the necessary minimum budget of $25,000 to establish such a social research laboratory. Had I succeeded, this laboratory would have been set up as an integral part of the University from the outset, and its work would have proceeded in familiar, academic form.

I did not believe then, nor do I believe today, that there was the slightest chance that this would come about. As if I had known that one day I would write the present memoir I put on record my strategy and my confidence in it:

> But because I was too impatient, or too pessimistic, or too sharply aware of how new institutions develop, I took a different course. The present Bureau was built up around an original Rockefeller grant, without budgetary assistance from the University. Service jobs for commercial and governmental agencies were the main sources of income. Practically all of these studies had scientifically valuable aspects, but only surplus time and money could be devoted to completely scientific purposes. Nevertheless, the Bureau now exists as a social science laboratory and is at the full disposal of the Department.

I then played my final gambit. Can a modern university really do without something like our Bureau? If not, could I take a chance on something very close to blackmail? I tried, along the following line:

> Perhaps the unorthodox operation of the Bureau creates problems which outweigh its advantages. It seems to me perfectly legitimate to consider whether it might not be better to close it and wait until the time is ripe for it to be resumed on the basis of full support by the University. If, on the other hand, one agrees that new insitutions are often created first and then legalized, the work of your Committee might be looked at as a part of this process.

This letter was written in January 1945. Twenty-three years later I find myself chairman of a board of sixteen distinguished representatives of professional schools and graduate departments at Columbia—a board which the Cheatham Committee, when it legitimized the Bureau, set up to keep close watch on its risky director. It would be nice if this symbolized the final victory of an idea born in Vienna almost half a century ago. But it does not. Today scores of such bureaus exist throughout the country, many of them directed by alumni of the Columbia prototype, but they are not yet really integrated into the university structure. The effort continues. This year I induced the Columbia administration to appoint a new committee to see how the position of our Bureau could be improved. To bring them up to date I distributed to the members of this body copies of the letter from which I just quoted.

APPENDIX
THE SOCIAL RESEARCH INSTITUTE IN THE
AMERICAN UNIVERSITY
Reprinted with permission from *American Sociological
Review* (1962).

You are all aware of the controversies which have grown up
around these institutes. On the positive side, we may note the
following. They provide technical training to graduate students
who are empirically inclined; the projects give students opportunities for closer contact with senior sociologists; the data collected for practical purposes furnish material for dissertations
through more detailed study, or what is sometimes called secondary analysis; the members of a department with an effective
institute can give substance to their lectures with an enviable
array of actual data; skills of intellectual cooperation and division
of labor are developed; chances for early publications by
younger sociologists are enhanced.

On the other side of the debate, the argument goes about as
follows. Students who receive most of their training on organized
projects become one-sided; instead of developing interests of
their own, they become mercenaries of their employers; where
institutes become influential, important sociological problems
are neglected because they do not lend themselves to study by
the "research machinery"; people who work best on their own
find themselves without support and are regarded as outsiders.

The situation, as I see it, is promising but confused. We allow
these institutes to develop without giving them permanent support, without integrating them into the general university structure, without even really knowing what is going on outside our
immediate academic environment. As a bare minimum it is imperative that a more detailed study of the current situation be
carried out. This would, I hope, lead to recommendations for
university administrators, for members of our own association,
and for all others concerned with the basic problem of how the
avalanche of empirical social research can be fitted into current
educational activities without having careless institutional improvisations destroy important traditional values or hinder creative new developments. True, we have no perfect formula for

incorporating institutes into our graduate education. But pluralism is not the same as anarchy, and it is anarchy with which we are faced at the moment. Some form of permanent core support, assimilation of teaching and of institute positions, a better planned division of the students' time between lectures and project research, a closer supervision of institute activities by educational officers, more explicit infusion of social theory into the work of the institutes—all this waits for a systematic discussion and for a document which may perform the service which the Flexner report rendered to medical education fifty years ago.

In such a report the role of the institute director will have to figure prominently. Let me place him in a broader framework. We are confronted nowadays, in our universities, with a serious problem which can be classified as an "academic power vacuum." When graduate education in this country began, no one doubted that the university president was an important figure. Gilman at Johns Hopkins and White at Cornell were intellectual as well as administrative leaders. Stanley Hall at Clark was impressive both as a president and as a psychologist. Inversely, individual professors were deeply involved in organizational innovation. John W. Burgess forced the creation of a graduate faculty upon the Columbia trustees. In his autobiography he describes movingly what this meant to him as a teacher and scholar. Silliman sacrificed his private fortune to establish a physical laboratory in his home and finally convinced the trustees at Yale that natural sciences were not a spiritual threat to young Americans.

Today, however, we witness a dangerous divergence: academic freedom is more and more interpreted in such a way as to keep the administration out of any truly academic affairs; and the faculty, in turn, has come to consider administration beneath its dignity. But educational innovations are, by definition, intellectual as well as administrative tasks. And, so, they have fallen into a no-man's land: the president and his staff wait for the faculty to take the initiative; the professors on their side consider that such matters would take time away from their true scholarly pursuits. As a result, many of our universities have a dangerously low level of institutional development.

One institutional consequence of research institutes is that they inevitably train men who are able and willing to combine intellectual and administrative leadership. An institute director, even if his unit only facilitates faculty research, must train a staff able to advise on important research functions. It is not impossible that, on specific topics, the collective experience of the institute staff exceeds the skills of the individual faculty member. One who has lived with scores of questionnaires can help write a better questionnaire on a subject matter in which he is not expert. Having helped to dig up documents and sources of data on many subjects makes for greater efficiency even on a topic not previously treated. In an autonomous unit this is even more pronounced. Here the staff carries out a self-contained work schedule. A hierarchy is needed, proceeding often from assistants to project supervisors, to program director, and, finally, to the director himself. The latter is at least responsible for reports and publications. But the director is also concerned with maintaining what is sometimes called the "image" of his operation. Its prestige, its attraction for staff and students, and its appeal for support are self-generated, not derived only from the reputation of the teaching departments. The professional staff sees its future career closely bound up with the destiny of the unit, a fact which sometimes makes for challenging problems in human organization.

At the same time, the director must develop the coordinating skills so necessary in a modern university. Often the place of his unit in the organization chart is not well defined. The novelty of the whole idea makes for instability and requires considerable institutional creativity. And, finally, we should frankly face the fact that in our system of higher education the matching of budgetary funds with substantive intellectual interests is a characteristic and enduring problem. The institute director knows the skills and interests of the faculty members, and he brings men and money together. This is not badly described as the role of "idea broker." Often he will have to work hard to obtain funds for a more unusual research idea suggested to him; at other times a possible grant looks so attractive that he will try to discover, among some of his faculty colleagues, what he would diplomatically call a "latent interest."

I am afraid this is not the appropriate forum for reforming university presidents. But I can at least try to convince some of you that directing a research institute is no more in conflict with scholarly work than is teaching. The director is faced with a variety of research problems which permit him to try out his intellectual taste and skills, while the individual scholar might find himself committed to a study prematurely chosen. The multitude of data passing through the director's hands considerably broadens his experience. Staff conferences provide a unique sounding board for new ideas. Even negotiations for grants open vistas into other worlds which a sociologist can turn to great advantage in his own work. Undoubtedly not every personality type is suited for this role, and even the right type of man needs proper training. But the opportunities for self-expression and for intellectual growth are considerable, and sociologists, in particular, should not be misled by the prevalent stereotype of administration.

[2]

The Obligations of the 1950 Pollster to the 1984 Historian

The meetings of the American Association for Public Opinion Research give testimony to the great progress which its members have made in two respects: our work has shown great technical improvement over the last few years and we have tried to make it ever more useful. Those of us who work at universities, however, often have to meet the criticism that technical excellence and usefulness are not enough. The significance of our work is doubted.

It is not always easy to say exactly what critics mean by lack of significance, but in many of their comments we find them asking that research work be undertaken for other than immediate practical purposes. This "transcendency" is looked for in at least three directions. Some feel that too much polling work is done for private clients and not enough in the public interest. This is certainly true and many of us wish the availability of funds would make possible a different state of affairs. Others mean that our work does not contribute enough to general theoretical knowledge. In this respect we ourselves have started to improve matters. The program for our meetings this year shows clearly that we are looking more and more on public opinion research as part of an analysis of political behavior on the one hand, and as part of a general theory of opinion formation and decision making on the other.

But there is at least one more aspect of this quest for significance. This has to do with the choice of specific topics in even

From *Public Opinion Quarterly* (1950), 14:618–38. Reprinted by permission. Presidential address to the American Association for Public Opinion Research.

the simplest opinion poll. Even if we do not work for a specific client, do we not have a tendency to ask questions which will make interesting reading in tomorrow's newspapers? Don't we overlook the fact that, in a way, the pollster writes contemporary history? Might not the 1984 historian reproach us for not having given enough thought to what he will want to know about 1950?

Here we might explain why 1984 has been chosen for our title. In the late George Orwell's novel, the hero, Winston Smith, has grave doubts whether the world of dictatorship and thought police in which he lives is really as wonderful as the tele-screens in every other corner tell him it is. He is consumed by a desire to find out how life looked forty years earlier. But he cannot find out. A Ministry of Truth operating in Orwell's nightmare employs many historians whose sole task is to change and adapt history to the vacillating needs of the dictator. Old issues of the *London Times* are continuously rewritten so that anyone who wants to consult the past will find that it supports the party line of the day. The despair of not being able to compare the present with the past is one of the most haunting features of Orwell's story.

The Historian's Attitude to Attitudes

We all hope that this picture of the future is purely fictional, and that the 1984 historian will not block the citizen of his day from understanding the past. But how much help will he be in 1984 if we do not help him in 1950? Let me begin with a more remote example in which a famous historian was confronted with exactly this problem of explaining the past to his contemporaries.

In the fifteenth century Machiavelli wrote what is probably one of the first examples of modern and careful analysis of political behavior. And yet, for several centuries afterward, "Machiavellian" stood for everything evil in public affairs. At the beginning of the nineteenth century a reaction set in, and in 1837 the English historian and statesman Macaulay wrote an essay to set the matter straight. He wanted to explain why Machiavelli was so misunderstood. His answer was that *The Prince* was written at a time and in a social setting where people had a very different way of looking at things. His argument runs about as follows: At the end of the Middle Ages the Italian cities had developed a middle-class culture of artisans and merchants, while the countries north of the Alps, like England, France, and Germany were still in a barbarous state. In the north, courage was the main means of survival; courage to withstand the hardships of life and courage to repel hostile hordes which were incessantly threatening each other with war. In the Italian cities, ingenuity was the most cherished ability; ingenuity in improving the protective value of the community, and ingenuity in meeting the competition of fellow citizens in an essentially democratic society. "Hence while courage was a point of honor in other countries ingenuity became the point of honor in Italy."

The pertinence of this passage to Macaulay's main topic is obvious. He feels that a great thinker living in what we today would call "an ingenuity culture" was judged by people who lived and are still living in the aftermath of a "courage culture."

From our point of view it is important to see what evidence Macaulay tried to adduce for his thesis. The great English historian struggles hard to make his point clear and convincing to his reader. First of all he compares an English and an Italian hero. Henry V was admired by the English because he won a great battle, in spite of his personal crudeness and cruelty. Francis Sforza was admired by the Italians because he was a successful statesman, in spite of his personal treachery and faithlessness.

And still, Macaulay is not yet quite sure that the reader has seen the matter clearly. He finally hits upon what seems to him a useful literary device, and what today we can consider probably the first projective test recorded in the literature. He writes:

> We have illustrated our meaning by an instance taken from history. We will select another from fiction. Othello murders his wife; he gives orders for the murder of his lieutenant; he ends by murdering himself. *Yet he never loses the esteem and affection of Northern readers.* His intrepid and ardent spirit redeems everything. The unsuspecting confidence with which he listens to his adviser, the tempest of passion with which he commits his crimes, and the haughty fearlessness with which he avows them, give an extraordinary interest to his character. Iago, on the contrary,

is the object of universal loathing. . . . *Now we suspect that an Italian audience in the fifteenth century would have felt very differently.* Othello would have inspired nothing but detestation and contempt. The folly with which he trusts the friendly professions of a man whose promotion he had obstructed, the credulity with which he takes unsupported assertions, and trivial circumstances, for unanswerable proofs, the violence with which he silences the exculpation till the exculpation can only aggravate his misery, would have excited the abhorrence and disgust of the spectators. The conduct of Iago they would assuredly have condemned; but they would have condemned it as we condemn that of his victim. Something of interest and respect would have mingled with their disapprobation. The readiness of the traitor's wit, the clearness of his judgment, the skill with which he penetrates the dispositions of others and conceals his own, would have ensured to him a certain portion of their esteem. (Emphasis mine)

It is clear what Macaulay is striving for. He wishes someone had conducted attitude studies in Florence and in London of the fifteenth century. Let us suppose that a polling agency existed at the time and was hired by Macaulay to test his hypothesis. In a somewhat facetious way, we can imagine how they might have proceeded. The Othello story could have been written up in one or two paragraphs, without giving either Othello or Iago any advantage. Pretests could have been conducted to make sure that the wording was quite unbiased. (Perhaps they might have concealed the fact that Othello was a Negro because that might bias some respondents.) The crucial question would have been: How many Florentines and Londoners, respectively, approve of Iago, how many of Othello, and how many say "don't know?" Nothing less, but hardly much more, would have been needed to provide empirical evidence for Macaulay's brilliant conjecture.

Few historians will make such elaborate efforts to document their statements about public attitudes. It is much more likely that we shall find statements which read like a Gallup release, except, of course, that the tables are missing. Take, for instance, the following account from Merle Curti's, "The Thrust of the Civil War into Intellectual Life."

A growing number of men and women in both sections, distrustful of their leaders, sympathetic with the enemy, or merely war-weary, preferred

compromise or even defeat to the continuation of the struggle. The fact
of war affected the thinking not only of these dissidents but of the great
majority of people who accepted it as inevitable and hoped that good
would come from it.

Here are all the ingredients of a statement on the distribution
of attitudes. We find quantitative statements like "a growing
number" or "the great majority of people." There are suggestions for comparisons between men and women and between
different sections of the country. The passage which we have
quoted even implies certain cross-tabulations between attitudes
toward the war and attitudes toward other issues of the day.

No wonder, then, that the historians of a later period for which
polls were already available would eagerly incorporate them into
their writings. Dixon Wecter writes *The Age of the Great Depression*. At one point he discusses the growing acceptance of birth
control. To document this trend, he first uses the traditional,
indirect methods of the historian, trying to derive attitudes from
their manifestations. He points to the change in terms, from
"race suicide" to "birth control" and finally to "planned parenthood." Then he goes at his topic more directly.

A poll among *Farm and Fireside* readers early in the Depression showed
two to one for giving medical advice on planned parenthood, and during
the thirties the Sears, Roebuck catalogue began to list contraceptive
wares. A straw vote of subscribers by the *Protestant Churchman* in January, 1935, revealed almost unanimous approval for birth control, while
in the next year, among all sorts and conditions, a Gallup poll agreed with
a *Fortune* survey in finding two out of three favorable. This majority,
moreover, rose steadily in later years, with women outranking men in the
warmth of their endorsement.

We could cite other, similar, examples to show further the
place of attitude and opinion research in historical studies; but
it might suffice instead to point out that some of the most enduring works of historiography, such as Taylor's *The Medieval
Mind* and Weber's *The Protestant Ethic*, are those which dealt
with the attitudes, value systems, and prevailing beliefs of the
period. By the historians' own testimony, there is a place for
attitude and opinion research in their field, but this still leaves
open the question of what kind of polling data the future historian

will need. How can we fit at least some of our findings into the stream of intellectual work as it extends into the future?

We can expect guidance from three directions. For one, we can study historical writings; secondly, we can turn to certain works on the contemporary scene; finally, we can scrutinize existing speculations on the probable course of the future. It should be helpful to illustrate briefly each of these points.

The Pollster Reads a Book

It would be worthwhile for a scholar to review typical historical texts from our point of view. Where do competent writers show, either explicitly or implicitly, the need for attitude material of the kind a sampling survey can furnish? Short of a careful scrutiny we cannot know the prevailing modes of analysis. Furthermore, the specific need for opinion data will vary according to the topic under investigation. But a few expectations are rather obvious.

In at least three areas the historian will be confronted with the need for opinion data. The most obvious, of course, is when "prevailing values" are themselves the object of his study. There are a number of classical investigations of major changes in the climate of opinion such as the transition from medieval traditionalism to the individualistic thinking connected with the Protestant Reformation. During the first half of the nineteenth century a countertrend started, stressing public responsibility for individual welfare. This trend could be observed in the United States as well as in other countries. Curti, for instance, points out that, before the Civil War, there was considerable resistance to accepting tax-supported public schools.

> Men of power and substance frequently argued that education had been, and properly so, a family matter. . . . What could be more potent than the certainty that if free schools were granted, the concession would not end short of socialism itself? To provide free schooling for the less well-to-do would result in the loss of their self-respect and initiative.

Today, hardly anyone feels this way. But how did this shift of public opinion come about? Among which groups did it start

and how did it spread? How long did it take for the initial resistance to disappear? What external events precipitated or re-
tarded the development?

Such knowledge would be of considerable practical importance today. If we substituted the word "housing" for "schooling" in the preceding quotation, we would describe the way in
which many people feel about public housing projects. It is probable that this sentiment is now in the process of historical change.
So far as public health insurance is concerned, the resistance is
still very great. More detailed knowledge of such developments
in the past would help us to predict better what turn our contemporary problems are likely to take. If we know better the
patterns of past change, we can perhaps extract from them some
recurrent paths of development. Therefore, incidentally, we can
expect that those historians who looked at history as one sector
of a general social science will be most likely to welcome attitude
data.

This leads to a second area in which the historian would undoubtedly need public opinion data. Wherever a new type of
institution or a major legislative development was investigated,
he would be greatly helped by data on the interaction between
the diffusion of attitudes and the sequence of social actions. One
of the most thoroughly investigated phenomena of this kind is
the turn from laissez-faire to social legislation, which took place
in England during the second half of the nineteenth century.
Karl Polanyi has pointed out that the free market system never
really worked well in any event. He summarizes Dicey's famous
investigation *Law and Public Opinion in England* in the following
way:

> Dicey made it his task to inquire into the origins of the "anti-laissez-faire"
> or, as he called it, the "collectivist" trend in English public opinion, the
> existence of which was manifest since the late 1860's. He was surprised
> to find that no evidence of the existence of such a trend could be traced
> save the acts of legislation themselves. More exactly, no evidence of a
> "collectivist trend" in public opinion prior to the laws which appeared
> to represent such a trend could be found.

Here is a challenging suggestion that major legislative events
may not be preceded, but rather followed, by changes in public

opinion. Before one could accept such a conclusion one would certainly want to know how safe it is to make inferences of this kind merely by examining newspapers, pamphlets, and recorded speeches. Could it not be the case that there was an undercurrent of public opinion in the direction of social legislation which did not find expression in the kind of material available to the historian, but which would have been caught by systematic public opinion research at the time?

A third area of overlay between the historian and the pollster ought to be those writings in which specific events are to be explained. There is virtually no American historian, for example, who has not tried at one time or another to explain the outcome of some presidential election. Robert Bower has collected a whole folklore of stories which have arisen in connection with elections of major importance, such as those of 1840, 1882, and 1896. He analyzes these explanations of election outcomes and shows that all of them imply the type of knowledge about issues and personalities of the day which might have been obtained through polls. Even with poll data it is not easy to arrive at safe conclusions. This is known by everyone who followed the efforts to understand Truman's election in 1948. Bower's "Opinion Research and Historical Interpretation of Elections" shows how much more tenuous the conjectures are for previous periods.

Historians themselves are, of course, aware of this task. A group of medievalists started, in their professional journal, *Speculum*, to appraise the status of their work. The first article, by J. L. LaMonte, was called "Some Problems in Crusading Historiography." It was of interest to read there that "the decline of the crusading ideal in spite of papal propaganda is a little known subject." One is reminded of the studies of returning veterans reported in *The American Soldier* when the author deplores how little is known about "the social effects of the change in material status of such crusaders as returned after considerably bettering their position in the East."

In such a reappraisal of historical writings, we should be sensitive to the effect which opinion surveys have had in changing the notion of a "fact." There was a time when only political documents found in archives were considered appropriate evidence for the historian. That made him focus on political events;

everything else was interpretation. Then the "new history" centered attention on data such as economic and social statistics.
This enlarged considerably the area of what were considered
facts. Still, sentiments and attitudes remained a matter of interpretation. Now, however, they too have become facts. The result of a public opinion poll is as much a fact as the content of
a political document or the crop and price statistics of a certain
region.

In turn, the term "attitude and opinion research" should not
be taken too narrowly. Let us remember that we have always
known and discussed among ourselves that much more than
simple "yes-no" questions belongs in our equipment. In connection with the historian's problem, two techniques in particular will certainly need considerable refinement on our part. One
derives from the problem of saliency. The fact that a respondent
answers a question which we put to him still does not tell us
whether he would have asked himself this question or whether
the matter is of particular concern to him. The historian will
certainly want to know what issues were in the foreground of
attention at various times and in various sectors of the population. Published polling material does not contain enough of
such information; as a matter of fact, considerable methodological progress on this point is still needed. The diffusion of opinion
in time and social space is a second problem which we do not
yet handle with enough emphasis or enough technical skill. In
many more of our surveys we should find out where people get
their ideas and how they pass them on. All of this has thus far
been a matter of conjecture for the historian; we are supposed
to turn it into an enlarged array of "facts." Thus the study of
historical writings will not only be a source of significant topics;
it could also be a spur for methodological improvements.

Signs of the Times

A second source of ideas, interesting hypotheses, and leads
for significant field surveys may be found in many efforts to
understand the meaning of what is going on around us right now.

It has been said that each generation must rewrite history, because hitherto unconsidered aspects of the past become interesting in the light of the changing present. But there is certainly a limitation to this rule. If there is no data at all on certain aspects of the past, not much can be done, even under the impetus of a strong new curiosity. The pollster as a contemporary historian thus takes on considerable importance. What he considers worthy of a survey will, in later years, influence the range of possible historical inquires.

Therefore, the question of where the pollster can get leads for significant investigations is an important one. Again, we cannot exhaust the possible choices, but a few clear avenues suggest themselves at the moment. There is, first, the critic of the contemporary scene. There are always social commentators who are especially sensitive to the shortcomings of our times; it is not unlikely that they hit on topics about which the future historian will want to know more. Let us quote passages which are characteristic of the type of statement we have in mind.

> Much too early do young people get excited and tense, much too early are they drawn away by the accelerated pace of the times. People admire wealth and velocity. Everybody strives for them. . . . Here they compete, here they surpass each other, with the result that they persevere in mediocrity. And this is the result of the general trend of the contemporary world toward an average civilization, common to all.

We can visualize translating this social comment into a research program. It would not be too difficult to develop an index of competitiveness, and to study at what age individuals exhibit a marked increase in their average scores. But that would not be enough. We are also called upon to follow the consequences of such developments for broader areas of society; for "not the external and physical alone is now managed by machinery, but the internal and spiritual also."

> Has any man, or any society of men, a truth to speak, a piece of spiritual work to do, they can nowise proceed at once and with the mere natural organs, but must first call a public meeting, appoint committees, issue prospectuses, eat a public dinner; in a word, construct or borrow machinery, wherewith to speak it and do it. Without machinery they were hopeless, helpless. . . .

Here a more sociological type of data is required; number and types of meetings, attendance figures, etc. Most of all we will want to study the statistical interrelationship between attitudes and kinds of social participation in intellectual enterprises.

Most interesting about these quotations, however, are their dates and their sources. The first is from a letter which Goethe wrote in 1825. The second is a characteristic portion of an essay written by Carlyle in 1830. Here are two leading minds in two different countries voicing the same apprehension in terms which might well be used today. Undoubtedly experts could provide us with similar statements for any other century, for we are always likely to find evidence of a feeling that matters were very different sometime ago. There are certain standbys which recur in many discussions; the tensions of daily living have become so much worse; people are now more apathetic politically than they were previously; the cultural taste of the country has been depraved. We shall not be able to decide the truth of such issues in retrospect, but we can at least lay the ground for more responsible discussion of the problem in the future.

The social critic will focus our attention primarily on certain contents and subject matters which are important for our times. There is another group of analysts who are more concerned with the kinds of dimensions which are useful in describing the social scene. They are likely to be interested mainly in comparisons between various countries, for instance, or between different social groups. It should never be forgotten how difficult it is to make the social scene "visible." When we deal with nature, many objects, like trees or stones or animals, force themselves on us visually. Social entities are much more the product of creative intelligence. The notion of a clique, for instance, or of a reference group, the inner gallery for which so many of us play the drama of our lives, or the distinction between an introverted and an extraverted personality are real conceptual inventions. In social observations we are often in the position of a bird which flies across the sky with a flock of other birds. For the external observer, the flock has a clearly visible geometric shape; but does the bird within the flock even know about the shape of his "group"? By what social interrelations among the birds is the form of the group maintained?

When we translate these sketchy considerations into problems of survey research, we meet them in a familiar form. Every self-respecting pollster will report his findings nowadays "sub-classified by age, sex, and socio-economic status." We know from our studies that these are useful classifications. But are they the most significant ones? Wouldn't we be helped in the work of today, and wouldn't we help readers of the future if we were alert to additional variables according to which we might classify our samples and analyze our findings?

It is on such an issue that we can get guidance from writers who have tried to obtain the best possible view of the contemporary scene. Let us turn for a moment to the patron saint of modern public opinion research, James Bryce. He makes an effort at one point to compare the political scene in England and that prevailing in this country. To this end he distinguishes "three sets of persons, those who make opinion, those who receive and hold opinion, those who have no opinions at all." After elaborating on this distinction, he comes to the conclusion that the first group is somewhat larger in England than in the United States of 1870, while the proportion in the second group is very much larger on the American continent than in Britain. From this he draws a number of interesting conclusions. The "power of public opinion in the United States," for instance, seems to him related to the inordinately large ratio of opinion holders to opinion makers.

To find significant variables for political classifications continues to be a challenge for writers of this kind. It is quite possible that an index of political participation and interest might prove a useful instrument for a great variety of surveys, on a national as well as on an international scale. As a matter of fact, some research organizations are reported to be working on the development of such devices.

In the writings of contemporary social scientists, the pollster will find other classificatory suggestions which are worth pursuing. David Riesman, for instance, has just published a book centered on the distinction between three types of social character. One is the tradition-directed type; the person who behaves as he thinks his social group expects him to, does not believe he should change anything in his environment, and feels shame if he violates any of the rules under which he lives. The second is the inner-directed type; the person who is guided by strong moral standards, has a kind of psychological gyroscope which controls his conduct, and who feels guilt if he does something which is not right. Finally, there is the outer-directed type; the backslapper who wants to get along with everyone, who has few convictions of his own, and who feels general anxiety if he is not successful in receiving all the signals which he tries to catch on his psychological radar system. In chapter after chapter of *The Lonely Crowd* Riesman tries to spell out the political correlates of these three types. He is especially interested in the outer-directed type, which he considers characteristic of modern American life. Riesman discovers in him a dangerous kind of political apathy. He wants to get all the inside dope on politics just as on baseball, but he has lost all belief that he, individually, has any influence and therefore refrains from giving public affairs any serious thought or any active devotion. A careful reading of Riesman's chapter on politics will show how much empirical research could and should be geared in with such speculations.

Finally, the literature of the so-called cultural anthropologists belongs here. They are not only concerned with singling out significant topics or finding variables which would be useful to make more clearly visible the main character of the contemporary scene. They also want to uncover the mechanisms by which the scene develops. Distinguished equally by brilliance and by irresponsibility of factual evidence, they challenge the pollster to try to bring about effective cooperation. But the challenge is worth accepting, for from an interaction between the two groups could develop really new insights into human affairs. No newspaper reader can be unaware of the writings on "national character." The main thesis is that each society and each national subgroup develops its own way of looking at the world, and its own way of giving satisfaction to basic needs. It is the function of the family to raise children in such a way that they "want to act in the way they have to act as members of the society or as a special class within it." Like a group of expert ball players giving a public exhibition, the anthropologists toss their variations on the basic theme from one to the other. Margaret Mead describes in great detail the small American family with its lack of tradition and its uncertain goals in a quickly changing world:

> while the child is learning that his whole place in the world, his name, his right to the respect of other children—everything—depends upon his parents . . . he also learns that his own acceptance by these parents, who are his only support, is conditional upon his achievements, upon the way in which he shows up against other children and against their idea of other children.

Gorer picks it up from Mead. He agrees with her that there is a strong element of uncertainty in the emotional life of the American family. The parents do not quite know what is right and therefore can love their children only if they are successful in their own peer group, the school class, or the gang. But Gorer does not think that ambition or success drive develops in children as a result; he has a different notion:

> The presence, the attention, the admiration of other people thus becomes for Americans a necessary component to their self-esteem, demanded with a feeling of far greater psychological urgency than is usual in other countries. . . . The most satisfying form of this assurance is not given by direct flattery or commendation (this by itself is suspect as a device to exploit the other) but by love.

The two writers, if confronted with their statements, would probably say that there is a strong relation between ambition and the desire to be loved. Yet how do they know that these desires are more frequent or more intense among Americans than among other people? They give many examples from Rotary meetings and from double dates in college which make their idea plausible. We pollsters are accustomed to asking for a better definition of terms and for more precise evidence; so we are inclined to criticize these anthropologists. But are we fully justified? Have they not seen here topics which are considerably more worthy of investigation than the rating of movie stars or even the attitudes of voters toward a local candidate?

Here are writers who have challenging ideas on the structure of our social relationships and their effect on attitudes and opinions. Does this not suggest that we have neglected the first link in this chain? To cite one specific example: in the writings of the social anthropologists, the authoritarian structure of the family plays a large role. Who among us, either in this country or abroad, has collected answers to questions like these: To what extent do young people make their own occupational choices and to what extent do their parents influence their decisions? In what countries and in what groups does a young suitor still ask the girl's parents for consent to marriage? How are conflicts between father and son resolved when they both want the car or both want to use the living room? Where do children still spend their holidays with their families, and where do they go off on their own? How much visiting of relatives is there, how frequent are family reunions, and so on? What would adolescents consider the main complaints as to the way they are treated by their parents? What activities are parents most eager to forbid in their young children and what principles are they most anxious to inculcate in their older ones?

Useful contributions along such lines could be made, especially by those among us who conduct international polls. But in this discussion we are not interested in the present for its own sake; we want to look at it from the point of view of tomorrow. What should we watch as the present slowly turns into the future?

Glancing into the Future

Scrutinizing writings on the past will give us an idea of the kinds of data which historians have missed prior to the appearance of the pollster on the scene. Studying the literature on present-day society will give us a chance to confront theoretical thinking with empirical data. A final, and probably the most important, possibility develops when we make efforts to guess what the future will want to know about today. Quite a number of political scientists feel that the best way to study the present is to see it as a transitional stage to future events. Harold Lasswell has emphasized the need of "developmental constructs."

In the practice of social science, . . . we are bound to be affected in some degree by our conceptions of future development. . . . What is the function of this picture for scientists? It is to stimulate the individual specialist to clarify for himself his expectations about the future, as a guide to the timing of scientific work.

We should form expectations of what major changes might come about within the next decades. It is in connection with these changing conditions that the historian will expect that we, today, have initiated a series of trend studies. This is undoubtedly the most difficult task. It not only requires of us pollsters that we translate more or less vague ideas into specific instruments of inquiry; there is so little thinking along this line that we shall even have to assume some responsibility for guessing what will be of importance a few decades hence. The best we can do in the present context is to give a few examples of the kind of effort which will be required.

There can be little doubt that the history of the next decades will be centered around the effects of the rapidly increasing industrialization characteristic of our times. Perhaps the reaction to contemporary mechanization will be found in strong religious movements. If this is the case, what will the future analyst, in retrospect, wish that we had ascertained today? An interesting lead for this is found in *The American Soldier*. The importance of this work lies in the fact that, for the first time, we really know something about the experiences and feelings of an important sector of the population. As far as religion goes, the following observation is reported. About three-fourths of the soldiers said that prayer was a source of strength in battle, but the minority who did not find this so had certain interesting characteristics: they experienced less fear, laid more stress on their relations with other soldiers, and seemed, in general, to be what modern psychologists would call better adjusted personalities.

Here, in one result, may lie the seeds of an important bifurcation. Increasing industrialization may lead to a compensatory dependence on religious beliefs. Or, it may create a new type of personality, differently adjusted to new social demands. We cannot tell in which direction the future will tend; as a matter of fact, we do not even know whether any really new developments will take place in the religious sphere; but general considerations and bits of research evidence seem to indicate that systematic work is called for.

At the same time that we try to answer these more general questions about the intensity of religious beliefs, we should analyze the specific character of religious movements as they develop. In this connection Julian Huxley has provided an impressive set of predictions. In his essay "Religion as an Objective Problem," he distinguished between the "old" religion and the "new." According to him, the old one developed as a result of fear and ignorance of the external physical environment. Modern science has given us enough insight into the control over the forces of nature so that religious beliefs as we have known them so far are likely to fade away slowly. Now we are faced with a new set of problems emerging from what he calls the "internal environment"; the disorganization of our economic and social life, war, poverty, and unemployment. New religious movements are likely to develop, centered less around the worship of a supernatural being than around the worship of a single solution for social evils.

> The process, of course, has already begun. Many observers have commented on the religious elements in Russian communism—the fanaticism, the insistence on orthodoxy, the violent "theological" disputes, the "worship" of Lenin, the spirit of self-dedication, the persecutions, the common enthusiasm, the puritan element, the mass emotions, the censorship.

The new religion is now in its most primitive form, with communism and fascism as typical examples. But just as the old religion moved from simple paganism to a refined monotheism, so will the new religion outgrow its present crudeness.

> Accordingly, we can prophesy that in the long run the nationalistic element in socialized religion will be subordinated or adjusted to the internationalist: that the persecution of minorities will give place to toleration; that the subtler intellectual and moral virtues will find a place and will gradually oust the cruder from their present pre-eminence in the religiously-conceived social organism. We can also assert with fair assurance that this process of improvement will be a slow one, and accompanied by much violence and suffering.

Here, indeed, is a research program. First we must find appropriate indices for the various shades of belief which Huxley distinguishes. Then we shall want to get our information separately from a large number of social subgroups. Trend data will have to be assembled over a long period of time; and wherever possible, these trends should be linked with external events. If a special movement starts somewhere, if a related book becomes a best-seller, if some special legislation is passed or a voluntary association established, we shall want to study the pertinent attitudes "before and after."

This is not the place to propose a concrete study design, but we should warn against oversimplifying the whole problem. The attitudes in which the historian will be interested are certainly complex in nature; and, in order to cover one single concept, it may be necessary to employ a whole set of interlocking questions. As a matter of fact, it might very well be that future trends will be different for different dimensions of the same notion. To exemplify what this means in terms of our work, we shall choose for our second example the problem of class tensions.

There is an abundance of prophecies in the literature which can be loosely labelled as Marxist. Conflicts of interest between the working class and the influential business groups will become more acute. The workers will become more class conscious, and more aggressive toward the privileged groups. The latter, in turn, will defend more strongly their class interests and more and more neglect the democratic forms of politics. These ideas are too well known to need further elaboration. Instead, let us pick out of this whole complex the notion of class consciousness, and see whether we can develop a kind of barometer by which to measure trends in the next few decades.

In recent years, a large number of business companies have conducted surveys to determine their standing with the public, but this by no means meets the task. There could very easily be an intensification of class consciousness among workers which does not express itself immediately in invectives directed toward General Motors or Standard Oil. Not even the recently increased interest of social psychologists in this problem covers it fully. Richard Centers, in his *The Psychology of Social Classes*, has developed a set of questions pertinent to two elements: readiness to accept the government as an agent in economic affairs; and a feeling that avenues of economic advancement are closing up, that social rewards are not fairly distributed.

The total picture has many additional aspects, however. We should study whether workers have a feeling of identification with their class. If a worker's son becomes a lawyer, should he work for a union rather than for a big corporation? Is there an increased interest in reading stories about workers rather than about movie stars? Is there an increased interest in leisure-time associations especially designed for workers? Another aspect of the problem would be whether workers are concerned with the power structure in the community. Do they think that the courts handle poor and rich alike? Do and can the councilmen in the city represent both poor and rich? Do they feel that the rich have special influence with the police? Even if there is growing uneasiness on this score, the question still to be raised is whether it is channeled into political reactions. Does "going into politics" become a more respected and desirable pursuit? Is voting the "right" way something which becomes an important criterion for judging people? Do political issues become a factor in one's own personal plans?

This example, incidentally, raises a serious problem of strategy for the pollster. Topics relevant to the work of the future historian are likely to come from the area of social change. Polls dealing with such areas can easily become suspect as "subversive" or "inflammatory." It will therefore be important to make clear, both to the general public and to specific clients, that the public opinion researcher is not taking sides when he focuses part of his attention on more unconventional issues. As a matter of fact, it might very well be that some of the work suggested here might best be done under the joint sponsorship of several agencies or perhaps under the aegis of a professional organization like the American Association for Public Opinion Research.

What Should Be Done?

We pollsters cannot be expected to tackle the whole problem by ourselves. We should seek the assistance of a "commission for the utilization of polls in the service of future historiography," whose specific task it would be to furnish us with appropriate ideas. This commission should consist, on the one hand, of historians and other social scientists who have given thought to questions such as those we have raised, and, on the other hand, of research technicians who can translate research suggestions into actual study designs.

There certainly will be no scarcity of topics. There is much evidence to show that people in this country were inclined to shy away from concern with international relations. Suddenly we are thrust into the position of being the leading power in the world. How will people in this country adjust to this change, and what will be the mutual interaction between the distribution of attitudes and the actions of our policy makers? At what rate will Americans really become aware of the existence of the Far Eastern people? When will they notice that the famous destruction of the "human race" by the atomic bomb might really mean the replacing of the Western sector of humanity by their Asiatic fellow men? Another element of our tradition is the belief that one man is as good as another. But in a society which becomes ever more complex, the expert plays an increasingly important role. How will this proverbial antiauthoritarian tradition adjust to the increasing, and probably unavoidable, "bureaucratization" of the modern world? Or one might turn from the political to a more personal sphere. Increasing amounts of available leisure time will force more people to review their "designs for living." How will they use the time over which they themselves have control: will they use it to have a richer personal life, to equip themselves better for competitive advancement, or will they just fritter it away? There is certainly an obvious interrelation between these questions and new technical developments such as television.

Whatever topic we select, the procedure for research will always be the same. We must first formulate clearly a number of alternative assumptions about future developments. Then we must decide on the kind of indices which are pertinent for the problem at hand; this is where the research technician can make his main contribution. To set up the machinery for collecting the data is a matter of decision and funds. As to the selection of respondents, a certain flexibility will be necessary. For some problems a national cross-section will be most appropriate. For other problems very specific population groups will command our interest. And at all times we shall want to collect "background information": documentation on major events, on the activities of organizations, community leaders, etc.

At this point, we should warn against a possible misunderstanding. Previously we stressed that attitude surveys provide a new type of "facts" for the historian. But this does not imply that they are more important than the more traditional kind of data. It is just the interplay between the "objective" facts and attitudes which promises a great advance in historiography. If for a given period we not only know the standard of living, but also the distribution of ratings on happiness and personal adjustment, the dynamics of social change will be much better understood. Let us add that sampling surveys will enlarge our ideas on social bookkeeping in still another way. Nothing is more characteristic of this trend than what has happened in the decennial census of the United States. As long as we thought only in terms of complete enumerations, we could afford to include only a few questions. Now that we use 5 percent and 1 percent samples on specific items, we are able to cover a much wider range of topics. This is undoubtedly only a beginning. Since small sample designs have been perfected, there is no reason why sociography should not develop on a much broader scale. Cultural activities and other living habits may soon be added to the more conventional trends in the birth rate or export trade. It is certainly no coincidence that the Kinsey reports did not begin to appear before 1948.

As early as 1908, in his *Human Nature in Politics*, Graham Wallas pointed to such changes in what he called the methods of political reasoning. He compared the reports of two Royal Commissions, both of which were concerned with the reform of the English poor laws, One was established in 1834 and the other in 1905. The earlier one dealt with "a priori deduction, illustrated, but not proved by particular instances." Now (in 1905) things are different.

> Instead of assuming half consciously that human energy is dependent solely on the working of the human will in the presence of the ideas of

pleasure and pain, the Commissioners are forced to tabulate and consider innumerable quantitative observations relating to the very many factors affecting the will of paupers and possible paupers. They cannot, for instance, avoid the task of estimating the relative industrial effectiveness of health, which depends upon decent surroundings; of hope, which may be made possible by State provision for old age; and of the imaginative range which is the result of education; and of comparing all these with the "purely economic" motive created by ideas of future pleasure and pain.

As can be seen, Wallas did not want to replace, but to complement, principles with social surveys. And so we too do not suggest that attitude data are better than "hard" facts, but that they add, so to speak, a new dimension.

There is one more suggestion for the work of the new commission on polling and historiography. We are all aware that prediction is one of the touchstones by which a science can justify itself. So far our predictions have been confined mainly to the outcomes of political elections; many have felt that this is a rather insignificant pursuit. There is no reason, however, that we should not predict future sentiments and then, later on, study whether we were right. One of the most impressive chapters in *The American Soldier* is "The Aftermath of Hostilities." In the summer of 1944, the Research Branch prepared a document predicting what attitudes they expected among soldiers at the end of the war. In 1945, many of those predictions were tested: At some points the predictions were correct, and at others, wrong. But no person reading this chapter can escape the feeling that here might be the substitute for laboratory experiments, so often impossible to carry out in the social sciences. Interestingly enough, without knowing about the experience of the Research Branch, a historian, Helen Lynd, saw this very link between her field and ours. In "The Nature of Historical Objectivity," she stated:

we know surely . . . that the future which lies ahead will become present, and that hypotheses which we may now make can be tested by the course of events. If we are in earnest about historical objectivity, why do we not more often frame precise hypotheses about what may be the course of events in a given area in a given time? . . . With all that can be said against the recent opinion polls in this country there is this to be said in their favor: they at least made their errors public so that they could be subject to the verification of events.

It is somewhat faint praise to say that we at least make our errors public. We deserve better. But it might be our own mistake that many people are not aware of the many implications inherent in our work. Public opinion research has the unique opportunity to increase self-awareness in the community, a self-awareness which is an important factor in individual as well as in collective health. The great contribution of modern psychoanalysis is that it has given us more understanding of what is going on in ourselves. Public opinion research can do the same for the larger community if it becomes more aware of its potentialities and more eager to develop them. We want all of our intelligent fellow citizens to have respect for the kind of work we are doing. One very good way to get this respect is for us to show that we recognize our common problems and can contribute to their clarification.

[3]
Notes on the History of Quantification in Sociology—Trends, Sources, and Problems

The three major nouns in the title of this paper are necessarily vague. Quantification in the social sciences includes mere counting, the development of classificatory dimensions and the systematic use of "social symptoms" as well as mathematical models and an axiomatic theory of measurement. The notion of history is ambiguous because some of these techniques evolved several hundred years ago while others were developed within the last few decades. Finally, there is no precise line between sociology and other social sciences; with the economist, the sociologist shares family budgets, and with the psychologist he makes the study of attitudes a joint concern.

The task of sketching out the history of quantification in sociology is made more difficult by the fact that it rarely has been seriously attempted. Both the history and the philosophy of science have been concerned almost exclusively with the natural sciences. Their discoveries have been linked step by step with their antecedents; their relation to the political, social, and religious events of the time has been spelled out; even their effect on belles lettres has been traced. The few comparable studies in the social sciences have usually been concerned with broad, semi-philosophical systems. There has been hardly any work on the history of techniques for social science investigation. In following some of these procedures back to their origins, it was often necessary to draw attention to historical situations or to

From *Isis* (1961), 52:277–333. Reprinted by permission.

men with whom the American reader is not likely to be familiar, and to report something about the broader political and ideological contexts in which the pioneers of sociological quantification worked.

The need for such details required a severe restriction in the scope of the paper. Actually, it deals with only three major episodes. They were selected because they carried the seeds of many subsequent developments and foreshadowed discussions which continue today. To give the three major sections of this paper a proper frame, a few words are needed about how a future history of quantification in sociology might look. It would begin with a preparatory phase lasting approximately from the middle of the seventeenth to the beginning of the nineteenth century. These first 150 years were dominated by the sheer difficulty of obtaining numerical information on social topics. Many historians of statistics and demography have described this period, and I shall not try to retrace the ground which they have covered. I shall, instead, suggest points at which sociological ideas entered into the work of some of the more famous writers on society of the period. But my main attention will be focused on the life, work, and followers of one man—Hermann Conring. As I slowly pieced together whatever information I could find about him, I became increasingly impressed with his importance. He saw the same problem faced by his British contemporaries whom we remember today as the founders of political arithmetic. But his efforts took a very different turn. The first section of my paper sketches his work, tries to explain it in the context of the times, and traces its consequences.

A second period in this history begins with the work of the Belgian Quetelet, and the Frenchman Le Play. Both men started out as natural scientists, acquiring their interest in the social sciences during the period of social unrest which culminated in the French-Belgian Revolution of 1830. Quetelet was an astronomer who wished to uncover for the social world eternal laws similar to those he dealt with in his main field of investigation. Le Play was a mining engineer and metallurgist who believed that the minute attention to concrete details which made him a success in his main occupation could also provide the foundations for a true social science. The spirit in which these two men worked and the role their ideas played in subsequent developments are correspondingly different.

Quetelet concerned himself almost exclusively with the interpretation of large-scale statistics which became available, at the beginning of the nineteenth century, as a byproduct of the rapidly expanded census activities undertaken by various government agencies. He anticipated with varying degrees of precision many basic concepts of quantification, and his writings led to sophisticated controversies which continued into the twentieth century. It seemed to me useful therefore to single out some of these ideas and to show how they were slowly clarified. Thus I will report the Quetelet story in reverse. My implicit starting point will be some modern ideas on quantification, and I shall trace these back to the writings of Quetelet, his opponents, and his commentators.

It is more difficult to fit Le Play into my narrative because, in spite of his many assertions, he never was nor really meant to be a detached scientist. During his lifetime he created a number of ideological movements, and these both attracted and distracted his followers. Those of his disciples who intended primarily to develop his ideas on social research could never free themselves entirely from the political position of the founding father. This was so in a twofold sense. They continued the organizational activities which Le Play initiated, and had an interestingly ambivalent attitude toward the methods which he had developed. They succeeded in making considerable improvements in these methods, but they experienced such achievements as impious disloyalty to their great master. The history of the Le Play school following his death is a curious example of what happens when a research tradition assumes a sectarian form. So far as I know, this story has never been traced, and later in this paper I shall give it somewhat more attention than strict adherence to the topic of quantification would require.

My paper thus concentrates on the development of some of the basic notions and broader ideas which introduced quantification into the study of social affairs. Any history of science must include at least three elements: the intrinsic intellectual nature of the ideas, their historical social context, and the peculiarities of the men who made the major contributions. It will become obvious why I concentrate first on the historical, then on the intellectual element, and finally on the biographical.

Throughout the paper, I have had to discuss repeatedly the historiography of the field itself. Because professional historians of science have paid so little attention to the social sciences, their history was often written by amateurs—specialists in social research who only occasionally looked into its past. As a result, quite a number of legends have been passed on from one to the next. While I am an amateur myself, I have for the major parts of this paper gone back to the original sources, including the commentators who previously have given them careful attention. At points where I felt that a further pursuit would exceed the time or the material available to me, I have brought specific unsolved questions to the attention of the reader. In a post-scriptum to this paper, I shall indicate the topics I have not dealt with, my reasons for their exclusion, and the places where one can find pertinent information.[1]

The Preparatory Period

The Political Arithmeticians

The idea that social topics could be subjected to quantitative analysis acquired prominence in the first part of the seventeenth century. There are conventional explanations for this emergence: the rational spirit of rising capitalism; the intellectual climate of the Baconian era; the desire to imitate the first major success of the natural sciences; the increasing size of different countries which necessitated a more impersonal and abstract basis for public administration. More specifically, one can point to concrete concerns: the rise of insurance systems which required a firmer numerical foundation, and the prevailing belief of the mercantilists that size of population was a crucial factor in the power and wealth of the state.[2]

Problems of demographic enumeration were the first topics to be discussed systematically. No reliable data were available, and no modern census machinery was in sight. Two obstacles are mentioned by the authors who have dealt with the work of this period: the unwillingness of the population to give information, because of their fear of increased taxes; and the tendency of governments, whenever statistical information was available, to treat it as highly classified, because of its possible military value.[3] Thus, the ingenuity of early scholars was directed mainly toward obtaining estimates of population size and age and sex distributions from meager and indirect evidence. Multiplying the number of chimneys by an assumed average family size or inferring the age structure of the population from registered information regarding age at the time of death were typical procedures in what was then called political arithmetic.

Today it is hard for us to imagine the lack of descriptive information available in the middle of the seventeenth century. The ravages of periodic outbreaks of the plague, for instance, made it impossible for anyone to know whether the population of England was increasing or decreasing. As a matter of fact, the first mortality tables, published in 1662 by Graunt, who is considered the originator of modern demography, were based partly on public listings of burials; they had acquired news value for the average citizen—somewhat comparable to the list of victims which nowadays is published after an airplane accident.

But soon the supply of facts increased, the analytical techniques were improved, and by about 1680 the art of "political arithmetic" was well established under English leadership. I have the impression that something like a community of *aficionados* developed: all over Western Europe, empirical data were traded for mathematical advice. Thus, for instance, in 1693, the English astronomer Halley published a paper on mortality based on registration figures of births and funerals in the city of Breslau. How had Halley obtained these figures? German historians discovered that Leibnitz was an intermediary. He had learned about the material through a friend, a clergyman in Breslau who, together with a local physician, was an ardent and capable amateur demographer. Leibnitz brought the data to the attention of the Royal Society, which asked Halley to express an opinion.[4]

A century later natural scientists still considered descriptive social statistics appropriate topics to be worked on. In 1791, Lavoisier, the chemist who was to be guillotined three years later, published a treatise for the National Assembly dealing with the population and economic condition of France; in this he expounded the idea that a revolutionary government had the opportunity and the duty to establish a central statistical bureau. At the beginning of the nineteenth century, the mathematicians La Place and Fourier dealt with population statistics; and, as we shall see, their work played an important role in Quetelet's life.[5]

I do not intend to pursue the development of political arithmetic in this paper. But I want to suggest that the sociological implications of some of these early writings be reexamined. To indicate the kind of analysis I have in mind, I shall briefly sketch out the work of two men. One of these is William Petty (1623–1687) who worked with Graunt and created the term "political arithmetic." After the Restoration, he decided to use his experience in Ireland to formulate a general theory of government based on concrete knowledge. He was convinced that to this end "one had to express oneself in terms of number, weight, and measure." He argued that Ireland was a good case study, not only because he knew it so well, but because it was a "political animal who is scarce twenty years old," and a place, therefore, where the relation between the social structure of the country and the chances of good government could be studied more closely. Thus originated his *Political Anatomy of Ireland* (1672).

A sensitive biography by E. Strauss[6] describes the political and social settings of Petty's work: for this reason alone it makes very worthwhile reading. Two chapters provide a more detailed guide through those parts of Petty's writings which are relevant to my paper. He anticipates ideas which only recently have been considered noteworthy intellectual discoveries. A few years ago, the Harvard economist Dusenberry argued that sociological factors must be taken into account in the economics of saving. He pointed out that whites save less than Negroes on the same income levels, because white people have a broader range of social contacts and therefore must spend more money on conspicuous consumption. Compare this with the following passage from Petty:

When England shall be thicker peopled, in the manner before described, *the very same people shall then spend more, than when they lived* more sordidly and inurbanely, and further asunder, and *more out of the sight, observation, and emulation of each other*; every man desiring to put on better apparel when he appears in company, than when he has no occasion to be seen. (Emphasis mine)[7]

During the depression of the 1930s, a number of studies appearing in this country and abroad made it clear that, for psychological reasons, work relief is preferable to a straight dole. Petty also argued for unemployment benefits, and, while he phrases his beliefs in less humanitarian words than we would use today, the psychological foundations of his argument that even "boondoggling" is preferable to dole are certainly very modern:

tis no matter if it be *employed to build a useless pyramid upon Salisbury Plain, bring the stones at Stonehenge to Tower Hill, or the like*; for at worst this would keep their minds to discipline and obedience, and their bodies to patience of more profitable labours when need shall require it. (Emphasis mine)[8]

The second exhibit in my appeal for a sociological reconsideration of some of the early political arithmeticians is the German J. P. Suessmilch (1707–1767), who too first studied medicine. But he then turned to theology, and spent most of his adult life as a pastor, first with a Prussian regiment and later at the court of Frederick the Great. In 1741, a year after Frederick II ascended the throne, Suessmilch published his book *Divine Order as Proven by Birth, Death and Fertility of the Human Species* (Geschlecht).[9] In his work, Suessmilch collected all the data published by his predecessors, and his book is considered the most complete compendium of the time. In addition, historians of statistics credit him with having been the first to focus attention on fertility (in addition to birth and death rates). But all of these reviews omit any reference to Suessmilch's broadgauged interpretation of his findings. For instance, Westergaard[10] says at one point when describing Suessmilch's major work, "the succeeding chapters are uninteresting to the history of statistics insofar as Suessmilch here briefly presents arguments against polygamy, discusses proposals as to supporting married couples with numbers of children, as to hygienic matters, luxury, etc. After this long digression, the author resumes his statistical investigations."

Even a cursory look at this part of Suessmilch's text shows that much would be gained by a careful examination. For example, when he finds that the number of marriages has declined in a certain part of Prussia, he offers a variety of explanations: an increase in the number of students attending universities and of people called into military service, a shift to industrial work, increases in food prices, and so on. All in all, the *Goettliche Ordnung* is filled with social analysis. Suessmilch considers a growing population of crucial political importance; he therefore tries to uncover the political and social conditions which make for such growth, so that he can advise the king effectively.

It is true that Suessmilch frequently turns to theological arguments. He finds that slightly more boys than girls are born; he attributes this to the wisdom of the Creator, because young boys, who grow up under less sheltered conditions, have a somewhat higher mortality rate than do girls. At the time of marriage, the two sexes are in balance. At the time of widowhood, however, there are more women than men; but widowers have a greater chance of remarrying repeatedly (he created the term "successive polygamy"); in other words, even in the later phases of life, the sex ratio is functionally useful. Altogether, one could probably find surprising parallels between modern functionalism and Suessmilch's efforts.[11]

Having done no special research myself on the political arithmeticians, I feel somewhat hesitant about making one more suggestion before I leave the topic. Given the fact that political arithmetic, especially in its early phases, was equivalent to obtaining a quantitative foundation for broad social problems, it is surprising that it seems to have had so little relation with another stream in English intellectual history—the Scottish moral philosophers. Some of them, like Adam Ferguson, are cited as the precursors of modern empiricism, mainly because they wanted to substitute concrete anthropological observations for mere speculation about the origins of society.[12] But they were also much concerned with human nature. And, for these concerns, they could have derived much information from the work of the political arithmeticians, which was well developed by the middle of the eighteenth century. Yet, I have not been able to find a study of the points at which these two traditions merged, and, if they did not, an explanation of what accounts for this separation.

The Story of the Two Roots

In 1886, August Meitzen, a professor at the University of Berlin, published a book on statistics.[13] The first part of the volume dealt with the history of the field. It contains no detailed analysis of specific writings, nor does it pretend to be a history of ideas. Meitzen's main aims were to record the times and circumstances under which the early statistical organizations were founded, to list and describe the early publications of statistical data, and to provide brief sketches of the major writers who made notable contributions. The book apparently seemed important at the time, for in 1891 the American Academy of Political and Social Science published an English translation in two supplements to their regular series. (The second part contains sound advice on the collection, tabulation, and interpretation of demographic and social data, which might explain why the translation seemed desirable.)

In describing the main historical trends, Meitzen put forth the idea that the statistics of his time developed from two different roots. One was represented by the political arithmeticians whom I have just described. He correctly places their origins in the middle of the seventeenth century. The other root was an intensive interest in characteristic features of the state, from which the term "statistics" was derived. This brand of statistics considered anything which seemed noteworthy about a country, and was in no way restricted to the topics now covered by the term. As a matter of fact, numerical data played only a small role in this tradition.

Sometime toward the end of the eighteenth century, Meitzen writes, the English root of political arithmetic and the German root of university statistics (as it came to be called) became involved in a controversy about which of the two was more scientific and more useful. The battle was won, in Germany as well as elsewhere, by the political arithmeticians. From the beginning of the nineteenth century onward, they also monopolized the title of statisticians. Whatever was left of the former activities of university statisticians was thereafter considered a part of political science.

Meitzen designated a Göttingen professor, Gottfried Achenwall (1719–1772), as the founder of the German nonquantitative root. In 1749, Achenwall had published a book which included in its title the phrase *The Science of Today's Main European Realms and Republics.* He is, says Meitzen, *"therefore called the father of statistical science."* This paternity has been accepted by many contemporary writers. Thus, George Lundberg follows Meitzen's example.[14] While his sympathies, of course, are on the side of the victorious party, he acknowledges that Achenwall's book "gained such general recognition when it was translated into all languages that Achenwall was long hailed as the father of science." George Sarton[15] and Nathan Glazer[16] write in the same vein.

There is something strange in this story, however. What happened in Germany during the ninety years between Graunt and Achenwall? Why did the political arithmeticians have so little influence in the German universities? How could the Göttingen professor create a "second root" so quickly that, within a few decades, it acquired equal standing with the English tradition to the point that, as we shall see, the final battle was fought in all the countries of Western Europe?

Part of the answer was given in another book which actually appeared two years before Meitzen's but which did not come to the attention of American social scientists for a long time. In 1884, Victor John, docent at the University of Bern in Switzerland, also published a history of statistics, but of a very different kind. He properly calls his work a source book,[17] and it is indeed a volume of remarkable scholarship in which he either summarizes or quotes sources that today are quite inaccessible.[18] He had noticed the queer hiatus between 1660 and 1750, left unexplained by traditional stereotypes. He was able to fill in this gap by focusing attention on the work of Hermann Conring (1606–1681). Conring was one of the great polyhistors of his time, holding three professorships at the Brunswick University of Helmstedt: first in philosophy, then in medicine, and finally in politics. In 1660, at practically the same time that Graunt and Petty started their work, he began a series of systematic lectures under the title "Notitia Rerum Publicarum." These lectures were first published as notes taken by his students, but later appeared, at the beginning of the eighteenth century, as part of a multivolume collection of Conring's writings and correspondence. He had a large number of important students, some of whom went into public service and some of whom taught at other German universities. Many compendia of his system were in use throughout the Empire. And as John proves convincingly, the book which Achenwall published in 1749 was essentially the first systematic presentation in the *German* language of the Conring tradition which until then was available almost exclusively in Latin. John demonstrates that all of Achenwall's basic ideas had been explicitly developed by Conring. As a matter of fact, Achenwall always conceded this: he was a pupil once removed of Conring's and wrote his dissertation about him, still in Latin, incidentally.

Thus, John clarifies at least one point. There was no hiatus. The English root of political arithmetic and the German root of university statistics developed at the same time. But this fact only raises a number of new and more interesting questions. For one, why did the two countries develop such different answers to what was essentially the same intellectual challenge? Compare the programmatic statements of the two authors:

Petty	Conring
Sir Francis Bacon, in his "Advancement of Learning," has made a judicious parallel in many particulars, between the *Body Natural and Body Politic, and between the arts of preserving both in health and strength*: and as its anatomy is the best foundation of one, so also of the other: and that to practice upon the politic, *without knowing the symmetry, fabric, and proportion of it, is as casual as the practice of old women and empirics.* (Emphasis mine)[19]	Just as it is impossible for the doctor to give advice for the *recovery or preservation of health when he does not have some salient knowledge of the body,* so it is also impossible for anyone who does not have *knowledge and awareness of the facts of public life to cure it* either in its totality or in some of its parts. (Emphasis mine)[20]

Here were two men, equally concerned with problems of government, both trained in medicine and intermittently acting and thinking as physicians, both bent on finding empirical foundations for their ideas. And yet they took two completely different roads. The Englishman, citizen of an empire, looked for causal relations between quantitative variables. The German, subject of one of three hundred small principalities and, as we shall see, involved in the petty policies of many of them, tried to derive systematically the best set of categories by which a state could be characterized. As I sketch out a tentative explanation of this difference, a collateral problem will arise. Once the German tradition was established, why was it so impermeable and, in the end, even so hostile to the quantitative tradition of the political arithmeticians? This second question is highlighted by the fact that 100 years later Suessmilch, writing in German at the same time as Achenwall, made no dent on the work of the German professors. And, finally, what was it in the European intellectual scene which kept Conring from having any international influence as a statistician when, at the time of the great battle 150 years later, German university statistics and English political arithmetic were pretenders of equal strength and prestige throughout Western Europe?[21]

Hermann Conring and German Universitätsstatistik

It is difficult to visualize intellectual life in Germany in the decades following the Thirty Years' War. The educated layman knows the connection between Locke and the Glorious Revolution; he is aware of the brilliance of the French theater when Louis XIV established his hegemony in Europe through a series of wars. But who remembers that at about the same time (1683) the imperial city of Vienna was besieged by the Turks and saved in the nick of time by a Polish army—except, perhaps, if he has heard that this brought coffee to Europe and thus greatly affected the intellectual life of London?

The physical devastation of large parts of Germany at the time of the Westphalian Peace (1648) and the drastic decline in the population would lead one to expect a complete blackout of the mind. And yet, recovery had to come; and indeed, it did come, but it gave German intellectual activities a peculiar complexion. First of all, there was abject poverty. It is true that both Petty and Conring were involved in shady financial transactions, but the differing social contexts affected the scale of their misdeeds. Petty dealt in huge fortunes, while Conring's correspondence resounds with begging and waiting for a few gold pieces promised to him for some political service. In the two-score German universities, professors remained largely unpaid and the life of the students was at an all-time low. No middle class existed, no intellectual center, no national aristocracy which might have supported the work of artists and scientists. Whatever help there was had to come from the three hundred princes who ruled their ruined little countries with absolute power.

These princes were, by and large, all concerned with the same problems. One was to maintain their independence against the Emperor, whose power had been greatly weakened by the great war. At the same time, there was enough national feeling to make a possible invasion by France a common concern, especially in the western part of the realm. The relation between Catholics and Protestants, although formally settled by the peace treaty, was still very much in flux. And finally, the jealousies and battles for prestige between the various courts kept everyone on the move. This competition is especially relevant for my narrative. As one could expect in as many as three hundred principalities, there was a typical distribution of ability and culture among the rulers; for the better kinds, the advancement of knowledge and the improvement of government was a serious concern or at least an important competitive tool. It may sound somewhat strange to compare this situation with what happened in the Italian city states during the Renaissance. There was, of course, little money and probably less taste to build palaces, to paint murals, or to collect sculptures. But people were cheap. Therefore, if a man acquired some intellectual renown, several courts might bid for his services. The natural habitat for an intellectual was still the university corporation; so a relatively large number of small universities were created (and disappeared) according to the whims of some of the more enlightened rulers.

But again, what was expected from the learned doctors was colored by the peculiar situation. All in all, the critical German problem of the times was civic reconstruction. Problems of law and of administration had high priority. The competition between the principalities pressed in the same direction: the struggle over a little piece of territory; the question of which prince should have which function in imperial administration; questions of marriage and succession among ruling houses were discussed and settled in the light of precedent, and by the exegesis of historical records. International law started a few miles from everyone's house or place of business. No wonder then that it was a spirit of systematically cataloguing what existed, rather than the making of new discoveries that made for academic prestige. This, in turn, prolonged the life of the Scholastic and Aristotelian traditions which had dominated the medieval universities and by then had withered away in most other parts of Western Europe. In the second half of the seventeenth century, when English and French intellectuals wrote and taught in their own language, the form of communication among German academicians was still exclusively Latin, even in the numerous "position papers" they were asked to publish by the princes whom they served.

The life and work of Hermann Conring must be examined against this background. He was born in 1606 in Friesland, son of a Protestant pastor. His gifts were soon recognized and he was taken into the house of a professor at the University of Helmstedt. This town belonged at the time to the Duchy of Brunswick, which in turn was part of the general sphere of influence of the Hanoverian Duchy.[22] In 1625, Conring went to the University of Leyden, probably because his family still had many connections with the Netherlands from which they had originally come. (Four years before, Grotius, who was also a student at Leyden, had fled his native country because he had been involved on the liberal side of religious and political controversy.) The best source on Conring's study period in Holland is Moeller.[23] Conring stayed in Leyden for six years and was greatly attracted by the breadth of its intellectual life. He tried very hard to get a Dutch professorship, but did not succeed. So in 1631, he returned to Helmstedt as professor of natural philosophy and remained there for the rest of his life.

From what we know about him today, we can conclude that he would undoubtedly have become a European figure like Grotius, who was twenty years his elder, and Leibnitz, who was forty years his junior, if like them, he had spent part of his mature life outside Germany. I have no space here to document in detail what is known about Conring as a person. Instead, I shall briefly compare him with these two men with whom we are so much more familiar. Conring never met Grotius, but he came back to Helmstedt imbued with his ideas. Whenever it was not too dangerous for him, he stood up for religious tolerance and if possible, for reunification of all Christian churches. In many respects the two men seem to have been similar, as may be seen, for example, from a character sketch of Grotius by Huizinga.[24] Huizinga described how Grotius was "permeated in every fiber with the essence of antiquity": that in his writings on public affairs he mixed contemporary cases and "examples from antiquity in order to give advice to his own day"; that his knowledge in all spheres of learning was so great that "the capacity and the alertness of the humanist memory has become almost inconceivable." Practically the same terms are used of Conring by his contemporaries and by the historians who tried to reconstruct his image from his very extensive correspondence. The only difference is one of morality. All authorities on Conring agree on his veniality and servility, although some point out that this was characteristic of German academicians of the time.

Leibnitz and Conring had repeated personal contact. A brief summary of how this came about will bring the description of Conring's life one step further. From early in his Helmstedt career, Conring lectured on politics, although officially he was made professor of this subject only in 1650. One of his students was the young Baron J. C. Boineburg (1622–1672), who defended the dissertation he had written under Conring in 1643. A few years later, after having changed his religion, Boineburg entered the service of the archbishop elector of Mainz, who was one of the leading rulers of Germany in the period after the Westphalian Peace; and Boineburg became possibly the most prominent German statesman of the time. The crucial problem of the principalities in the Rhine area was how to contain the power of Louis XIV. The Mainz elector changed his position, being first in favor of appeasement and then in favor of organizing defensive alliances with Protestant countries. Boineburg remained an appeaser throughout his political career, which brought him repeatedly into conflict with his own prince, but at the same time made him an important bridge between Germany and the West. Whenever he had to make a political decision, he turned to his old teacher for advice. Many times he asked Conring to write pamphlets on current issues to support a specific position. Boineburg was also very much concerned with the possibility of reunifying the Christian churches which, incidentally, was also Grotius' main interest toward the end of his life (1645). At one time, Boineburg suggested an exchange of statements by relatively conciliatory representatives of the Catholic and Protestant positions. Again, he called upon Conring who wrote a number of monographs from the Protestant point of view; the whole affair came to nothing. These "expert opinions," always based on extensive historical and legal research, are one of the sources of knowledge about Conring. An instructive and well-organized inventory can be found in Felberg.[25]

At the same time that Boineburg turned to his teacher either for advice or for backing of his various political schemes, he was on the outlook for other intellectuals he could use for similar purposes. His attention was drawn to a young Saxonian who, at the age of twenty-four, had written a treatise, "A New Method of Teaching Jurisprudence" (*Methodus Nova*), a work in which he wanted to apply to legal studies and research the same ideas which Bacon had sketched in his *Novum Organum* for the natural sciences. Boineburg prevailed upon Leibnitz to enter the service of the elector of Mainz; he accepted and remained in this position for ten years—from 1666 to 1676. Boineburg wanted to be sure of his judgment and sent Leibnitz' drafts to Conring.[26] The latter was not overly impressed, but Boineburg retained Leibnitz nonetheless. As a result, Leibnitz and Conring came into continuous contact with each other. Both were Protestants, and the one was directly, the other indirectly, attached to a Catholic court. Boineburg called in Conring for informal or formal expression of expert opinion. Leibnitz he used more as a personal representative. For four years, beginning in 1672, Leibnitz was Boineburg's representative in Paris, a stay which was interrupted only by a brief visit to London. This was the period in which Leibnitz made contacts with French and British academicians and laid the foundations for his international fame. The only return Conring got out of it was a small French pension for which he was expected to contribute to the fame of Louis XIV in his public writings.

Leibnitz never completely escaped Conring's shadow. When he moved to Hannover in 1676 to become court librarian, a position he held until the end of his life (1716), his administrative superior was a man who again had been a student of Conring.[27] Between Conring and Leibnitz an atmosphere of mutual respect and ambivalence prevailed. The former was probably jealous of the rising fame of this new, and last, German polyhistor. He may also have had the feeling that he had been born a few decades too early. When he was thirty, Germany was still in the middle of the great war, and the main problem of a German professor was to keep out of the hands of various occupying armies and to clothe and feed his family. When Leibnitz was thirty, the agent of a German statesman could make trips all over Europe and take active part in public affairs. By then, Conring was old; and while he was famous, his participation in the recovery period was restricted to the written word.

Conring's isolation during a crucial intellectual period may also explain a final disagreement between Conring and Leibnitz. By the middle of the 1670s, Leibnitz was already deeply involved in mathematical studies and his reputation in this field, however controversial, was at least as great as his reputation as a social scientist. Conring thoroughly disapproved of all such mathematical ideas and advised Leibnitz not to waste his time on them.[28] This blind spot in Conring cannot, however, completely be attributed to Conring's age. All in all, he seems to have had only a limited understanding of mathematical thinking. A careful and systematic compilation of everything which Conring wrote on population problems[29] shows that he had a static view of the problems involved. While interested in studying size and social structure of populations in relation to public policy, he had no conception of or interest in birth and death rates or any of the other dynamic ideas so characteristic of contemporary British political arithmeticians.[30] Whether further research could explain these blind spots, I cannot tell. One rather obvious root is Conring's continuous concern with Aristotle's writings. They were the topic of his dissertation; later, he published many commentaries on and new editions of Aristotle's political texts; his own work, which created the tradition of German university statistics, was deeply influenced by Aristotelian ideas. I feel it was necessary to sketch this general background before I could turn to this part of Conring's efforts.

Conring wants to bring order into the available knowledge about various countries. His purpose is explicitly threefold: he looks for a system which should make facts easier to remember, easier to teach, and easier to be used by men in the government. To this end it is necessary to have categories of description which are not accidental but are deduced, step by step, from basic principles. His "model," as we would say today, is *the state as an acting unit*. The dominant categories are the four Aristotelian causae. His system is consequently organized under four aspects.

The state as an acting body has a goal or *causa finalis*. The second aspect is a *causa materialis* under which Conring subsumes the knowledge of people and of economic goods. The *causa formalis* is the constitution and the laws of a country. The *causa efficiens* is its concrete administration and the activities of its elite. Under each of these main categories, Conring systematically makes further subdivisions. The causa efficiens, for example, describes the concrete ways by which the state is governed. They are either principales or instrumentales. The former are the statesmen themselves; the latter are again subdivided into animatae (staff) and inanimatae. At the point where he has arrived at a "causa efficiens instrumentalis inanimata," his main example is money. And under this rubric he then develops elaborate monetary ideas which, I gather, were quite advanced for his time.

One should notice, behind this forbidding terminology, a number of very modern topics. Thus, contemporary social theory is much concerned with the goals (causa finalis) and subgoals of organizations, their possible conflict, and the duty of the "peak coordinator" to attempt their integration. The distinction between causa formalis and efficiens corresponds almost textually to the distinction between formal and informal relations, which is fundamental for all modern organizational analysis. The many examples which Conring attaches to his definition can be gleaned from Zehrfeld.[31] And Conring does not stop at a merely descriptive presentation of his categories. He often adds what we would call today speculative "cross-tabulations." For example, consider his conjoining the causa formalis and the causa materialis: in a democracy, all people should be studied; in an aristocracy, knowledge of the elite is more relevant.

These ideas are first developed as a general system and then applied consistently to one country after another. Stress is laid on interstate comparisons. Conring's richest material pertains to Spain, which he still considered the leading European power. It would not be too difficult to reconstruct from his very extensive comments an "anatomy of Spain." By comparing it with Petty's work on Ireland, one should get a better picture of the difference in style of thinking which distinguishes these two authors. Conring himself, incidentally, was very explicit about his method. He classifies the type of sources available to him and gives detailed criteria as to how to judge their reliability; he tries to separate his own work from that of the historian, the geographer, the lawyer, etc.; and again in the frame of Aristotelian logic, he discusses elaborately the kind of inferences which can be drawn from descriptive facts of rules of conduct for the responsible statesman.[32]

The first publication of Conring's on the "notitia rerum publicarum" was unauthorized notes by one of his students; the original manuscripts were published only after Conring's death. Soon, his students began to give the same course at other universities. Various compendia appeared, usually under a title such as "Collegium Politicalstatisticum." (It is controversial when and how the term "statistics" was introduced for this tradition.) By the beginning of the eighteenth century, the Conring system was taught all over Germany.[33] It had the advantage of being eminently teachable even by minor men and gave an academic frame of reference to the training of civil servants, which remained a common problem to all the little German states up to the end of their existence in the Napoleonic era. Conring's political activities helped in the diffusion of his main idea. He spent some time in about ten other German principalities in his capacity as temporary advisor; it can be taken for granted and could probably be proven from a perusal of his correspondence that on such occasions he established academic contacts.[34]

In any case, when Achenwall was a student at various German universities in the years around 1740, he met a well-established tradition. He began to collect statistical information in the Conring sense and when in 1748 he received a call to Göttingen, he was prepared to make it the base of his main course. As a matter of fact, his inaugural lecture was a defense of the whole system against representatives of related disciplines who feared the competition with their own prerogatives. I have already mentioned that Achenwall's writing in German helped to focus attention upon his work. But the image of a "Göttingen school of statistics," which got abroad rather quickly, was much strengthened by an institutional factor.

The Göttingen School

The University of Göttingen opened in 1737. To it, historians of higher education trace back some of the main ideas of nineteenth-century German university life. Professors should do original research, not only transmit available knowledge; sons of upper-class families, who traditionally were educated in private schools, should be attracted; and they should not only listen and recite, but be active in their studies. (The prestige of Göttingen was greatly enhanced by the creation of a library which was considered the outstanding one in Europe.) It is not surprising that this university became the center for the development of statistics understood as knowledge of the state. It was interesting to young men who came from a more literate background; it gave opportunity to do research in terms of the accumulation of more and more information about more and more countries; the material was useful for future civil servants.[35] In addition, however, it provided for several generations of professors a methodological continuity; and nothing is more conducive to institutional fame and stability.[36]

From Achenwall on, we are in often-described territory. He and his successors refined Conring's categorical system, raised new methodological questions (e.g., what is *relevant* for a necessary and sufficient description of a society), and added a great deal of substantive material. The main figures in the Göttingen tradition are Schloezer, Achenwall's successor, who in 1804 created the slogan that statistics is history at a given point in time while history is statistics in flux; and Nieman, who, in 1807, published the most elaborate classificatory system which he, incidentally called a "theory."[37] By then the confrontation with the political arithmeticians was in full swing. It developed by a somewhat roundabout route. Among the offshoots of the Göttingen group were men who were especially concerned with the *presentation* of comparative information on countries. This led to the idea of two-dimensional schemata: on the horizontal dimension, the countries to be compared and on the vertical dimension, the categories of comparison. Originally the entries in those "matrices" were verbal descriptions or references to sources. But this schematization was naturally conducive to the use of figures wherever they were available, if for no other reason than that they took less space. This in turn favored topics which lent themselves to numerical presentation (more and more such information became available due to the increasing number of government agencies collecting census materials). The guardians of the Göttingen tradition were afraid that this would give a "materialistic" flavor to the comparative study of states and deflect from the educational, social, and spiritual significance of their teaching. They invented the derogatory term, "table statisticians" which today would be considered a pleonasm, but was very apt in the context of the time. A distinction was made between "refined and distinguished" in contradistinction to "vulgar" statistics. John gives a number of quotations from the *Göttinger gelehrte Anzeigen* to indicate the vehemence of feelings at the beginning of the nineteenth century. The vulgar statisticians have depraved the great art to "brainless busy work." "These stupid fellows disseminate the insane idea that one can understand the power of a state if one just knows its size, its population, its national income, and the number of dumb beasts grazing around." "The machinations of those criminal politician-statisticians in trying to tell everything by figures . . . is despicable and ridiculous beyond words."[38] The only thing missing here is the apt expression of quantophrenia which Sorokin has recently created in a similar mood.[39]

In spite of John's very detailed documentation of this fight,[40]

I do not feel satisfied that it has yet been clarified. Thus, for example, it should not be forgotten that the period of the Napoleonic wars led to a temporary collapse of Göttingen and the meteoric rise of the University of Berlin after its foundation in 1810. It is also likely that the helplessness of the German states in the face of the Napoleonic onslaught discredited the claim of the Conring tradition that it provided the factual foundation for successful statecraft. And the beginning of a broader German nationalism probably made the academic world more receptive to the kind of general causal relations which the British political arithmeticians looked for under similar political circumstances 150 years earlier. There is here still a piece of history which deserves much more careful investigation than is available in the literature so far.[41]

But the story sketched in the preceding pages helps to explain why German academia was for so long a period impervious to the political arithmeticians. What Conring started served the most immediate needs of his country. It could not afford the intellectual investment which in England led to a better rate of growth in general knowledge; one can be concrete in surmising that Conring, even if he had thought of them, could not have afforded the computations with which Graunt started. Later the system served well the educational needs of the many little German universities, staffed by mediocre people. When Achenwall gave it additional prestige in Göttingen, something like vested interest began to play a role. Schloezer worked for a while in Berlin and knew of Suessmilch—yet why should a professor at the leading university pay attention to a military pastor?[42] But their king, Frederick the Great, did. Upon Suessmilch's advice he ordered a number of statistical surveys and therewith contributed to the downfall of the university tradition.

Meantime, the Germans had acquired an international audience. Things had greatly changed since Conring's time. In 1774, twenty-five years after Achenwall's first publication, Goethe published *Werther*. When Schloezer's book came out, Fichte's philosophy was well developed and the whole romantic school was in full flourish. I have no knowledge of an early contact between the Weimar-Jena humanists and Göttingen, which was the center of the German social sciences in the broadest sense.

(At the creation of the University of Berlin in 1810, the convergence is well documented.) But as the rest of Europe paid very serious attention to the German humanistic flowering, it should not be too surprising that even the more specialized efforts of the university statisticians were considered abroad as a major intellectual development which deserved as much attention as the contemporary work of the political arithmeticians in England. The fact that by now the former are practically forgotten while the latter are considered the foundation of the modern notion of statistics should not keep us from realizing that the intellectual balance might have looked very different at the end of the eighteenth century. It would not be too difficult to trace how influences from these two centers radiated to other countries and where and how they overlapped. From a cursory inspection, I have the impression that early Italian writers were especially influenced by the Germans, while in eighteenth-century France combinations began to emerge.

The question can be raised why I consider the development of classificatory systems a legitimate part of the history of quantification in the social sciences. I want to postpone my answer until I have described another effect of this kind by the Le Play school. First, I turn to the writer who marks the beginning of what one should consider modern efforts at sociological quantification. I agree with John's judgment that a major turning point came about when Quetelet's first publication appeared. "He is the focal point, at which all the rays of the first great period of statistical history converge, to be redirected through moral statistics and similar developments into many new fields."[43] While this simile too will need some correction, it is certainly a deserved tribute to the man who is the central figure of my next section.

Quetelet and His "Statistique Morale"

Life and Writings

Quetelet was born in 1796 in the Belgian city of Ghent. He grew up in modest circumstances, but his abilities were recognized early. He originally wanted to become a painter and sculptor, and for a while he was an apprentice in a painter's studio. He also had strong literary interests: he published poetry at an early age and had a play performed in a local theater. In order to make a living, he took a job at the age of eighteen as a teacher of mathematics in a lycée. When he was about twenty, he came under the influence of a mathematician at the University of Ghent who prevailed upon him to extend his mathematical studies. In 1819 Quetelet received his doctorate. His thesis, on a problem in analytical geometry, was considered a major contribution. However, he retained his humanistic interests, and up to 1823, when he was twenty-seven years old, he continued to publish essays on literary criticism and to translate Greek poetry into French. Many of his friends at this time were writers and philosophers.

Quetelet's thesis brought him to the attention of the Ministry of Education and in 1819 he was called to Brussels to teach mathematics at one of the several institutions of higher learning in the capital of the Belgian part of the Dutch kingdom.[44] Part of his teaching involved what we would today call adult education, and this seems to have fitted in well with his literary inclinations; repeatedly thereafter he wrote popular monographs on a variety of scientific topics. I am stressing Quetelet's many-sided and humanistic background, because the quality of his later work cannot be understood without knowledge of it.

Quite soon after coming to Brussels, Quetelet became deeply involved in a plan the origins of which are unknown: he wanted to start an astronomical observatory. For almost a decade until the plan became a fact, it had priority among all his activities. It also brought about the main turn in his intellectual life, although this occurred in an unexpected way. In 1823 he was sent to Paris to study astronomical activities and to find out what kinds of instruments would be needed for the Brussels observatory. While in Paris he became acquainted with the great French mathematicians whose headquarters were at the Ecole Polytechnique. He was especially impressed by Fourier and La Place and by their work on probability of which he evidently had known nothing before. Both of these men, as was mentioned earlier, had analyzed statistical social data. This combination of abstract mathematics and social reality obviously provided the ideal convergence of the two lines along which Quetelet's mind had developed. He quickly realized that a whole new field of activities, embracing all of his interests, could be opened up. In later reminiscences he said that after he had become acquainted with the statistical ideas of his French masters, he immediately thought of applying them to the measurement of the human body, a topic he had become curious about when he was a painter and sculptor. With his return from Paris in 1824 at the age of twenty-eight, the basic direction of his intellectual career was essentially set.[45] Soon the Dutch government gave him an opportunity to do something about it.

In 1826 Quetelet was asked to help the work of the Royal Statistics Commission, and he participated in the preparation of plans for a Belgian population census. His first publications covered quantitative information about Belgium which could be used for practical purposes including mortality tables with special reference to insurance problems. In 1827 he analyzed crime statistics but still with an eye to improving the administration of justice. In 1828 he edited a general statistical handbook on Belgium which included a great deal of comparative material obtained from contacts he had formed during his stays in England and France. The unrest leading to the Belgian insurrection in 1830 intensified Quetelet's interest in social topics.[46]

Quetelet's two basic memoranda appeared in 1831. By then he had decided that from the general pool of statistical data, he wanted to carve out a special sector dealing with human beings. He first published a memorandum entitled "The Growth of Man," which utilized a large number of measurements of people's size. A few months later he published statistics on crime under the title "Criminal Tendencies at Different Ages." While the emphasis in these publications is on what we today would call the life cycle, both of them included many multivariate tabulations, such as differences in the age-specific crime rates for men and women separately, for various countries, and for different social groups.[47] In 1832 a third publication, giving developmental data on weight, made its appearance. By this time the idea of a social physics had formed in his mind, and in 1835 he combined his earlier memoranda into one entitled "On Man and the Development of his Faculties," with the subtitle, "Physique sociale." With this publication all of Quetelet's basic ideas were available to a broader public.

Quetelet's literary background and the fact that his humanist friends remained an important reference group for him help to explain the manner in which he published his works. When he had new data or had developed a new technique, he first published brief notes about them, usually in the reports of the Belgian Royal Society, and sometimes in French or English journals. Once such notes had appeared, he would elaborate the same material into longer articles and give his data social and philosophical interpretations. He finally combined these articles into books which he hoped would have a general appeal. He obviously felt very strongly that empirical findings should be interpreted as much as possible and made interesting to readers with broad social and humanistic concerns.

The statistical data which he published in the period just reviewed were always averages and rates related to age and other demographic characteristics. Around 1840, however, he became interested in the *distribution* of these characteristics. It occurred to him that the distribution of the heights and weights of human beings, when put in graphic form, looked very much like the distribution of errors of observations which had been studied since the turn of the century. This led him to the conviction that the distribution of physical characteristics could be looked at as if they were binomial and normal distributions. They were currently discussed in terms of two models. One was the idea of trying to hit the bull's eye of a target with a rifle. Measuring the distance radially from the center, one would find that most of the hits were near the center and the less frequent the greater their distance from the center. This could be represented mathematically by assuming that a very large number of incidental causes, such as movements of the air, involuntary movements of the triggering finger, and so on, affected the tendency of the marksman to hit the center of the target. To obtain the proper derivation through the application of probabilistic mathematics, one had to assume that these incidental factors were independent of each other.

The other model used the time-honored urn of balls. Suppose

that in such an urn one has, say, one hundred balls, thirty of them black and seventy of them white. By drawing many samples of ten balls from this urn (always replacing the balls after each draw), one would find that most of the samples contained three black balls. The frequency of samples with very few or very many black balls would decline the more the number of black balls deviated from the "true number" in the urn, here three out of ten. The distribution of black balls in many samples could again be computed mathematically.

It was Quetelet's idea that the distribution of people's size originated in the same way. Nature, like the marksman, kept trying to hit a perfect size, but a large number of accidental and independent causes made for deviations in the same way that the rifle shots deviated from the bull's eye. Or using the urn scheme: the "true size" corresponding to the number of black balls in the urn was due to basic biological factors. People were samples in which varying numbers of black balls were drawn. This was just another way to account through probability theory for the actual distribution of size which Quetelet saw in his data.

In his earlier publications Quetelet had been primarily interested in the fact that the *averages* of physical characteristics and the *rates* of crime and marriage showed a surprisingly stable relation over time and between countries with age and other demographic variables. It was these relations which he had pointed to as the "laws" of the social world. By now, however, he was concerned with the distributions about the averages. He was convinced that if he could make enough observations, his distributions would always have the normal or binomial form. The notion of "law" was now extended: the distributions themselves and their mathematical derivations, as well as their constancy over time and place, became laws.

In the middle of 1840 Quetelet published a number of articles along these lines. One dealt with "probability as applied to moral and political sciences," another with the "social system and the laws which govern it." He now developed in addition another terminological distinction. Originally he had talked about "physique sociale" when he had dealt with people rather than with general statistical information about commerce, armament, and so on. He now distinguished within this area between physical and other characteristics of men and women. The quantitative study of nonphysical characteristics was called "statistique morale." The same data and the same ideas were again used and reused in a large variety of publications, including popular treatises on probability theory itself.[48]

In 1855 Quetelet suffered a stroke from which he recovered only slowly. After a while he resumed work, but never again developed any new ideas. His publications continued, however, and in them he reported new data and reiterated his basic propositions. In 1869 he published the two volumes on which his international fame is based, entitled *Physique sociale, or An Essay on the Development of Man's Faculties*,[49] thus reversing the order of the title used in 1835. The work was introduced by a translation of an article of the English astronomer Herschel who, writing in the *Edinburgh Review* in 1850, had drawn the attention of the English public to Quetelet's applications of probability theory to the social data. The first volume, divided into two parts, dealt in the main with population statistics, such as birth, death, fertility, and so on, and with the application of these statistics to public administration and medicine. The first part of the second volume dealt with physical characteristics, such as size and weight, and added some data on physiological investigations. It is the second part of this volume, book 4, which contained the material relevant to the social sciences. Intellectual abilities and insanity were treated in the first chapter. A second chapter deals with the development of "moral qualities." The emphasis was on crime statistics, but data on suicide and on all sorts of behavioral manifestations such as drunkenness, duels, were also included. These two chapters will serve as the basis for our specific discussion of Quetelet.[50]

Anyone who draws his information from this book, generally considered the standard source for Quetelet's writings, should be warned that it is a very confusing compilation. Large parts of it are verbatim reprints of previous publications, including the most important ones from the early 1830s. Sometimes footnotes are added to enlarge on an idea; in other places, Quetelet adds chapters containing more recent data and offers an interpretation which overlaps almost word for word with interpretations of similar data in other chapters. Furthermore, because his thinking on the social and philosophical implications of his work varied over the thirty years of his productive career, some statements on quite basic ideas contradict others made in a different part of the *Physique sociale*. Even in his lifetime the confusing nature of Quetelet's prodigious literary output had created concern. The German economist G. F. Knapp published in 1871 an analytical catalogue of Quetelet's publications in order to trace where various parts of his texts appeared for the first time and where he subsequently repeated them more or less verbatim in other publications. Knapp also wrote extensively on Quetelet's substantive ideas and created great interest in him among his own students and contemporaries.[51] A very helpful book on Quetelet was published in 1912 by a Belgian, Joseph Lottin.[52] This is an outstanding example of intrinsic analysis. Organized by topics, it combines and confronts extensive quotations in order to bring out what Quetelet most likely intended to convey. Lottin's book probably contains all available biographical material on Quetelet. It provides a well-organized chronology of his publications and, most valuable of all, it lists almost all the German, English, and French literature on the various debates which started during Quetelet's lifetime and continued well beyond his death.[53] English-speaking readers will find Frank Hankins' dissertation the best source of information about Quetelet.[54] This author was well aware that there is no English equivalent for the French term "statistique morale" or the German "Moralstatistik." He decided to use the phrase "moral statistics," and I shall follow his example.

Throughout his life Quetelet was active in many enterprises, such as the organization of international statistical congresses, the improvement of census work in his own and in other countries, and so on. Because of the specialized focus of my paper, I shall not give attention to these aspects of Quetelet's life and works but rather try to elucidate some of his ideas on quantification.

The Distribution of Nonphysical Human Characteristics

I mentioned previously Quetelet's work on the distribution of size and weight in large-scale human populations. He was convinced that similar distribution curves could be found for intellectual and "moral" characteristics if appropriate measures were used. He made explicit his belief that such measurements were possible in principle, and that the lack of data was due only to technical difficulties. Much of his general interpretive writing on moral statistics hinges on the kind of quantitative data he used as substitutes for the variables he felt would be really desirable. Debates about Quetelet's work usually focus on his idea of an "average man" or his shifting pseudo-psychological comments on his data. A careful reading would show, however, that his underlying theory of measurement, partly brilliant and partly a confused foreshadowing of latter developments, gives the clue to much of his work.[55]

On pages 148ff. Quetelet makes a statement not on his findings themselves nor their interpretation, but on the *formal* nature of the variables which can be used to *"measure the qualities of people which can only be assessed by their effects."* The passage which follows is a somewhat condensed summary of his presentation which I will reanalyze in the light of contemporary thinking about measurement in the social sciences.

One can use numbers without absurdity in the following cases:

1. When the effects can be assessed by a *direct* measure *which shows their degree of energy*: effects, for instance, which can be seen by strength, by speed, or by work efforts made on material of the same kind.[56]
2. When the *qualities* are such that their *effects* are about the *same,* and are *related to the frequency of these effects,* as, for instance, the fertility of women, drunkenness, etc. If two men placed in the same circumstances got drunk, the one once per week and the other twice, then one could say that their propensity to drunkenness has a 1:2 ratio.[57]
3. Finally, one can use numbers if the causes are such that one has to take into account the *frequency of their effects as well as their energy* . . . this is especially true when it comes to moral and intellectual qualities such as courage, prudence, imagination, and so on.[58]

When the effects vary as to their energy but appear in approximately the same proportions, the matter is greatly simplified. One can then disregard the element of energy, and work only with frequencies. Thus, if one wants to compare the propensity to theft of twenty-five-year-old and forty-five-year-old men, one could, without too much error, just consider the frequency of thefts committed at these ages. Variations in the degree of seriousness of these infractions can be assumed to be about the same in both age groups.

I think that *all the qualities of people which can only be assessed by their effects can be classified in the three categories which I have just established*; I believe also that the reader will feel that the temporary impossibility of using numbers in such assessments is due to the *unavailability of data rather than to shortcomings in the methodological idea*.

For the moment, let us disregard the references to cause and effect, a topic to which I shall return presently. The three types of variables described here are then quite familiar. The first is a continuous variable which we would exemplify today in the "moral" area by the amount of time an individual watches television, the distance a child walks on an errand without being distracted by something which makes him forget his original goal, and so on. Whether a variable is continuous or not is a question of empirical fact, which has nothing to do with the substantive content of the subject matter to which it is applied.

The same is true for the second of Quetelet's types. These we would call discontinuous variables (or rather, variates, if we wanted to be very precise). Examples would be the number of times per year that an individual buys a weekly magazine, the number of times he goes to the movies, and so on. The natural sciences also deal with such discontinuous variables and do so for a broad range of phenomena, whether it be the number of meteorites in a certain sector of the sky or the number of atoms per section of a bombarded screen.

Finally the third, or mixed, type is well known today. A price index combines price changes of a variety of products; a scholastic aptitude test counts the number of mistakes made, and might give different weights to different items. To simplify matters, we shall forget about the mixed type for the time being, and just distinguish between continuous and discontinuous variables.

Why were these distinctions important to Quetelet? The answer is simple. The type of discontinuous variables which Quetelet had in mind plays an important role in the social sciences. But the observations needed to establish them usually require a considerable amount of time. They have nevertheless one great advantage: if we wish only to compare subgroups in a population, we can often *substitute a one-time observation of many people* for *repeated observations of one person*. This is especially true if we are concerned only with averages, which in this case take the form of rates. Suppose we want to know whether men or women are more faithful readers of a particular weekly magazine. The logically correct procedure would be to select a sample of both sexes, find out from each person the number of weeks in a year he had bought the magazine, and then compute the average. This would be the number of weeks per year the average person of both sexes performed this act. Dividing this average by the number of weeks in a year gives us the probability that the average man (or woman) will buy the magazine. Instead of proceeding in this way, under many conditions we can approach the problem differently. We can interview a sample of men and women *just once* and ask them whether they have bought the magazine *this week*. The proportion of positive replies will be the same as the probability obtained through the more precise procedures.

It is this substitution of observations over people for observations over time which is one of Quetelet's central ideas. And as long as one wishes only to compare averages, this is the standard procedure in social research today. But when it comes to measuring *distributions* of these discontinuous variables, we are of course in a very different situation. In these cases we would need the full variable over time for each person and therefore observations over time. In many of the major writings of Quetelet and his commentators, the existence of such distribution is implied. A digression on two of these commentators will be enlightening at this point.

Lottin states repeatedly that Quetelet never wanted to make measurements of such discontinuous variables on *single* individuals. This is one of the few points on which Lottin is wrong. As the preceding quotation shows, and as can be corroborated in many other citations, Quetelet considered such measurements desirable and, in principle, feasible. One would misunderstand much of his writing if one overlooked this point, for Quetelet was convinced that, if such measurements were available, they would show distribution curves just like the ones he published for size and weight.[59] He gave these hypothetical distributions exactly the same interpretation that he gave his biological data, substituting society for nature. Society aims at a certain average which it obtains in a majority of cases but from which it deviates up and down according to the laws of probability. Today we deal with many empirical distributions of the sort which Quetelet had more or less clearly in mind. These include scores on intelligence tests, frequencies of sociometric choices addressed to each of a group of individuals, the number of times an individual did not vote in a series of elections, and so on. Within the range of precision which Quetelet thought of, the distributions of such measures do indeed look like distributions of physical characteristics.

Yet there is an important difference between the first two types of measurements in Quetelet's list; this leads to an interesting episode in the criticism of Quetelet. Durkheim's disciple Halbwachs wrote a monograph on Quetelet in 1912.[60] He was not clear about the important difference between looking at averages of discontinuous nonphysical variables and studying their distribution, just as Quetelet himself was never really explicit about this distinction. But one can deduce from Halbwachs' text that he had these distributions in mind when he launched his main attack on Quetelet. The distribution of physical characteristics, he argued, might be accounted for in the same way as are shots or astronomical observations, namely as the effect of a large number of minor *independent* factors which make for deviations from the average. But clearly this could not be true for data in the area of moral statistics, because here the interdependence of social action becomes crucial. Halbwachs stated and restated the notion that individuals influence each other, that the various sectors of society are dependent upon each other, that contemporary society is affected by past ideas and experiences. From such considerations he developed an argument against Quetelet's basic idea of probabilistic analysis which rests on a serious misunderstanding. Because of the dominant position of the Durkheim school in French and in modern sociology, it is worthwhile to consider this point in some detail. We are confronted here with the following situation. An early author, Quetelet, has a correct idea which he develops, however, only within certain limits. A subsequent author, Halbwachs, instead of adding what was missing, misjudges the partial contribution which his predecessor had made. As a result, instead of steady progression, we find temporary discontinuity in intellectual developments. Only many decades later when the idea of stochastic processes developed was the trend resumed. And it is fairly safe to say that the modern version was created by men who knew nothing of Quetelet's work.

Typical of Halbwachs' arguments are the following:

All these circumstances *preclude the idea that the laws of chance play a role in the social sciences.* Here the combination of causes (represented by individuals) are connected with and dependent upon each other, because, as one of them comes about, similar ones are reinforced and tend to occur more often; therefore, we are not in the same situation here as we are in games of chance, where the players as well as the dice are not supposed to acquire habits, to imitate each other, or to have a tendency to repeat themselves.[61]

Society and the moral acts of its members are probably, of all phenomena, the area in which it is least possible to consider an individual and his acts in isolation from the behavior of all others; this would mean leaving out what is really essential. *This means, at the same time, that this is an area in which the calculus of probabilities is least applicable.*[62]

The crucial sentences are those I have italicized. Halbwachs sets up an antithesis between social interaction and the application of probability mathematics. This has been proved to be completely wrong in more recent applications of mathematical models in the social sciences. Let us consider an example. Suppose that we are observers at a ball attended by men and women who do not know each other, and suppose moreover that more women than men are present. As the music starts, each man chooses a partner at random by drawing a woman's name out of a hat, and this is repeated for ten dances. At the end of the ten dances, we can classify the women according to the number of times they had partners. We will find a normal (more exactly, a binomial) distribution: the women will have had some average number of dances, the lucky ones who exceed this average being balanced by the number who were more or less out of luck. This would indeed be a situation corresponding to an error curve of the kind Quetelet had in mind.

Now let us change the situation slightly. At the time of the first dance each woman has the same probability of being chosen by chance. But suppose that the men watch the situation and believe that the women chosen the first time are the more desirable partners; a first choice thus increases their chances of being selected a second time. One might assume, to translate this situation into probability terms, that at the second dance the names of the women chosen the first time are put into the proverbial hat twice. Then even if the partners for the second dance are again chosen at random (by drawing slips from the hat), obviously the women who were chosen the first time will be more likely to be chosen again. Suppose that we allow this process to repeat itself for ten dances, and, after the tenth dance, we make a statistical count of how often each woman was chosen. The number of women with very many and with very few partners will now be clearly larger than in the previous "model," although the average number of "successes" will be the same.[63]

Here then is a situation in which, contrary to Halbwachs' opinion, social interaction is taken into account and probability considerations are still applicable. In the same way there is no difficulty in developing so-called stochastic processes in which probabilities of individual choices at time (t + 1) depend upon the total probability distribution at time (t). Modern mathematical sociology has proven the Durkheim school wrong and Quetelet right. It is true, however, that Quetelet himself was unaware of the fact that his sociological thinking exceeded the specific mathematical model upon which he drew. In his discursive writings, Quetelet often talks about social interaction and the effects of the past. As far as I am aware, however, he never went beyond the classical normal distribution which, indeed, makes no provision for these more complex processes.

Let us return now to the way Quetelet worded his distinction between the three types of measurement. He talked of "qualities . . . which can only be assessed by their effects." Today authors would talk interchangeably of hypothetical constructs, disposition concepts, underlying characteristics, or mathematical latent structures. But his three types of measurements classify manifest, observable data, not the underlying qualities themselves. Quetelet thought that certain things, such as size and weight, were human qualities that could be measured directly. Other qualities, such as a tendency to suicide or marriage or, most of all, to crime, could be measured only indirectly. Now here he obviously confused two completely different problems. Certain variables are quite conventional: an individual's height, the prices of commodities, or the amount of income. As one turns to the new area of social investigation, other variables have to be developed: the number of times a man gets drunk or the amount of money a person contributes to charity (another example which Quetelet himself gives). These variables may somehow sound different, but as far as the required observations go, all are on the same level of reality. A difference arises only *if one wants to make different uses of such information.* One might be interested in the size of people; then that is all there is to it. Or one might be interested in the charitable tendencies of people; then the amount of money they give to organized charity is an *indicator,* perhaps only one of several that might be used. This fact, of course, is equally true for physical characteristics. Suppose one were interested in a child's "propensity to physical growth." Then actual size would be a reasonable indicator, although physical anthropologists could certainly give us many others. The relation of propensities (or tendencies or however else one wants to translate Quetelet's favorite term, *penchant*) to manifest data is always the same, regardless of subject matter. It is true that in the social sciences the inferential use of manifest data is more frequent than in the natural sciences. But medicine is an interesting borderline case: diagnosticians use manifest physiological data to make inferences regarding unobservable physiological propensities. It is this general problem and its partial misconception which we now have to trace in Quetelet's writings and the subsequent literature they inspired.

Propensities and Their Measurement

The matter is best explained in connection with Quetelet's writings on criminal tendencies (*penchant au crime*) which fill the largest part of book 4 of his *Physique sociale* (pp. 249–363).

What he had before him were crime rates carefully computed for a large number of subsets in the population. However, he was not satisfied with what we today would call descriptive correlations. He wanted to fit his findings into a much broader picture. In order to do so, he considered his rates as measures (*échelles*) of underlying tendencies. From his point of view, this had two advantages. He could talk about his findings in more dramatic language, and he could speculate on interpretations which seemed to him of great human interest. If murder was more frequent among younger than among older people, that gave occasion to write about the violent nature of youth. The higher crime rate among men allowed him to speculate about the restrained nature of the female personality.

Quetelet constantly refined his arguments. Often he stresses the comparative uses of his data. It is true, he would say, that crimes are committed more often than criminals are caught. But, as police vigilance is a rather constant phenomenon, this plays no role if we just want to *compare* the criminal tendencies of various age or other population groups. It is true that the same criminal tendency can lead to manifest crime under one set of conditions and not under another. So we measure only the *penchant apparent* and not the *penchant réel*. But for comparative purposes, either serves equally well. On page 343, he demonstrates this interchangeability by analyzing the age distributions of indictments, convictions, and acquittals.

At other points, Quetelet met a more general statistical difficulty. He looked at crime rates as probabilities. In order to compute this probability for a specific group, he had to know both the absolute size of the group and the number of crimes committed by its members. But often he only had data on the criminals themselves, without the corresponding population figures. Thus, for instance, he could distinguish his criminals according to whether they were illiterate, could read and write a little, or had a considerable amount of education (*l'influence des lumières*). But no educational statistics were available for the country as a whole. Again, relative rates were the solution. He gives a table cross-classifying French crime reports by sex and level of education (and, incidentally, for two different years).

And then follows a typical interpretation (p. 297):

> I think that one could explain these findings by saying that in uneducated strata, the habits of women are similar to those of men; in more educated strata, women have a more retiring style of life and consequently have less opportunity to commit a crime, all other things being equal.

But none of this touches on the central issue: What is implied when one makes inferences from a committed crime to a criminal tendency? Does Quetelet do more than substitute for the observed crime rate the *words* criminal tendency? It is not difficult to gather his own position. For him, the crime is an *effect* of the tendency, which he thinks of as a *cause*. Today, we would talk of a propensity and its indicator rather than of a cause and its effects. This may be only a difference in linguistic fashions; I would follow the modern usage without attaching any importance to the difference.[64]

Quetelet assumes a *deterministic* relation between the hypothetical construct and its manifestations. This obviously derives from his training as a natural scientist. In the natural sciences, for example, the acceleration of an object is related to a force in a deterministic way. But in the social sciences, indicators or symptoms have a *probabilistic* relation to the underlying propensity. It is curious that Quetelet never hit on this idea in view of the fact that he was so imbued with probabilistic thinking in other contexts. Much of what I quoted before should have led him to this notion. Crimes are not always detected; whether or not they are committed depends on opportunity—all this would be best formulated by saying that the individual criminal tendency should be measured by the probability of committing a crime. This would have clearly raised the question how such probabilities assigned to individuals could be ascertained.

But Quetelet overlooks this question because of another idea which he repeats many times in his writings. He continually stresses that the only assumption he introduces—we would call it an axiom today—is that "the effects are proportional to the causes." To put this in modern terminology again, he assumes a *linear* relationship between the latent continuum he tries to measure and the probability of the manifest indicator he can observe. Even in the deterministic world of classical physics, this is undoubtedly wrong; the angle by which the needle of an instrument deviates is by no means always linearly related to the strength of an electric current which is to be measured. Measurement theory, as developed in modern social science, has made it quite obvious that such linearity does not prevail. The matter is important enough to justify two examples.

Suppose we want to develop a conventional test to measure conformity toward social regulations. One item in the test might be the question "Are there situations in which white lies are justified?" The probability of a positive answer will be great all along the intended continuum: only at the extreme, let us say, right end, where people have very strict feelings about always doing the right thing, will this probability be small. A graph relating these probabilities to the underlying axis—authors call it variously a traceline or an operating characteristic—will look convex upward. Take then the question "Are people entitled to break rules if it is clearly to their advantage?" The probability of a positive reply will be high only at the extreme left where people have quite loose moral standards; it will then rapidly decrease and remain low along the rest of the continuum. The corresponding graph will look concave upward. In other words, the relation between the effects (the answer to the question) and the cause (the underlying attitudes) can take various forms.[65] The situation becomes even more interesting when we look for an example which comes closest to Quetelet's use of rates. He takes it for granted that a high aggregate rate of criminality indicates a high average criminal tendency in a given population. He would certainly also take it for granted that a high proportion of male births expresses a high average tendency to have male children mediated "obviously" by the tendency of families to go on having children until at least one of them is a boy. But Leo Goodman has recently shown that the relation can be the reverse (personal communication). If all families pursue this practice, the couples who biologically are likely to have more girls would produce more children. The "effect," the rate of male births, would go in the opposite direction to the "cause," the *penchant* to have male children. Quetelet thus makes a much oversimplified assumption on the relation between a tendency and its manifestation.

The matter becomes even more complex if more than one indicator is at stake. On page 224 Quetelet talks about the possibility of measuring foresight (*prévoyance*) especially in its economic implications. He argues that the propensity to foresight existing in a certain country can be measured and he gives a series of examples on what data could be used: the amount of savings people have, the amount of insurance they purchase, how often they use pawn shops (because they do not properly balance their income and their necessary expenses in advance), the frequency of gambling, the number of bankruptcies; even visits to nightclubs are suggested as measures.[66] At this point, where Quetelet is only speculating, he sees that the "cause" he wants to measure, lack of foresight, can have a variety of effects or indicators, and that the inference as to the underlying tendency would be the safer the more of these indicators were used. But how would they be combined? Quetelet is dimly aware of this problem and this is obviously why he introduces his third type of variable as described in the main quotation above. He would probably correctly say that crude measurements of "lack of foresight" would be an additive counting of all these instances just listed. But he does not see the implication this has for the criminal tendencies in which he is interested.

Measuring the productivity of writers or the lack of foresight of householders is an *intrinsic procedure*. A measurement has to be constructed either by a mathematical model or by some cruder kind of reasoning; but there is no *outside* criterion by which it could be validated. No single one of the eligible indicators is a priori more relevant than any of the others.[67] The same idea would have to be accepted for the measurement of criminal tendencies. Starting out with a conceptual analysis, one would have to look for indicators of aggression, contempt for law, and so on. One *might* include the actual performance of a criminal act as one of the indicators. But this would spoil the main use to which such a measure could be put. What we would like to know is the *empirical* relation between the criminal tendencies, measured independently, and the frequency of criminal acts in various populations and under various social circumstances. Actually Quetelet at one point adopts (p. 250) a conceptual distinction which really implies what has just been said here. He states that the criminal act is the resultant of three factors: the *general* criminal *tendency,* the *skill* to perform a certain *class* of crimes, and the *opportunity* to go ahead and do it on a *specific* occasion. But Quetelet never proceeds from this formal distinction to a clear awareness that therefore *indepen-dent measures of propensities have to be developed.* He thought that in his comparative rates he had partialled out skill, oppor-tunity (and chance of detection) and that they measured there-fore dispositions, tendencies only. Subsequent research has shown that these assumptions are wrong. It is necessary to de-velop measures of criminal tendencies independent of the crim-inal act itself—provided that the notion of *penchant* is to be maintained.

But should it be maintained at all? This was the question raised by the German philosopher and mathematician, M. W. Drobisch, one of the first who brought Quetelet to the attention of his German colleagues by a review published in 1849. In 1867 he wrote a monograph,[68] the first part of which brings the review of Quetelet's work up to date and focuses on the question of whether criminal tendencies could be imputed to all people or should be considered restricted to criminals only. He argues strongly for the latter position: "the regularities demonstrated by moral statisticians have bearing only on certain classes of arbitrary human action and refer always to small proportions of a country's people who are especially disposed to these ac-tions."[69] Such a statement is trivial if it means that the crime rate pertains to criminals only. But if it implies something about criminal dispositions then it has to be tested empirically. An independent instrument of measurement to support Drobisch would have to show a *bimodal* distribution of these tendencies; on the contrary if the tendencies of criminals—whatever their origin—are only extreme forms of everyone's experiences, then the distribution should be unimodal. As long as only *rates,* or to put it more generally, the *averages* of propensity distributions, are known, the issue cannot be decided. A unimodal and bimodal distribution might well have the same average. It is surprising how many prominent writers participated in a "discussion bi-zantine" as Lottin calls it in a review of the pertinent literature.[70]

Halbwachs drew another conclusion from Quetelet's analysis

without noticing that he here accepted probabilistic thinking
which he disapproved of so strongly in other contexts. Combining his functionalism with Quetelet's idea of normally distributed
criminal tendencies (and elaborating on a remark made by Durkheim in his *Rules of Sociological Method*), he makes the following statement:

> In order to suppress all crimes, it would be necessary to instill in all people
> a deep collective aversion against the qualities leading to such acts, such
> as ruthless ingenuity, a spirit of intrigue and manipulation. But this maybe
> is not desirable; in fact, *as society permits the regular occurrence of a
> stable proportion of crimes, it undoubtedly feels that it would do more
> harm than good if this number were further reduced.*[71]

In quantitative terms, what Halbwachs says is this: One cannot just cut off the extreme tail of a distribution of attitudes or
traits; if one wants to curtail certain *excessive* degrees of vitality,
one would have to move the *whole* distribution of the relevant
propensities toward a lower level of intensity. While substantively Halbwachs' take-off from Quetelet seems less realistic
than the one Drobisch made, it certainly is logically more in the
spirit of what Quetelet was driving at.

It took a hundred years after Quetelet before his effort to
quantify *penchants* was taken up again in Thurstone's well-
known paper, "Attitudes Can Be Measured."[72] I am confident
that Thurstone did not know about Quetelet; even Allport, who
traces the conceptual antecedents of the notion of attitude measurement, finds the first seeds in Spencer.[73] I have the impression
that this discontinuity is greater in the social than in the natural
sciences. But I have no evidence on this; nor do I have a good
explanation, even if I should be right.[74]

After Quetelet

From time to time Quetelet published speculations on the
philosophical implications of his work. Did the apparent constancy of crime, marriage, suicide, and other rates over time
imply that human beings have no free will? He never could make
up his mind, but he certainly engendered a large literature on
the topic. The debate led to the formation of a "German school"

of moral statisticians which fought a rather imaginary "French school" with undertones quite explicitly related to the Franco-Prussian War of 1870. One gets a good idea of this rather curious discussion from a survey paper by Knapp, who also refers to the main literature up to 1871.[75] The topic would deserve a new review in the light of modern ideas on the role of mathematical models as mediating between statistical findings and theories on human behavior; in the confines of my present paper I cannot do more than draw attention to the matter.[76]

Moral statistics as a topic of empirical research expanded rapidly during the nineteenth century. Also, more and more areas of social life were made the object of enumerations: literacy, the circulation of newspapers, voting, and so on. Correspondingly, new substantive fields of statistics were created parallel to or as subdivisions of moral statistics: thus came into being educational statistics, political statistics, social statistics, and so on. The Germans were particularly apt in thinking of appropriate classifications. The most comprehensive effort is undoubtedly the voluminous textbook by George V. Mayer. Meantime, sociology as a discipline had penetrated the universities and its relation to the data collected by descriptive statisticians became a topic of discussion. Quite a literature on "sociology and statistics" emerged written by representatives of both disciplines; in a way it can be considered the beginning of the modern debate on the role of quantification among sociologists. An especially perceptive contribution, containing also interesting historical material was a short monograph by the Austrian Franz Zizek.[77] The most creative effort to give structure to the ever-increasing mass of data was made by the Italian Alfredo Niceforo. From the end of the nineteenth century on, he had been interested in what he called "the measurement of life."[78] He finally exemplified his main ideas in a small book on the measurement of civilization and progress, published in French.[79]

The title is characteristic: instead of just classifying available data, Niceforo starts out with the problem of how one would characterize quantitatively a civilization in "space and time." In chapter 2, he defines what he means by civilizations, and in chapter 3, he proposes what today would be called the dimensions of this concept. For each dimension he then proposes a number of crucial (*signalétiques*) indicators. In his first chapter there is an especially clear discussion of this three-level relation between concepts, dimensions, and indicators. He calls his whole effort "social symptomatology," and the logical clarity of his ideas is remarkable. Niceforo incidentally is the earliest sociologist I found who used correlation coefficients explicitly, and who competently demonstrated their place in such a study.[80]

One cannot talk today about a Quetelet school; his thinking, his way of analyzing data have become an integral part of empirical social research.[81] In one respect, however, he did not transcend the intellectual climate in which he worked. While he repeatedly mentioned the idea that special data could be collected to form the empirical basis of a new concept, he never set a concrete example; he only reinterpreted material collected by the social bookkeeping procedures of contemporary society. The tradition of starting with an idea and collecting observations under its guidance must be credited to the man to whom the last section is devoted.

Le Play and His "Méthode d'Observation"

Le Play's Life and Writings

Le Play was born in 1806, and thus was ten years younger than Quetelet. He grew up in a small Norman fishing village and received his early education at various regional schools. In 1824, at the age of eighteen, he moved to Paris where he soon thereafter graduated as a mining engineer. In his early jobs, he had to inspect mines and pass judgment on the possible commercial values of mineralogical deposits. In 1829, he made a trip through Germany in the company of a friend from his student times with whom he had hotly debated social issues over the years. They stayed for a while with the family of a miner and wrote down detailed observations on its way of life. This became the first of several hundred family monographs which formed the body of Le Play's empirical social research.

In 1830, during the July Revolution, Le Play was hospitalized because of an accident in a laboratory experiment. The turbulent events of the day reinforced his decision to devote himself systematically to the study of social conditions. For eighteen years, he was equally active in both of his chosen fields. He became a professor of metallurgy, head of the official committee on mining statistics, but at the same time, continued his travels, collecting his family monographs and pondering their use for the sake of social reform. In 1848, the second revolution occurred in his lifetime. He decided to give up his regular profession and to devote himself completely to the cause of social reform as he understood it. In 1855, he published a selected number of his monographs under the title of *The European Workers*. A year later, he founded an international society for social economics which organized the collection of family monographs all over the world and published them under the title *The Workers of Two Worlds,* a series which continued until after the First World War.

After 1848, Le Play's source of income came partly from the Academy of Science and partly from public offices which were entrusted to him by Napoleon III. Most conspicuous were his activities as French representative for a series of international exhibitions. The reports on these exhibitions stress his organizational ability and describe him as a master of classificatory devices which facilitated the exhibition of products and the orientation of visitors among the vast variety of activities going on at these international affairs. In 1864, he was appointed senator by Napoleon III. By that time, he was a well-known public figure and had published a large number of books and pamphlets on current affairs.

In 1871, the Paris Commune was the third upheaval which Le Play witnessed at close range. From then on, he devoted himself completely to the setting up of various reform organizations, supervised the writing and distribution of numerous pamphlets, and finally founded a periodical, *La réforme sociale.* His travels brought him repeatedly to England, which he admired because of its social stability; among his many publications is one on the British constitution. Beginning in 1877, he published the six volumes which form the basis for our subsequent discussion. The work is known as the second edition of *The European Workers.*[82] The first volume was newly written and presents in 650 pages an autobiography, a detailed account of the methods he used in his social investigation, and numerous prescriptions about how the results should be used for public policy. The other five volumes reprint the family monographs as they were presented in the first publication of 1855, including the earlier introductions. In addition each volume contains a newly written appendix which comments on the changes which had taken place between 1855 and 1877 in the regions he had studied. The family monographs themselves contain a great many policy considerations which are either summarized or extended in the new appendixes. The cases are classified according to what Le Play considers their degree of social disorganization. In the second volume he starts with families from Eastern Europe, where he sees the highest degree of social stability; he then moves to the Scandinavian and English countries, where he still finds a considerable amount of stability (volume 3); volumes 4 and 5 then divide the Western continent into two groups of increasing difficulties; the sixth volume is devoted to family monographs mainly collected in the Mediterranean region, and they all are examples of disintegration.

In scrutinizing the literature about Le Play, I have found that many authors refer to the first volume only; it is indeed an impressive document. But as to his research techniques it tells what Le Play thought he did, not his actual procedure; this can be gathered only from a reading of the monographs themselves. I shall, when I discuss his methodology, also draw on volumes 2 to 6. It is necessary to describe the rigid external form in which the fifty-eight family monographs are presented. At the center of each, as sections 14, 15, and 16, one finds the famous budget, divided by accounts of incomes, expenses, and supplementary details. The budget is preceded by thirteen sections which again are divided into four groups under the following headings:

> Description of the locality, the occupational organization,
> and the family itself (sections 1–5)
> Sources of subsistence (sections 6–8)
> Style of life (sections 9–11)
> History of the family (13)

Each of the first eleven sections is about a page long and consists in the main of vivid descriptive detail, the purpose of which is to help interpret the main budget account. Beginning with section 17, each monograph is followed by about four to eight additional sections headed by the general title: "Various Elements of the Social Structure (*Constitution Sociale*)." The impact of the monographs derives mainly from these miscellaneous sections which range in length from two to ten pages. Some of them are based on direct personal observations to which I shall come back presently. Others are summaries of what today we would call organizational and institutional arrangements: descriptions of the steps by which a young worker in a certain region advances from apprenticeship to the status of master; classification of the kind of contracts which existed between workers and entrepreneurs; detailed information on the economic and technical aspects of the industry in which the family worked; wherever possible, Le Play draws attention to the inheritance laws or customs to which he attaches great theoretical importance. The sources of these descriptions are sometimes quotations from books. Another group of these accessory paragraphs consists of interesting but uncorroborated statements on what we would today call empirical correlations. He classifies workers into certain categories and claims that they vary according to the rate of illegitimate births; he divides the population of an area according to their ethnic characteristics and states that they also vary according to their colonizing ability—the topic of emigration is of great interest to him. Still another type of comment deals with one of the central topics of all his writings: What is it in the personal habits of a family or the conditions of their work which facilitates or inhibits their rise in the social scale?

The purpose of these sections of the family monographs is quite easily discernible. Le Play is not concerned with the families for their own sake. He is convinced that his case studies are the best means of understanding the working of the whole social system. He therefore wants to link the individual facts he has established up to section 16 with whatever information he can gather about broader social structures. His contemporaries understandably admired him equally for his naturalist approach to the individual family and for his ability to abstract, during a relatively short trip, an enormous amount of information from crucially located informants and from literature only locally available. Even now, readers will be captivated by the vividness of his descriptions and the plausibility with which he argued connections between phenomena observed on very different societal levels. It is no wonder, then, that it took quite a while, as we shall see, before anyone asked whether his stories were correct and his interpretations sound. I am confident that much of his contemporary fame was due to the fact that he never just reported something the way a traveler would tell about a "cute" observation. Everything was part of a description of the functioning or malfunctioning of a coherent social system.[83]

Le Play tried to make each volume of *The European Workers* self-contained. As a result there is much repetition in explaining the purpose of his work and emphasizing the conclusions he wants drawn. Here is a brief summary of his main position.[84]

1. Le Play was convinced that he was creating an objective social science similar to the kind of mineralogy so familiar to him.

> In order to find the secrets of the governments which provide mankind with happiness based on peace, I have applied to the observation of human societies *rules analoqous* to those which had directed my own mind in the *study of minerals and plants*. I *construct a scientific mechanism*. (Vol. 1, first page of the foreword)

He stated repeatedly that "the conclusions of *The European Workers* are logically derived" (vol. 1, pp. 432, 436).

2. He did not see any contradiction between his claim to objectivity and the many statements that his personal history made him discover so many "truths" (*les vérités*) overlooked by other students.

> My first impressions, which I mention here because they are so vivid, *developed over the salutary influence* of religion, national catastrophe and poverty. (Vol. 1, p. 400)

He always disliked Paris. It is easy to explain why some people disagree with him.

> They were educated in urban agglomerations, and in educational institutions where in France all forms of error are accumulated; *they have*

acquired preconceived ideas, the sinister influence of which I have just
explained. (Similar references—vol. 1, pp. 41, 432; vol. 6, p. 32)

Both statements are in the tradition of good sociology of knowledge. It is just not clear why the environment in which Le Play
grew up led to truth while the upbringing of his adversaries bred
error.

3. Le Play was quite explicit about the use he wanted made
of his monographs. In his opinion, they bring out, by comparative analysis, the conditions under which people are happy or
unhappy. This knowledge was to be conveyed to the elite of a
country (*les classes dirigeantes*). They, in turn, were supposed
to take the necessary measures so that favorable conditions prevailed. This is the main sense in which he uses the term "reform." The word he often uses to describe the groups responsible for the well-being of a society is "patronage." *Patron* is
the French word for the small entrepreneur who still has quite
close contact with his workers; he uses the term also to include
the resident landlord. Occasionally, however, he personalizes
this social function of a specific group:

> I clearly understood that the greatest interest of my fellow citizens is to
> *escape the errors which push them to disaster*; and I have even clearly
> seen that for someone who is in a favorable situation and has the qualities
> necessary for our times, it would have been easy to lead our people (*race*)
> back on the road to salvation. *I have not stopped looking for such a
> saviour.* (Vol. 1, p. 428)

I cite this quotation, not only because of its characteristic wording, but because it appears in a chapter (vol. 1, chap. 13) which
for more than forty pages details his relations with various public
figures of the July Monarchy and the Second Empire. His reports
are undoubtedly biased; but a historian acquainted with the period will find in these pages important leads to study the relation
between public policy and the beginning of social research in
that period.

4. The large majority of the working people should contribute
to the stability of society by conducting their family life according to two major principles: observance of the Decalogue and

strengthening of paternal authority. These two terms are repeated well over a hundred times through the six volumes of *The European Workers*. They are reiterated in the introductions and appendixes to each volume; they are likely to appear in any of the sections of the cases themselves; and they form almost the theme song of the first volume. The word *Decalogue* is not used in any metaphorical sense; Le Play is convinced that the Ten Commandments do indeed contain the essence of social wisdom.

5. Actually Le Play is concerned with the life of people at a relatively early period of industrialization in Western Europe. But he describes it in exclusively moral terms. People have vices and are corrupt; evil prevails in all strata of society; the population is degraded and offers no resistance to the "invasion du mal"; the "pratique du bien" disappeared; we live in an "époque d'erreur et de discorde"; only the "reform" which is derived from Le Play's "méthode d'observation" can bring help. Even the most descriptive parts of his monographs are so permeated by this terminology that it is quite pointless to pick out specific page references. The reader cannot glance at any three pages without meeting this vocabulary; in addition, each volume registers the terms in the glossary.

6. None of these evils is explained in terms of social and economic dynamics or as due to changes in technology. They are the result of "false teachings" and "fundamental errors" which have been disseminated. There are essentially two sources of these social heresies which have infected all strata of society. One is the writings of Rousseau, and especially his idea that man is born good; the child is a "dangerous barbarian" and it is the main task of a strict paternal regime to teach him order, obedience, and submission to authority. The second source of all false ideas is Thomas Jefferson with his insistence on equal rights. He speaks of Jefferson's "deplorable presidency" (vol. 3, p. 426; for other examples of attacks on Jefferson, see, for instance, vol. 1, p. 626; vol. 6, pp. 23 and 546; I am sure that I have by no means caught all of them). Le Play considered the United States the most vicious social system of all he knew, and predicted for it an early and complete disintegration. This was

his position in the 1855 edition of *The European Workers* and it is reiterated with even more emphasis in the second edition (1877).[85]

7. According to Le Play, the success of his reforms will depend on the outcome of an "eternal battle between the good and the evil": the good is defined by the "hommes de tradition"; they stand for the "éternelles verités." The enemy are the "hommes de nouveauté." Most of them are intellectuals—the "lettrés." One repeatedly finds the opposition of "les lettrés" to "les sages," the men who are usually old and without formal education but imbued with the wisdom of the past. In chapter 4 of the first volume, Le Play deals with the contributions which various occupational groups make to the welfare of society; it is no surprise to find that the liberal professions have a bad record, indeed. They come about as part of a necessary division of labor. "But earlier or later they misuse their authority; they oppress those whom they should protect, and they become dissemination points of corruption" (vol. 1, p. 131). A reference to the glossaries will round out the picture. Under the heading, "écoles," Le Play stresses that professors do harm if they do not consider themselves supplementary agents of parental authority; otherwise, they diffuse bad principles. . . .

8. Le Play can in no way be seen as a defender of vested interests. He continually stresses the moral duties of the "patronage." He considers Adam Smith a sinister influence (vol. 1, p. 124) because he encourages the entrepreneur to be guided only by his economic interests. He feels that the absentee landowner neglects his moral duties. He is against the repression of free speech; but he argues characteristically that, if there were no free speech, the authorities would be deprived of sources of information which would help them to exercise their functions better.[86] He approves strongly of the incipient British factory legislation, but again, mostly because it sets limits to the freedom of the individual manufacturer (vol. 3, pp. 432ff.).

We are thus faced with a very strange phenomenon. Here is a natural scientist successful as a man of affairs and organizer of great public enterprises. He wants to develop an objective social science, to be based, as we shall see, on quantitative evidence. But the purposes to which he wants to put this knowledge are seen in a system of ideas which is not only conservative in terms of a Burke tradition but which in modern usage can only be described as "fascistic." Much of the later history of the school which he created (and I shall talk only about those of his followers who continued his empirical investigations) can be understood only if all this is kept in mind.

The Purging of the Saint

From the middle of the nineteenth century, Le Play attracted waves of men who wanted to learn his research techniques. They shared his political and religious convictions. But in addition, they always looked at the social science which they wanted to practice as a kind of revelation which they were called upon to develop and pass on to subsequent generations. During Le Play's life, they were his apostles, grouped around the organization and the magazine *Réforme sociale.* In 1886, four years after his death, those who considered themselves scientists as much as reformers started a new journal called *La science sociale,* which appeared in monthly issues up to 1915. Its approximately 40,000 pages deserve intensive study because of their strange intertwining of a charismatic tradition and empirical research. There does not exist careful analysis of the Le Play tradition similar to Lottin's work on Quetelet. This may be due partly to the fact that Le Play described so extensively his own life and the development of his ideas as he saw it; existing accounts are essentially summaries of what Le Play had written himself. But also the mere labor of going through the thirty years of *Science sociale* may have appeared too staggering. Nevertheless, I hope that such an effort will be made one day; it would contribute much to the main topic of this paper. The following pages try to indicate its possible value.

The journal *Science sociale* was subtitled "According to the Method of Le Play." The articles most interesting in the present context were the elaborations on the method and the periodic reviews of the organized efforts to apply Le Play's ideas to the empirical study of concrete situations.[87] A second group of contributions are new family monographs in the Le Play tradition. A third kind of paper reanalyzed earlier writings: thus, for instance, we find an interesting series of papers on Montesquieu and the kind of evidence he adduced in the *Esprit des lois*; another scrutinized Necker's writings on public opinion. A fourth group of efforts were devoted to the social interpretation of literary products: What was the social context of the *Iliad*? What was Balzac's image of the French middle class? The fifth type of essay deals with the historical record of whole cultures like the Assyrian or the ancient Chinese. Finally, there are discussions of contemporary problems, such as the early difficulties in the colonization of Algeria, the reform of the French educational system, the question of anti-Semitism, etc.

All these contributions presume that the Le Play school had developed a method by which social subject matters could be treated in an objective and definitive way. Many of these articles contain valuable factual information or lucid insights into other people's writings; all of them reflect a considerable amount of righteousness and self-assurance. The whole style of writing is quite reminiscent of contemporary Christian Science literature. Instead of talking about "la science sociale," they just refer to it as "la science"; "la méthode d'observation" becomes "la méthode." And yet, if one scrutinizes the articles carefully, a very significant change in tone becomes noticeable. To make the drama of this play more understandable, some of its actors must first be introduced.

The editor of the journal, up to his death in 1907, was Edmond Demolins. Almost forty years younger than Le Play, he was a historian trained in a provincial Jesuit college who came to Paris in 1873. He soon fell under the spell of Le Play and began to give public lectures on his methods. During the early years of *Science sociale,* he wrote periodic reviews on the progress of the movement. He was clearly the public relations agent for Le Play; some of the foreigners, who later on disseminated the ideas of the group in their own countries, never met Le Play and refer to Demolins as their main source of inspiration. He was always engaged in a diversity of activities. In the early 1890s, he created an antisocialist league and tried for a while to use the journal as its communication center.[88]

While Demolins was the activist of the group, the man who was increasingly considered the intellectual heir of Le Play is Henri de Tourville (1843–1903). He was an abbé who lived most of his life in seclusion, trying to make Le Play's work more systematic. His great contribution was a classificatory system which was always reverently called the Nomenclature, with a capital "N." During the first two years of the journal, de Tourville wrote a series of articles entitled "Is Social Science a Science?" His answer was, of course, affirmative. But he made the point that the genius of Le Play could be utilized by his disciples only if his system was made more explicit. His starting point was the way in which the family monographs were reported. He pointed out that while the first thirteen paragraphs were fairly systematic, the richest insights of Le Play are found in the supplementary paragraphs for which the founder had never provided a systematic guide, thus leaving future workers somewhat up in the air. De Tourville wanted to work out a system of categories which would give a place to every relevant observation Le Play made. I shall come back to this idea presently.

The next major figure in the sequence is Paul de Rousier. His contribution lay in further clarification of the core of Le Play's family monographs—the budget. In issues of *Science sociale* appearing around 1890, he suggested certain improvements to which we also shall return later. At about the same time, de Rousier also made several trips to the United States, which were to become very important in the further history of the school. His main move at the time was to show that Le Play had been too harsh on the Americans. Here were all these rich people like the Carnegies and the Goulds who had just the sense of responsibility which, according to Le Play, was the duty of the elites. The same men on whom we today look back as economic robber barons de Rousier described in *Science sociale* as the true modern aristocrats. The youngest among the more prominent men in this sequence is Paul Bureau; he joined the group a few years after Le Play's death. By introducing explicitly psychological elements, he was the first to bring about a major change in the Nomenclature. His new category was what he called "representation de la vie," which he proposed as the translation of the German word *Weltanschauung*.[89] Bureau was considerably influenced by Gabriel Tarde and, later, wrote an interesting account of the way in which his ideas developed.[90]

Beginning in the late 1890s, a tone of aggression enters into the writings of the group; increasingly a strong ambivalence is apparent. Le Play is still compared with Newton and Galileo and any other great scientific hero who comes to mind. But, in fact, he is being purged. Beginning in 1904, the subtitle of the journal is no longer "According to the Method of Le Play" but "Selon la Méthode d'Observation." The new series starts with a review of the present state of "la méthode sociale." The achievements of the last twenty years are no longer described as explications and clarifications of Le Play's own ideas, but as important discoveries made by the younger men. The master left grave gaps in his monographs; his use of the budget implies a series of errors; his family monographs are monotonous; his family types are badly defined; de Tourville's work is "more scientific and more interesting" (de Rousier). Le Play made intuitive observations but does not tell on what he based his conclusions; his analysis was oversimplified and incomplete; he was badly deceived and made grievous errors (Demolins). Le Play's family types were quite wrong; he based his classification on the way property was transmitted, but the correct principle of classification would be the kind of educational tradition a family has; his stem-family covers a variety of quite different phenomena. He was especially wrong in his anti-Americanism. Not only are the people in the United States not decadent, their spirit of individualistic enterprise is the best bulwark against the spread of socialism (Pinot). This is the mood in which *La science sociale* is written until 1915.[91]

We are thus faced with the following situation. Here is a school created by a charismatic personality who makes an important innovation in social methodology and intertwines it with very strong and activistic ideological beliefs. One group of his disciples share his beliefs and want at the same time to make methodological progress. Under normal circumstances, a scientific innovator is respected by his students, and it is taken for granted that his successors make continuous advances beyond the teacher. In a charismatic context, this leads to a tension between the scientific and the sectarian element in the tradition. This would be a matter of only secondary interest if it were not for the fact that rather suddenly, the Le Playistes disappeared from the French sociological scene. At least as far as one can see from a distance, the school which was so extensive and articulate up to the First World War has been completely replaced by the Durkheim tradition to which only casual and rare attention was paid in the *Science sociale*. In various reviews of French sociology which Frenchmen have recently written the Le Playistes are not even mentioned.[92] Do we face here a political phenomenon? Did the few relevant university posts all go to the Durkheim group at a time when the French government had an anticlerical tendency? Did the descriptive fervor of the Le Playistes exhaust its potentialities and make it less attractive than the conceptualizing of the Durkheim school to a younger generation? Do we face here the difficulty a charismatic movement has: In spite of their ambivalence to the founder, did the Le Playistes form too much of a sect to be acceptable to the regular academic bureaucracy?

I cannot tell. Certainly the methodological ideas of the school were interesting and susceptible of further development as I shall discuss presently. But first, I must trace briefly the effect which Le Play had abroad, especially in England and in the United States, and here, strangely enough, the theme of the purge can be continued. While we find outspoken and clamorous admirers of his in the two Anglo-Saxon countries, they changed his ideas even more than did his French disciples, each in his own way and perhaps without knowing it.

Ramifications Abroad

In 1878, a young Scotch biologist by chance visited a lecture of Demolins. He was deeply impressed, spent the remainder of his Paris study trip in contact with Demolins—he seems never to have met Le Play personally—and in his later writings always described himself as a Le Playiste. There are several biographies of Patrick Geddes, the Edinburgh professor of botany who, in 1902, joined with Branford in creating the Sociological Society in London. All stress Geddes' magnetic personality, his great schemes, and his tremendous energy; but they offer little information on his intellectual development.[93] I must therefore depend upon Geddes' own story in *The Making of the Future,* which has a special chapter on Le Play and his method and many references as to how Le Play's French background can save the social sciences from the evils of "Prussianism" (the book was written during the First World War).[94] I come reluctantly to the conclusion that Geddes never really read Le Play's monographs. In vague terms, he speaks of him as a regionalist and praises him for his fine maps;[95] Geddes, himself, was famous for his graphical presentation of social facts, but Le Play never published a map, except one indicating the geographical location of the families he studied. Geddes thinks of Le Play as a kind of rural sociologist and seems unaware of the master's political views, which certainly were not congenial to his own position. He and his students[96] kept hammering upon a presumed central formula of Le Play—(place-work-folk)—which does not play any role in Le Play's monographs and which can at best be read into some chapter headings in the first volume of the second edition of *The European Workers.* Geddes kept in touch with Demolins—he had him as lecturer in summer schools organized by the Outlook Tower, the famous Edinburgh building where his farflung activities as city planner were centralized. I guess that the charismatic atmosphere engendered by Le Play appealed greatly to Geddes, who himself had the same effect on his disciples. One of them, Victor Branford, was a wealthy businessman who in 1920 donated a house for the work of the British Sociological Society and called it Le Play House. Yet from available literature I cannot trace any concrete influence of Le Play's actual research upon the city surveys of the Geddes school. Perhaps British colleagues can provide further clarification.[97]

Another British social scientist presents a more puzzling problem. Charles Booth, the organizer of the great survey *Life and Labour of the People in London* (the enterprise started around 1880), did work quite reminiscent of Le Play in two respects. He was an avid and skillful observer of family lives, an ability which is well documented by the examples in a biography written anonymously by his wife;[98] and he did at certain points of his work study budgets. Strangely enough, however, I have in all the writings on Booth not been able to find any evidence that he was even aware of Le Play. The latter is neither mentioned in the chapter of Beatrice Webb's *Autobiography* devoted to her collaboration with Booth nor does he play a role in a recent biography by Simey and Simey.[99] They point out that very little is known about the origin of his ideas; this might be an explanation for this gap in the evidence. But one should also keep in mind that there are vast differences in the basic approach of the two men in spite of the external similarity of their procedure. Booth's thinking was centered around the problem of poverty and he tried to measure it as precisely as possible. Le Play was guided by a vague notion of corruption and never had the idea that some systematic classification of families could ensue from it. Booth is much nearer than Le Play to modern procedures of translating a concept into a well-defined system of indices. The difference in technique has a consequence which might exemplify the interplay of ideology and methodology. Both men were started on their inquiries by discussions with friends who were of a radical political persuasion; Le Play and Booth believed that the consequences of industrialization did not require the remedies advocated by their interlocutors. Booth, as a result of his own studies, became convinced that he was wrong; Le Play never changed his belief in his own righteousness. The difference is of course mainly due to the general attitudes of the two men. But actually Booth's procedure permitted a check on the amount of existing poverty, while Le Play's observations could neither settle how much "evil" there was, nor to what it was due.

I shall show presently that Le Play and Booth make very different uses of their budget data. Whether their qualitative monographic work is similar or not I cannot tell. The answer would have to come from a very detailed comparison of some of their cases. This has not been done yet but would certainly be worth the effort. The Simeys point out that Booth is badly neglected by contemporary sociologists, and I very much agree with them. When, however, they call him "the founding father of the empirical tradition in the social sciences," they certainly do a great injustice to Le Play.[100]

In the United States in 1897 the *Journal of Sociology* published a set of instructions for the collection of family monographs.[101]

But already, a few years earlier, American social scientists seemed to have become interested in the Le Play school. At the time of one of his visits to the United States, de Rousier was asked to describe its activities; his report was published by the American Academy of Political and Social Sciences.[102] This publication is interesting because it already foreshadows the subsequent ambivalent criticism of the Le Play disciples. To have overlooked this point is the only objection I would raise against the best available English-language presentation of Le Play's own work and that of his followers. Sorokin in his book *Contemporary Sociological Theories* devotes more space to them than to Durkheim and Weber taken together.[103] He is mainly concerned with substantive ideas and not with methodological matters; a review of his analysis therefore does not fall within the scope of this paper. Two of his students, however, made themselves the American exponents of Le Play's family studies and their enterprise requires a more detailed discussion.

In 1935, Zimmerman and Frampton published a book entitled *Family and Society*.[104] The last part of it consists of a 240-page condensation of the first volume of *The European Workers*. The original translation was made by Samuel Dupertuis, and the American version carries the introductory note that the condensation was done "without destroying a single idea." A comparison with the original text shows, however, that somewhere along the line a strenuous effort was made to attenuate Le Play's position so as to make it palatable to an American academic audience. All attacks on America are omitted, the word "Decalogue" never appears—in its place are terms like "moral law," "mores," "universal moral code," etc.; sometimes the phrase "Decalogue and paternal authority" is presented only by the second term. One should also know that Le Play's careful editorial structure, so characteristic of him, is destroyed; in the American version, occasionally a major chapter of Le Play's original begins in the middle of a paragraph. What most emphatically has been eliminated are Le Play's major obsessions without which he cannot be understood at all. Because the Dupertuis version provides American readers with their only access to the French author, I give one example in some detail. Here is a passage from page 453 in Zimmerman-Frampton, corresponding to about pages 167–69 in volume 1 of Le Play's *The European Workers*.

> The sophists of England and Germany inspired by the eloquence of Rousseau, have tried to meet the situation. They conclude that social disorders come especially from the constraints prescribed by the mores [!] and exercised by the family heads, and by the civil, religious and political hierarchies which increase the strength of paternal authority. They seek to abolish these constraints by overthrowing the rulers, if necessary.

Now this statement reads as if it belonged to a distinguished conservative tradition à la Burke (whom Le Play indeed quotes in a footnote). But in the original text the first sentence is preceded by a lengthy passage beginning with: "Around 1750, thinking began to be misled in the literary academies and in the Parisian salons, where the intellectuals, the aristocrats and the financiers met together." The imagery of a conspiracy, the notion that social changes are fostered by "people in the backroom," can never be found in the American version, although it is so characteristic for Le Play; as a matter of fact, a few lines later, the French author repeats that these people "began to pervert the minds of their contemporaries with their sophistries." The first sentence of the Dupertuis translation is correct but he omits about ten lines coming before the second sentence. These Rousseauian opinions are described as "absolutely false" and "contrary to the opinions of all thoughtful men (*sages*) and to the evidence available daily to the mothers of babies and their nurses." This anti-intellectual element in Le Play's text is avoided throughout the Dupertuis translation. And in the same ten omitted lines, we find still another of Le Play's favorite themes: "Logic applied to Rousseau's fundamental error [leads] to conclusions from which, as a fatal consequence, derives the ruin of any society adopting it." The idea that there are fundamental errors and verities from which logical inferences lead to wrong or correct views about society is the counterpart of Le Play's drive toward empirical observations: a reader cannot really assess the latter if he does not at the same time become aware of Le Play's pseudo-logic which permeates all his arguments. Even the last sentence in our quotation has in its original form an additional implication. The original says: "[the sophists think] that these constraints and hierarchies should be abolished; and if the rulers hesitate to accomplish this task, they should be overthrown." Le Play imputes even to the revolutionaries that they first would try to make the rulers change their evil ways and then only, if this does not work, would they be overthrown.[105]

The French disciples of Le Play were much concerned with the methodology of his work. They were exasperated by the fact that his monographs made fascinating reading while his procedures were loose and often manifestly faulty. The whole history of the *Science sociale* group can be understood as an effort to capture his spirit and to make it transmittable to others. His Anglo-Saxon admirers probably hardly knew his actual studies which to my knowledge are even now accessible only in French. They were fascinated by his programmatic writings and transmitted them in varying degrees of vagueness and distortion.

The first check by an outsider was published in 1913 by Alfons Reuss.[106] His important monograph deals with Le Play's significance in the development of methods in the social sciences. However, it is not so much concerned with his procedures as with the reliability of his observations and the relation between his data and his conclusions. The most startling part is Reuss' reanalysis of one of the family descriptions that Le Play had made (volume 4, case 6). Reuss went back to the German village in which two children of an observed family still lived, and he made use of a great deal of available documentation on local social conditions. He provides a fifty-page translation of the original case study and then confronts it with the material which he himself collected. The discrepancies are of various kinds. Thus, the budget figures make it appear that the man's only recreation was drinking, while actually he was active in a number of civic organizations, interests which are nowhere mentioned by Le Play, which do not show up in the budget, but which in the light of local political habits explain the large amount of money spent in pubs. (Germans use the term "Bierbank Politiker" to describe a local worthy of this kind.) Le Play's more general considerations made him overlook facts which happened not to fit in with his preconceived notions. Thus, he was greatly concerned with the negative effects of the French inheritance

laws which led to the progressive splitting up of farms. In the
area on which Reuss checked, Le Play had remarked how the
family life of the oldest son had benefited from his being able
to keep his parents' farm intact; but Le Play neglected the bad
effects that this had had on the lives of the younger children
about whom, according to Reuss, there was ample evidence. As
one would expect, the worst misperception occurred on what
we today would call labor relations. Reuss documents from contemporary newspapers the occurrence of repeated local riots
because of low wages, exploitation by company stores, and un-
sanitary working conditions. Nothing of this is mentioned by Le
Play. Reuss' monograph still deserves careful reading; in our
context, pages 84–88, "The Significance of Figures in Le Play"
are specially worthwhile.[107]

One final example combines the charismatic role of Le Play
and what happens when "outsiders" enter the scene. In 1886,
some years after Geddes, a young French Canadian spent a few
months in Paris and fell under the spell of Demolins. Upon
leaving France, he pledged that he would devote his life to the
study of Canada in Le Play's spirit. Leon Gerin, who became
a distinguished civil servant, collected monographs which were
published in *Science sociale*. He also revisited families which
had been first reported in *The Workers of Two Worlds*; he never
doubted their authenticity. The official obituary speaks of him
as the founder of Canadian sociology. At the age of seventy-
five, he published a selection of his cases, several of them introduced by devoted memories of his initiation by Demolins.
Since Gerin's death, however, younger Canadian sociologists
have cast grave doubts on the Le Play–Gerin approach. The
discussion deals less with research methodology than with controversial interpretations of Canadian social history; I therefore
mention it only in passing.[108]

Le Play's monographs captivate the reader by his insights, his
reckless generalizations, his stream of alleged evidence, his su-
perb style, the clear structure of his writings, and, even if one
disagrees with it, the consistency of his philosophical position.
Outsiders have sided with or against him mainly on emotional
grounds, since, except for Reuss, none of them has analyzed his
empirical work; and Reuss wrote at a time when methodological

thinking on social research was still in its infancy. The following pages are intended to give an outline of the direction in which a systematic study of Le Play's monographs holds promise.

Quantification and Diagnostics in Le Play's Monographs

Le Play is probably best remembered as the man who introduced the family budget into the tool chest of the empirical social scientist. He is quite outspoken about its central methodological role. One finds many remarks like the following:

> Every action which contributes to the existence of a working family leads more or less directly to an item of income or expense. (Vol. 1, p 225)

> There is nothing in the existence of a worker, no sentiment and no action worth mentioning which would not leave a marked clear trace in the budget. (Vol. 1, p. 237)

He repeatedly compares budgetary analysis with the work of the mineralogist which he knew so well.

> The surest way an outside observer has to know the spiritual and material life of people is *very similar to the procedure which a chemist uses to understand the nature of minerals*. The mineral is known when the analysis has isolated all the elements which enter into its composition, and when one has verified that the weight of all these elements adds up exactly to that of the mineral under analysis. A similar *numerical verification is always available to the student who analyzes systematically the social unit represented by the family*. (Vol. 1, p. 224)

Le Play wrote in great detail about the best way to classify and compute the budget items he obtained in periodic talks with his respondent. In this sense he can indeed be considered the fountainhead of an important quantitative technique. But his analysis of the data was quite peculiar and it took others to develop the whole range of possibilities.

In principle, there are three major ways to use budget data; these may be tagged as the analytical, the synthetic, and the diagnostic procedure. By *analytical* is meant the study of specific expenses, either in relationship to each other, or to the total income of the family, or to some of its general characteristics, such as occupation, age of children, etc. Already, during Le

Play's lifetime, the interest of some of his contemporaries shifted toward the search for such generalizations. In 1857, the German economist Ernst Engel published his famous law stating that the proportion of income spent on food increases as the total income of a family decreases. His data were taken in part from Le Play's monographs.[109] Since then, this kind of generalization has been the main objective of an ever-increasing number of budget studies. They represent early forms of multivariate analysis; on the same income level, for example, white collar families spend more on rent than manual workers. I know of no evidence that Le Play was aware of this use of his material. There is very little doubt that he would not have thought well of it. He, as well as his students, found statistical generalization quite pointless.[110]

In the *synthetic* mode of budget analysis one combines all the information to form what in principle are types, although often the information is finally translated into uniform money terms. The best example for our narrative is the way Booth, in his first social survey of life and labor of the people in London, tried to establish his poverty line. For a large number of items of food, clothing, shelter, etc., he listed the minimum supply which, by expert opinion, was needed for the sustenance of a family of given size. If a family's income did not permit the minimum supply of these items, it was classified as poor. To find the extent and distribution of poverty was the main purpose of this enterprise, as was mentioned before.[111]

What then did Le Play himself do with the pages of budgetary information covered in sections 14–16 of each monograph? In his methodological introduction, he gives the following example:

> Often a single figure says much more than a long discourse. Thus, for instance, one cannot doubt the degradation of a Paris worker after one has learned from the study of his budget that each year he spends 12% of his income to get drunk, while he does not devote a cent for the moral education of his five children of ages 4–14. (Vol. 1, p. 226)

In other words, he selects specific items and uses them for what is best called diagnostic purposes. Space does not permit us to discuss the logical foundations of this kind of social symptomatology. I can list only a few examples here. Le Play uses specific budget items as indicators of broader sentiments or social configurations. A French tinsmith pays high dues to a labor union, which shows how aggressive he feels against upper-class people; the family of a London cutlery worker spends much money on food, which allows one to infer that they will have little chance to advance on the social ladder; a German worker's income derives partly from gardening, which accounts for the moral stability still prevailing in his type of family. Most of these observations refer to moral issues: too much money for drink, not enough for religious practices and education, too much for "useless recreations." One has to keep in mind that these budget items are mentioned as part of general observations and discussions which go far beyond the quantitative evidence. One can get the full impact of Le Play's monographs without ever looking at the dreary pages of balance sheets for earnings, occasional incomes, fringe benefits, and expenses.[112]

The later Le Playistes increasingly abandoned the budget; as a matter of fact, they became highly critical of it. The nature of this criticism in itself deserves some attention because it signals an interesting trend in the whole history of quantification. When de Rousier in the first issue of the new series of *La science sociale* listed all of Le Play's shortcomings, he quoted many examples of the kind which were exemplified above by the summary of Reuss' reanalysis. He thought that Le Play was just following the "habit he had acquired during his professional studies (as a mineralogist)." According to him, Le Play was "seduced by this desire for numerical verification and as a result left aside the phenomena *which cannot be expressed in numbers and therefore elude such verification*" (emphasis mine). But if one looks at some of de Rousier's examples, one notices that today they would in no way be considered unquantifiable. Thus, for instance, he says that many families do not spend money, but time, on the education of their children. He obviously did not consider the possibility of a time budget, which today has become quite conventional. He says that expenses for devotional candles are not an appropriate measure of religious devotion, but he does not consider the possibility that records of church attendance or family prayer might at least enlarge the scope of quantitative measurement. In other cases, statistical records of the kind of personal contacts a family has would cover well de

Rousier's examples of phenomena which supposedly are accessible only to qualitative comments. Le Play, incidentally, often reports what the members of his families talk about with each other. Even quantified inventories of conversations, although still rare, have cropped up in recent empirical studies.

We face here an episode in the history of quantification which has many parallels. Le Play proposes budget items as a social measure. After a while, the instrument proves deficient and so time budgets or sociometric records are proposed. They cover more ground but after a while, they too, appear to leave out some significant parts of social reality. Bureau, for instance, reproaches the Le Playistes for being materialistic because they fail to consider what today we would call attitudes. Now attitudes are being measured and the objection is that this is an atomistic approach and that it does not take into account "climates of opinion" or "collective norms." These periodic waves of optimism and pessimism are one of the topics which the history of the Le Play school suggests for further investigation.[113]

I now return to another aspect of Le Play's diagnostic procedure. Anyone who has done field work or who has reported to sociologically minded friends about a personal trip hopes to find incidental observations which throw light on a complex social situation. Professors at the Sorbonne do not list their telephone numbers in the directory; how well does that indicate their exalted status and their social distance from students? In some American towns, families do not lock their doors when they leave the house; to what extent is this an indicator of mutual trust? Anthropologists developed great skill in such observations because of the language barrier between them and the people they visited. In contemporary society, students like Riesman and Margaret Mead have come to symbolize the art of making such incisive diagnostic observations. The logic of the procedure is by no means yet clarified and I will not try to discuss it here.[114] But Le Play's monographs certainly contain pertinent examples. To show the religious indifference of a London cutlery worker, he mentions that the man did not even know how to find a minister when a family member who was ill requested religious consolation (vol. 3, case 6). The high status of women in a nomadic family of the Urals is demonstrated by a description of how the wife interfered when Le Play interviewed the husband (vol. 2, case 1). The social alienation of a tinsmith in French Savoy is exhibited by the fact that he and his wife collect mischievous gossip about dignitaries of the town (vol. 3, case 4). An impoverished family who won a special prize spend most of the money buying new clothes, which shows that they hope to regain their former social status (vol. 6, case 7). Living with the family of a Viennese carpenter (vol. 6, case 1), Le Play tries to teach the wife an economic lesson: he lends her money so that she can buy sugar wholesale. The experiment fails because the children keep begging for more and it is easier for the mother to refuse when she can point to an empty cupboard. For Le Play this is a sign that the family will never become an economic success, but at least he appreciates the tender heart of the mother.

What one might call the global indicator game is something which binds together whole generations of would-be Le Playistes. Lewis Mumford wrote a short essay on Patrick Geddes and Victor Branford, both of whom he knew in connection with his interest in city planning.[115] He makes the usual undocumented and stereotyped references to Le Play's influence on the two men,[116] but he certainly catches the spirit of the affinity when he characterizes a typical stroll with Branford.

> He would gleefully point out some sinister exhibition of the social process, as in the combination of a bank with a meeting hall in the Methodist Center in Westminster, or the juxtaposition of the bust of Cecil Rhodes with the new examination buildings in Oxford, which sorted out the brains of an imperial bureaucracy.[117]

It would clarify the nature of Le Play's work and the logic of this diagnostic procedure if one were to collect and analyze systematically all pertinent examples in Le Play's monographs. I have the impression, however, that they are not very numerous. Le Play gives much more space to observations which go beyond the individual family and link it to broader sociological statements. Or, to put it more precisely, he soon leaves the specific family and focuses his attention on broader contexts. Thus, in the case of the London cutlery worker, he tells us that the poorer workers in his neighborhood go to church in the evening, while the middle-class people go in the morning; the preacher is aware of this stratification, and custom tailors his sermons accordingly. The social *ressentiment* of the Savoy tinsmith leads to an instructive digression on the spreading power of the labor unions in this area. One of the most interesting examples can be found in paragraphs 18 and 19 of case 7 in volume 6. Le Play obviously selected this family because it got a prize for having produced a large number of children and bringing them up decently under very restricted economic conditions. In four pages, Le Play makes ten statements as to the factors which account for high fertility. Formulated as hypotheses, they would do honor to any modern textbook, and most of them would be controversial even today after a century of empirical research has piled up. Le Play is of course convinced that his opinion is the only one conceivable.

The French disciples of Le Play were very much concerned about the loose connection between the family monographs themselves and the broader social observations which were considered Le Play's most important contributions. This explains the dominant role which de Tourville's "Nomenclature" played in the pages of the *Science sociale*. De Tourville wanted to provide a system of categories which would give a place to every relevant observation and at the same time permit a reorganization of the original work of Le Play. He was also confident that his system would facilitate comparative analysis. The Nomenclature consisted of twenty-five major categories, which approach the families under study, so to say, from two sides. The first nine corresponded approximately to the first thirteen paragraphs of the original monographs: the geographical setting and the type of work done by the family members (a and b), its sources of income, properties, expenses, and savings (c–f), the obligations and rights of the family members, the style of life, and its history (g–i).

The remaining categories tried to see the family in ever-broadening circles of its social context: the technical, commercial, and cultural conditions of the industry in which they worked (j–l); the religious practices, the neighborhood relations, and the professional and communal organizations in which the family was embedded (m–q), the broader characteristics of the country in which the family lived, the city, the province, and the laws of the whole state inasmuch as they had bearing on the life of the family (r–u); finally, the broad history of the country, its national composition, and its relation (especially emigration or immigration) with other countries (v–z). For a long while, de Tourville's Nomenclature was considered the perfect key to all social analysis. The general argument went about as follows: it guaranteed, so to say, the basic elements needed to describe any social system. After they have been provided, the task of the analyst is fairly easy. He has to find how these elements are related to each other in a specific case and how they vary from one to the next.

Here again is another major wave of categorization, so characteristic of the history of the social sciences. The reader will undoubtedly have anticipated the parallel with Conring and the school of German university statistics. Their aim was certainly the same as the one of the Le Play group, although we can take it for granted that the latter did not know of this earlier effort. It is not too difficult to pinpoint the major difference between the two approaches. The starting point for the Conring school was the state and the administrative tasks of the statesman. In a cameralistic system, he took it for granted that the welfare of the state depended upon the activities of the rulers. Their activities, therefore, were the starting point for the relevant categories: increase of population, defense against potential enemies, improvement of agriculture, monetary policy, and so on. Matters like the family would be derivative problems related, for instance, to the number of available conscripts; individual characteristics of diverse population groups would be worth knowing if the statesman wanted efficient compliance with his administrative measures. The Le Play group took the reverse view. The welfare of the country depended upon the morality, the industry, and the submissiveness of the citizens at large and upon the sense of responsibility of the elite. These qualities were formed in the confines of the family. The system of categories, therefore, had to start out with a description of this primary group; it drew in the characteristics of the larger context only to the extent that this explained what happened at the social core. Le Play, so to say, saw society from within outward. Conring and his school

looked at society as a large social system, the main characteristics of which they wanted to describe; they paid attention to
the primary group only to the extent to which it would affect
the actor on the big scene. Anyone who knows the literature of
modern sociology is aware that the development of nomenclature
is still an honorable pursuit. One might say that recent literature
is trying to combine the Conring and the Le Play traditions.

Postscriptum

What other major episode might have belonged in this introductory survey? I have not described in detail the coming of the
British social survey; recently, good summaries have become
available, especially Abrams' introductory chapters to his book
on social surveys and McGregor's paper on the social background of the survey movement.[118] The development of quantification in Germany is a complex topic. Toennies, best known
for his conceptual distinction between Gesellschaft and Gemeinschaft, was for years a vigorous promoter of an empirical
"sociography"; but twice, once before the First World War and
again before the rise of Hitler, this development was cut short.
Max Weber is the great symbol of broad-scale historical research. Only rarely is reference made to his periodic interest in
quantitative research and the ambivalence of his efforts. Space
limitations have forced me to reserve the German materials for
a future publication.[119] The Italians have an empirical tradition
of their own. Not knowing their language, I had to leave their
side of the story to other students; Niceforo's books provide
many leads to historical sources. Americans came later onto the
scene, of course. Nothing is stranger than the idea often expressed by European colleagues that quantification is a U.S.
export endangering their tradition. It is true that when this country took over the European empirical research techniques, it did
so on a large scale. But the steps by which this came about are
little known. Here is a vast area for further inquiry; I have not
touched upon it in this paper, because the tracing of institutional
and personal contacts, as well as analysis of the literature, would
be required.

Some time at the end of the nineteenth century, quantification in sociology takes on its modern function: to translate ideas into empirical operations and to look for regular relations between the variates so created.[120] Histories of specific techiques will be needed to clarify this general trend. Helen Walker has done it for correlation analysis and Frederic Stephan for sampling.[121] The use of questionnaires has a long past which still waits for its recorder. Mathematical models of social behavior have a curious history. At the end of the eighteenth century, men like Condorcet worked on them very seriously. For a long while thereafter, the idea was monopolized by the economists. In very recent years, psychologists and sociologists have reentered the scene. The literature increases rapidly; but it is still an object for the book reviewer rather than the historian.

In any case, much work must be done if we want to match the increasing quantity of sociological quantification by better quality of insight into its history.

PART TWO
The Logic of Method

[4]
Problems in Methodology

The Scope of Methodology

Tired social scientists and hostile outsiders sometimes ask: What has social research all added up to in the last fifty years? Is there any sociological finding that has not been anticipated by philosophers or novelists? The answer has to be qualified. True, it is unlikely that any surprising "discoveries" will be made for quite some time to come. But it is this very fact that forces the modern social scientist toward his main tasks: parsimonious organization of knowledge through systematic theory, and development of empirical methods to gauge how much regularity there is in the social world, to find the conditions under which these myriad proverbs, aperçus, and visions are true.

If coherence and precision are among the main objectives of the contemporary sociologist, then the very nature of his work involves decisions as to the direction of efforts, the selection of topics, the merit of procedures themselves. Sociologists are supposed to convert the vast and ever-shifting web of social relations into an understandable system of manageable knowledge. To discover and appraise the way in which this is being done is the object of methodological analysis. The sociologist studies man in society: the methodologist studies the sociologist at work.

The topics of methodology cannot be specified precisely, because they depend upon the development of the social sciences

From Robert K. Merton, Leonard Broom, and Leonard S. Cottrell, Jr., eds., *Sociology Today: Problems and Prospects* (New York: Basic Books, 1959). Copyright © 1959 Basic Books. Reprinted by permission. Work on this paper was in part supported by a Ford Foundation grant to Columbia University for the study of advanced training in social research. I am indebted to Patricia Kendall for much editorial help.

themselves. It is possible, however, to identify at least six major themes which occupy today's methodologists:[1]

1. *Location of topics.* Authors have a tendency to express themselves on selected aspects of a problem without specifying where they have "cut in" on the broader concern which underlies their treatment. Thus, as Merton has found,[2] writers on the sociology of knowledge may emphasize the social base of an ideology, its specific structure, or the link between the two. MacIver has brought order into the controversy between pollsters and political scientists by suggesting the notion of "public opinion system" consisting of three parts: the basis of consensus, the alignment of opinion, and the structure of communication. In the first part he locates the study of value systems and climates of opinion; the second part covers today's public opinion polls; the third calls for the study of leadership, pressure groups, and the effect of opinion distribution on legislation.[3] Although the interrelations of these parts have by no means been worked out, the scheme succeeds in preventing a too narrow delineation of a concrete inquiry.

2. *Clarification of terms.* Clarifying terms is probably the oldest duty of the methodologist and, unfortunately, one which never ends. Zetterberg has noted how many sociological terms fuse description, evaluation, and prescription. The very term "value," for example, sometimes stands for an evaluation by actors and sometimes for a prescription by the community. The term "social roles" is sometimes used in a descriptive sense (what people in a certain status do) and sometimes in a prescriptive sense (how others expect them to do it).[4] Rommetveit has pointed to the ambiguity in the social psychologist's use of the term "frame of reference." Sometimes it means that the measures on a given dimension depend upon the subject's location or situation: the same house appears luxurious to the poor man and drab to the rich man. At other times the emphasis is on multidimensional objects, of which different observers choose different dimensions; the much-quoted forest which the farmer perceives as a source of lumber and the hunter as an animal's abode is an example.[5] Lazarsfeld has shown how many typologies are defective because the authors fail to specify the dimensions, and the combinations thereof, from which the typol-

ogies implicitly derive.[6] Some of the most interesting of the recent publications came about when the authors, engaged in a piece of empirical research, reviewed the pertinent literature. They often found that they had to refine traditional definitions and reconcile contradictions within the same texts before they could use general ideas in a specific inquiry. I refer especially to the rapidly growing literature on the concepts of "role" and "rational choice."

   3. *Explication of research techniques.* The construction of scales, sampling, and avoidance of interviewer bias are not aspects of methodology as we propose to define the term. The implications of a specific technique, however, are the methodologist's concern. Lindzey, for example, has developed ten assumptions which underlie the use of a thematic-apperception test. The basic assumption is, of course, that an individual reveals his own strivings in his interpretation of an unstructured situation. But, in addition, use of the technique involves the assumption that the clinician can tell with what figure in the picture the subject identifies himself; that he can distinguish the part of the story that reflects enduring dispositions from those that reflect some force in the immediate present; and so on.[7] Clausen and Kohn's discussion of ecological studies has rendered a similar service. They show that two sets of assumptions are implied in the literature. One set is of a statistical nature— for example, the assumption that it is possible to determine which one of a cluster of variables that characterize an area is responsible for the area's high or low rate of mental disorders. The other set has to do with substantive interpretation: the assumption that the "effect of the area" can be attributed to an interplay with hereditary factors, to social interaction (for example, isolation), or to the development of peculiar value systems in certain areas.[8] It seems that such explications are especially difficult for qualitative procedures. There does not exist, for example, a satisfactory discussion of what the field worker does when he observes that residents of forty-year standing are called strangers or that bad reputation in one town does not keep a boy from being acceptable in a neighboring one.[9]

   4. *Interrelation of research techniques.* There is no royal road to the solution of a research problem; heated procedural dis-

cussions spring up all the time. The methodologist tries to bring out the specific features of controversial techniques and, as he does so, also advances the explications we have mentioned. His work might be restricted to rather specific techniques, such as Stouffer's et al. comparison of the Guttman scale and a scale derived from a latent dichotomy, based on the fact that both are special cases of a broader model.[10] Or it might deal with more general issues. Meehl's discussion of clinical versus statistical predictions is itself based on a bibliography of 104 items. He makes essentially two contributions: he distinguishes clearly between the question of what are in practice more successful, actuarial or clinical predictions, and the question of whether the two methods proceed in a basically different way. On the latter point, he remarks that in both procedures statistical relations between variables are implied; but the clinician has a flexibility which the statistician lacks in that he can enlarge the inventory of such relations as he studies a case.[11]

As empirical work progresses, it may develop that a whole area is treated by two different techniques which await coordination. Such, at the moment, is the case with selective perception. Attitude surveys have shown how perception of other people's vote intentions or political apprehensions depend upon the perceiver's corresponding predispositions. Similar data are available from laboratory work on the determination of perception by experimentally induced motivation. In surveys we usually have many more cases and can therefore bring many more variables into play; in the laboratories there are fewer variables but they are more carefully controlled. What is the relation between the findings brought to light by these two traditions?[12]

5. *Systematization of empirical findings.* Much scientific work progresses from isolated studies to generalizations and theoretical systems from which existing and future knowledge can be deduced. Sociological theories in this strict sense are slow to develop. It is possible, however, to organize an array of empirical findings so that they can be compared and loosely related to one another. Sometimes this is done by culling out some salient elements which reappear in many interpretations. Thus Lipset and his associates, in a review of voting studies in many countries, have suggested that groups vote for leftist par-

ties if their income is uncertain, their prestige is low, and their social situation facilitates communication among them while it curbs contact with other strata in the society. They end up with a tableau which, as a substitute for a multiple-correlation analysis, corresponds to the crude data available. For various occupational groups, they indicate the presence or absence of the factors listed above and show that the frequency of leftist voting corresponds roughly to the pattern so developed.[13] Festinger, using experimental studies on social communication, proceeds differently. He takes a number of factors which make for "pressure to communicate" and lists their effect in a series of separate propositions: that this pressure increases with the relevance of the topic, the cohesion of the group, the perceived discrepancy of opinion, and so on. Each proposition is exemplified by a number of experiments. He proposes similar sets of factors affecting the change of opinion among members of small groups.[14]

Compared with the usual bibliographical reviews, such "propositional inventories" have great merit in that they suggest a small and possibly crucial number of concepts and relations among them. This kind of endeavor is, however, better described as methodology than as theory. The derivation of the findings from the general propositions is necessarily vague, and data are grouped by analogy rather than by precise transformations. This comment should not detract from the merit of the effort. To explicate the characteristics of productive inventories of this kind would, incidentally, be an important task.

6. *Formalization of reasoning.* The vague relations among propositions which are an unavoidable aspect of propositional theories, even if ostensibly stated "more geometrico," can be improved by mathematics and even by simple formalizations. The introduction of sociometric matrices permits the ordering of more complex relations among people than can be managed by using the first Moreno diagrams or by early computations. The simple operation of matrix multiplication makes it possible to count various types of clique, for example.[15] The use of formalism in sociological data is not yet likely to lead to new findings. But it can disclose hitherto unnoticed implications or clarify the relation among propositions. The latter point becomes especially clear in the few cases in which we have a subsequent

mathematization of a systematic inventory, as Herbert Simon has provided for Festinger's paper on communication. One of Festinger's formal propositions, for example, is that pressure to communicate increases with the relevance of the topic. In an explanatory aside, he adds that this comes about via a desire of tbe group members to achieve uniformity of opinion. Simon shows that the whole system becomes more complex if such asides are formally incorporated into it, but that at the same time some of the propositions turn out to be logical derivatives of a smaller subset. One remarkable feature of Simon's formalization is, incidentally, that he uses only very general mathematical ideas which are independent of the specific indices used in the original studies.[16]

The foregoing outline of six problem areas suffers from the difficulties inherent in any job description. Inevitably, some areas are overlooked, others are included without clear justification, and the subdivisions are somewhat arbitrary and indistinct. Still, such a classification of a field increases the chances that at least some readers will think of similar problems and activities when they use the term "methodology."

For better understanding, it is necessary to discuss in detail one specific topic. I have selected for this purpose an issue which has many ramifications. From the time empirical social research first became popular, a sense of uneasiness has been abroad. Is it possible that the traditional richness of social thought can be translated into a language which considers the objects of social inquiry to be combinations of isolated properties—I shall call them "variates"—and in which general ideas are expressed by relations among these variates? Is the IBM card about to deprive the social sciences of all meaning? Part of this fear derives from an imputation of imperialism which any sober empiricist will want to deny. Broad historical studies and intuitive analyses of specific cases will remain an important part of our field. But this same suspicion also results from a misunderstanding of the methodology of social research. Modern methods of quantitative research are considerably more subtle and flexible than the inexperienced critic assumes. To demonstrate this, I shall discuss what happens if concepts are transformed into "measurements" during the course of empirical research. Some aspects of this transformation—especially the final stages of index formation—have been covered extensively in recent literature;[17] my emphasis will be on the less explored phases of the flow from concepts to variates. I shall then show how this explication clarifies a few issues which remain cloudy as long as they are discussed on too general a level.

The following section corresponds to the explication of qualitative procedures discussed in the foregoing section as the third problem area. In the final section I shall go one step further. I shall consider such notions as "structure" and "process," which supposedly are threatened by atomistic quantification; I shall show that no such danger exists and that "variates" and their interrelations do justice to the complexity of these ideas. This section thus exemplifies the role of a simple formalism in organizing a series of complex ideas—the sixth area in my list. It will also have bearing on the second item, the clarification of terms.

Two preliminary remarks are necessary. By "variate" I mean any classificatory or ordering device by means of which distinctions can be made among people or collectives: the size of a city, the financial status of a company (in the red or in the black), the IQ of an individual—each of these is a variate. The term "variable" is sometimes used for such "measures" and sometimes for their quantitative version only. The term "variate" seems more neutral and more general. The term "concept" will be used in a somewhat restricted sense. I shall concentrate on what might be called classificatory concepts—for example, the "cohesiveness" of groups, the "aggressiveness" of people, the "bureaucratization" of an institution. In this way I shall exclude concepts which are verbally defined without being used directly for classificatory purposes, as, for example, the notions of "role" or "frame of reference."[18]

I shall occasionally speak of these classificatory concepts as "traits." In the case of individuals, this is quite conventional. We are accustomed to distinguishing traits as more permanent dispositions in contrast to particular manifest behavioral episodes. On the collective level, the same relation exists. The traits of collectives are the more permanent social relations and prevailing belief systems as compared with the occasional performances, decisions, or movements of the group. Some traits of collectives have been studied in great detail—for example, degree of bureaucratization, by Max Weber and his spiritual descendants, or the counterpart, degree of feudalism, by historians interested in comparative analysis.[19] Other such traits have turned up as ad hoc improvisations, but now they add up to a rather interesting list.[20]

However we try to define a trait clearly, our words remain necessarily imprecise. They neither convey our own conceptual intentions fully nor provide the listener or reader with an unambiguous device for deciding when a certain person (or collective) possesses this trait, let alone to what degree he possesses it. The translation of a verbalized trait into a variate—a device to classify concrete objects according to this trait—is always more or less indeterminate. The translation of traits into variates is the topic of the next section.

The Birth and Growth of Variates

Classificatory concepts arise from many sources. The wisdom of everyday language and experience suggests some: the honesty of a man, the exclusiveness of a school. The needs of the practitioner give birth to others: What is an efficient worker—one who works quickly, one who makes few mistakes, or the optimal combination of both? How about an efficient organization? It does not consist of efficient people only; ease of communication among its members, the absence of internal conflicts, and many other features come to mind. On a somewhat more sophisticated level we have new kinds of conceptualization: the backslapper becomes an extravert; the unmanageable crew has low morale. Teachers have known for many centuries that students vary in their abilities. One day two French psychologists translated this familiar observation into a program of intelligence testing, and we have not yet heard the last of it. Administrators have noticed that some colleges receive many more applications for admission than others. This raises the question of whether colleges have something resembling a quality level. Attempts to measure this level are now the object of many, often controversial, efforts.

Behind any such classificatory effort stands what we shall call an *originating observation*: variations and differences exist which are to be explained. The "explanation" consists of a vaguely conceived underlying or latent property in regard to which people or collectives differ. Four steps can usually be discerned in the translation of this imagery into empirical research instruments:

1. The original imagery, the intended classification, is put into words and communicated by examples; efforts at definition are made.
2. In the course of this verbalization, often called conceptual analysis, several indicators are mentioned, and these help to decide where a given concrete object (person or group or organization) belongs in regard to the new classificatory concept. As the discussion of the concept expands, the number of eligible indicators increases; the array of these I shall call the *universe of indicators*.[21]
3. Usually this universe is very large, and for practical purposes we have to select a *subset* of indicators which is then made the basis for empirical work.
4. Finally, we have to combine the indicators into some kind of index.

As I have said, the last step has been treated extensively in existing literature on measurement. We might think of very simple procedures, such as the summation of correct answers to measure the extent of knowledge of geography; or procedures which require mathematical models, which would be the case if we used paired comparisons to order pictures according to their beauty; or a combination of data which require decisions on the weighting of several indicators, such as the standard-of-living index.

In the present paper I shall not be concerned with this fourth step.[22] I want, rather, to concentrate on the earlier phases about which there has been very little systematic thinking. In particular, I shall raise two questions: How is the original universe of indicators established (steps 1 and 2)? What are the consequences of choosing one specific subset of indicators rather than another (step 3)? By scrutinizing some pertinent evidence, we shall be able to draw a few general conclusions, but it will soon become clear that much uncertainty remains.

Expressive and Predictive Indicators

Although we are obviously most interested in concepts appearing in sociological literature, we shall start with a psychological concept. This is advisable partly because the notion of "traits" is in many respects a paradigm for our problem and partly because we have available a case in which the authors have documented unusually well the way in which they made their decision. I am referring to the notion of an authoritarian personality and the way in which it was translated into the famous F-scale by a group of social scientists working at the University of California in Berkeley.[23]

The authors of *The Authoritarian Personality* deserve credit for having provided a detailed account of why they chose the items included in their instrument. They start by saying that they found, in clinical and statistical sources, many characteristics which disposed individuals to anti-Semitism. They believed that these characteristics pointed to a basic trait for which they wanted to develop a test, subsequently labeled the F-scale. The items of this test were required to satisfy one or both of two criteria: (1) they should be expressive of the personality structure which was surmised on the basis of previously collected material; and (2) they should make probable the presence of anti-Semitism in the tested person. The first purpose is clearly stated at the beginning of chapter 7: "The task was to formulate scale items which, though they were statements of opinions and attitudes, would actually serve as '*give aways' of underlying trends* in the personality" (p. 223, italics mine). At the same time, the items should be correlated with anti-Semitism: "For every item there was a hypothesis, sometimes several hypotheses, stating what might be the nature of its *connection with prejudice*" (p. 225, italics mine). We might say that the indicators chosen according to these criteria play an expressive role in regard to the underlying trait and a predictive role in regard to the originating observation which the trait is supposed to explain.

The items of the test fall into two main groups. One group is supposed to indicate the "lack of integration between the moral agencies by which the subject lives and the rest of his personality" (p. 234). An example is the overemphasis on conventional values, such as good manners and hard work. The other group refers to "weakness in the ego" whereby strong impulses are repressed and displaced "because they are affect-laden and potentially anxiety-producing" (p. 236). No amount of verbal definition could make this kind of imagery really focused.[24] But the discussion of the contemplated universe of indicators gives a vivid idea of how prejudice and aggression against outgroups could be generated by a personality type, where "outside agencies are depended upon for moral decisions" (p. 234) and where props are needed "for keeping id drives ego-alien" (p. 240).

We are not concerned here with the question of where these basic traits reside: whether they represent biochemical structures not yet discovered or whether they are to remain hypothetical constructs. For the present discussion the important thing is this: in the stream leading from basic traits to the manifestation of anti-Semitism, the indicators can be taken by dipping, so to speak, nearer to its origin or to its terminus. One item reads: "Obedience and respect for authority are the most important virtues children should learn." Agreement can indicate uneasiness in handling one's own moral problems; but the relation to anti-Semitism is certainly not obvious. Another item reads: "Most people don't realize how much our lives are controlled by plots hatched in secret by politicians"; from agreement with this statement, it is only a small step to belief in the Protocols of the Elders of Zion.

I shall distinguish two types of indicators: expressive and predictive ones. Of the two examples just given, the first is the expressive, the second the predictive type. Many others are mixtures. This distinction, like all such dichotomies, is one of convenience, focusing on the extremes of a serial order. It refers to the place the indicators have in the hypothetical processes which mediate between the originating observation and the conceptual imagery that is developed to organize it.

Before I discuss some of the consequences of this distinction, a second example should help to clarify it. In this example the units to be classified are not individuals but collectives of great complexity—whole industries. My purpose is to show that sociological authors, even if they deal with very different material and have very different goals in mind, go about forming classificatory concepts in much the same way as psychologists do when they establish a trait. The study on which my test case is based does not carry out the final index formation (step 4), but it is especially detailed on the first steps.

Two scholars assembled the strike rates of various industries in eleven countries and found that a fairly stable ordering could be established among industries, from those with a consistently high to those with a consistently low propensity to strike.[25] They then raised the following question: "Is there any single theory which will largely explain the facts which we have found? Can we, at one and the same time, explain the high propensity to strike of miners, longshoremen, sailors, and loggers and the low propensity of government employees, grocery clerks, railroad employees, and garment workers?" They give this answer: "The first hypothesis is that the *location of the worker in society* determines his propensity to strike. . . ."

Here we find clearly the idea that industries can be classified according to their "location in society." How can this notion be transformed into a classificatory device—a variate? The authors themselves give a detailed verbal elaboration of their idea which suggests how they would proceed if further empirical work were their goal. First, they give distinct names to what they themselves call the two "ends of our scale." At the strike-prone end, workers form an "isolated mass"; at the other end, an "integrated group." They then proceed to describe these two situations in correlative terms. It will suffice here to give examples for the isolated mass; the reader can easily derive the opposite characteristics of the integrated industries.

The workers who are on the isolated end of "location in society" have little social, geographical, or occupational mobility. "Just as it is hard (for miners, etc.) to move out, so also is it difficult for them to move up." There is, further, little contact with other occupational and social groups. "In these communities there are not the myriad of voluntary associations with mixed membership." Finally, they are "as detached from the employer as from the community at large" because of absentee ownership and the absence of "small-scale employing units."

In verbalizing their concept of "location in society," the authors give several good reasons why the strike rate should be affected by the presence or absence of the situational characteristics just mentioned. The lack of contact with other groups makes the isolated mass more prone to strike because "these workers don't count on public opinion to support their grievances" and "they do not aim to be more considerate of the general community than they think the general community is of them." For the integrated group, on the other hand, the "individual grievances are less likely to coalesce into a mass grievance which is expressed on the job level . . . they are more able to escape job situations without striking than are the workers in the high propensity industries." For the latter the union also becomes more important, and this too increases the probability of strikes. (The importance of the union can be recognized by the fact that on the one hand union meetings are more adequately attended and on the other hand personal and ideological factionalism is more frequent.) The pages in which this explanatory hypothesis is developed (pp. 191–95) provide, then, a large inventory of indicators which could be used to classify industries according to their location in society.

Again, some of these indicators express the underlying trait while others have the function of justifying the prediction that the described condition would affect the strike rate. And it can easily be seen how this distinction refers to imputed processes. Take this sequence: occupational isolation makes for a strong feeling of shared grievances; this leads to receptiveness to unionization; union leaders have a tendency to organize strikes; ergo occupational isolation is likely to lead to strikes. From this argument we can derive at least three layers of indicators: lack of contact with other elements in the community; sentiments about grievances; and attitude toward unions. An indicator is more likely to be of the predictive type if it is taken from the end of such implied arguments: attitude toward unions in this context is much more predictive and contact with other occupational groups much more expressive. As a matter of fact, in the frame of the Kerr-Siegel analysis, one would probably exclude attitude toward strikes as an indicator of "location in industry" because it would be considered almost identical with the originating observation, the strike rate. Altogether, it would be better to say that indicators can have more or less expressive and predictive functions; but it did not seem worthwhile to complicate this discussion by too careful a terminology, so long as the main idea is brought to proper attention.

The Drift of Indicators

The observations made in connection with these two examples can be generalized. Almost all classificatory concepts derive in the following way: some empirical variations are observed; they are to be explained by a more general notion, an "underlying trait." The indicators for this trait point to the new unit to be construed, but their choice is also dictated by the originating observation.

In many measurements of this kind there is probably a secular drift toward dominance of expressive over predictive indicators. Originally the same conceptual imagery—and the corresponding expressive indicators—is coupled with *different* empirical observations which it is supposed to explain. This leads to distinct subsets of predictive indicators. Finally these are fused and take on expressive functions for a *generalized* variate. Two examples should help to shed some light on this rather subtle process.

It is little known in this country that the notion of the authoritarian personality originated in another context. Around 1930 a group of sociologists at the University of Frankfurt were concerned about whether the German workers, organized largely in the Social Democratic Party, would resist the Hitler movement. Their fear was that many workers would submit to the dictatorship, despite ideological differences, because they had "authoritarian personalities." The indicators for this personality type were derived partly from a somewhat modified psychoanalytic model of the ego: the sado-masochistic character then described by Fromm and subsequently developed in his *Escape from Freedom*. For all practical purposes, this imagery is not very different from the moral predicament and the weak ego-structure of the authoritarian Berkeley man. Consequently, the expressive indicators in the two studies are approximately the same. Although the German sociologists never developed a formal instrument, they did carry out an empirical survey with German workers and published the elaborate questionnaire that they used.[26] The expressive indicators there are much the same as those subsequently used in the Berkeley study. Conventionalism was tested by asking the respondents how they decorated their rooms and how they felt about the then new style of short hair and lipstick for women; superstitiousness was discovered by asking about belief in prophecies; and projectivity by questions such as "Who has the real power in the country?" and "Who is responsible for the inflation?" (a major problem in Germany at the time).

But when it comes to predictive items, the differences are as marked as the differences between the originating observations which motivated the two studies. If workers presumably differed in their willingness to defend the German republic, it was appropriate to ask such questions as "What do you think of German justice?" "Who were the greatest personalities in German history?" "What is the best constitution for a country?"—all items as closely related to the issues of the times as they could be without explicitly referring to the political Nazi program. Inversely, the questions regarding outgroups or the violation of values by alien elements which characterize the F-scale are missing. This is interesting, because Hitler's anti-Semitism was of course well known at the time, but it is never mentioned in the 600-odd pages of the German report; the all-important question was whether there would be organized resistance to Hitler.[27] Since the Berkeley study was published, the notion of the authoritarian personality has been so greatly extended that both sets of originating observations have been virtually forgotten. Current modifications of the F-scale treat it as a general variate. One day they may contain anti-Semitic and anti-democratic statements as expressive items and may be used to study the contributors of money to the Boy Scout movement.

A second example shows how a misunderstanding of this drift can lead to a confused controversy which, if my analysis is correct, can easily be resolved. I refer to the discussion between Schachter, on the one hand, and Gross and Martin, on the other, concerning the concept of group cohesiveness.[28] To pinpoint the issue I shall assume (although it is historically incorrect) that Durkheim developed his notion of integration only in order to explain variation in the suicide rate.[29] Sampling the ways in which Durkheim describes integration in a group, we find that he uses two main sets of indicators: frequency and closeness of social contact among people in a group, and the existence of norms which are accepted by the large majority of the group. Durkheim himself did not develop measures of integration; in this respect the state of his book on suicide is logically the same as that of the Kerr and Siegel paper. It contains detailed verbal descriptions of what he meant by integration, and especially by malintegration. From this imagery, indicators for a variate could easily be culled, and they would clearly be distinguishable as to their expressive and their predictive function. Consider the following passages as examples of the first type.[30]

> There is, in short, in a cohesive and animated society, a constant interchange of ideas and feelings from all to each and each to all.

> What constitutes this [integration] . . . is the existence of a certain number of beliefs and practices common to all the faithful, traditional, and thus obligatory. The more numerous and strong these collective states of mind are, the stronger the integration of the community.[31]

There are other parts of the picture which are much closer to the originating observation. The man in an integrated society, where solidarity encompasses him at all points,

> will no longer find the only aim of his conduct in himself and, understanding that he is the instrument of a purpose greater than himself, he will see that he is not without significance.[32]

And speaking of the existence of norms:

> this relative limitation, and the moderation it involves, make men contented with their lot, while stimulating them moderately to improve it.[33]

An analogy with the history of the "authoritarian personality" leads to the following expectation. If the notion of integration were to reappear in other contexts, the expressive indicators should show greater stability than the predictive ones, which would correspond to our last two quotations and would imply greater immunity to suicide. What actually happened was that Durkheim's predictive indicators, related to moderation and freedom from anxiety, were forgotten by some students. The expressive indicators, related to social relations and dominance of values, were so extended that the ensuing variate acquired a vastly generalized character. And, in reaction, a quest for restriction and for attention to more specific originating observations was undertaken.

Group dynamics is the American heir of integration under the name of cohesion.[34] In an unpublished but recorded panel discussion, Festinger stated that the group-dynamics tradition started with the problem of why some groups have a great influence on their members while others do not. To explain this variation, it was necessary to find "a force located in the group, to provide a concept that will permit predictions to be made about the power of the group to assert influence on its members with respect to behavior and attitudes."[35] This is obviously what Durkheim meant to do in regard to a specific behavior, suicide. But in the group-dynamics tradition, the range of observations to be accounted for is so large that the whole emphasis has shifted to expressive indicators. It is as if it were forgotten that Kerr and Siegel wanted to account for strike rates, and that subsequent writers made efforts to measure "location of industry" for a large variety of purposes—for example, to predict vulnerability to Fascist movements. Although the group-dynamics writers have not constructed a general index of cohesiveness, it is easy to deduce from the publications how they might have done so. Such an index would be an aggregation of the answers of group members to such questions as "Do you like group X?" "Do you enjoy the activities of the group?" "Are most of your friends recruited from there?" "Does membership in group X increase your own prestige outside?" "Does it help you to achieve some of your goals?" (We are not concerned here, of course, with correct wording or with appropriate procedures for forming a final index or scale.)

In a variety of experiments, the group-dynamics people show how cohesion so conceived is related to opinions, to efficiency, to amount of communication, and so on. To this approach Gross and Martin object on two grounds.[36] They feel that, in each specific group-dynamics study, too small a subset of indicators is being used to measure cohesion, a point to which we shall return presently. But they also propose what they call "an alternative nominal definition of cohesiveness" (p. 553). They want to adhere more closely to the notion of "sticking togetherness" and propose, as a definition, "resistance of a group to disruptive forces." Now, it would certainly be possible and desirable to set up "a continuum of relevant weak and strong disruptive forces and to observe at what point the group does actually begin to disintegrate." But this would be an originating observation, corresponding to variation in strike rate or anti-Semitism. Cohesiveness would be the classificatory concept developed to explain these variations, and it would have to be established independently. A clear distinction between the originating observation, the conceptual imagery, and the proposed universe of items would have shown that the two parties to the controversy are largely talking past each other.

Gross and Martin do not suggest how they would "measure" this group trait independently of their proposed experiment on resistance to break-up. But, from their discussion of the group-dynamics studies, we can make a pretty good guess: their *expressive* indicators would be about the same as the ones listed above. But they would add more *predictive* indicators, such as, "What would you be willing to do to keep the group from dissolving?" "What would induce you to leave the group?" "What members would you want to take with you if you had to move to another place?" In other words, Gross and Martin want to reverse the drift which has made current cohesion measures relatively general by confining them more closely to one specific set of originating observations. Thus there is no real disagreement between them and the writers they criticize. The group-dynamics imagery of "the total field forces which act on members to remain in the group" and the supposedly opposed one of "sticking togetherness" is very much the same—even though the terminology of the latter smacks of paste and glue while that of the former is reminiscent of semimodern physics. The choice of indicators would hardly be affected by this difference; as a matter of fact, Schachter, in his rejoinder, stresses the fact that in some studies he and his colleagues ask specific questions regarding the eagerness of group members to preserve the group against outside obstacles.[37]

Incidentally, a third point of seeming disagreement between

Gross-Martin and Schachter can also be clarified if it is put in terms of methodological distinctions. A collective trait can be analytical, structural, or global. In the first case, information about individual members is aggregated; an example would be a measure of group morale based on the aggregate morale score of each member. In the second case, we aggregate some kind of information about relations between individual members; for example, groups can differ according to the number of reciprocated choices they contain in their sociograms. Finally, a global characteristic deals with a collective product irrespective of its relation to individual members; examples would be the folktales of tribes or the number of playgrounds in cities. Gross and Martin prefer relational, or perhaps global, to analytical characteristics of groups; this is their right, and maybe even their duty, as sociologists. They object to an "additive conception, where cohesiveness of the group is regarded as an average of the attractiveness of the group for the individual members." They want more emphasis put on "the importance of the relational bonds between and among group members."[38] However, the formal nature of a variate has no necessary relation either to its originating observation or to its corresponding conceptual imagery. We need not discuss this point further, because it has been clarified by numerous authors.[39]

There are limiting cases in which certain classificatory concepts begin and largely remain at one of the two extremes of the expressive-predictive continuum. An index of "ability to be a pilot" is likely to consist mainly of elements which, for all practical purposes, are tantamount to a set of predictors for a rating of pilot efficiency. In contrast are such traits as honesty, which have long been embedded in our language. We could engage in one of those evolutionary speculations of which sociologists were so fond fifty years ago: how the notion of honesty got into the language because of certain originating observations which were of practical importance for the community. Actually, however, today an index of honesty is put together as the result of contemplations of what is meant by honesty and how one could recognize an honest person; in other words, it consists of expressive indicators which are virtually tantamount to what is often called an operational definition.

One final qualification is needed. I have restricted myself

to those variates which are empirical counterparts of conceptual imagery. Much social research starts at the other end. One finds, for example, that Catholics are more likely to vote Democratic than are Protestants; then the question arises as to what religious affiliation means in this context. Merton has called this reverse process "respecification."[40] It consists in providing a conceptual imagery by turning an incidental classifier into a variate. I do not know whether this idea of respecification is exhausted by reversing the present discussion. In any case, I must emphasize the fact that all my examples are restricted to transforming concepts into variates and not to the post hoc interpretation of empirical findings, a problem which has been discussed elsewhere.[41]

The distinction between expressive and predictive indicators permits us to relate various studies to one another and to locate problems and controversies so that their "hidden agenda" become more explicit. The discussion thus far has dealt with the first two steps in the flow from concepts to variates. We now turn to the third step, the choice of a subset or sample from a large universe of items to form the basis of a specific classificatory instrument. What are the implications and consequences of this sampling of items?

The Sampling of Indicators

Discussions regarding any particular variate often have the tinge of a Pirandello play. Someone suggests some reasonable indicators and someone else objects that they fail to catch the "whole meaning" of the intended classification. As more indicators are added the objection is raised that this is not a "unitary concept," that it must be divided into three or four more "real" units. In this atmosphere it is surprising that anyone ever has the courage to go ahead and carry out a piece of research. But it has been done. And, as a result, there has slowly developed the doctrine of the interchangeability of indices. Experience has shown that, given a large universe of items, it makes little difference which sample of items is selected to form the classificatory instrument. In order to assess the validity and the limitations of this doctrine, we shall discuss a concrete example.

In a recent study, an index for the "eminence" of college

professors of the social sciences was needed.[42] The following information about the 2,451 respondents was available:

1. 2,003 had written a dissertation.
2. 1,697 had a Ph.D. degree.
3. 1,758 had published at least one scholarly paper.
4. 1,377 had published three or more scholarly papers.
5. 1,601 had read at least one paper before a convention.
6.   977 had read three or more papers before a convention.
7. 1,210 had held office in a professional society.
8.   861 had published at least one book.
9.   857 had served as consultant to a business organization.

For a pool of items to indicate eminence, one would also want to include something about the success of these men as teachers; but no information on this factor was available. For my present purpose, this does not matter, because I want to discuss, not an extension, but a sampling of the available set of items. We could form two indices by picking two smaller subsets at random. To make the argument more pointed, we make a biased selection. Items 1, 3, 5, and 8 are combined into a *productivity index*— they all deal with publications. Three others, items 2, 7, and 9, deal with honors; they are combined to form an *index of honors*, together with item 4, the publication of three or more papers, which is used here on the somewhat weak assumption that many publications make a professor better known.

By intent, the indices have two partially overlapping items: anyone who has a Ph.D. has, of course, written a dissertation; publication of three or more papers implies the publication of at least one. The remaining pairs of items differ in manifest content.

Table 4.1 classifies all respondents in two ways: according to their productivity scores, and according to their scores on the honors index.

In the main diagonal we find all the people (789 + 214 + 535) who have the equivalent level of eminence on either index. The remainder, 36 percent of the total, are classified differently by the two indices. At first glance this looks like a discouraging result; the "eminence" measured by one index is in more than a third of the cases not the same as that measured by another.

This outcome, however, is both unavoidable and of limited

Table 4.1
Interrelation Between Two Indices of Eminence

Productivity Score	Honors Score			
	4,3 (High)	2	0,1 (Low)	Total
4,3 (High)	789	261	64	1,114
2	196	214	201	611
0,1 (Low)	20	134	535	689
Total	1,005	609	800	2,414*

* Complete information was lacking in 37 cases.

consequence. It is unavoidable because indicators can at best have only an inferential relation to the underlying factor sought. Whether a man is liberal, whether he has status in the community, whether an army unit has morale, or whether an educational system is a success—none of these questions can ever be answered unequivocally and absolutely, because morale or status cannot be measured with the degree of agreement and precision with which weight or length of an object can be measured. This has nothing to do with the fact that some of the things we want to classify are social or psychological intangibles. Whether two men are friends is, indeed, often a matter of external observation, but friendship itself is not a concrete object to be perceived directly. Indicators are still needed to infer its existence. To label the whole procedure one might use the term "diagnostic process."

The certainty of the inference from manifest data to latent characteristic depends upon many factors. One of these is the degree to which an indicator question is subject to varied interpretation. It is rarely possible to formulate a question to which the answers allow of only one meaning. Respondents' experiences immediately prior to the interview may enter in. A man who belongs, by and large, in the middle range of the authoritarian scale might give unusually restrictive answers on a morning when his children have irked him a great deal, and unusually permissive ones just after an excellent dinner. In short, all indicators are related to an intended underlying classification only with a probability. All classifications of this kind in social research have to be "impure."

The consequences of this fact are twofold. One of these is encouraging. If we have a reasonable collection of indicator items, then for most purposes it does not matter much which subset we use to form our index. This is true so long as our aim is to find statistical relations among a number of variables, not the correct classification of each person. To show this, I shall raise a problem in which "eminence" is one of the variates involved. We shall then look at the data twice: first using the productivity index as a measure of eminence and then using the honors index. The purpose of the comparison will be to see what difference this makes to the final result.

Our problem is to weigh the relative importance of eminence and age in a college teacher's chances for reaching that measure of "success" in the professional hierarchy represented by becoming a full professor. How do age and eminence together affect the speed of promotion? Table 4.2 gives the answer we get if we use our productivity index as the measure of eminence.

Table 4.2 tells a rather interesting story. Reading along each row, we see that, regardless of eminence, the proportion of full professors increases sharply with age. Within columns, we also learn that teachers who are more eminent in terms of productivity have, at any given age, more often been made full professors. The table also suggests how age and productivity can compensate for each other. On the highest productivity level, about two-thirds have become full professors by the time they reach fifty, whereas in the middle productivity range the same proportion is reached only in the oldest age group. However, even in the lowest productivity group almost half the teachers

Table 4.2
Percentage Who Are Full Professors in Groups Classified
According to Age and Eminence
(Productivity Index)

Eminence in Terms of Productivity Score	Age		
	Under 40	41–50	51 or older
4,3 (High)	15%	63%	87%
2	7%	39%	65%
0,1 (Low)	2%	24%	45%

past the age of fifty have become full professors. Many of these men and women doubtless earn their promotion to top rank by their excellent service as teachers.

What would have happened had we used the honors index as a measure of eminence? Table 4.3 gives the answer, which is much like the other using the productivity index.

Again, age is more important than eminence. Only in the second row is there a noticeable difference between tables 4.2 and 4.3. Productivity seems to be more helpful in the forty-one to fifty age group; honors play a greater role among the oldest teachers.

In spite of the fact that the two indices are not highly correlated with one another, as we have seen in table 4.1, they produce much the same result when they are related to an outside variable. This *interchangeability of indices* reappears again and again in empirical social research. Studies have shown, for example, that different social strata have sharply contrasting attitudes toward economic and political issues. But what are "social strata," and how should they be measured? We could use as indicators such things as people's possessions, their income, or their education. In most studies it has turned out that, whichever is used, the correlation between strata and any particular attitude is about the same. In other words, the findings of empirical social research are to a considerable extent invariant when reasonable substitutions from one index to another are made.

This, then, is a general rule based on diversified research practice. To translate a rather broad but nonspecific concept into an empirical research instrument, there will always be a

Table 4.3
Percentage Who are Full Professors in Groups Classified
According to Age and Eminence
(Honors Index)

Eminence in Terms of Honors Score	Age		
	Under 40	41–50	51 or older
4,3 (High)	18%	65%	88%
2	6%	28%	73%
0,1 (Low)	2%	22%	44%

large number of indicators eligible for a classificatory index. A relatively small number of such items is practicably more manageable. If we choose two sets of reasonable items to form two alternative indices, we will usually find that (1) the two indices are related, but they do not classify all the people in a study in precisely the same way; and (2) the two indices lead to similar empirical results if they are separately cross-tabulated with a third, "outside" variable.

While this rule of the "interchangeability of indices" is one of the foundations of empirical social research, a serious and unavoidable price is exacted for its beneficial consequences. Because we never can reach "pure" classifications, a certain number of cases must always be misclassified, and therefore the empirical findings are less clear than they would be if we could somehow have precise measures for the variables with which a study is concerned.

The notion just developed sheds some light on another issue discussed in current literature. This has to do with the debate about "operationalism," centering on the question of whether intelligence is what an intelligence test measures. If so, then there are as many kinds of intelligence as there are tests. If not, what is the relation between the various tests and the "underlying" concept? A precise answer could be given only in terms of mathematical models which show that an intended classification consists of parameters which are related by equations to empirical data and can be computed from them.[43] But even without such precision one can easily understand the three-cornered relation which emerges from a careful analysis of actual research practice.

So-called nominal definitions are essentially declarations of intent; the investigator conveys as well as possible the classification he is driving at when he talks of intelligence, social cohesion, or location in society. He then proceeds to a *specification of meaning* as he evolves his universe of items, a process which is, in principle, unlimited.[44] For research purposes we then have to work with subsets of this universe—samples of items, if the word "sample" is used rather loosely. The various intelligence tests, for example, are different samples of this kind. Although they may correlate only moderately with each other, they are interchangeable in their predictive function for, say, success in college. For more specific purposes they could well serve different functions. Thus professors in the upper-right and lower-left corners of table 4.1 may well show differences, despite the fact that both are in the median range of eminence. Unproductive men with many honors, for example, could be found in smaller provincial colleges where the general atmosphere is not conducive to research but where a college position has regional advantages which it would lack in more competitive cosmopolitan centers. Such additional differential findings do not contradict the "general duty" aspect of our over-all index of eminence.[45]

As I mentioned before, the sampling theme appears also in the controversy over measures of social cohesion. Gross and Martin have shown that various measures of cohesion used in group-dynamics studies do not have a high correlation with one another. In my opinion, Schachter missed the right answer in his reply. It is not the relation of the indices to one another which is the crucial problem but their relation to outside variables. And on this point, none of the discussants provided information. This is a shortcoming, incidentally, that characterizes quite a number of recent publications. Kahl and Davis have studied the interrelation of various indices of socioeconomic status; March has similarly investigated different indices of personal influence.[46] Neither of them has proceeded to the crucial issue of whether it makes any difference which of the indices is used in establishing empirical propositions—that is, when we relate the indices to outside data.[47]

We have by no means fully covered the explication of index formation. Some of the missing links have been discussed elsewhere. Thus, in most careful studies, prior to the listing of indicators there is a specification of "dimensions" along which items should be sought.[48] Other problems have not yet been properly analyzed. In what sense, for example, does a broad concept such as authoritarian personality or location in society "explain" the originating observation? And the interchangeability of indices certainly has exceptions which deserve more systematic discussion. In addition, one general note of restraint must be sounded.

We have analyzed procedures that now prevail in social research; they are likely to lead to an oversupply of concepts and variates. Which of them will survive in a more systematic phase of empirical sociology cannot be predicted. In the near future we can expect greater interplay between empirical studies and more abstract reflection. The exigencies of specific problems will press toward the formation of ad hoc variates. Through inventories and theoretical efforts, they will be classified and the more basic ones selected; sometimes a conceptual idea will suggest a new variate which can replace numerous earlier classificatory devices. Whatever the trend, a major methodological issue will remain: Given a universe of discourse in which people and collectives are characterized by variates, what ideas can be developed in such a language? Its power is often underestimated by outsiders, and often not fully exploited by practitioners. The combination of several variates—we shall call it multivariate analysis—has a surprising flexibility. The final section of this paper is devoted to some of its elements.

Multivariate Analysis

A fitting introduction to this section is a reference to Herbert Blumer's 1956 presidential address to the American Sociological Society.[49] In his speech, which he called "Sociological Analysis and the 'Variable,'" he deplored the trend of empirical social research on many grounds that we cannot consider here. But in one respect his discussion is relevant to our topic. It assumes that empirical propositions consist of correlations between no more than *two* "variables." The following quotations are characteristic:

> In a variable analysis one is likely to accept the *two variables* as the simple and unitary items they seem to be. (p. 689, italics mine)
>
> The variable relation is a *single* relation. (p. 685, italics mine)
>
> The independent variable is put at the beginning part . . . and the dependent variable at the terminal part. . . . (p. 686)

In this picture of variate analysis, the real issue is lost from the very beginning. Competent social research deals with more than two variates; consequently it emphasizes, not a single relation, but a system of relations, and often it studies their interaction over time. Much of this can be demonstrated by consideration of not more than three variates, for they create "conditional relations" and, if properly chosen, "structures" and "processes."

Conditional Relations

Let us take as a first example a study reported by Pelz.[50] He classified directors of scientific research teams according to the degree of independence they provided. If the scientists had little freedom to make their own work decisions their productivity was relatively low. If they had a high degree of independence their productivity was the greater the closer the consulting contacts the director maintained with them. The value of greater independence was thus conditional upon a third factor: personal contact.

Consistent with our previous procedure, we look for an analogous finding in an area where collectives form the unit of analysis. In *The Academic Mind*, colleges were classified according to the amount of pressure politicians brought to bear on them and the amount of support the administration gave to the faculty.[51] Both classifications were based on the judgments of social scientists; this raises interesting problems which are discussed in appendix 5 of the book. For our present purposes we can take the information at face value and report the findings for fifty-nine colleges in which at least thirteen professors were interviewed. Table 4.4, in which the colleges are classified according to the pressures brought to bear by politicians and the protection given to the faculty by the administration, seems to indicate that

Table 4.4

Protection by Administration	Pressure by Politicians	
	High	Low
High	13	16
Low	15	15

Table 4.5
**Data of Table 4.4 Reported Separately for Public and
Private Colleges**

Protection by Administration	Pressure in Public Colleges		Pressure in Private Colleges	
	High	Low	High	Low
High	5	10	8	6
Low	11	5	4	10

there is scarcely any relation between outside pressures and administrative performance.

If, however, we distinguish between public and private schools, the picture looks quite different, as shown in table 4.5. In state universities, the administrators, having closer ties to a political network, tend to yield to political pressure; in private institutions, they tend to resist and even to counteract this pressure.

A set of data like that shown in table 4.5 can properly be called a *conditional relation*. It starts out with two variates, but then indicates that, under varying conditions, the original relation can be very different indeed.

Such conditional relations are the most elementary form of "systems," properly dear to the heart of the theorist who stresses the complexity of social phenomena. Multivariate analysis can reproduce this complexity in two ways. For one, the number of variates can be increased; and, for another, the types of variates can be variously combined to represent different aspects of a social situation.[52] This latter point deserves to be pursued one step further.

Contextual Propositions

An individual can be classified by the collective(s) to which he belongs. We can then talk of this person's contextual property. Being a teacher in a conservative college or a worker in a large plant are contextual properties; being young or an extravert are not but might, instead, be called primary properties. Now consider propositions about individuals who have been

characterized partly by primary and partly by contextual properties. Such propositions describe in various ways the interplay
between persons and collectives and are thus one way in which
structural ideas can be expressed. In recent years such contextual propositions have become increasingly available because
social research has been extended to simultaneous sampling of
collectives and individuals. To illustrate, I shall take another
example from *The Academic Mind*, concentrating first on two
variates.

In this study, two variates were developed. One, called actual
apprehension (AA), classified professors of the social sciences
according to how worried they were about their own job security
and how careful they were not to get into political hot water.
The other, called perceived intimidation (PI), summarized the
same information about other faculty members, as judged by
each respondent. There was a strong tendency for a teacher with
a high AA score to have a high PI score; the more apprehensive
social scientists tended to consider their colleagues intimidated.
This might be expected for at least two reasons: first, projection
of one's own experience; and, secondly, the fact that in a relatively endangered college the average professor would be more
apprehensive and would realistically think that his colleagues
were too. But the role of the reality situation was more interesting than that. A contextual variate was introduced by classifying seventy-seven colleges according to the number of incidents involving academic freedom that took place on each
campus. Both AA and PI were found to increase with the number
of incidents, as can be seen from columns IV and V of table 4.6.
But in the quiet colleges there was a great discrepancy between
the two scores: the proportion of apprehensive teachers was
much greater than the proportion of those who considered their
colleagues intimidated (top of column VI). As long as little happens at a college, many a teacher thinks that he himself is apprehensive—probably as a result of knowledge about the national scene—but does not realize that his colleagues are too.
When local trouble starts, feelings become more manifest and
perceived intimidation resembles actual apprehension (bottom
of column VI). The difference between AA and PI is clearly
affected by a contextual variate, the college climate within which

Table 4.6
Actual Apprehension (*AA*) and Perceived Intimidation (*PI*) of Social-Science Teachers in 77 Colleges, Classified by the Number of Academic-Freedom Incidents which Occurred on Each Campus

I	II	III	IV	V	VI
				Proportion Regarding	Difference
		Professors	Proportion	Their Colleagues as	Between IV
Incidents	Schools	Interviewed	Apprehensive*	Intimidated*	and V
Less than 3	5	87	38%	24%	14
3–5	14	256	42%	22%	20†
6–10	32	680	51%	42%	9
11–15	10	225	54%	50%	4
16–20	9	281	56%	54%	2
21 or more	7	325	47%	50%	−3†

Note: There are more colleges here than there were in tables 4.4 and 4.5 because denominational and teachers colleges have been included.
* The proportions were computed for each college individually and then averaged over schools so as not to overweight the larger schools in which a larger number of social scientists were interviewed.
† No explanation comes to mind for the especially large difference in the second line. In the last entry for this column, however, we are dealing with large and distinguished colleges which, on the one hand, came under special attack, and in which, on the other hand, the administrations protected the faculties quite well. As a result, both *AA* and *PI* scores decrease, but the former somewhat more; the teachers still suspect that their colleagues are rather scared.

these respondents work and which is reasonably indicated by the number of incidents that took place.

Table 4.6 compares two primary characteristics of the same people in varying contexts. A somewhat different contextual proposition emerges if the comparison is made on the same characteristic but in regard to two (or more) subsets of individuals. In *The Academic Mind* the professors were also classified according to an index of conservatism. The apprehension of conservative teachers was found to be more highly correlated with the number of local incidents than was that of the less conservative teachers; the latter were more apprehensive to begin with, and what happened at their own college made far less difference. Corresponding propositions have been reported by Lipset and his collaborators.[53]

The size of the shop in which printers work has an effect on all sorts of variates and their relations to one another. The larger the shop, for example, the more active in and the better informed are the printers about union politics. But the effect of size is more marked upon the chairmen of the local union unit than upon the rank and file (pp. 178f). The increase of union activity with shop size is also more pronounced for printers whose primary friendship groups are mainly composed of fellow printers than for those whose social relations are away from their place of work (p. 164). It should be noted that these findings trace not only the effect of shop size on average activities or attitudes but also the *differential effect* of size upon various subsets of printers. In this sense, they establish conditional relations.

The complexity of contextual propositions can go quite far, even with only three variates. In *The Academic Mind* it was found that the older a professor, the more likely he was to be conservative. The same index of conservatism was used to classify colleges according to the average conservatism of their social-science faculties. The more conservative the college, the more rapid the increase of conservatism with age. This is a type of proposition which deserves particular attention because it has an especially strong sociological flavor. Its main feature is the fact that the contextual variable is an aggregate of the variates which are also used to classify the individuals involved. The results are all the more striking if the individual variations within collectives are in the opposite direction from the aggregate variations between units. In an unpublished study, H. Zeisel found that the greater the average wealth of a county, the larger are the awards juries make in accident cases; but within counties the richer jurors make smaller awards, presumably because they identify more closely with the insurance companies. The interpretation points to an interplay between collective norms and individual frames of reference. In the same class of results belongs Stouffer's famous finding that, within military units, morale is higher among soldiers who have been promoted; but, between units, morale decreases with the number of promotions, presumably because the nonpromoted soldiers feel especially deprived when a general expectation is frustrated for them individually.[54]

Contextual propositions go far toward catching what authors have in mind when they use such "holistic" expressions as "taking the total situation into account" and "considering structures." But, again, much work remains to be done before this somewhat vague resemblance is turned into a systematic and creative correspondence. On the one hand, a more systematic classification of contextual propositions is needed. I mentioned that the contextual variables could be aggregates or not. The difference between table 4.6 and Lipset's findings on the role of shop size was pointed out. Then, with even three variates, two could be contextual; this is the case when Lipset compares the effect on the opinion of individual members of the majority vote in the union local and that of the majority vote in the whole union.[55] Many more such distinctions are necessary to order the available empirical findings. On the other hand, the writings of theoretically inclined authors must be scrutinized in order to form a clearer picture of all that is meant by concern with structures.[56]

One does not need to wait for such a confrontation to recognize that contextual propositions have one major limitation: they suggest interpretations which cannot be checked by cross-sectional data. Do chairmen of union locals become more informed in large shops? Or is being informed a prerequisite of their election? Do academic-freedom incidents really make faculty intimidation more visible, or are teachers in the turbulent colleges more likely to take it for granted that their colleagues are apprehensive? This is what critics of survey studies mean when they say that the dynamics of a situation, the process by which a relation comes about, are not accounted for. But this objection can be met at least partly if multivariate analysis is extended so that it includes repeated observations on the same variate. Such procedures are known as panel observations, and a few remarks about the analysis of the resulting kind of data will conclude our discussion.

Panels

The essence of panel analysis is as follows. A person or a collective is characterized by a number of variates. At periodic intervals, measurements are taken on these variates. At least four types of sequences can then be examined: (1) changes over time for each variate; (2) correlations between variates and their changes over time; (3) conditional relations, especially differences in (1) and (2) between subgroups which differ initially according to a specific variate, the qualifier; and (4) concurrent changes of two or more variates. The last type of sequence has been selected for exemplification.[57]

Pairs of individuals can be characterized by the degree of their personal contact and their agreement on certain topics. This permits us to study what Merton has called value homophily—the many ways in which agreement leads to friendship and in which, in turn, friendship reinforces similarity of attitudes.[58] In the study of voting behavior, many such relations have been examined. Expectations as to who will win an election affect the vote intentions of some people (the so-called bandwagon effect); at the same time, prospective voters often overrate the chances of the candidate they favor (projection). And the effect of political propaganda is difficult to assess because of a similar mechanism: at one point in time, exposure to a party's propaganda is highly correlated with intention to vote for that party; but, studied over time, vote intention affects exposure more than the other way around.

Such analysis is not restricted to two variates, or to the study of individuals. As a matter of fact, some rather involved discussion in macrosociology can be greatly clarified if it is couched in terms of panel analysis. We shall take our example from an anthropological topic.

The folk-society idea states that primitive communities can be characterized by a number of properties: isolation, homogeneity, traditionalism, nonliteracy, lack of conflict, absence of specialization, and so on. As time goes on, their development tends to bring about the disappearance of these characteristics. A community in which they are completely absent has become part of modern urban society. A considerable amount of debate has centered on two points: What if change in the various properties occurs at different rates? How does change in one affect the trend of change in others? Several aspects of the problem have been summarized by Miner,[59] as follows:

> The problem is seen as one of the relation among variables. No one of these is the sole cause of the others, but it is assumed, subject to proof, that, as certain of these vary, so do others. (p. 336)

Some of the traits seem to presuppose others. For example, great heterogeneity in the division of labor requires a large population, while a large population may exist with a relatively unelaborate division of labor. (p. 338)

Some of the criteria used in the definition of the folk society are treated by Redfield as linked or interdependent variables, but might better be treated as independent variables. . . . [It is not required that they] change at the same rate or that they are all interdependent in the same way in all circumstances. (p. 339)

The underlying concern can be stated more formally. Over periods of time, primitive communities are subject to a variety of changes which are engendered partly by outside factors (the introduction of new tools or increased contact with other communities) and partly by intrinsic developments (an increase in population density or the improvement of skills over generations). After a while, these changes affect other aspects of community life. Each of these "traits" can be in the lead as far as change is concerned, or it can be affected by earlier changes in some other trait. The first type of change cannot be foreseen and must be accepted as a "given" in the analysis. But the changes in a trait that are conditional on changes in other traits can be analyzed by observing the communties repeatedly. These conditional changes are *mutual effects* inasmuch as the influence moves back and forth between all the traits. Yet some traits dominate others, in the sense that changes in them have stronger net effects. How can we establish a hierarchy of traits in terms of such mutual effects? To the best of my knowledge, there is too little "timed" material available to carry out such an inquiry into changes of the folk society. But in a simpler area a pertinent procedure can be suggested. As a paradigm it should help to clarify some of the problems which Miner raises; but I shall restrict myself to a formal parallel and not try to draw substantive conclusions for a field in which I do not have enough first-hand knowledge.

During the presidential campaign of 1940, a sample of 600 respondents was interviewed repeatedly. At that time, Willkie had emerged as a new political figure, and citizens of various political persuasions had to make up their minds about him. Whether they liked Willkie as a person was, of course, closely

related to their vote intention. Table 4.7 contains all the combinations that can be derived from our basic information and is
known as a sixteenfold table.[60] Ninety percent of the respondents in the first and fourth lines do not change, while in the two
middle lines only 60 percent maintain their original pattern. If
people have a tendency to "harmonize" their attitudes as the
campaign goes on, in which direction do they move? Do they
adjust a specific opinion to their vote intention, or does the
process go the other way? The crucial answer comes from the
twenty-four cases which are characterized as follows: they are
"divergent" at the first interview in the sense that they are not
following the majority pattern—Democrats who are for Willkie
and Republicans who are against him. At the second interview
they are "in harmony"—their opinions and attitudes match.
(The four groups of cases are indicated by asterisks in table 4.7.)
It is easily seen that the majority of this small but critical group
retains its vote intention and adjusts its opinion about Willkie.
Party loyalty is more deep-rooted than is the attitude toward a
newly emerging political figure.

Altogether, repeated data are available on the following issues:
vote intention; personal liking for Roosevelt; personal liking for
Willkie; attitude toward the third term; and opinion on the importance of government versus business experience in a President. On these five issues, ten sixteenfold tables similar to table
4.7 can be set up. The argument following table 4.7 may be then
translated into an index to express the "relative strength" of the

Table 4.7
Concurrent Change in Vote Intention and Personal Liking for Willkie
(Erie County, Ohio, 1940 Election)

			Second Interview				
		Party	+	+	−	−	
		Willkie Attitude	+	−	+	−	Total
	(+ +)	Republican for Willkie	129	3	1	2	135
	(+ −)	Republican against Willkie	11*	23	0	1*	35
First Interview	(− +)	Democrat for Willkie	1*	0	12	11*	24
	(− −)	Democrat against Willkie	1	1	2	68	72
	Total		142	27	15	82	266

two variables in each pair. (The details of this index will be omitted here.)

The data showed that the complex aggregate of attitudes making up party loyalty, and thus vote intention, was stronger than any single campaign issue. Of all the specific items, attitude toward President Roosevelt was the most important. Next came the "opinions on third-term issue," which was itself determined largely by both vote intention (i.e., party loyalty), and opinion on Roosevelt. Opinion on Willkie was much less important, as we should expect, since Willkie was comparatively unknown. The "government versus business experience" question turned out to be by far the weakest of all the attitudes analyzed: it was dynamically dominated by all other items. [61]

The formalism exemplified here gains strength when it is considered in relation to the types of variate to which it may be fitted. Some can be of an anticipatory psychological nature, such as expectations and intentions; others may be external events, such as contacts with people, rules promulgated by an institution, rewards and punishments meted out, or communications received; a third group might be "mediating" variates, the way and extent to which these external stimuli are perceived. It is obvious how very complex sociopsychological processes can then be represented by panel analysis. And the units of such an analysis need not be people; they can be collectives, such as small groups, counties, or primitive communities.

Then we find a link with the types of problem raised in the folk-society discussion. Some of these problems refer to the rate of change for the separate dimensions. But the most vexing ones—often phrased in the misleading form of cause and effect—require a reformulation in terms of mutual-effect analysis and its extension over more than two time periods, a topic which we cannot consider here. As a matter of fact, I venture to guess that the traditional chapter on social change in most sociological textbooks would benefit by being recast in terms of the panel formalism.

The teaching of methodology is handicapped by a lack of appropriate material. Not only are there many unsolved problems,

as indicated by this introductory review; good expository statements are scarce, even on topics which are fairly well clarified.
Actually, expositions are not all that is needed. During his few
years of graduate work, no student can acquire much research
experience. He would be greatly helped if there existed analytical
documents analyzing major published research studies, their
merits and shortcomings, and, most of all, the decisions lying
behind the final product. Something like the commentaries on
court decisions available to the law student is needed. And there
is no reason why some of this exegesis should not be written by
the authors themselves. We shy away too much from intellectual
autobiographies, such as W. F. Whyte's appendix to the second
edition of *Street Corner Society* or Edward Shils' reminiscences
on his studies of small groups—published, characteristically
enough, in a foreign journal.[62] A finished product tends to conceal the difficulties behind its creation. Students are deprived
of the opportunity to learn the intricacies of social research to
such an extent that often they cannot even read a study properly,
let alone profit from it. At least some methodological sophistication (different from the knowledge of technical skills) should
be part of every sociologist's training, and this is made difficult
if no appropriate teaching material is available. Of course, only
a small number of sociologists will or should make methodology
their main interest. But the mixture of contempt and anxiety
which the term "methodology" so often evokes should be replaced by a better understanding of its intent. T. S. Eliot has
caught it well: ". . . the end of all our exploring/Will be to arrive
where we started/And know the place for the first time."

[5]
The Interpretation of Statistical Relations as a Research Operation

The Role of Test Factors

The starting point for the present discussion is a research procedure which is applied almost automatically in empirical research. Whenever an investigator finds himself faced with the relationship between two variables he immediately starts to "cross-tabulate," that is, to consider the role of further variables. The procedure may be demonstrated by using data that represent in somewhat stylized form the results obtained in many studies of radio listening tastes. By relating age of respondent to the program to which he usually listens, it is found that older people listen more to religious programs and political discussions on the air than do younger people, while there is practically no age difference in listening to classical music (see table 5.1).

Every research man knows that age is related to education; because of the recent extension of formal education, younger people in a community are usually better educated than older ones. In the present sample the relation between age and education is shown in table 5.2. We thus deal with three variables: age, education, and type of listening. To simplify matters, we convert each variable into a dichotomy. Education, which is introduced here to elaborate and to clarify the original relationship, is called the test variable (t). Age is conventionally called

From Paul F. Lazarsfeld and Morris Rosenberg, eds., *The Language of Social Research* (Glencoe, Ill.: The Free Press, 1955). Copyright © 1955 by The Free Press, a Corporation. Reprinted by permission of The Free Press, a division of Macmillan Publishing Co., Inc. From an address given at the Cleveland meeting of the American Sociological Society in 1946.

Table 5.1
Proportion of Listeners in Two Age Groups

	Young % Listen	Old % Listen
Religious programs	17	26
Discussion programs	34	45
Classical music programs	30	29
(Total Cases)	(1,000)	(1,300)

the independent variable (*x*) and listening the dependent variable (*y*). Sometimes for brevity of expression we will use the symbols *xyt*, in the sense indicated in the previous sentence. But, otherwise, no mathematics will be used in this exposition.

Simple reflection will show that three relations can be drawn between three such variables. One relates age to listening: [*xy*], and the corresponding information has been given in table 5.1, for each of the three program types. Then we have the relation between age and the test factor, education: [*xt*]. This is, of course, the same for all program types and the figures, rounded out but substantially correct, are reported in table 5.2. Finally, we have [*ty*], the relation between education and listening. This again is different for all the programs, and the data will be given presently.

For better understanding, one should take into account at this point that the entire fourfold table 5.2 and any one line in table 5.1 give the same type of information. The content of table 5.2 could be summarized by stating that 60 percent of the young people but only 31 percent of the old people are in the high education group. Inversely, we could convert any line of table 5.1 into a fourfold table, giving for the two age classes the number

Table 5.2
Relation Between Age and Education

	Young	Old	Total
High Education	600	400	1,000
Low Education	400	900	1,300
(Total)	(1,000)	(1,300)	(2,300)

Note: The education break is between those who completed high school and those who did not; the age break is at forty.

of people who listen or do not listen to a certain type of program. I shall use both types of presentation, according to which is convenient.

Various coefficients have been developed to "measure" the relation between two such dichotomies. For our present purpose, the only distinction we will need is whether the two are unrelated or related in some substantial way. Therefore, the simplest index will be best and this is the so-called standardized cross-product. For table 5.2, for example, it is

$$[xt] = \frac{600 \cdot 900 - 400 \cdot 400}{2300^2} = .08$$

(The value of this cross-product, incidentally, is about one-fourth of what the so-called point correlation would show.) There does exist a relation between education and age, for otherwise the cross-product would vanish.

The research operation I am describing here thus starts out with an original relation $[xy]$, then introduces a test variable, and thus creates two more relations $[xt]$ and $[ty]$. But the most important results obtained with the help of the test variable are two *partial relations*. We can now raise the following question. If we study people in the high education and low education groups separately, what happens to the relation between age and listening? The answer is given in table 5.3. The figures pertain to religious programs. To make them more comparable with the first line of table 5.1, we use the percent presentation in table 5.4 and then see that *within each educational group the relation between age and listening has practically disappeared.* (The first line of table 5.4 repeats information presented in table 5.1.) We

Table 5.3
Relation Between Age and Listening to Religious Programs, by Education

	High Education			Low Education		
	Young	Old	Total	Young	Old	Total
Listen	55	45	100	115	285	400
Don't Listen	545	355	900	285	615	900
(Total)	(600)	(400)	(1,000)	(400)	(900)	(1,300)

Table 5.4
Percentage of Listeners to Religious
Programs
Young 17%   *Old 26%*

High Education		Low Education	
Young	Old	Young	Old
9%	11%	29%	32%

can now perform the same analysis for the other two program
types listed in table 5.1. The results are reported in tables 5.5
and 5.6 without discussion of all the intermediate steps. The
main point to note is how different the role of the test variable
is from one example to the next. We begin with listening to
discussion programs on the radio.[1]

The data of table 5.1 are repeated in the first line of table 5.5,
as they were in table 5.4. Table 5.5 shows that, *within* educational
groups, age makes an even larger difference than for the sample
as a whole.

Now, how about listening to classical music? From table 5.1
it might appear that age plays no role here. However, notice:
note 1 (p. 375) shows that educated people listen more to this
type of program, and we know that younger people are more
highly educated.

Carrying out the full tabulation scheme reveals indeed a rather
complex structure, exhibited in table 5.6.

Table 5.6 shows that age plays a different role for high and
low educated respondents. In a more sophisticated environment,
maturation leads to more attention to such cultural matters as

Table 5.5
Percentage of Listeners to Discussion
Programs
Young 34%   *Old 45%*

High Education		Low Education	
Young	Old	Young	Old
40%	55%	25%	40%

Table 5.6
Percentage of Listeners to Classical Music
Young 30%   *Old 29%*

High Education		Low Education	
Young	Old	Young	Old
32%	52%	28%	19%

good music. In a "culturally impoverished" environment, the peak of such interest seems to come near to the age when school influence still prevails; with increasing age, cultural interests decline.

It is the logic, not the substantive details, of these three examples, to which one should attend. The introduction of age had a different effect in each example cited in table 5.1. With religious programs it decreased the original difference; with discussion programs it led to an increase; with classical music it brought to light two countertrends which were concealed in the original findings.

A General Scheme for the Relation
Between Three Dichotomies

The gist of the preceding examples can be put into a general formula. In order to understand its importance, we must first give more consideration to what was variously called partial associations, partial fourfold tables, or partial differences. There are always two of them, as can be seen from table 5.3 and from tables 5.4 and 5.5. The original relation [xy] is split into two conditional relations for high and low education people separately, and an obvious symbolism to be used for the two of them is [xy;t]' [xy;t]''. Their meaning is similar to the statistician's partial correlation; the latter, however, really corresponds to an average of our two partials. The very fact that we can separate them and can have different relations on each side of the test factor is of the essence for our present purpose.

The whole structure consisting of the two original variables and the test variable can be formulated as follows:

(Form 1) $[xy] = [xy;t]' \oplus [xy;t]'' \oplus [xt] \cdot [ty]$

This shows that the original relationship can be described as the sum of the two partial relationships and an additional factor which is the product of what are called the marginal relationships between the test factor and the two original variables. One remark as to the arithmetic of this formula. The plus signs are encircled because it is not really a straight sum: a weighted sum has to be used. However, this has no bearing on our later discussion and it is not worth complicating the matter by introducing the two weight factors that belong here.

The formula can become more vivid if one applies it to a number of well-known cases. It is known, for instance, that in counties where there are *more storks* there also are *more children*. This somewhat puzzling result is made more acceptable if a *distinction* between *rural* and *urban* counties is introduced as a test factor. It then turns out that within the two groups of counties the relationship between storks and children disappears: the two partials are zero. The original relationship emerges as the product of the fact that in rural counties there are more storks, and in these same counties the birth rate is higher.

Our introductory examples can also be easily reproduced in this formula. With religious programs the product of the $[xt]$ $[ty]$ relationships is positive, and the two partials very small; with discussion programs the product is negative and therefore, by necessity, the partials have to be larger than the original relationship. In the case of classical music the salient feature is that one partial is positive and the other negative. The top rows of figures in tables 5.4–5.6 correspond to $[xy]$. The figures in the bodies of the tables correspond to the partials. $[xt]$ can be obtained from table 5.2. In table 5.3 and in note 1 (p. 375), we have the data to compute $[ty]$ for each of the three program types.

Just to become better acquainted with the general formula, the reader is asked to apply it to a type of argument which is especially frequent in Durkheim's writing. At one point he says in essence: "Idiocy seems to be a deterrent of suicide. The idiots are much more common in the country than in the city, while suicides are much rarer in the country." A similar example can be found when Durkheim tries to prove that less literate people commit fewer suicides by the following argument: "We have seen that in all countries of the world women commit many fewer suicides than men. Women are also much less educated . . . they do not have strong intellectual needs. . . ." It will be noted that Durkheim never considers the partial relations. What effect does this have on his argument?

There are two cases in which the formula takes on a very characteristic form and which, therefore, deserve special attention. One case happens in a *controlled experiment* where we have two matched groups, one of which is exposed to a stimulus and the other is not. Let us call the exposure stimulus x. The essence of matching can be precisely formulated in the frame of our discussion. For any conceivable test factor, the two matched groups should be alike, or, in other words, $[xt]$ equals zero; therefore, the third member in our basic formula will always be zero (matching is required for relevant test factors t only). Relevant factors are those which do have, or might have, a relationship with criterion y. In the case of an irrelevant test factor, $[ty]$ would be zero, and again the final item in the formula would disappear.

In the case of the controlled experiment, therefore, the result of introducing a relevant test factor would be exemplified by

(Form 2) $\qquad [xy] = [xy;t]' \oplus [xy;t]'' \oplus [0] \cdot [ty]$

The other case of special interest occurs when the two partials are zero and the original relationship is equal to the product of the relationship between the test factor and the two original variables. It is found, for instance, that men have more automobile accidents than women. If, however, the amount of mileage driven during the year is introduced as a test factor, it turns out that the partial relationship between sex and accidents disappears. In this case, then, the original relationship is shown to be equivalent to the product of two new ones which in turn might be made the object of further elaboration. The two relationships remaining here are usually called the marginals. They come about if we cross-tabulate the test variable against the two original variables; they do not require simultaneous tabulations of three variables, or in other words, they do not require partials.

(Form 3) $[xy] = [0] \oplus [0] \oplus [xy] \cdot [ty]$

The difference between the last two cases is easily remembered. In form 2, the partials remain and one of the basic relations $[xt]$ disappears. In form 3, the marginals remain and the partials disappear. It is useful, therefore, to call the first case elaboration by partials (P), and the case of form 3, elaboration by marginals (M). (The term "marginals" becomes appropriate if one inspects table 5.3 more closely. $[xt]$ and $[yt]$ are formed by comparing age and listening habits of the two educational groups. This means comparing the marginal sums of the two partial fourfold tables.)

For one who does not like to think in statistical terms, it might be easier to put it this way. In case P, the original relationship is maintained even after the test factor is introduced. In case M, the original relationship disappears and is substituted by new marginal relationships into which the test factor enters.

Here, then, is brought down to its logical skeleton a research operation familiar to every research laboratory. It consists of elaborating on a relationship between two variables by introducing a third one. We have already applied it to a number of concrete examples which, however, were all taken from empirical studies. Still, the way our examples run has a familiar tinge; going to texts that are held in high esteem by theorists, we find the same pattern. Dollard argues that upper-class whites are fairer to Negroes than lower-class whites because the former have less to fear from competition with the Negroes. Durkheim suggests that Catholics commit less suicide as compared with Protestants, because the Catholic community is more cohesive. These are important theoretical discussions, but if one looks at them quite closely, they too boil down to one scheme: two variables analyzed in the light of a third.

We already know everything that can be done with three variables. It is expressed in our main formula. Therefore, we ought to be able to derive from our formula anything which the theorists can do with two original variables and one additional variable. Or, in other words, we should be able to classify all theoretical thinking on three variables into a few major types, derived from the conditions of our main formula. This can actually be done, but, before proceeding, an additional consideration has to be introduced.

(To simplify the discussion, this analysis is restricted to three variables; if more than three variables are linked together, nothing changes basically, as can be shown fairly easily. We also restrict ourselves to dichotomies. If variables were introduced with three or more steps—for instance, young, middle-aged, and old people—the discussion would only become somewhat more complicated, but would not take a different form.)

The Role of Time Order Among Variables

A new aspect is introduced if we consider the time order between variables. The basic research operation from which we started required the classification of people according to certain attributes. The same classification is done mentally when we talk of people who do or do not live in competition with Negroes, or of the poor and rich neighborhoods, or of cohesive and uncohesive groups. (For the sake of simplicity, we shall restrict our examples to individual people.)

Very often these attributes are acquired at different times and therefore can be ranked accordingly. If, for instance, we relate length of engagement with subsequent marital happiness, the length of engagement comes earlier in the time order. If we relate parole breaking to some conditions of a criminal's adolescence, the latter again is prior in the time sequence.

Sometimes the time order is not as obvious, but it is clear enough for our purpose. Take such a result as that low-income people join fewer organizations. Even though a few people might have lost their money after they had joined, by and large we can assume that present economic status is acquired prior to present membership. The same would be true in many studies when we relate fairly permanent personality traits to achievements in school or on the job.

Some variables can be used in different ways, and therefore might change their place in a time sequence, according to the problem under investigation. The most typical example is age. People who are sixty years of age are characterized by certain physical handicaps, as compared to the twenty year olds. But, they are also characterized by the fact that they have been born and have grown up in the nineteenth century rather than after the First World War. Therefore, the timing of the variable depends upon the context. When we mentioned previously that older people are less educated, the thing that matters obviously was the period during which the people grew up. Therefore, age, as the indicator of time of birth, is prior to education. If, on the other hand, we relate the age at which people die to the kind of climate they live in, age is subsequent to climate. A similar distinction can be made when we compare married people with single people. Being married can either mean the ability to have acquired a spouse, or it can mean living together under specific conditions as family members.

Finally, there are variables with undetermined time sequence. If we find, for instance, that the Democrats are more in favor of government interference in business than the Republicans, we cannot say offhand what the time sequence of party affiliation and opinion is. The same is true when we find that people use a certain product and listen to a certain radio program on which it was advertised. Very often, we have to use variables in our studies for which the time sequence is dubious. But this is due either to deficiencies in the manner in which we collect our information or to the fact that we use data that had been collected for other purposes. As a matter of principle, it is always possible to establish the time sequence of variables. Progress in research consists in getting this point straightened out. Although what one does with variables that are hazy regarding the time sequence would be an interesting topic of discussion it is not the topic of our present note. For the rest of the discussion, we shall assume that we deal with variables whose time sequence is established, and we shall choose our examples accordingly.

The Main Types of Elaboration

We are now ready to present the decisive point. It is claimed that there are essentially four operations which can be performed with two original and one test variable. It makes no difference whether these operations are performed with actual data or whether they take the form of theoretical analyses. If a relation between two variables is analyzed in the light of a third, only these four operations or combinations thereof will occur irrespective of whether they are called interpretation, understanding, theory, or anything else.

The way the four cases originate will now be described. Let us assume that we start out with a relation between the two variables, x and y, with x being prior to y in the time sequence. Then test variable, t, is introduced. Two time relations are possible: either t lies in sequence between x and y, or it lies prior to x (including "simultaneity" of x and t here). Upon the introduction of t, two things can happen: either $[xt]$ equals zero, or it does not equal zero. If $[xt]$ is not zero, we shall assume for simplicity's sake that the partial relations between x and y are zero. This gives four main configurations which are described in the following scheme by the symbols *MA, PA* [marginal antecedent, partial antecedent], etc. We shall turn to a description and exemplification of these four patterns (see table 5.7).

In cases of the type *PA*, we usually call the test variable t a "condition." General examples easily come to mind, although in practice they are fairly rare and are a great joy to the research man when they are found. For example, the propaganda effect of a film is greater among low than among high educated people. The depression had worse effects on authoritarian families than on other types.

Table 5.7

Position of t	$[xt] = 0$ $[xy; t] \neq 0$	$[xt] \neq 0$ $[xy; t] = 0$
Antecedent	PA	MA
Intervening	PI	MI

Three general remarks can be made about this type of finding or reasoning: (a) It corresponds to the usual stimulus–disposition–response sequence, with x being the stimulus and the antecedent t being the disposition. (b) The whole type might best be called one of *specification*. One of the two partials will, by necessity, be larger than the original relationship. We, so to speak, specify the circumstances under which the original relationship holds true more strongly. (c) Usually we will go on from there and ask why the relationship is stronger on one side of the test dichotomy. This might then lead into one of the other types of analysis. Durkheim uses type *PA* in discussing why married people commit suicide less than unmarried people. He introduces as a test variable "a nervous tendency to suicide, which the family, by its influence, neutralizes or keeps from developing." This is type *PA* exactly. We do not experience it as much of an explanation because the introduction of the hypothetical test variable, like the tendency to suicide, sounds rather tautological. We want rather to know why the family keeps this tendency from developing, which as we shall see later leads to type *MI*.

The type *PI* is also easily exemplified. We study the relationship between job success and whether children did or did not go to progressive schools. We find that if the progressively educated children come into an authoritarian job situation, they do less well in their work than the others; on the other hand, if they come into a democratic atmosphere, their job success is greater.

The relation between type of education and job success is elaborated by an intervening test factor, the work atmosphere. Following the example of Paul Horst, we call such a test factor a "contingency." He points out that in many prediction studies, the predicted value depends upon subsequent circumstances which are not related to the predictor. Another example of this kind is given by Merton, who studied the relation between occupational status and participation in the life of a housing community. White-collar people participate more if they are dissatisfied, whereas manual workers participate more if they are satisfied with their jobs.

Just for the record, it might be mentioned that types *PI* and

PA have a simple relationship. If *t* is the condition (type *PA*) then *x* is a contingency. If *t* is a contingency (type *PI*) then *x* is a condition.

Actually, then, we have here only one major type of elaboration for which the word "specification" is probably quite appropriate. There are two subtypes of specification according to the time sequence of *x* and *t*.

Type *MA* is used mainly when we talk of rectifying what is usually called a *spurious relationship*. It has been found that the more fire engines that come to a fire, the larger is the damage. Because fire engines are used to reduce damage, the relationship is startling and requires elaboration. As a test factor, the size of the fire is introduced. The partials then become zero and the original result appears as the product of two marginal relationships; the larger the fire, the more engines—and also the more damage.

When we start with a relationship which is psychologically puzzling, we usually stop at that point, but this same mode of elaboration is also used under different psychological circumstances. More people commit suicide during the summer than during the winter. (Incidentally, for a precise formulation, this relationship would have to be put somewhat differently: among the people sampled during the summer we find more suicides than among people sampled or counted during the winter.) Durkheim suggests, as a *t* factor for elaboration, increased social activities going on during the summer. (This is a nice example of how a concrete formulation clarifies the time sequence; the intensity of social life precedes the counting of people as well as the suicides.)

Our interest immediately shifts to the [*ty*] relationship, to wit: to the presumed fact that greater intensity of social life leads to more suicides. Actually, of course, whether this explanation which comes from Durkheim is correct would depend upon a disappearance of the partials. Durkheim would have to show that if intensity of social life is kept constant, the season does not make any difference in suicides.

Because he has no data on this point, he rather looks for other situations where he can presume that intensity of social life varies. He finds that there are more suicides during the day as compared with the number during the night, which he again explains with the help of the same test factor. This leads into the whole question of probability of inference which we do not follow up here.

At this point a terminological remark is in place. We use the term "elaboration" to describe the research operation expressed in our main formula. We also show that there are certain ways of reasoning that are identical with this formula; the only difference is that in reasoning we do not use precise figures—we make statements which essentially imply that certain partial or marginal relationships are larger or smaller than others, or they are approximately zero, or different from zero.

The term "elaboration" is useful because it is so colorless that it probably does not connote too many associations which would detract from the precise meaning it has in this paper. The terminology becomes more "touchy" when it comes to distinguishing the four types of elaborations. They too are precise as long as we realize that they represent certain research or reasoning operations. When we give them names, however, we are in danger of losing the focus of our discussion. It seems, for instance, reasonable to call type MA an "explanation," because this word seems to be used often to describe the operation MA. But there is no doubt that many people have used the word "explanation" in different ways. It is, therefore, important to remember that "explanation" in this context is identical with the too-cumbersome term "elaboration of the type MA." Whether the term should be used this way or not is a more psychological question. Should future experience show that the term misdirects the reader, it could be dropped without any change in the argument.

This terminological difficulty becomes immediately apparent when we now turn to type MI, for which many people will certainly have used the term "explanation." We, here, shall use the term "interpretation" for type MI. The difference between "explanation" and "interpretation" in this context is related to the time sequence between x and t. In an interpretation the t is an intervening variable situated between x and y in the time sequence.

Examples of type MI have been given all through the paper. Living in a rural community is related to a lower suicide rate when compared with city dwelling. The greater intimacy of rural life is introduced as an intervening variable. If we had a good test of cohesion we would have to find that type of settlement is positively correlated to degree of cohesion, and degree of cohesion with suicide rate. But obviously some rural communities will have less cohesion than some urban communities. If cohesion is kept constant as a statistical device, then the partial relationship between the rural-urban variable and the suicide rate would have to disappear.

It might be useful to exemplify the difference between type *MA* and type *MI* by one more example. It was found during the war that married women working in factories had a higher rate of absence from work than single women. Here are two possible elaborations:

1. Test factor: more responsibilities at home. This is an intervening variable. If it is introduced and the two partial relationships—between marital status and absenteeism—disappear, we have an elaboration of type *MI*.
2. Test factor: physical handicaps, as crudely measured by age; because it stands for amount of time, the physique of the respondents has already been exhausted. This is an antecedent variable. If it turns out when age is kept constant that the relation between marital status and absenteeism disappears, we would have it explained, probably call it spurious, and forget about it: type *MA*.

The latter case suggests again an important point. After having explained the original relationship, our attention might shift to [*ty*]: the fact that older people show a higher absentee rate. This, in turn, might lead to new elaborations: is it really that older women have less physical resistance, be they married or single? Or, is it that older women have been born in a time where work is not as yet important for women and, therefore, they have a lower work morale. In other words, after one elaboration is completed, we will, as good scientists, immediately turn to a new one; but the basic analytical processes will always be the same.

An important statistical observation is in place here. In types *MA* and *MI*, the two newly emerging relationships are always larger than the original one, as can easily be seen arithmetically. Therefore, we find that every elaboration has at least one correlation that is higher than the one with which we started. This has important psychological and logical implications but there will not be space to discuss them here.

One final point can be cleared up, at least to a certain degree, by this analysis. We can suggest a clearcut definition of the *causal relationship* between two attributes. If we have a relationship between x and y, and if for any *antecedent* test factor the partial relationships between x and y do not disappear, then the original relationship should be called a causal one. It makes no difference here whether the necessary operations are actually carried through or made plausible by general reasoning. This general reasoning, incidentally, will always consist of using one of the four basic operations discussed here, except in those cases where the reasoning is directed toward the disentangling of time sequences among badly chosen variables.

This definition has special bearing on the following kind of discussion. It is found that in densely populated areas the crime rate is higher than in sparsely populated areas. Some authors state that this could not be considered a true causal relationship, but such a remark is often used in two very different ways. Some authors suggest an intervening variable: for instance, the increased irritation which is the result of crowded conditions. Even if their interpretation is correct, that does not detract from the causal character of the original relationship. On the other hand, the argument might go this way: crowded areas have cheaper rents and, therefore, attract less desirable elements. Here the character of the inhabitants is antecedent to the characteristics of the area. In this case the original relationship is indeed explained as a spurious one and should not be called causal.

[6]

On the Relation Between Individual and Collective Properties

with HERBERT MENZEL

Purpose

Social scientists often make use of variables to describe not only individual persons but also groups, communities, organizations, or other "collectives."[1] Thus one reads, for example, of "racially mixed census tracts," of "highly bureaucratized voluntary organizations," or of a "centrally located rooming-house district." At other times the variables, although describing individuals, are based on data about certain collectives, as in a comparison of "graduates of top-ranking medical schools" with "graduates of other medical schools." This paper attempts to clarify some of the operations involved in the construction and use of such variables in empirical research, and provides a nomenclature for the different ways in which information about individuals and about collectives may be interwoven in these properties. The properties will be classified according to the measurement operations involved in their construction.

Some Features of Generalizing Propositions

The intended meaning of the variables often remains ambiguous if they are not examined in the context of the propositions

From Amitai Etzioni, ed., *Complex Organizations: A Sociological Reader* (New York: Holt, Rinehart and Winston, 1961). Copyright © 1961 Holt, Rinehart and Winston, Inc. Reprinted by permission of Holt, Rinehart and Winston. Written in 1956. (Ed. note: the final section has been omitted.)

225

in which they are used. It is therefore necessary at the outset to highlight certain features which are common to all generalizing propositions, whether or not they involve collectives. (As an illustration, reference is made to the proposition "Children of rich parents go to college in greater proportion than do children of poor parents.")

1. Generalizing propositions assert something about a set of *elements* (children).
2. For the research purposes at hand, these elements are considered *comparable*. In other words, the same set of *properties* (wealth of parents; going to college) is used to describe each element.
3. Each element has a certain *value* on each property. The values (rich parents, poor parents; going to college, not going to college) may be quantitative or qualitative.
4. The propositions assert interrelationships between the properties of the elements.

Present Concern

The propositions with which the present discussion is concerned have the additional characteristic that their elements are dealt with either as collectives or as members of collectives. An example of the first kind is "There is a negative correlation between the rate of juvenile delinquency of American cities and the proportion of their budget given over to education." An example of the second kind is "Those recognized as leaders do not deviate very far from the norms of their group."

Special Meaning of "Collective" and "Member"

The terms "collective" and "member" are used here in a specific sense which needs clarification. A collective may be an element of a proposition; that is, it is one of a set of units which are regarded as *comparable* in the sense specified above: the same set of properties is used to describe all the elements. These elements are *collectives* if each is considered to be composed of constituent parts, called *members*, which are regarded as comparable in their turn. "Comparable" is used in the same sense as before: all members are described by a single set of properties.

(This is usually not the same set as that used to describe the collectives.)

In other instances members are the elements of the propositions. Elements will be called "members" if they are considered to be constituent parts of larger units, called "collectives," which are regarded as comparable in the same sense as before.

Thus one set of properties is always used to describe or classify all the members, and another single set of properties is used to characterize all the collectives. It is clear that under these definitions one can speak of "collectives" only when their "members" are also being referred to, and of "members" only when their "collectives" are also involved. Furthermore, there must be a multiplicity of members if the term "collective" is to be meaningful. It is perhaps less obvious but will be seen later that there must also be a multiplicity of collectives—i.e., the members of more than one collective must be referred to—if the distinctions between properties to be described below are to be relevant.

By contrast, the notion of "element" is needed to characterize any generalizing proposition whatsoever. It is applicable even in situations where the notions of "member" and "collective" are not involved at all.

Distinction Between "Individuals" and "Members"

In the examples that come to mind most easily, the members of collectives are individual persons. Thus, for example, cities are the collectives and people are the members in the following two propositions: (1) "The oldest settlers of cities are most likely to hold political office," or (2) "The more industry there is in a city, the higher the proportion of Democratic voters." The first proposition has members and the second has collectives as elements. In the same sense, a precinct can be treated as a collective, with the inhabitants as members. However, the members of a collective are not necessarily individual persons. A city, for example, can be described as a collective with the voting precincts as members. It follows that what appears as a collective in one context (e.g., precincts), can appear as a member in another. In any analysis of a piece of writing in which some of the elements are collectives, it is always necessary to specify clearly of what members the collectives are composed (for the purposes at hand).[2]

The graph below will help to keep this terminology in mind. The circles symbolize the collectives, the crosses within them their members. The dashes indicate that we are dealing with collectives as elements of a proposition. This is the situation with which we deal in the first part of this paper. In later sections

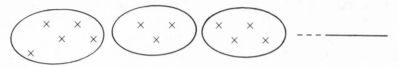

we discuss research where members are the focus of attention. They are then the elements of propositions, but their membership in one of a series of collectives is one of their characteristics.

Possibility of "Three-Level" Propositions

In some studies, more than two levels appear: for example, inhabitants, precincts, and cities may all be elements of the same study. This whole matter could, therefore, be elaborated by pointing out the various relationships which can exist between inhabitants, precincts, and cities. The next few pages are restricted to collectives which have only one kind of member; the members in most illustrations will be individual persons, but we will also present some examples in which the members themselves are larger units.

Propositions About Collectives as Substitutes and in Their Own Right

Propositions about collectives are sometimes made as substitutes for propositions about individual persons, simply because the necessary data about individual persons are not available. For example, a high Republican vote in "silk-stocking" districts is sometimes accepted to show that wealthy people are likely to vote Republican, when no records about individual votes and individual incomes are available.[3] For this reason it is often not realized that a large number of sociologically meaningful empirical propositions can be made of which only collectives are intended to be the elements. Thus, for example, an anthropologist may show that the political independence of communities is correlated with their pattern of settlement. A student of social disorganization may ask whether city zones with a high incidence of juvenile delinquency also show a high incidence of commitments for senile dementia. A small-group experimenter may hypothesize that "the probability of effective utilization of the insights that occur is greater in certain communication patterns than in others."[4] Much discursive writing also consists, in a hidden way, of such propositions.

A Typology of Properties Describing "Collectives" and "Members"

Properties of Collectives

It is often useful to distinguish three type of properties which describe collectives: analytical properties based on data about each member; structural properties based on data about the relations among members; and global properties, not based on information about the properties of individual members.[5] The following examples may clarify these distinctions:

1. *Analytical.* These are properties of collectives which are obtained by performing some mathematical operation upon some property of each single member.[6]

   The average rental paid in a precinct and the proportion of its inhabitants who have "Old Immigrant" (English, German, Scottish, Scandinavian) names are analytical properties of a collective (precinct) composed of individuals.[7] The proportion of the communities of a given state that have their own high school is an analytical property of a collective (state) the members of which are communities. The diffusion of a message in a city, defined as the percent of the target population knowing the message, is an analytical property of the city.[8]

   The standard deviation of incomes in a nation appears as an analytical property in the following example. The effect of post-

war legislation in Great Britain was to make the income distribution much narrower. Economists have predicted that under
these conditions people will save more, because they will spend
less money on display consumption which might help them be
socially acceptable in the higher strata.

Correlations are sometimes used to characterize collectives and
then also constitute analytical properties. The correlation of age
and prestige in a given community, for example, has been used
as a measure of its norms regarding old age. Sometimes more
indirect inferences are involved. MacRae shows that in urban
areas voting is highly correlated with occupation, while this is not
the case in rural districts. He concludes from this vote that in
rural districts there is a stronger spirit of community and
cohesion.[9]

2. *Structural.* These are properties of collectives which are obtained
by performing some operation on data about the relations of each
member to some or all of the others.

Assume, for example, that a sociometrist has recorded the "best-
liked classmate" of each student in a number of classes. He can
then describe the classes by the degree to which all choices are
concentrated upon a few "stars." Or he might, alternately, classify them according to their cliquishness, the latter being defined
as the number of subgroups into which a class can be divided so
that no choices cut across subgroup lines. In these examples the
collective is the school class, and the members are the individual
students; "concentration of choices" and "cliquishness" are
structural properties of the classes.

For an example in which the members are larger units, consider
a map of the precincts of a city, which indicates the number of
Negroes residing in each. Let a "Negro enclave" be defined as
a precinct in which some Negroes live, but which is completely
surrounded by precincts without Negroes. The proportion of the
precincts of a city which are Negro enclaves would then be a
structural property of the city.

3. *Global.* Often collectives are characterized by properties which are
not based on information about the properties of individual members.

American Indian tribes have been characterized by the frequency
with which themes of "achievement motive" make their appearance in their folk tales.[10] Societies have been classified as to the
presence of money as a medium of exchange, of a written language, etc.[11] Nations may be characterized by the ratio of the
national budget allotted to education and to armaments. Army

companies may be characterized by the cleanliness of their mess equipment.

Voting precincts have been classified according to the activities and attitudes of their Republican and Democratic captains, including hours spent on party duties, number of persons known to the captain personally, and his expressed commitment to the party.[12] In experiments in message diffusion by leaflets dropped from airplanes, cities have been treated to different degrees of "stimulus intensity," defined as the per capita ratio of leaflets dropped.[13] All these are global properties.

The density of settlement is a global property of a district. Having a city manager form of government is a global property of a city.

The insistence on specified initiation rites as a prerequisite to membership is a global property of a religious cult or of a college fraternity. Accessibility from the nearest big city is a global property of a village. A scale score assigned to each state according to the combination of duties assigned to the state board of education (rather than left to local authorities) is a global property of each state.[14]

"Emergent," "integral," "syntalic" and other terms have been used in meanings very similar to that of our term "global." It is not at all certain which term is most useful.[15]

Notice that all three of the above types of properties—analytical, structural, and global—describe collectives.

A Subsidiary Distinction Among Analytical Properties of Collectives

An interesting distinction may be made among the analytical properties. The first two examples given above were the average income of a city, and the proportion of the communities of a given state that have their own high school. These properties of collectives have what one might call a similarity of meaning to the properties of members on which they are based. The wealth of a city seems to be the same sort of thing as the wealth of an inhabitant. The endowment of a community with a high school and the rate of high school endowed communities in a state have a parallel meaning. This is not true for the remaining examples of analytical properties given above—the standard deviation of incomes in a nation, or correlations like that between age and prestige in a given community. Correlations and standard deviations can apply only to collectives and have no parallel on the level of members. The standard deviation of incomes in a city, for example, denotes something quite different—lack of homogeneity, perhaps—from individual income, the datum from which it is computed.

Another variable of this sort is "degree of consensus." When a Democrat and a Republican are competing for the mayoralty, the degree of political consensus in a particular club might be measured by the extent of the club's deviation from a fifty-fifty split. In this instance the analytic property is measured by a proportion, but it is not the simple proportion of adherents of either party; clubs which are 80 percent Democratic and those which are 20 percent Democratic are regarded as equal in consensus.

Whereas correlations, standard deviations, and similar measures always have a meaning peculiar to the group level, averages and proportions may or may not have a parallel meaning on the individual and collective levels.[16] Lack of parallel meaning is perhaps most clearly illustrated in the concept of a "hung jury," that is, a jury rendered indecisive by its inability to reach the required unanimity. Such a state of affairs is most likely when the individual jurors are most decisive and unyielding in their convictions.

Properties of Members

Another set of distinctions can be made between properties describing members in contexts where collectives have also been defined.

1. *Absolute* properties are characteristics of members which are obtained without making any use either of information about the characteristics of the collective, or of information about the relationships of the member being described to other members. They thus include most of the characteristics commonly used to describe individuals.

   In the proposition "Graduates of large law schools are more likely to earn high incomes at age forty than graduates of small law schools" income is an absolute property of the members (the individual students).

2. *Relational* properties of members are computed from information about the substantive relationships between the member described and other members.[17]

> Sociometric popularity-isolation (number of choices received) is a relational property. Many other sociometric indices fall into this category. For example, if each member of a small group has rated each other member on a five-point scale of acceptance-rejection, each member can be characterized by the total score he received (popularity), by the total score he expressed (active sociability), by the average deviation of the scores he accorded the others (discrimination in his acceptance of other members), etc.[18] In a study of the diffusion of the use of a new drug through a community of doctors, the physicians were classified according to whether or not they had a friend who had already used the new drug on a certain date.[19]

Some investigators have clarified the structure of relational properties by the use of matrices.[20] This new device can be fruitfully applied to some older papers.[21] The distinction between relational properties of individuals and structural properties of collectives deserves emphasis. The former characterize members of collectives in their relations to one another. The latter characterize collectives and are aggregates over the relational properties of their members.

3. *Comparative* properties characterize a member by a comparison between his value on some (absolute or relational) property and the distribution of this property over the entire collective of which he is a member.

> Sibling order is a comparative property of individuals in the proposition "First-born children are more often maladjusted than intermediate and last-born children." Note that each individual is characterized by comparison with the age of the other individuals in his family; in the resulting classification, many of the "last-born" will be older in years than many of the "first-born." Being a "deviate" from the majority opinion in one's housing project unit is a comparative property.[22]

> Another example is contained in the following proposition: "Students who had the highest I.Q. in their respective high school classes have greater difficulty in adjusting in college than students who are not quite at the top in high school even when their actual I.Q. score is equally high." Here the comparative property (being at the top in high school or not) is established in terms of the I.Q. distribution in each student's respective high school; the proposition pertains to a set of college students which includes boys and girls from several high schools (collectives).

4. *Contextual* properties describe a member by a property of his collective.

> Consider an example cited previously: "Graduates of large law schools are more likely to earn high incomes at age forty than graduates of small law schools." In this proposition, "being a member of a large law school" is a contextual property of individuals.
>
> Contextual properties are also used in the following propositions: "Union members in closed shops are less militant than union members in open shops." "Residents of racially mixed districts show more racial prejudice than those of racially homogeneous districts." "The less the promotion opportunity afforded by a branch (of the army), the more favorable the opinion (of soldiers) tends to be toward promotion opportunity."[23] In these propositions, being a member of a closed shop, residing in a mixed district, or being a soldier in a branch with frequent promotions are all examples of contextual properties.

Contextual properties are really characteristics of collectives applied to their members. Thus the classification of "collective properties" developed above could be repeated here as a subdivision of contextual "individual properties."[24] Note also that a contextual property, unlike a comparative property, has the same value for all members of a given collective.

Contextual and Comparative Properties Meaningful Only Where More Than One Collective Is Involved

It is not meaningful to speak of contextual or comparative properties when the elements under study are all members of the same collective—for instance, when only graduates of one law school are being studied—for the following reasons. Any *contextual* property would, in that case, have the same value for all the elements; hence nothing could be said about the interrelationship of this property and any other property. Any *comparative* property would, under these circumstances, classify the elements in exactly the same way as the absolute property from which it was derived, except that the calibration may be grosser. (If only children of one family are considered, the classification into "first-born," "intermediate," and "last-born" differs from that by age only in the grosser calibration. Similarly, if I.Q. scores of graduates of one law school are replaced by classification into lowest, second, third, and highest I.Q. quartile within their school, nothing will change except that the number of categories is reduced.)

Special Case Where the Typology Can Be Applied in Two Alternate Ways

A difficulty comes about when all the members of a set of collectives (or a representative sample of the members of each) constitute the elements of a proposition which includes a contextual property. Suppose, for instance, that the income ten years after graduation is recorded for all who graduate from fifty law schools in a certain year. A possible finding might be, "The income of law school graduates is correlated with the size of the school they graduated from." This is a proposition about students, relating their income (an absolute property) to the size of their law school (a contextual property). The same proposition could be interpreted also as one where the elements are the law schools; the average income of the students would then be an analytical property of each law school; its size would be a global property of these collectives.

The Present Classification Is Formal Rather than Substantive

As stated at the outset, the scheme suggested above is intended for the classification of properties according to the operations involved in their measurement. Although a classification by the underlying concepts or forces that the properties may be intended to represent might have numerous parallels to the present classification, it would not be the same.[25] In the present methodological context, for example, "number of libraries in a community" and "occurrence of aggressiveness themes in folk tales current in a tribe" are classified as global properties because they are not based on information about the properties of individual members. Yet it would be convincing to argue that these properties are relevant to the behavioral sciences only because properties of individuals, of the relations among individuals, or of the resulting social structures are inferred from them. Similarly, the title of office held by a person in a hierarchy

236 The Logic of Method

would here be classified as an "absolute" property, even when the researcher is actually interested in the incumbent's power over subordinates, which the title implies.

At some points arbitrary decisions have to be made. On an intuitive basis we decided to consider the number of members in a collective (e.g., population size) as a global property, although one might argue that it is analytical, obtained by counting the "existence" of each member. Even more ambiguous is the classification of rates based on the behavior of ex-members— for example, suicide rates. No definitive practice is proposed for such borderline cases.

PART THREE
Qualitative and Quantitative Analysis

[7]
Some Functions of Qualitative Analysis in Social Research

with ALLEN H. BARTON

The advancement of research procedure in social science as elsewhere depends on making explicit what researchers actually do and systematically analyzing it in the light of logic and of substantive knowledge. Such a "codification" of procedures points out dangers, indicates neglected possibilities, and suggests improvements. It makes possible the generalization of methodological knowledge—its transfer from one specific project or subject matter to others; from one researcher to the scientific community. Finally it makes possible a more systematic training of students, in place of simply exposing them to concrete cases of research in the hope that they will somehow absorb the right lessons.

Such a recording and analysis of procedures has gone quite far in certain parts of the social research process—in the design of experiments, in the analysis of survey data, in the scaling and measurement of social and psychological variables, and in sampling. But codification has been very unevenly applied; important parts of the research process have been neglected.

This is particularly true of the analysis of nonquantified data, "qualitative analysis," as it is often called. A great deal of social research operates with qualitative descriptions of particular institutions, situations, or individuals, rather than with "largely

From *Frankfurter Beiträge zur Soziologie* (1955)1:321-61. Reprinted by permission.

239

quantified data accumulated by structured observation in empirical situations approximating (with specified deviations) the model of controlled experiment."[1] Not only is this type of research large in volume, but it plays important roles in the research process, by itself and in connection with quantitative research. This paper aims to make a start at the systematic analysis of "qualitative procedure."

The question which we would like to answer is: What can a researcher do when confronted by a body of qualitative data—detailed, concrete, nonmetric descriptions of people and events, drawn from direct observation, interviews, case studies, historical writings, the writings of participants? The methodologist's first step toward a systematic answer is to examine what researchers in fact have been doing with qualitative material. About 100 studies were culled for characteristic examples. An effort was then made to organize these cases in order that the most characteristic types of qualitative work would be distinguished and documented. This paper presents the resulting organization.

The reader will have no difficulty in noting that this "guide through qualitative research" is itself guided by proceeding from simple to ever more complex procedures. We begin with a discussion of the value of simple observations. We then proceed to those studies which center on ordering and classification. Our next group of examples demonstrates the various ways in which several variables are interrelated through qualitative analysis. Next we discuss cases where the analyst wants to encompass such a great number of dimensions that he cannot make them all explicit, but tries to sum them up in a general "pattern." This is probably the point at which qualitative research is most creative, most controversial, and most difficult to describe. It will be seen that we had to use a special term, "matrix formula," to bring into relief this means of seeing the social world in a new way. Finally, we touch on the role of qualitative data in the support of theory, a topic so large that we did not dare to pursue it to any extent.

It should also be kept in mind what this paper does not attempt to do. First of all, it does not describe how qualitative research should be done; it is restricted to an organized description of what is actually being done, without expressing any judgment.

Secondly, this paper, but for one point, does not make any attempt at formalization. The exception is in the section where the use of typologies is discussed. The logic of typologies is by now so well developed that it was simple to include it in this paper. Such formalizations have considerable advantages. They indicate the underlying assumptions in a given piece of qualitative work, what points the author might have overlooked, at what points he might have contradicted himself, and so forth. There is no doubt that additional formalizations will be needed. We have, for example, distinguished various ways in which a single observation can be fruitful; however, we have not tried to bring the different possibilities into a more general context from which they can be derived. As a matter of fact, one of the hopes for the present survey is that it will facilitate further work in this direction.[2] We have also not dealt with the problem of evidence. Under what conditions in the social sciences an assertion is proved is a very difficult question, not restricted to qualitative research. It seemed best not to touch on this issue, in a context in which all emphasis was placed on providing a picture of a kind of work which is usually considered so "private" that it defies all systematic presentation.

Analysis of Single Observations

When one examines qualitative reports, one of the first types of material which catches our attention is the "surprising observation." Like the nets of deep-sea explorers, qualitative studies may pull up unexpected and striking things for us to gaze on. We find that there are people who believe that they are being educated by the unrelated and trivial information presented by quiz shows.[3] Interviews with people deprived of their newspaper by a strike disclose that some do not turn to alternative sources of news, but to reading anything which is lying around the house; a major function of newspaper reading seems to be simply to fill in "gaps" in the daily routine.[4] Observers of the underworld tell us that professional thieves constitute a rather exclusive social group, with exacting standards of membership strongly reminiscent of those of lawful professions.[5] Anthropological data of course are full of surprising observations: that Eskimos lend their wives to guests without any jealousy, that Fiji Islanders kill their chiefs when they grow old, and so on.[6]

These phenomena are of various levels: some are individual beliefs and behaviors, some are a matter of group standards and structures within a society, some involve the norms of a whole culture. In each case the qualitative researcher has simply disclosed that such-and-such a phenomenon exists. And in one way or another, to be told that such things exist has a strong impact on the reader. They all have an element of surprise.

In the next few pages we will try to clarify what this impact is, and what research functions are served by these qualitative observations which simply state the existence of something surprising. We can distinguish at least two different uses for such observations. First, the existence of a phenomenon may raise problems—that is, compel us to look for explanations, to explore its consequences, to try to fit it into our scheme of knowledge. Second, we may find in the qualitative observations an indicator of some general variable which we want to study, but cannot measure directly.

Observations Which Raise Problems

Some observations are surprising because they conflict with our expectations, either commonsense or theoretically derived. Other observations surprise us by bringing to light phenomena which are simply new and unexplained, which challenge our curiosity. Yet another important type of problem-raising observations is that which brings together under a clear label a body of "familiar" experiences which had not previously been seen as a definite, generally occurring social phenomenon—which forms for the first time, so to speak, a "social object" to be studied.

In any of these cases the result is that a problem is raised. Our attention is focussed on a phenomenon, and we are stimulated to seek explanations and inquire into consequences. To make such a problematic observation is to initiate a research process which may lead to significant advancement of our understanding of social phenomena. (Some kinds of observations no doubt raise more significant questions and lead to more valuable findings than others. It would be of great value to develop "screening principles" which can direct our attention to the more significant of the surprising observations; this cannot, however, be gone into here.)[7]

To give concrete meaning to the notion of a problematic qualitative observation, and to provide material for its further development, a number of examples can be given.

As is well known, the original experiments of the Western Electric researchers led to highly surprising quantitative results: the experimental changes in physical conditions of work in no way accounted for the changes in production in the experimental group of workers. At this point the researchers decided to go back to the very first stage of the research process and simply gather observations about what goes on in a normal working group in a factory. This exploratory research turned up a number of surprising qualitative observations.

> Some work groups were characterized by a lack of ambition and initiative and a complacent desire to let well enough alone.
>
> The supervisory control which is set up by management to regulate and govern the workers exercises little authority. . . .
>
> They [the employees] firmly believe that they will not be satisfactorily remunerated for any additional work they produce over the bogey.[8]

All of these facts were in conflict with what the management and the researchers had expected. By following them up the researchers were led to their now well-known discovery of the importance of informal groups in formal organizations, and of the barriers to communication which exist between levels within organizations.

Communications research offers many examples of surprising qualitative observations. We have already mentioned the discovery of unexpected motives—for listening to quiz programs and for reading newspapers. Unexpected responses to communications are another important example. A broadcast warning the public to patronize X-ray operators and avoid "quacks" left some listeners afraid of any X-ray treatments and others doubting whether there could be any X-ray machines in the hands of incompetent operators.[9] A film designed to impress

Americans with the British war effort left some more convinced than ever that America was bearing all the burden.[10] The discovery of such anomalous responses led to more detailed investigations of the communications process, which turned up some important general principles—for example, about the need to relate the message to the experience-world for the audience, which may be quite different from that of the communicator.

A study of how prejudiced people respond to cartoons ridiculing prejudice found an unexpected type of response.[11] Some people were neither shamed out of their prejudices nor insulted; they simply did not understand what the cartoons were driving at. When this response was investigated in detail, the "derailment mechanism" of motivated misunderstanding was revealed (see the section "Qualitative Suggestions of Process," below).

Listeners to Kate Smith's war bond "marathon broadcast" placed remarkable emphasis on her "sincerity."[12] Considering that other professional entertainers drew no such response, and that the respondents were generally suspicious of advertising and propaganda manipulation, this seemed worth investigating. Further study suggested the importance of "the propaganda of the deed" in a propaganda-wary society—in this case, Kate Smith's presumed strain and sacrifice in making the eighteen-hour broadcast.

The examples so far have involved unexpected phenomena which stimulated a search for causal explanations. In other instances the problem which is raised is in the other direction—an investigation of the consequences of a certain phenomenon is stimulated. Thus one researcher interested in problems of the profession noted an "obvious" fact as raising a problem: while all professionals meet a certain proportion of failures, the trial lawyers as a group necessarily lose half their cases.[13] What must be the consequences of such a high rate of failure for these professionals, and how do they deal with it? The answers to these problems might throw light on some important problems of the professional role. The ability to take a commonplace fact and see it as raising problems is important because it can lead ultimately to such enlightenment.

Another such observation was made by Merton in his study of the Kate Smith war bond marathon. In the content of the broadcast there was no reference to the real economic purpose of war bond buying as an anti-inflation measure. Merton saw this fact as raising problems of consequences: an opportunity to educate a large and attentive audience in economic realities had been neglected, and reliance had been placed instead upon "large delusive statements" playing upon the anxieties of those with loved ones overseas. What were "the further, more remote but not necessarily less significant effects of these techniques upon the individual personality and the society?" "Does the unelaborated appeal to sentiment which displaces the information pertinent to assessing this sentiment blunt the critical capacities of the listeners?"[14]

An example of the forming of commonplace experiences into a clearly labeled social phenomenon, and thereby creating a new object for investigation, is Adler's formulation of the concept of the inferiority complex.[15] Everyone at one time or another has experienced feelings of being inadequate, unworthy, etc., but until these private sensations had been pointed out and labeled, they could not be investigated by social science. Other examples which might be called to mind are Veblen's formulation of the concept of conspicuous consumption,[16] or Sutherland's labeling of certain categories of business behavior as "white collar crime."[17] Without having actually discovered any new facts, simply by directing attention to familiar facts placed for the first time within a distinctive category, these investigators were able to raise important problems and initiate fruitful study.

The reader may have noticed that some of the examples of "surprising observations" cited are no surprise at all to him. This is as it should be. The point is that one time they were surprising and initiated further investigation which has been sufficiently successful to render them familiar and understandable today. Another problem is that an observation may be surprising to the particular researchers, while other social scientists have known about it all along. Thus the Western Electric researchers made the "surprising discovery" that informal social organization existed among workers. Other sociologists had long been aware of the problem of informal groups; however, the special preconceptions of American industrial sociology up to that time had kept it unaware of this whole realm of phenomena. In a still more extreme case, a finding may be new only to one particular researcher; in which case it might better be termed "self-education" than a scientific discovery.

Is there anything which a researcher can do toward making "surprising observations" other than to maintain an alert state of mind? It may seem contradictory to speak of giving instructions for making surprising observations. However, there are ways in which one can at least increase the probability of making such observations. Some of these are discussed by Jahoda, Deutsch, and Cook under the heading "The Analysis of 'Insight-Stimulating Cases.'"[18] Strangers or newcomers to a community or a country, it is suggested, may be able to pick out problematic facts which are simply taken for granted by those accustomed to the locale. Marginal individuals, or cases in transition from one stage or status to another, may present much more clearly certain problematic features of a personality-type or social system. Deviants, extreme cases, or "pure, ideal-typical" cases may have a relatively high efficiency in indicating problematic facts.

Observations Which Serve as Indicators

The first type of surprising observations discussed were those which were anomalous and unexplained, which served the function of stimulating a search for explanations. Another type of qualitative observations are challenging because we see in them indications of some large-scale phenomenon which we cannot perceive directly. Thus the occurrence of riots and protest meetings in the North during the Civil War serves as an indication that opposition to Lincoln's war policy existed; bits of shell or pottery found in graves mark the routes of trade and cultural contact in the prehistoric world; a peculiar military custom indicates the castelike nature of army organization; modes of speech may indicate complex mental patterns or cultural emphases.

Three situations can be pointed out in which one pays particular attention to qualitative indicators. They are distinguished in terms of the kind of obstacle which prevents direct observation and measurement of the underlying variable:

1. Situations in which qualitative evidence substitutes for otherwise simple statistical information relating to past ages or inaccessible countries.
2. Situations in which qualitative evidence is used to get at psychological data which are repressed or not easily articulated—attitudes, motives, assumptions, frames of reference, etc.
3. Situations in which simple qualitative observations are used as indicators of the functioning of complex social structures and organizations, which are difficult to subject to direct observation.

The underlying assumption in all these cases is that a phenomenon which cannot be directly observed will nevertheless leave traces which, properly interpreted, permit the phenomenon to be identified and studied. A great historical movement, a basic personality characteristic, an essential characteristic of organizational structure, should all leave their imprint on almost any documentary material, accounts by observers, or even physical refuse, which they leave behind.

Examples of the first class (qualitative substitutes for unavailable statistical or descriptive material) would include the use of newspaper stories or other contemporary records of public demonstrations as indications of public opinion in past times of crisis;[19] Frazier's use of advertisements for slaves in ante-bellum Southern newspapers to find out about the structure of the slave family;[20] the use of reports of refugees, Soviet press materials, and the contents of Soviet literature to provide information about life in the Soviet Union;[21] the use of archeological remains to indicate culture contacts or religious beliefs in prehistoric times.

Examples of the second class (qualitative indicators of psychological variables) include formal projective testing, the psychological analysis of personal documents or artistic works, the analysis of items of literature or entertainment as presumed projections of the traits of their audience,[22] and of course the analysis of qualitative interviews or records of participant observation. A good example of the use of indicators for a psychological concept is found in the study of antiprejudice cartoons mentioned earlier:

> In tracing the process through which these 68 respondents arrived at their misunderstanding, we find our starting point in the fact that most of

them *identified* with Mr. Bigott. [Footnote:] By "identification" we mean
the mental process through which a subject assumes the role of another
person to such an extent that actions, either verbal or behavioral, directed
toward the object of identification are experienced as directed toward the
identifying person. Evidence of identification with Mr. Bigott was man-
ifested by the subject's acting in one or more of the following ways: (a)
explicitly affirming identification, saying, for example, "I guess I'm a Mr.
Bigott"; (b) consistently and openly sympathizing with Mr. Bigott, expressing sorrow, for example, that Mr. Bigott looked so weak and sick
in the "transfusion" cartoon; (c) interpreting a threat to or criticism of
Mr. Bigott as referring to himself, as, for example, becoming emotionally
upset by the cobweb on Mr. Bigott's head.[23]

A single conversation reported by the authors of *Deep South*
bears witness to the depth of feeling involved in white attitudes
toward Negroes in this deeply prejudiced area: A social worker
described a poor-white family in which two girls

"are having babies and are not married. . . . That isn't the end by any
means. . . . Somebody told me that this older girl was sleeping with the
father. . . ." After the recitation of the case, when the social worker was
out of the room, a woman whispered to the interviewer: "Mrs. Wilson
says *those girls have Negro men too*, but Miss Trent [the supervisor]
won't let me say anything about that. . . . *Isn't that awful?*" It is significant to note from this interview that the incest situation was viewed with
less horror than the infraction of the caste sex taboos.[24]

On the basis of his long participant observation, William
Whyte was able to report the following striking indicator of the
complete acceptance of gambling in Cornerville:

When a mother sends her small child down to the corner for a bottle
of milk, she tells her to put the change on a number.[25]

Investigators studying the effects of unemployment on the
psychology of the people of an Austrian village had the school-
children write essays on the theme "My Future Occupation."
The pervasiveness of the insecurity of the children of the unemployed, its corrosive effect on planning for the future, was
indicated among other things by the very language used. Children
of employed workers would write, "I will be . . ." or "I want
to become. . . ." Children of the unemployed tended to use

phrases like "I might become" or "I would like to be. . . ." In the same study a small boy remarked to one of the investigators that he would like to be an Indian chief, "But I am afraid it will be hard to get the job."[26]

The third situation—the use of simple qualitative indicators to show the attributes of complex social structures—is very clearly exemplified in Blumenthal's study of a small mining community. The speed and inclusiveness of interpersonal communication in the community was indicated

> by the fact that should a death occur at nine o'clock in the morning and the information not reach a resident until late in the afternoon, his usual expression is, "I can't understand why I didn't hear that sooner," and others say to him, "Where have you been? Everybody knew that by noon."[27]

At another point Blumenthal notes the existence of conflicting qualitative indicators of the social contact between Mineville and its nearest neighbor, and concludes that one has the greater weight:

> During the heyday of Crystal her people and those of Mineville were not so well acquainted as might be supposed. . . . Hotly contested baseball games and the communities having celebrated together on the main day of festivities for each—Miner's Union Day—were not indications of far-reaching personal relations. This is shown by the measure of social distance evidenced by the fact that a young man whose reputation was such in one town that its "respectable" girls refused to associate with him could go to the other and fraternize with its "best" young women.[28]

The existence of primary group relations within smaller units of the American army can be inferred from the following qualitative indications drawn from an interview:

> We bunked together, slept together, fought together, told each other where our money was pinned in our shirts. . . .If one man gets a letter from home the whole company reads it.[29]

The authors of *The American Soldier*, wanting an indicator for the complex notion of the "Army caste system," pointed to an institutionalized symbolic act:

Enlisted men selected for officer candidate school were first discharged
from the Army and then readmitted in their new and very different status.

Just as it is impossible to move from one caste to another in
an ethnic case situation, so an enlisted man about to become an
officer must leave the army system before reentering in his new
status. The continuation of this custom is a certain indication
of the continuation of the attitudes of a "caste system" in the
army.[30]

In discussing the family structure found in Middletown's various classes, the Lynds suggest a possible indicator of the position of the husband in the family:

> It may not be wholly fantastic to surmise that there may be some
> significance for the understanding of local marital association in the hi-
> erarchy of terms by which local women speak of their husbands. There
> is a definite ascent of man in his conjugal relations as one goes up in the
> social scale, from "my old man" through "the man," "he" (most fre-
> quent), "the mister," "John," "my husband," to "Mr. Jones." The first
> four are the common terms among the working class families, and the last
> two among business class families.[31]

The indicators which have been referred to are of many different forms. Some are linguistic, some are symbolic acts, some
are documentary, some are physical objects. As substantive
knowledge of linguistics, social organization, and technology are
applied to the problem, one may expect ever more sensitive and
reliable interpretations of such qualitative indicators. To what
extent interpretation of indicators will have to remain an art,
and to what extent it can be made a science, is one of the
important problems of qualitative research which we cannot attempt to discuss here.

Construction of Descriptive Systems

The previous section discussed what can be done with a single
"point" of qualitative data; the present section considers what
one does when confronted by a whole array of qualitative observations. As a first step toward understanding a field of human

activity, one must organize the raw observations into a descriptive system. In some cases one has only to apply categories already set up by previous investigators or by the society itself, and proceed with the further stages of analysis. In other cases previously existing categories are clarified and revised by the attempt to apply them to a concrete body of data. And in some cases the researcher must create his own classification system for the material under study. It is this latter case which will be particularly considered here.

In terms of their formal structure, the descriptive systems created by investigators can range from crude lists of "types," each defined individually without clear logical relationship to the others, to fully systematic typologies in which each type is a logical compound of a small number of basic attributes. Between these end points are all intermediate degrees of "partial" systematization, including some sets of types which include in their definition virtually all the logical elements necessary to set up a multidimensional "attribute space," but in which the logical analysis has not been explicitly made. Descriptive systems may also vary in terms of their degree of concreteness or generality. A fully systematic typology may be based on dimensions of a highly limited, concrete nature, while a preliminary classification can be broad and general.

Preliminary Classifications

A classification which falls toward the unsystematized end of the continuum can be called a preliminary one, since it represents an essential first step toward the ideal of a fully systematic one. The importance of this first step from completely unordered data to a preliminary classification must never be underestimated. Until the data are ordered in some way, the analysis of relationships cannot begin; more refined categories normally develop out of the attempt to analyze relationships between preliminary categories; there is an interacting process between refinement of classification and the analysis of relationships.

A good preliminary classification must provide a workable summary of the wealth of elements in the original data, and include—even if in unsystematic form—the basic elements nec-

essary for understanding the situation. A bad preliminary classification is one which is poor in elements and suggestiveness,
which omits so many important aspects of the situation that
analysis reaches a dead end, and one must go back to the original
data for a new start. So long as the essential elements are suggested somewhere in the initial classification, they can be picked
and recombined more logically as the analysis proceeds. The
question of what it takes to make fruitful preliminary categories—whether the process can be systematized and taught, or
whether it is wholly an individual art—is one of those which
most needs exploring. The present discussion can only raise this
question and present a number of examples of the process.

Good examples of the use of this form of qualitative analysis—
the formation of relatively unsystematized but fruitful classifications of people and situations—can be found in the work of
the Chicago urban sociologists. Such an instance is Louis Wirth's
suggestive notes in "Some Jewish Types of Personality." Wirth
defines his purpose in using this technique as follows:

> The sociologist, in transforming the unique or individual experience
> into a representative or typical one, arrives at the social type, which
> consists of a set of attitudes on the part of the person toward himself and
> the group and a corresponding set of attitudes of the group toward
> him. . . . The range of personality types in a given social group is indic-
> ative of the culture of that group.[32]

Wirth's gallery of "characteristic and picturesque personalities that are met within the average community" includes:

the *Mensch*, a person of superior economic status who has "achieved
his success without sacrificing his identity as a Jew"

the *allrightnick*, who "in his opportunism, has thrown overboard most
of the cultural baggage of his group"

the *Schlemihl*, who belies the stereotype of the Jew as "the personi-
fication of the commercial spirit" by being "quite shiftless and helpless,
failing miserably in everything he undertakes"

the *Luftmensch*, who moves easily from one unsuccessful project to
another, and whose "only apparent means of subsistence is the air he
breathes"

the *Yeshiba Bochar*, literally the talmudical student, the young man
whose learning gives prestige irrespective of wealth or origin

the *Zaddik*, the "pious, patriarchal person . . . whose exemplary conduct is pointed to as an example"; and so on.[33]

The purpose of presenting these types, drawn largely from the folklore and literature of the subject group, lies in the fact that

> they are as complete an index as any at present obtainable of the culture pattern of the group. . . . Together they constitute the personal nuclei around which the fabric of the culture of the group is woven. A detailed analysis of the crucial personality types in any given area or cultural group shows that they depend upon a set of habits and attitudes in the group for their existence and are the direct expressions of the values of the group.[34]

Starting from these types, therefore, one can derive a classification of the values, habits, and attitudes which are important to the explanation of the behavior of the group.

In much the same way, from folklore and literature as well as personal observation, C. Wright Mills draws a gallery of "white-collar types." There are types of managers:

> the "glum men" on the top of the white-collar pyramid, harassed, cautious, careful to stay in line with the aims of the employers or other higher ups
>
> the "old veterans" just below the top, who seek security in closely following explicit instructions, and strive for deference from those below
>
> the "live wire," the younger man on his way up
>
> the "new entrepreneur," who prospers as a fixer and go-between in a world of huge and complicated organizations, mass manipulation, and general insecurity.[35]

There are types of intellectuals,[36] of academic men,[37] and—all the way down at the bottom of the white-collar pyramid—of salesgirls: "the wolf," "the charmer," "the ingenue," "the social pretender," and so on.[38]

There is a serious purpose in pinpointing these picturesque types:

> By examining white-collar life, it is possible to learn something about what is becoming more typically "American" than the frontier character probably ever was. What must be grasped is the picture of society as a

great salesroom, an enormous file, an incorporated brain, a new universe of management and manipulation. By understanding these diverse white-collar worlds, one can also understand better the shape and meaning of modern society as a whole, as well as the simple hopes and complex anxieties that grip all the people who are sweating it out in the middle of the twentieth century.[39]

The general run of preliminary categories will not be as colorful and rich in suggestions as these just quoted, but they will be of the same formal nature: a simple list of discrete "types." Thus we will have lists of "types" of comic-book readers,[40] types of client-professional relations, types of appeals in a certain propaganda broadcast,[41] types of communities, etc., representing a preliminary ordering of material into a simple list of headings. As the analysis progresses, either within the original study or in the work of replication or secondary analysis, these simple lists may be developed into more systematic and more general descriptive systems.

Somewhat further along the road to generality and systematization are the kinds of "types" found in the great deal of the speculative and theoretical literature. Typical examples here are Spranger's six "value types"—the theoretical, economic, aesthetic, social, political, and religious[42]—or von Wiese and Becker's four types of religious organizations—the ecclesia, the denomination, the sect, and the cult.[43] Merton, in discussing the forms of interpersonal influence, lists the following types: coercion, domination, manipulation, clarification, provision of prototypes for imitation, advice, and exchange.[44] Kingsley Davis classifies social norms in traditional categories: folkways, mores, law, custom, morality, religion, convention, and fashion.[45] Lasswell sets up eight basic categories of values which he uses to classify institutions and leaders;[46] Malinowski sets up seven "basic needs" in terms of which cultural phenomena can be classified;[47] and so on.

All of the above mentioned sets of categories are of far greater generality than those which arise in the analysis of a single empirical study of limited scope. They are the result of attempts at general analysis of a wide range of situations. On the other hand, in their formal aspect, they are similar to the other forms of preliminary categories discussed earlier. Some of them are quite unsystematized; others include in their definition most of the elements required to set up a logical structure of basic attributes from which they could be derived, but this has not been explicitly done.

A special kind of descriptive system which might be mentioned under this heading consists of ordered categories, which are set up as developmental stages or degrees along a continuum. Thus Piaget distinguished the stages of development of children's attitudes toward the rules of conduct, from "moral realism" in which the letter of the rule is absolute to "autonomous rationality" in which blind acceptance "withdraws in favor of the idea of justice and of mutual service."[48] Scheler sets up seven categories of knowledge which he orders along the dimension of increasing "artificiality": (1) myth and legend; (2) knowledge implicit in the natural folk-language; (3) religious knowledge; (4) the basic types of mystical knowledge; (5) philosophical-metaphysical sciences; (6) positive knowledge of mathematics, the natural and cultural sciences; (7) technological knowledge.[49] In such sets of categories an ordering along one dimension is explicitly stated, while the other attributes characterizing the categories are simply listed or suggested without any systematization.

Systematic Typologies

The most highly developed form of descriptive system which can arise in a qualitative analysis is one in which each type is explicitly derived from the logical combination of basic attributes or dimensions. A simple example is the logical scheme set up by Riesman in his study of political participation.[50] By examining a set of concrete "type cases" Riesman was led to break the concept of participation into two basic elements: emotional involvement and competence, or more simply, "caring" and "knowing." Taking each of these elements as a simple dichotomy, Riesman obtained four types of relations to politics (see table 7.1). Merton employs this technique in his typology of prejudice and discrimination. He starts from the usual formulation of two types of people: people who live up to the American creed of nondiscrimination, and people who violate it. Merton suggests a further elaboration: that people be distinguished on

Table 7.1

Competence

		+	−
Affect	+	"involved"	"indignants"
	−	"inside-dopesters"	"indifferent"

one hand by whether they personally believe in the creed or not, and, on the other hand, by whether they practice discrimination or not.

> This is the salient consideration: conduct may or may not conform with individuals' own beliefs concerning the moral claims of all men to equal opportunity. Stated in formal sociological terms, this asserts that attitudes and overt behavior vary independently. Prejudicial attitudes need not coincide with discriminatory behavior. The implications of this statement can be drawn out in terms of a logical syntax whereby the variables are diversely combined, as can be seen in the . . . typology [table 7.2].[51]

A mere list of the "folk-labels" of each type would appear superficially like one of the preliminary lists of categories; they are fundamentally different, however, since they are systematically derived from the cross-tabulation of two basic dimensions.

The most elaborate use of systematic typologies is found in Talcott Parsons and Edward Shils's work.[52] They set forward five dichotomous attributes:

1. Affectivity—Affective neutrality
2. Self-orientation—Collectivity orientation

Table 7.2
A Typology of Ethnic Prejudice and Discrimination

ATTITUDE DIMENSION

	Non-Prejudiced	Prejudiced
Non-discrimination	Type I: The All-Weather Liberal	Type III: The Fair-Weather Illiberal
BEHAVIOR DIMENSION Discrimination	Type II: The Fair-Weather Liberal	Type IV: The All-Weather Illiberal

Source: Adapted from Merton, "Discrimination," p. 103.

3. Universalism—Particularism
4. Ascription—Achievement
5. Specificity—Diffuseness

By combining these five "pattern variables" Parsons has been able to construct general categories for describing social relations, cultural systems, and personality systems.

The process of constructing systematic typologies need only be briefly summarized here. The starting point is often a good preliminary set of categories. By examining them one derives a small number of attributes which seem to provide the basis for the distinctions made and sets these attributes up as a multidimensional system (an "attribute-space"). This operation has been termed the "substruction" of an attribute space to a typology. One can then examine all of the logically possible combinations of the basic attributes. This serves to locate the original set of categories within the system; it often shows that some combinations have been ignored (appear as blank cells), while in other cases distinctions have been missed (the original category will overlap several cells). Of course not all of the logically possible combinations may be important or even empirically possible; it will often be necessary to restrict the combinations to be studied, or to recombine several categories to simplify the analysis. Such a recombination has been termed a "reduction," and is closely related to the operation of index formation.[53]

Partial Substructions

There remains to be mentioned a type of operation which is very frequent in qualitative analyses: the partial systematization of a concept or a set of categories. A good introduction to this operation is the well-known discussion by Simmel of envy and jealousy.[54] The situations in which these feelings arise are quite complex, and Simmel does not give an exhaustive account of them. What he does, however, is to indicate one important aspect in which the two attitudes differ: in the case of jealousy the person feels that he has a claim on the object of his desire, while in the case of envy he has no claim, only desire for the object. Simmel has thus partially substructed the attribute-space by which envy and jealousy could be systematically defined; he has not done so completely, but rather only enough to make one major distinction.

A more elaborate but still partial substruction is presented in Werner Landecker's discussion of "Types of Integration and Their Measurement." Landecker begins by indicating his discontent with the undifferentiated concept of "social integration." To study the relation of integration to other variables, to find its necessary conditions and its consequences, the broad abstraction must be broken down:

> Early in the exploration of a type of phenomena it seems advisable to break it up into as many subtypes as one can distinguish and to use each subdivision as a variable for research. This appears to be a more fruitful procedure than to attempt immediately to generalize about the generic type as a whole. The main advantage of subclassification in an initial phase of research is that it leads to problems of relationship among subtypes which would evade the attention of the investigator if he were to deal with the broader type from the very beginning. Generalizations on the higher level of abstraction will suggest themselves as a matter of course once regularities common to several subtypes are discovered.[55]

In analyzing the concept of social integration, Landecker first breaks down society into two types of elements: cultural standards, on the one hand, and persons and their behavior, on the other. The logical interrelations among these two elements give him three types of integration:

"Cultural integration": integration within the realm of cultural standards

"Normative integration": integration between cultural standards and the behavior of persons

"Integration among persons": integration within the realm of behavior

This last type in turn is broken down in terms of two types of human behavior: the interchange of ideas and the interchange of services. Integration within the realm of communication is termed "communicative integration"; integration within the realm of services is termed "functional integration."

Since "integration" is a relational concept, Landecker's types can be easily represented by a relational matrix—a table, along each side of which we list the elements involved in interrelationships. The interior cells of the table then indicate the logically possible connections, including, in the main diagonal, the internal relationship within each element (see table 7.3).

This relational scheme allows us to locate all of the types of integration proposed by Landecker. It also raises the question of further relationships not discussed and distinctions not made: for example, the possible subdivision of "normative integration" in terms of the two spheres of behavior, the relationship between the two forms of behavior themselves, and indeed the possibility of distinguishing still other major spheres within the realm of behavior, for example, the sphere of government, religion, or family life. For this reason we refer to Landecker's scheme as a "partial" substruction, one which is not fully worked through in all its logical possibilities.

An even more elaborate relational scheme is implicit in a discussion of "craftsmanship" by C. Wright Mills:

> Craftsmanship as a fully idealized model of work gratification involves six major features: (1) There is no ulterior motive in work other than the product being made and the processes of its creation. (2) The details of daily work are meaningful because they are not detached in the worker's mind from the product of the work. (3) The worker is free to control his own working action. (4) The craftsman is thus able to learn from his work; and to use and develop his capacity and skills in its prosecution. (5) There is no split of work and play, or work and culture. (6) The craftsman's way of livelihood determines and infuses his entire mode of living.[56]

In effect, Mills proposes six attributes by which a job situation

Table 7.3

	Persons and Their Behavior		
	Cultural Standards	Communication	Work
Cultural Standards	1. Cultural integration	2. Normative integration	
Communication		3. Communicative integration	5. ?
Work			4. Functional integration

can be described. If all six of these attributes have the values indicated above, we have the ideal-type situation of "craftsmanship." The situation of the modern industrial or office worker, Mills implies, is the opposite of the idealized craftsman in all these respects. Actually the six attributes give sixty-four logically possible combinations of values; the intermediate, mixed combinations, however, do not enter into Mills' present discussion, which deals only with the ideal-type cases and not with the whole attribute-space.

In this case each of the six attributes actually refers to a relationship—between a worker's capacities and his work, between work and leisure, etc. They can be derived from a relational matrix consisting of four elements: the worker (his capacities, his character); the work activity; the final product; and the worker's leisure activities (his "play," "culture," "general mode of living"). Each of these can act on any of the others, as summarized in the relational scheme (table 7.4).

This scheme might suggest additional dimensions of the man-job relationship to be taken into account, to make for a more systematic classification of work situations. Still more elements might also be added—for instance, the "external rewards," which are not supposed to dominate the craftsman's approach to his work but which are obviously primary for many kinds of jobs.

Formal devices such as attribute-space and relational matrices can often help to clarify concepts which are not systematically

Table 7.4

	Worker	Work Activity	Final Product	Leisure
Acting on: Worker	—	(1) Gratifies (4) Develops	(1) Gratifies	
Work activity	(3) Freely controls	—		(5, 6) Contributes to
Final product		(2) Visibly related to	—	
Leisure		(5, 6) Contributes to		—

presented; sometimes they can even suggest significant possibilities not originally considered. They are not, however, a substitute for careful study and sensitive thinking about a problem. There are any number of possible relationships or attributes which might be picked out and put into a formal scheme; the strategic act is to "feel out" those which are important, which will ultimately help to solve the problems in which we are interested. Formal analysis can then be used to clarify, develop, and communicate the results of qualitative insights.

Qualitative Data Suggesting Relationships

The only fully adequate way to test the existence of a relationship between two variables is through statistical analysis; to test cause-and-effect relations requires either a controlled experiment, or a rather large number of cases of "natural change" observed over time. But research which has neither statistical weight nor experimental design, research based only on qualitative descriptions of a small number of cases, can nonetheless play the important role of suggesting possible relationship, causes, effects, and even dynamic processes. Indeed, it can be argued that only research which provides a wealth of miscellaneous, unplanned impressions and observations can play this role. Those who try to get suggestions for possible explanatory factors for statistical results solely from looking at tabulations of the few variables which were deliberately included in the study in advance often can make no progress; sometimes even a single written-in comment by a respondent will provide a clue to additional factors.

Finding "Factors" Influencing Action

A classic case of the use of qualitative observation to disclose possible factors influencing behavior is the Western Electric study.[57] When the experimental group of workers maintained their high production even when physical conditions were made worse than before the experiment began, it was clear that something else was affecting their production. What the real factors were was first suggested by informal conversations with and observations of the experimental group, and from then on the main research effort was focussed on qualitative interviewing and observation to discover social factors and processes.

A recent study, the main focus of which was to uncover possible factors rather than strictly to test them, is Merton's *Mass Persuasion.* Here some seventy-five people were selected who were known to have bought bonds through a Kate Smith war bond "marathon" broadcast, and interviewed in such a way as to reconstruct their experience during the broadcast as spontaneously as possible. Among the factors which stood out as possibly influential were the fact that "the all-day series of appeals emerged as a dramatic event . . . a single unified pattern"; "there was reciprocal interplay, for the audience was not only responding to Smith, but she was also responding to her audience and modifying her subsequent comments as a result"; "there was considerable qualitative evidence that belief in Smith's disinterestedness and altruism played an integral role in the process of persuasion"; "the audience's images of Smith, the class structure of our society, the cultural standards of distinct strata of the population, and socially induced expectations, feelings, tensions were all intricately involved in the patterns of response to the bond drive"; "but the cumulation of affect and emotion was not the major function of the marathon broadcasts. Above all, the presumed stress and strain of the eighteen-hour series of broadcasts served to validate Smith's sincerity . . . for an understanding of the process of persuasion, the most significant feature of these responses to the marathon is the effectiveness of this propaganda of the deed among the very people who were distrustful and skeptical of mere exhortation."

A study applying the same technique to a broader historical situation was that of Elizabeth Zerner on the factors in recent history which influenced attitudes toward Jews in France.[58] By a very small number of detailed interviews with people who were presumed to be good observers (about half concierges of apartment houses, the other half intellectuals), it was suggested that there were four main events influencing attitudes toward Jews in one manner or another: the persecutions outside France, which made people more aware of the Jews as a special group;

the appearance of Jewish refugees from other countries, who were a clearly visible, different group in French society; the persecution of the French Jews during the occupation, which aroused certain feelings of guilt and a certain real danger for those who helped the Jews; the restoration of Jewish jobs and property after the Liberation, which obviously caused loss and disturbance to some non-Jews.

One special technique for discovering additional factors relevant to a given type of behavior is the examination of cases which deviate from the behavior expected in terms of known factors. Thus a purely economic-interest explanation of voting leaves poor Republicans and rich Democrats as "deviants"; by qualitative interviewing one may be able to get some idea of the factors other than economic interest which motivate voting. In the "Mr. Bigott" study of the response of prejudiced people to antiprejudice cartoons, it was expected that the prejudiced would misunderstand the message of the cartoons—as indeed almost two-thirds did. But there remained deviant cases who understood the "hostile" meaning. To explain these cases, qualitative interviews were used. It appeared that such factors were involved as the degree of security in one's attitudes, the feeling that one's beliefs were socially caused and not a personal responsibility, the fact that the subject totally disidentified himself from the caricatured figure of "Mr. Bigott" and therefore was under no threat.[59]

Qualitative Suggestions of Process

The simplest form of a "process" analysis is that which looks for an intervening variable which "explains" the correlation between two other variables. In his study of an East Coast slum neighborhood, William Whyte arrived (on a qualitative basis) at the following relationship: the socially aspiring "college boys" clubs seemed to be more unstable and subject to internal conflict than those of the non-mobile "corner boys." To explain this relationship (which could be considered quite "upside-down" from a middle-class viewpoint) Whyte introduced a third variable, "informal organization." The corner boy clubs could draw for cohesion on already existing informal organization:

The daily activities of the corner boys determined the relative positions of members and allocated responsibilities and obligations within the group.

Among the college boys on the other hand,

Outside club meetings the members seldom associated together except in pairs. Since there was no informal organization to bind the men together, there was also no common understanding upon matters of authority, responsibility, and obligation.[60]

To be able to assert this explanation with any certainty, it would be necessary for Whyte to have observed corner boy clubs which were weak in informal organization and college boy groups which were strong in it; if the former were also unstable, while the latter were stable, it would constitute a certain test of the hypothesis. Whyte does not record whether he sought out such "test situations" or was familiar with a range of such cases.

In the same way the relation between membership in a corner gang and failure to rise economically was explained in terms of the impact of group relations on saving and spending habits. Whyte denies that preexisting differences in intelligence and ability explain the whole relation (again on the basis of qualitative observations which presumably held ability constant for a number of cases in each group). Whyte goes on to suggest:

The pattern of social mobility in Cornerville can best be understood when it is contrasted with the pattern of corner-boy activity. One of the most important divergences arises in matters involving the expenditure of money. The college boys fit in with an economy of savings and investment. The corner boys fit in with a spending economy. The college boy must save his money in order to finance his education and launch his business or professional career. He therefore cultivates the middle-class virtue of thrift. In order to participate in group activities, the corner boy must share his money with others. If he has money and his friend does not, he is expected to do the spending for both of them. . . . Prestige and influence depend in part upon free spending.[61]

This observation indicates some of the factors in the process of social mobility. Of course behind each such factor uncovered are other factors—the variables which for instance determine who sticks with the boys and spends, and who breaks away, saves money, and rises.

The uncovering of possible processes can go much further than inserting a third variable in a chain. The study of antiprejudice cartoons mentioned previously suggested a whole chain which led up to misunderstandng among the nondeviant two-thirds of the prejudiced people who misunderstood:

1. Identification with Mr. Bigott and momentary understanding
2. Desire for escape from identification
3. Disidentification mechanism (caricaturing Mr. Bigott, making him intellectually or socially inferior)
4. Derailment of understanding: absorption in the derogatory characteristics of Mr. Bigott to the exclusion of understanding the point of the cartoons[62]

In the Whyte study one finds the process of the rise of a local corner boy to political leadership traced out through a series of steps, with interacting forces noted.[63] To get a start, the corner boy must demonstrate his loyalty and ability to get results for his immediate circle of friends. Yet "if he concentrates on serving his own group, he will never win widespread support." "In order to win support he must deal with important people who influence other groups." Since he has only limited resources in terms of energy and access to official favors, he must "betray" his original friends by neglecting their interests and using his resources to help outsiders and big-shots. The result is a widespread cynicism toward "politicians" among the rank and file, which might be expected to cause constant turnover. However, according to Whyte, the politician is normally able to "trickle down" enough benefits to his followers in the district as a whole to prevent a revolt, even though his closest original friends who had the highest expectations may be badly disillusioned. The process reaches a kind of equilibrium, presumably at a level determined by the political abilities, initial "connections," and good luck of the individual politician.

In exploring for possible factors affecting some given variable, or for chains of causes and effects constituting a "process," there appear to be two basic techniques. The first attempts to obtain objective information about the sequence of events, particularly what events preceded the response under investigation.[64] The typical questions, whether addressed to a subject or used by an observer to guide his observations, are: "What happened before X? What happened just before the subject made his decision to move, vote, buy, steal, etc.? What was the frame of mind? What had been going on in the family, neighborhood, nation, world? Had he been talking with anyone, reading anything, listening to anything?" Some responses will look like causal factors immediately, on the basis of our past experience or general hypotheses about human behavior. Others will only become prominent when we notice an apparent correlation between them and the criterion behavior in several cases.

The second technique is to ask people themselves to explain what happened and to give their reasons for acting as they did.[65] The basic question here is always Why? This technique has obvious limitations: people are often unaware of the real motives, of indirect influences, of the precise chain of causes and effects, of underlying necessary conditions. On the other hand it stands to reason that the participant knows a good deal about his own behavior, particularly about attitudes, motives, influences, "trigger events," and so on, and often can tell the outside investigator about things which he would never have guessed by himself. "Reasons" may not be the whole story, but they are an important source of information on possible factors, and in some cases a quite indispensable source, especially in the early stages of investigation. By adding to the general "why" query a set of more specific questions, focussing the respondent's attention on each of several basic aspects of the situation, reason questions can obtain more adequate coverage, although still limited to what the respondent himself is in a position to know.

Both of these techniques are combined in a technique of qualitative exploration of causal relations known as "discerning." This has been carefully described in Mirra Komarovsky's study of the effect of unemployment on the family status of the husband.[66] With only fifty-nine case studies to analyze, it was not possible to undertake a full-scale statistical analysis of the interrelations between all the possible variables. What was done was to take each case of apparent change due to the husband's unemployment and subject it to systematic checks: Had the change already begun before the unemployment? Did other factors arise concurrently with unemployment which might have been the real cause? Are the participants able to trace the step-by-step development of the change, the detailed links between unemployment and the altered role of the husband? If the respondents believe that unemployment was the reason for a certain change, on what evidence do they base their opinion? By these techniques it was possible to isolate with considerable promise of validity the causal relations between unemployment and family structure. The search for "possible factors" and "possible consequences" was made systematic; within the limitations of the data real precautions were taken against spurious relations.

Quasi-Statistics

Previous sections have dealt with operations of qualitative analysis which are essentially prior to quantitative research: observations which raise problems, the formulation of descriptive categories, the uncovering of possible causal factors or chains of causation for a particular piece of behavior. These operations stimulate and focus later quantitative research, and they set up the dimensions and categories along the "stub" of the tables, into which quantitative research may fill the actual frequencies and measurements.

However, one encounters very frequently in social science literature studies which do not use the mechanism of quantitative data collection and statistical analysis, and still make the kind of statements which quantitative research makes. These statements may be simple frequency distributions (i.e., "most Trobrianders" or even "the Trobriander" knows or believes or does so-and-so); they may be correlations (corner boys have a spending economy, while college boys have a saving economy); they may be statements of causal relationships ("If [the politician] concentrates upon serving his own group, he will never win widespread support. . . . In order to win support, he must deal with important people who influence other groups"). Such statements, based on a body of observations which are not formally tabulated and analyzed statistically, may be termed "quasi-statistics." They include "quasi-distributions," "quasi-correlations," and even "quasi-experimental data."

Nonquantitative research of this sort is no longer logically prior to statistical research. It rather directly substitutes for statistical research, making the same kind of statements but on the basis of a recording and analysis of cases which takes place largely within the mind of the observer. This kind of research has obvious shortcomings, but it also has a place in the research process, viewed as a continuing and increasingly refined pursuit by the whole community of social scientists.

An example of the dangers of impressionistic "quasi-statistics" is given by Bernard Barber in an article on participation in voluntary associations:

> American observers themselves were overwhelmed by what they did not fully understand: instance the following from Charles and Mary Beard's *The Rise of American Civilization*: "The tendency of Americans to unite with their fellows for varied purposes . . . now became a general mania. . . . It was a rare American who was not a member of four or five societies. . . . Any citizen who refused to affiliate with one or more associations became an object of curiosity, if not suspicion." Although in comparative perspective the United States may well be a "nation of joiners," a survey of the available data on the number of people with memberships in voluntary associations reveals the little-known fact that many have not even a single such affiliation. This uniformity too holds for all types of areas in the United States, whether urban, suburban, small city, small town or rural.[67]

Barber then quotes statistics showing that in these various areas and strata of the population from one-third to over two-thirds of the people do not belong to any voluntary associations. As one proceeds from simple frequency distributions to correlations and then to systems of dynamic relationships between several variables, impressionistic "quasi-statistics" become steadily less adequate.

On the other hand it is argued that a careful observer who is aware of the need to sample all groups in the population with which he is concerned, who is aware of the "visibility bias" of the spectacular as opposed to the unspectacular case, who becomes intimately familiar with his material over a long period of time through direct observation, will be able to approximate the results of statistical investigation, while avoiding the considerable expense and practical difficulty of quantitative investigation. It has been claimed, for instance, that to provide a fully statistical basis for the conclusions which Whyte was able to draw from his observation of corner gangs and college boys groups, would require hundreds of observers studying hundreds of gangs and neighborhoods over many years.

There are some situations in which formal quantitative methods are apparently less necessary than others. When one is dealing with primitive groups with a nearly homogeneous culture, in which one set of prescribed roles is just about universally carried out by the population, it may require only the observation and interviewing of relatively few cases to establish the whole pattern. The same argument can be applied to studies of a quite homogeneous subculture within a civilized society. These methods seem to have succeeded in presenting a good first approximation at least in the description of the culture and behavior of such groups. When anthropologists now call for formal sampling, data recording, and statistical analysis it is either to catch up finer details—the small number of deviant individuals, for instance—or to deal with situations of culture groups with less homogeneity—with groups in process of acculturation, breakdown of old norms, or the development of strong internal differentiation.

In situations of less homogeneity and simplicity, it is doubtful that quasi-statistics are anything like a full substitute for actual statistics. However, they can still play an important "exploratory" function. Statistical research is too expensive and time-consuming to be applied on all fronts at once; like the 200-inch telescope, it must focus on a few areas of particular interest for intensive study. Quasi-statistical studies can run ahead of the more cumbersome quantitative procedures to cover wide areas of social phenomena, and to probe into tangled complexes of relationship in search of possible "processes." They serve as a broad scanner and "finder" like the wide-angled but less powerful Schmidt telescope of Mount Wilson and Palomar. Moreover, the gathering and analysis of "quasi-statistical data" can probably be made more systematic than it has been in the past if the logical structure of quantitative research at least is kept in mind to give general warnings and directions to the qualitative observer.

Systematic Comparison

There is one special form of research into relationship which stands on the border between statistical and quasi-statistical methods. This involves the systematic comparison of a relatively small number of cases. It differs from quasi-statistics in that the cases are processes along lines closely approximating those of a statistical survey or controlled experiment. However, it involves too few cases to actually apply statistical tests, and it involves natural situations in which one cannot be certain that "other factors are equal" for the various cases beyond those factors specifically analyzed. It is as though one set up the tables for a statistical or experimental research, but had only one or two cases to fill in each cell, and perhaps had to leave some entirely empty.

This form of "comparative research" is the only one possible when the "cases" to be studied are social phenomena of a high order of complexity, such as wars, revolutions, large-scale social systems, forms of government. There do not exist very many cases in recorded history of such phenomena. Toynbee faced this problem in his classic "comparative analysis" of "Great Civilizations"—there were only about twenty-one such civilizations, along with a number of abortive or arrested civilizations.[68] Weber faced the same situation in dealing with the role of religious systems in the development of society.[69] Besides the total number of available cases being small, each is a very large and complex unit which requires great time and effort to analyze. Even where there are a large number of cases, this factor may compel the researcher to restrict himself to the systematic comparison of a few. This situation arises in studying communities or large institutions. To describe any one community's social structure is such a large job that most studies have been of single cases. Only after different researchers over a generation have produced a dozen or so such studies can a "secondary analyst" undertake a comparative analysis. In the long run, it is to be hoped that data-gathering procedures on such complex "cases" can be so simplified that statistical studies will become possible. Then the intensive study of one community, factory, union, government agency, or voluntary association can give way to a quantitative study of a sample of such cases, testing the hypotheses derived from single-case studies. Of course, where the difficulty lies in the fact that there is only a handful of cases at all, the comparative method is the best we can do.

An example of systematic comparison of a small number of cases is offered by Lipset's study of the Canadian province of Saskatchewan.[70] The population of the province, mainly wheat farmers, had a remarkably high level of participation in political affairs and, in seeking explanations for this unusual behavior, comparisons were first made with areas where participation was known to be low.

The amount of participation in public affairs in the large cities of Canada and the United States is notoriously low. This is true even of cities like Toronto and Vancouver, which resemble Saskatchewan in giving a large vote to the new, radical Cooperative Commonwealth Federation (C.C.F.) party. Comparing Saskatchewan with these large cities, Lipset was struck by the smallness of political units in Saskatchewan and the large number of offices to be filled in each. The average rural municipality had fewer than four hundred families, with over fifty elective posts on municipal council and school boards to be filled, while most large cities elect no more officials than that to represent their hundreds of thousands of families.

Besides the small size of Saskatchewan communities, they were relatively lacking in social stratification—almost everyone was a working farmer. In this respect too Saskatchewan is at the opposite pole from the cities, with their wide differences in incomes and their staffs of specialists for performing normal public services. In the cities the positions of responsibility which are available tend to be monopolized by upper-class people and professionals; in Saskatchewan schoolboards, telephone companies, marketing agencies, etc., had to be staffed by ordinary farmers, who thereby acquired organizational and political skills unknown to the average city dweller.

Certain rural areas also are highly stratified, and in such areas the rate of mass participation is also low.

> Within the rural areas of the Southern States or in parts of California, where significant social and economic cleavage exists within the rural community, the wealthier and upperclass farmers are the formal community leaders, and the bulk of the poorer farmers are politically apathetic.[71]

A third structural factor distinguishing Saskatchewan is its exposure to extreme economic fluctuations, due to the unstable price of its one main crop and to the recurrence of drought. In this it can be contrasted with its eastern neighbor, Manitoba, which has more diversified crops, stable markets, and more reliable weather. And it is notable that Manitoba today has much less community and political activity. Low participation is also found in the Maritime Provinces, where the farmers generally have a low standard of living, but do not experience the chronic alternation between wealth and poverty of the farmers of Saskatchewan.

Having isolated these possible sources of high participation by comparing the social structure of Saskatchewan with that of areas of low participation, we can now look for other areas which have equally favorable patterns of social characteristics. The neighboring wheat-belt areas of North Dakota and Alberta have virtually the same characteristics: small political units, little social stratification, and highly unstable economies. And both these areas have widespread community participation through local government and cooperatives, and a readiness to develop new political movements when confronted by economic crisis. The same structural characteristics were found in Manitoba in the 1890s, at which time the Manitoba agrarian political movement evoked widespread participation. When Manitoba's society changed through the development of a large urban center with an upper class and specialized services, and through the diversification of agriculture, which ended the complete dependence on the wheat crop, mass participation in politics fell off. Manitoba thus provides a natural "before-and-after" experiment.

Lipset notes that the same pattern of structural characteristics which exists in Saskatchewan can also be found in communities far removed from the specific conditions of the wheat belt. Merton studied an American industrial community, "Craftown," which was small in size, relatively unstratified, being mainly inhabited by workers, and faced with a series of pressing social and economic problems. This community was found to be much more politically active than neighboring urban areas; its widespread political participation resembled that of the Saskatchewan farmers.[72] The generalization of explanatory factors from "the wheat economy" to attributes applicable to any community obviously opens up a much wider range of cases for use in comparative analysis.

This comparative analysis of areas of high and low participation can be summarized in table 7.5.

In the study just discussed it appears that comparisons were used not only to suggest explanatory factors but also to offer supporting evidence, as a kind of quasi-experimental test. One of the most celebrated instances of such quasi-experimental tests is found in Malinowski's study of the use of magic in the Trobriand Islands.[73] Malinowski wanted to test the old theory that primitive man uses magic because of a childlike confusion of the

Table 7.5
Scheme of Factors Accounting for Political Participation

Economic Fluctuations	Small Social Units	Little Stratification	Cases	Participation
+	+	+	Saskatchewan	High
			North Dakota	"
			Alberta	"
			Manitoba, 1890–1910	"
			"Craftown"	"
(+)	(+)	–	Rural South	Low
			Rural California	"
(+)	–	–	Large cities in U.S. and Canada	"
–	(+)	(+)	Maritime Provinces	"
–	–	–	Manitoba today	"

Note: Attributes in parentheses were not explicitly discussed in the comparisons.

real and the imaginary or because of some instinctive belief in the supernatural. He found the Trobrianders engaging in some activities—for instance, fishing within the lagoons—for which their technology was adequate to permit certain economic returns and personal safety. Other activities—for instance fishing in the open sea—involved uncertainty of return and risks to life which could not be eliminated by available technological means. In the safe and certain activities, no magic was used; in the unsafe and uncertain ones, magic was used a great deal. This supported Malinowski's contention that magic was not a substitute for rational techniques, but a supplement to them when dealing with situations which were beyond the power of available rational technology and which created severe emotional strain.

Of course the use of comparisons of small numbers of cases as tests requires great caution; care must be taken to see that other significant factors are in fact equal, and that cases are selected in an unbiased manner.

Matrix Formulations

Sometimes the analysis of qualitative observations confronts a mass of particular facts of such great number and variety that it seems quite unworkable to treat them individually as descriptive attributes or in terms of their specific interrelationships. In such a situation the analyst will often come up with a descriptive concept on a higher level which manages to embrace and sum up a great wealth of particular observations in a single formula. Take for instance, Ruth Benedict's description of the Zuni Indians, which mentions their avoidance of drugs and alcohol, their lack of personal visions, their placid response to divorce, their "mild and ceremonious" relation to their gods, and so on. After presenting a great many such particular facts, Benedict is able to sum them up in a single formula: The Zuni culture has an Apollonian pattern—that is, a central theme of avoidance of emotional excess. This pattern or theme permeates every aspect of Zuni life.[74] Such a formula capable of summing up in a single descriptive concept a great wealth of particular observations may be called a matrix formulation. This definition covers the notion of a "basic pattern" of a culture, a "theme," an "ethos," a "zeitgeist" or "mentality of the time," a "national character," and on the level of the individual person a "personality type."

Matrix formulations may be applied to complex units at any level. In a study of an unemployed village in Austria, the researchers made a collection of separate "surprising observations." Although they now had more time, the people read fewer library books. Although they were subject to economic suffering, their political activity decreased. Those totally unemployed showed less effort to look for work in other towns than those who still had some kind of work. The children from the unemployed village had more limited aspirations for jobs and for Christmas presents than children of employed people. The researchers faced all kinds of practical difficulties because people often came late or failed to appear altogether for interviews. People walked slowly, arrangements for definite appointments were hard to make, "nothing seemed to work any more in the village."

Out of all these observations there finally arose the overall characterization of the village as the "Tired Community." This formula seemed clearly to express the characteristics which permeated every sphere of behavior: although the people had nothing to do, they acted tired—they seemed to suffer from a kind of general paralysis of mental energies.[75]

In a study of a particular group—people who had been designated as "influentials" in an American community—Merton confronted the problem of explaining their diverse behaviors. Various classifications proved of no avail in accounting for the wide range of observations available. The particular behavior on which the research was focused—the reading of news magazines—remained unexplained. In trying to order the "welter of discrete impressions not closely related one to the others," the researchers finally came up with one general "theme" which distinguished the influentials: some were "cosmopolitan," primarily interested in the world outside the local community, while others were "local," primarily interested in the local community itself. Merton clearly indicates the typical function of such a matrix formulation when he declares:

> All other differences between the local and cosmopolitan influences
> seem to stem from their difference in basic orientation. . . .The difference
> in basic orientation is bound up with a variety of other differences: (1) in
> the structures of social relations in which each type is implicated; (2) in
> the roads they have travelled to their present positions in the influence-
> structure; (3) in the utilization of their present status for the exercise of
> interpersonal influence; and (4) in their communications behavior.[76]

The bulk of the article is then taken up with an elaboration
of this dual matrix formulation in terms of all the specific behaviors which fit into one or the other type of orientation, the
local or the cosmopolitan.

Matrix formulations can thus vary in the level of the unit which
they describe, from a whole culture to a community and to a
status group within a community. They are used right down to
the level of individual personalities, where, for instance, a great
variety of particular behaviors will be summed up in the matrix
formula of an "anal personality" or a "cerebrotonic tempera-
ment." At the personality level they are often referred to as
"syndromes," a term arising out of the physiological level where
it refers to just the same kind of complex of individual facts all
of which can be summed up in one single formula.

Another way in which the matrix formulations can vary is in
terms of the relations between the elements. The elements which
went into Benedict's formulation of an Apollonian culture were
all alike in terms of the variable "emotional tone"—their emotional tone was low in intensity. They all went together in the
same sense that one can classify in a single group all regions
with a very even temperature, or all people with high blood
pressure. In a matrix formulation such as Toennies's gemeinschaft, the elements seem to be involved in causal relations and
processes with one another.[77] The element of "reciprocal trust,"
for example, can be considered as growing out of the element
of "prolonged face-to-face association with the same people,"
as can a great many of the other characteristics of a gemeinschaft
situation. In the matrix formulation of an "anal personality,"
the behavior characteristics are thought of as all arising out of

a single basic factor, the fixation of the erotic development at a certain childish stage. In many of the culture-pattern formulations since Benedict's purely descriptive ones, we find the idea that all of the elements in the pattern are products of the pattern of child training—or even of a single element in the child-training pattern. Some matrix formulations involve a mixture of descriptively related and causally related elements.

Yet another way in which matrix formulas can be differentiated could be called their "projective distance." The following examples should indicate what is meant by this dimension. In Merton's et al. study *Mass Persuasion*, it was found that a wide variety of remarks made by the Kate Smith devotees could be summed up in the notion of "submissiveness to the status quo."[78] They believed that it was right for some to be poor and others rich, they accepted their position in the system of stratification, they rationalized that the rich had so many troubles that it was just as well to be poor. The more general descriptive concept follows very directly from the manifest content of the respondent's statements; they could almost have made the generalization themselves.

In *The Psychology of Social Movements*, Hadley Cantril confronted a collection of interviews and observations of people who join all sorts of marginal political cults like the Townsend groups, Moral Rearmament, the Coughlinites, and so on. Out of the welter of characteristics there emerged the general notion that all of these people were suffering from a lack of orientation in the complexities of the modern world; a need for a frame of reference within which the events of their lives and world affairs could be understandable. The matrix formulation of "need for orientation" seemed to tie together a great many diverse forms of behavior, attitudes, and beliefs on the part of the members of these groups. Now this matrix formulation is further removed from the manifest content of the material than was the formulation in the previous example. There is a greater gap between the formula and what the people actually said in talking about troubles they had and how good it made them feel that their movement told them what was wrong with the world and how it could be corrected. Here the statements and observations collected by the field work are interpreted as projections of a somewhat complex psychological state, which very few of the respondents themselves could directly articulate.

A still greater distance between the manifest content of the material and the matrix formulation which is constructed to express its basic pattern is often found in the characterization of personality types or of the ethos of a culture. In these cases, guided by general theoretical orientations, one may use subtle indicators as a basis for a formulation which appears in some ways contradictory to the manifest content of the material. Verbal expressions and actual behavior patterns apparently indicative of feelings of superiority are interpreted, when seen in the context of more subtle indicators, as evidence of quite the opposite basic outlook. In Benedict's characterization of the Zuni as basically Apollonian, she has to explain away—on the basis of looking beneath the surface—various apparently "Dionysian" elements.[79]

There is a good deal of similarity between the rationale of the matrix formulation and Parsons' discussion of the place of "secondary descriptive systems" in his scheme of social systems based on the unit act:

> When a certain degree of complexity is reached, however, to describe the system in full in terms of the action scheme would involve a degree of elaboration of details which would be very laborious and pedantic to work out. This is true even if description is limited to "typical" unit acts and all the complex detailed variations of the completely concrete acts are passed over. Fortunately, as certain degrees of complexity are reached, there emerge other ways of describing the facts, the employment of which constitutes a convenient "shorthand" that is adequate for a large number of scientific purposes.
>
> . . . It has been seen that the acts and action systems of different individuals, in so far as they are mutually oriented in one another, constitute social relationships. In so far as this interaction of the action systems of individuals is continuous and regular these relationships acquire certain identifiable, relatively constant properties or descriptive aspects. . . . It is not necessary to observe all the parties to a relationship, or all their attitudes, etc., but only enough to establish what is for the purpose in hand the relevant "character" of the relationship. . . .
>
> Thus the primary function of such a secondary descriptive scheme as that of social relationship is one of scientific economy, of reducing the

amount of labor of observation and verification required before adequate judgements may be arrived at. A second function . . .[is] to state the facts in a way that will prevent carrying unit analysis to a point where it would destroy relevant emergent properties.[80]

Parsons gives as examples of secondary descriptive schemes typologies of social relationships, personality types, and descriptive categories applied to groups. While Parsons' concept is not entirely identical with that of the matrix formulation, it illustrates much of the reasoning behind such complex descriptive concepts, which sum up and render manageable a large and varied body of individual points of data.

Qualitative Support of Theory

So far we have mainly discussed ways in which qualitative data can contribute to the formulation of problems, classifications, and hypotheses. Qualitative materials are particularly suitable for this exploratory phase of research: their wealth of detailed descriptive elements gives the analyst the maximum opportunity to find clues and suggestions. For testing hypotheses, on the other hand, the ideal model would be the controlled experiment, with precise measurements on a limited number of preselected variables.

The use of controlled experiments in social science is increasing, but it remains severely limited. Recent years have also seen a great development of quantitative research, employing such rough approximations of the experimental design as the controlled observation of natural processes, or the correlational analysis of cross-sectional surveys. These techniques provide tests for certain theories. There remain, however, major areas in which theories are supported mainly by qualitative data.

The General Problems of Qualitative Support

The word "theory" has actually a number of different meanings, ranging from broad general orientations to precise propositions.[81] The theories for which qualitative support is most often used are relatively large-scale, wide-ranging systems or relationships. For example, large-scale theories of social change must rely upon the qualitative data of historical records; theories of the functioning of organizations and institutions are based largely on qualitative descriptions; theories of personality development grow out of clinical case materials. One calls to mind at once the historical theories of Marx, Weber's institutional analysis, Freud's personality theory, and the later work in their traditions.

In discussing the use of qualitative data to support theory, it should be made clear that more is involved than mere illustration. For illustration, intended to help the writer communicate the meaning of his concepts, purely imaginary examples can be used. Durkheim, for instance, in describing types of suicide, drew on examples from literature as well as real case histories.[82] But for the use we have in mind it is important that the examples be real. Since they are not systematically sampled or precisely measured, they do not offer rigorous proof in any statistical or experimental sense. Yet according to their number, range, and relation to the reader's own experience they offer varying degrees of support or corroboration. It is this function which we wish to examine.

Psychoanalysis, Marxism, and other theories of history in general or of overall personality development are large and complicated structures. The use of qualitative data in supporting such complex theoretical systems is one of the major undeveloped areas for methodological analysis. In order to find manageable illustrations of the use of qualitative data to support theory, we will restrict ourselves to a much simpler type, which may be called "trend theories." These are theories which call attention to one particular trend in society, usually derived from some underlying change in the economic or demographic structure.

We will consider three such theories. Erich Fromm has suggested that a major tendency of our time is "self-alienation," resulting from the insecurities and disruption of social bonds brought about by the rise of the market economy and industrialization. C. Wright Mills suggests that the rise of the big city and the standardization of tastes subject increasing numbers of people to status insecurity. Lasswell proposes the "developmental construct" of the garrison state, which attempts to work out the logical implications of the tendency toward an increasing reliance on military force in international relations.

"Signs of the Times": Qualitative Observations
Supporting Trend Theories

Fromm's theory as a whole is relatively complicated, dealing with the interaction of economic structure, personality, and systems of belief.[83] We will consider one particular aspect of that theory: that the individual, rendered isolated and powerless in the face of impersonal market forces, monopolies, mass organization, and recurring wars, develops "automaton conformity" as a mechanism of escape:

> This particular mechanism is the solution that the majority of normal individuals find in modern society. To put it briefly, the individual ceases to be himself; he adopts entirely the kind of personality offered to him by cultural patterns; and he therefore becomes exactly as all others are and as they expect him to be.[84]

Let us see how Fromm goes about supporting this contention derived from his trend theory. First of all, he wants to demonstrate that it is possible for a person to think thoughts and feel feelings which are not his own but induced from outside. This he does by describing a common hypnotic experiment where it is suggested to a subject that he will do certain things and have certain feelings upon awakening from the hypnotic sleep. This establishes that the phenomenon can exist; however, it involves very special conditions.

Fromm then attempts to show that the same kind of behavior occurs in the daily life of many individuals. To specify what this would involve, he gives a hypothetical example of "pseudo-thinking" in daily life: the man who makes a weather prediction which he believes to be his own thinking, when he is simply repeating what he heard on the radio. He then proceeds to actual observations:

> Many persons looking at a famous bit of scenery actually reproduce the pictures they have seen of it numerous times, say on postal cards. . . .

Or, in experiencing an accident which occurs in their presence, they see or hear the situation in terms of the newspaper report they anticipate.

The average person who goes to a museum and looks at a picture by a famous painter, say Rembrandt, judges it to be a beautiful and impressive picture. If we analyze his judgement, we find that he does not have any particular inner response to the picture but thinks it is beautiful because he knows that he is supposed to think it beautiful.[85]

Fromm gives a number of other observations of pseudo-thinking and feeling: the man whose face goes solemn after he leaves a party where he was "gay"; children who say they "like" to go to school every day; people who believe they are marrying because they want to, while they are only conforming to other people's expectations; the case of a man who "voluntarily" follows the career set by his father but suffers strange difficulties.

Of course Fromm's examples do not provide rigorous proof of the assertion that "the majority of normal individuals" are self-alienated. What Fromm has done is, first, to establish thoughts and feelings. Then he presented a hypothetical example to show how this might happen in daily life. Finally he mobilized a wide range of common observations to show that it actually does occur frequently.

Let us take another example. C. Wright Mills holds that the white-collar worker in urban, mass-production society suffers from an increasing ambiguity and insecurity of social status; he or she is unable to develop a stable self-esteem or a secure prestige status in the eyes of others.[86] Mills presents qualitative observations from various sources. Strategically placed specialists—e.g., personnel directors—report such surprising behavior as the following: a girl typing in a large office was deeply hurt when her chair was replaced with a new one, because the old one had her nameplate on the bottom; office workers attach great importance to objectively meaningless changes in the location of desks, etc. This suggested to Mills the intensity of the effort to retain some identity and status in a standardized environment.

Detailed interviews found other phenomena which fitted in with the notion of a "status panic": routine clerical workers tried to conceal the nature of their own work, and borrow prestige from the firm or industry, by identifying themselves with such phrases as "I am with Saks," or "I work at Time." They saved up their salaries and spent them for an evening at expensive places of entertainment, or for a vacation at a costly resort, in order to "buy a feeling, even if only for a short time, of higher status." A salesgirl dealing with "Park Avenue" customers will try to behave with greater dignity and distinction in her off-the-job contacts than the girl who works on 34th Street.

Such qualitative observations provide support for a theory in several ways. Aside from their own weight, they may call the reader's attention to certain areas of his own experience, which may provide much additional support. Furthermore, when the observations cover many different areas of behavior they gain additional weight, because they indicate that the theory has the ability to account for a wide range of phenomena.

The notion of the "garrison state" as formulated by Lasswell also suggested a trend growing out of basic social changes; however, it was unusual in being formulated not ex post facto but at a very early stage in the process. This is what Lasswell meant in describing it as a "developmental construct"—a trend theory referring not only to the immediate situation but to the future. The substance of Lasswell's theory was a set of consequences which could be expected if the world situation stimulated modern great powers, with modern economies and technology, to all-out development of military strength. Some of these consequences were relatively logical and obvious: the entire labor force would be put to work, political conflicts would be minimized in the interests of national unity, the government would become involved more and more in previously private activities. Others were more of a symbolic nature:

> The distinctive frame of reference in a fighting society is fighting effectiveness. All social change is translated into battle potential.

> The military are therefore compelled to become competent in the skills of technology, administration, and public relations; there is a "merging of skill" between the professional soldier and the manager of large-scale civilian enterprise.

> There is intense concern with public morale and its manipulation; the military "are compelled to consider the entire gamut of problems that arise in living together under modern conditions."[87]

If one wanted in 1953 to see to what extent the predicted trend had become a reality, the developmental construct provides a guiding framework for observation. "All social change is translated into battle potential"—a study of illiteracy in America is discussed mainly in terms of "how many divisions" it costs the army. "The merging of skills"—generals appear on boards of directors of large corporations, and large corporation executives appear in the defense departments. "Intense concern with public morale"—the traditional concern with the morality of school-teachers in terms of smoking, drinking, and sex shifts to a concern with treasonable ideas. In politics the traditional charges of corruption and inefficiency against opponents are replaced by charges of treason, or of failure to build enough air groups.

One or two of these might be isolated events; taken together they begin to build up a "pattern," giving some plausibility to the theory. At this point it becomes important to undertake more systematic studies of the actual extent and degree of militarization, to distinguish its progress in different spheres, etc.

From the few examples presented here, it is hoped that the reader has been able to get an idea of the intermediate role played by qualitative observations in relation to theory—as more than simply illustration, but less than definitive proof. It is likely that there are several degrees or stages of qualitative support, ranging from an initial encouragement to go on with a certain line of speculation, to a systematic examination of case material which offers some approximation to the classical canons of proof. There also may be differences in function according to the type of "theory" involved. The present analysis is only a tentative beginning; there is a great need for intensive work on additional examples of qualitative support of theory.[88]

Now that we are at the end of our survey, it is necessary to add that some of the areas we have distinguished inevitably overlap at their borders. It would be easy to find examples in which it would be difficult to decide whether they have the complexity of a matrix formula. Another set of uncertainties will sometimes arise when we have to decide whether the writer is arguing for a relationship between a few variables or whether he is supporting a rather general theory. Even the very notion of qualitative research has its haziness on the fringes; it would not be easy, for example, to say when the comparative analysis of a few cases shades over into statistical treatment.

The present discussion is a beginning only. It has started from a simple position: that there exists this area of research which is generally considered important but which has not been analyzed methodologically. It has set forward a collection of examples both as an extensional definition of "qualitative analysis" and as material for further study. Besides collecting this material, it has made a preliminary organization of it. There are many problems left unsolved in the discussion.[89] The tentative classifications set forward here need to be tried out on additional materials; more good cases need to be collected and examined. Only after many successive phases of logical formulation and attempted application will the methodology of qualitative techniques come to possess the same usefulness to the research worker which is today possessed by quantitative methodology.

[8]
The Use of Panels in Social Research

The following remarks are designed to draw attention to a fairly recent development in social research. In its bare essentials, the type of study to be discussed consists of repeated interviews made with the same group of persons. The people participating as subjects in such studies are commonly known as panel members and the whole procedure has become widely known under the name of panel technique.

There are two main types of research problems in which the panel technique is likely to be applied. If the effect of some specific event or series of events is to be studied, then we have the first type of situation in which the panel technique may be used. In one such case, a sample of voters in an Ohio county was kept under observation for six months during the 1940 presidential campaign, the purpose being to study what effect the propaganda of the two parties had upon the way people made up their minds.[1] In another case, the American Association for the United Nations wanted to find out the best way of getting Americans more interested in the progress of UN activities. A sample of persons in a Midwest city of about 800,000 was interviewed about their attitudes toward the United Nations and the actions of the United States in foreign affairs. An intensive informational campaign was conducted by this organization and after the campaign was over the same sample was interviewed again.[2] In a similar way, advertising agencies sometimes use panels to study the effectiveness of their promotional efforts.[3]

The other main type of panel study is somewhat more difficult

From *Proceedings of the American Philosophical Society* (1948), 92:405–10. Reprinted by permission. Read February 7, 1948, in the Symposium on Research Frontiers in Human Relations.

to describe because no major findings are yet available in the literature. In a society as complex and changing as our own, the individual is continually placed in a situation where he must reconcile the different and variant elements of his experience. A Quaker who is a convinced pacifist sees the country endangered by an enemy. How will he resolve the conflict between his pacifism and his patriotism? A convinced Communist sees the Soviet Union making moves which he considers imperialistic. How will he reconcile his party loyalty and his intellectual judgment on a specific political issue? But we don't need to remain in the area of big issues to look for problems of this kind. In everyday life almost everyone is continuously under cross-pressures of some kind. People belong to different social groups which may have conflicting interests. The individual must make all sorts of choices among his needs, desires, and situational demands, some of which are relatively important, others relatively insignificant.

The study of people under cross-pressures is one of the major concerns of social science today. In going through recent social science literature one often comes across statements of the following sort, "In getting higher education the English Catholic must choose between ethnic affiliation and religion; he generally chooses to study with his Protestant ethnic fellows at McGill University. . . ."[4] The application of the panel technique to problems of this sort allows a greater degree of analytical precision. It would allow us to state, for example, the proportion of English Catholics who go to McGill for their higher education and the proportion who go to Catholic institutions, and to compare intensively those who resolve the conflict between their ethnic affiliation and their religion in one way with those who resolve this conflict in another.

The understanding of what actually transpires in such situations will make for tremendous gains in the understanding of social change. The application of the panel technique to this area of social science interest will be one of its major contributions. By keeping sets of people under repeated observation, we can register the changes they make in their attitudes, affiliations, habits, and expectations. We can learn which of the various attitudes, affiliations, etc., are more basic and hence more constant and which are more superficial and changeable. We hope to determine, if elements change, which element in a psychological or social situation is the more dominant one controlling the changes in the other factors.

The outstanding example of such a study is that undertaken by Theodore Newcomb of the students of a "progressive" college attended by the daughters of well-to-do families. The faculty of this college was quite liberal but the background of the girls quite conservative. For four years the investigators observed the various ways in which one group of girls resolved this conflict.[5]

The reader who is somewhat acquainted with social science literature will at this point raise a justified question especially with reference to the first type of study. If we want to know the effect of a political campaign or a similar event, why do we have to reinterview the same people? Couldn't we interview one group of respondents before the event and a similar one after the event. By comparing the two, the argument runs, we would get a fairly good idea as to the influence which the event had. Numerous examples of this kind come to mind. Many of us have seen public opinion polls taken, for instance, before and after the President made a major public announcement. If people think better of him after the speech then we are sure the speech was a success. Poll data are available which show that the attitude of the average American to the Russians improved every time they were victorious in a battle during the war and slumped every time the Russians, after the war, made a move against one of their neighboring countries. This type of study is undoubtedly of very great value and is usually called a trend study.[6]

It is important to consider the differences between such trend studies and the panel technique. A considerable amount of additional information is obtained by reinterviewing the same people. The most important difference is our ability to single out in a panel study exactly who are the people who change. Once singled out, the changers can be subjected to more intensive study to determine the psychological and social-psychological elements which operated to produce the changes in question. A trend study may show us the net impact of events on opinion. A panel study can allow us to single out the individuals who changed their opinion in the course of the repeated interviewing, to probe for the psychological meaning of the event, and the role played by the various mass media of communication in the change. By interviewing the same people at least twice, we can answer questions such as the following: Are people more likely to change when they are very interested in an event and follow it in great detail; or when they are only slightly concerned and know of it only in a casual way? Some preliminary evidence seems to show that the latter is more likely to be the case. There are many proverbs which claim that men are more apt to shift than women and many others which claim the exact opposite. The panel technique permits us to say whether men or women are more likely to shift their opinions. Incidentally, the results so far do not seem to point to any sex differences.

The study of actual changes often leads to unexpected results. At the time that Senator Black was appointed a judge of the Supreme Court, he was accused of having been at one time a member of the Ku Klux Klan. It happens that there is some information available on who was affected by this allegation which suddenly threatened to change the image of a liberal into that of a reactionary. Although Senator Black received about the same amount of approval before and after the allegation, a kind of game of musical chairs took place. Jews and Catholics turned against him while about an equivalent number of Protestants were more in favor of his appointment than before the storm broke.[7]

The last example points to a second value of the panel technique. Trend studies often indicate that an event has not brought about any net change in opinion. But it might very well be that underneath this apparent constancy, there is a great amount of shifting of positions which can only be found out if the same people and their attitudes are traced over a period of time. At the beginning of the present 1948 presidential campaign, there is some indication of a new development in American politics. As long as Roosevelt was alive, there was a strong feeling in the population that the Democratic Party was the party of the common man whereas the Republicans represented more the interests of the wealthier sections of the population. There are indications that this appraisal of the two parties has changed somewhat and that voters, especially among the working class, are less sure than before which of the two parties represents their interests better.

Suppose that one further development takes place (for which there is no evidence but which we bring in to make our example more dramatic); some sections of the business community might feel that their interest in an active recovery program in Europe is better served by a Democratic administration. Then we might have at this moment an internal shift in the social stratification of the two parties which might go beyond any net change in both which polls or the election might show up. Such a social restratification of the major parties has taken place several times in the political history of this country. The historian looking back over this period many decades hence will not miss such a development. But if we want to know and understand it at the time it happens, we have to make studies of repeated interviews with the same people.

This is not the place to go further into detail on the comparison of panel and trend studies.[8] We shall turn rather to the other type of panel study in order to show briefly some of its considerably more complex technical aspects. Table 8.1 exemplifies some of the technical difficulties. It is taken from a small group of people who were interviewed twice during a presidential election. Each respondent was asked two questions: how he intended to vote and whether he felt that the Republican candidate if elected would make a good President. Because both questions were each answered on two different occasions by each respondent we have four pieces of information about each member of the panel. Table 8.1 classifies these replies first according to

Table 8.1

First Interview	Second Interview				
	Dem. Ag.	Dem. For	Rep. Ag.	Rep. For	Total
Dem. Against	68	2	1	1	72
Dem. For	11	12	0	1	24
Rep. Against	1	0	23	11	35
Rep. For	2	1	3	129	135
Total	82	15	27	142	266

whether they were obtained at the first interview or at the second. For each interview we can then subclassify the respondents into four groups: those who wanted to vote Democratic and who were also personally opposed to the Republican candidate; those who wanted to vote Democratic but personally respected the opposing candidate; those with Republican vote intentions who, however, disapproved of their party's candidate; and, those with Republican vote intentions who also approved of the candidate.

All the information which can be obtained from two questions and two interviews with the same respondents can be represented in the type of table shown as table 8.1. Let us first look at the last column. Most Democrats are against the person of the Republican candidate and most Republicans are for him. But 59 of the 266 respondents have a kind of personal detachment. Twenty-four Democrats think that the opposing candidate is all right while 35 Republicans, although they intend to vote for their party, obviously wish that another candidate had been put up.

Now let us look at the bottom row of figures which come from the second interview. The number of people with such detached views has decreased. Obviously, what the campaign has done is to intensify partisan feeling. Only 15 Democrats now have a good word to say about the Republican candidate and only 27 Republicans have any doubts left about him.

But that is not all that we would like to know from this table. How do people reconcile their vote intention and their opinion on a specific issue? Do the Democrats who like the opposing candidate shift to him or do they remain Democrats and start to see him in a darker light? The answer is given in the second row of our table. There is only 1 case of the former, but 11 cases of the latter type. And it so happens that similar figures prevail for the Republicans. Let us look at the third row where we find the respondents who at the first interview intended to vote Republican but didn't like their candidate. One of them switched to the Democrats but 11 now feel better toward their candidate. In this one case there is no doubt that most people adjust their cross-pressures in a one-sided direction. If their party loyalties are in conflict with a specific opinion of their own they are rather more likely to maintain their party loyalties and change their opinion.

This is of course just one example from which no general conclusion should be drawn. But it shows the type of problem and the type of procedures which derive from the use of the panel technique. Just for the record it might be mentioned that the statistical analysis of tables like table 8.1 is quite difficult and proper procedures are still in the process of development. It can easily be seen how many more problems would arise if we had more than two interviews and more than two questionnaire items to deal with.

Besides the difficulties in analysis discussed above, there is one other drawback of the panel technique. There is a danger that we may change our respondents' attitude by the very fact that we reinterview them repeatedly. In some cases the danger is obvious. Suppose, for example, we interview people during a vaccination campaign. If we repeatedly ask people whether they have been vaccinated, our interviewers will probably act as reminders and speed up the success of the campaign in our panel beyond the performance of the population at large. In this case, then, the results of our study will be quite misleading. It could of course happen that our interviewers antagonize the respondents and as a result they might be less likely to get vaccinated. In other cases the panel bias is not likely to be marked. If interest in an election is high and everyone talks about it, the fact that a respondent has been asked about his vote intentions is not going to influence him very much. In any case this is a matter for concrete study. We cannot tell in advance whether bias is likely to exist or not.

Actually, a few such studies of bias have been made. The technique used is fairly simple. At the time the panel is picked out a second group of respondents known as a "control group" is set up as closely matched to the panel as possible. This second group, however, is not interviewed until the whole panel study nears its end. At the time the last interview is made with the panel, the control group is also interviewed. From a statistical point of view the two groups were originally alike and should therefore at the end of the study show the same distribution of attitudes were it not that the panel group was interviewed repeatedly. Whatever significant differences show up between the two groups can be attributed to the effect of the panel bias.

Two examples should give an idea of how much work there is still to be done in this direction. During a presidential campaign it was found that the distribution of opinions in the panel was no different than in the control group. But the panel made up its mind somewhat quicker. Under the impact of the repeated interviews the "Don't Knows" in the end were less numerous in the panel than in the control group. This is a very encouraging result. On the other hand it was found that if people were repeatedly interviewed about their newspaper reading habits the panel group was likely to do more newspaper reading than the control group. The reappearance of the interviewer obviously stimulated the reading interests of the panel members. There was some indication, however, that approximately from the third interview on this effect became less and less marked. It might very well be that if the panel had gone on longer, the panel bias would have disappeared in the end.

There are many operational problems involved in panel studies just as in any other large-scale research operation. How can we get people to participate in a panel and to stick to it? How do we substitute for unavoidable losses? Is it sometimes possible to correspond with panel members by mail rather than to make personal contacts? Should we handle a panel as the American Senate is handled, always substituting new members for part of it?

Finally, there are a number of serious statistical problems to be dealt with. They all center around the concept of turnover. Tables 8.2 and 8.3 exemplify the problem. They each represent one question on which people have been interviewed twice.

In the first question (table 8.2) 100 people changed their minds one way or another. On the second question (table 8.3) 200

Table 8.2

First Interview	Second Interview		
	Yes	No	Total
Yes	50	50	100
No	50	850	900
Total	100	900	1,000

Table 8.3

First Interview	Second Interview		
	Yes	No	Total
Yes	400	100	500
No	100	400	500
Total	500	500	1,000

people did so. One might feel that the turnover on the second question is therefore greater. But one must consider that many fewer people said yes to the first question at the time of the first interview. One therefore cannot expect as many people to change as in the second case. It might be more advisable to compute the turnover as percentage of the people who said yes both times. This would give a turnover of 200 percent for the first and 50 percent for the second table and now we would have to say that the first question has the larger turnover. There are obviously still many other ways in which turnover can be described. What index we can use to describe best the turnover in such tables is a very vexing problem, especially because most all of the statistical treatment of panel data goes back to this one point. But this is not the place to deal with such technical matters at length. It is preferable to end up with some more general theoretical considerations which will show the place panel studies are likely to hold in the social sciences in the coming years.

Basically, what we do in a panel study is relate information obtained at one time to information obtained at a subsequent time. We are in the center of what has come to be called dynamic social research. We study changes and we want to explain these changes. We know who changed and we have information on people prior to their change. Explaining the change necessarily means to relate this previous information to the subsequent change. Everything will depend therefore upon how ingenious we are in deciding what information we should gather at different time periods. To exemplify the problem more clearly, let us assume that we are dealing with a panel of people who are about to move into a public housing project where Negroes and whites will live together.[9] If we center our attention on the whites then we know in advance that some of them will get along with their Negro fellow tenants and some will not. Some will improve their ability to get along with people of other races and some will not. What information should we collect from all these prospective tenants prior to the time they move into the housing project to help us explain what shifts in racial attitudes will take place?

We will obviously want to know their race attitudes prior to their entrance into the housing project. But it will also be important to know their *expectations*. It may turn out that the greater their initial uneasiness the more will they be pleasantly surprised by reality. On the other hand we know that some people have a hard time experiencing "reality," and if they enter a situation with apprehension they behave nervously and start trouble. Some sort of index of psychological flexibility is needed.

Pieces of information about the psychological predisposition of the respondents have been called *intervening variables* because they intervene, as it were, between the individual's reaction and the situation in which he is placed.[10] In the example given above, where a group of individuals are about to enter a public housing project, we have people who will be subject to the same external experience. They will, however, react differently. Between the external situation and the individual response there intervene certain psychological and social characteristics which channel the response in an individually characteristic fashion. Social psychologists in recent years have developed out of their experience many hypotheses as to which intervening variables are of importance. We talk of a person's *level of aspiration* or of a person's *expectations*, indicating that we consider that such information will be of value in interpreting how the individuals will react to the situations in which they are placed.

The important intervening variables have to be ascertained before expected changes take place. To follow through with the example given above, we should know as much as we can about the panel members before they move into the interracial housing project. Once they have been living there it is too late to look for such information, for we can never know then whether what we have found has not already been influenced by their new experience. This is, of course, exactly where the importance of the panel technique lies. We periodically study people's attitudes, expectations, and aspirations. We find out what has happened to them between interviews: what they read, with whom they talked, what external events impressed them, etc. Both the situational factors and the intervening variables change continuously. Our analysis would weave back and forth from these two series of data, expressing, in one case, reaction to the situation as a function of some psychological predisposition, and, in another, the psychological predisposition as a function of the changing situation. We would want to know how people's expectations affect the way they react to changes in their environment; and how the environment experienced changes their hopes and concerns.

On more than one occasion it has been said that one of the difficulties which impede the progress of social science is the fact that we cannot experiment with human beings in the same way that the agricultural station experiments with animals and plants. It should not be overlooked, however, that life itself is in a very real sense a continuous series of experiments. In the course of time, almost everything conceivable and sometimes things previously inconceivable happen to one group of persons or another. Although many of these events are, as yet, unpredictable, some events, fortunately for our purpose, occur with sufficient regularity or frequency so that if we know just what sort of persons will be subject to them, we can observe the various ways in which they will respond. Panel studies are conducted, usually, on the impact of events of a given predictable regularity such as voting in a presidential election, exposure to certain advertising, etc. If we find the right statistical technique we will be able to interrelate "stimulus, predisposition, and response" and with time and experience our hope is to understand, predict, and control human behavior more successfully.

The panel technique discussed here is an expensive and rather slow research operation. A social science, unfortunately, will not develop overnight, and, if we want to develop one, we will have to pay for it in time and money. We cannot prefer mere speculation because it comes to us quickly or simpler methods like cross-sectional polls and artificial laboratory experiments because they are cheap. The panel technique is just in its beginnings—we have just begun to explore some of the implications of its use—and most of its future development will require long and arduous work. Among the many lines along which the methods of the social sciences are developing, the panel technique seems to be one of the most promising for the future of a fuller understanding of human behavior.

Friendship as Social Process:
A Substantive and Methodological
Analysis

with ROBERT K. MERTON

In certain respects, the field of sociology can be aptly described in terms of numerous schools of substantive theory. In a book such as Sorokin's *Contemporary Sociological Theories,* for example, each school is marked off from the others by the substantive class of "factors" which it provisionally takes as the basic determinant of social and cultural patterns; factors such as the geographic or the biological, the demographic, economic, or technological. Increasingly, however, such a description needs to be supplemented by others. Not, of course, that these schools of thought have dropped from sight, but only that they no longer constitute the major forms for organizing the greater part of work now going forward in sociology. Indeed, the major alignments are not so much in terms of schools emphasizing different substantive factors as in terms of what might be called styles of intellectual life.

One such line of division is that between the generalizers and the empiricists, between the sociologists primarily concerned with developing substantive doctrines which go well beyond presently available data and the sociologists primarily concerned with extending the range of certified facts in hand. Another line of division, and the one most in point for this paper, is that

From Morroe Berger, Theodore Abel, and Charles Page, eds., *Freedom and Control in Modern Society* (New York: D. Van Nostrand, 1954). Copyright © 1954 D. Van Nostrand. Reprinted by permission.

between sociological theories which, comprised of concepts and propositions about social behavior, are substantive in character, and methodology which, comprised of statements about the logic of inquiry, is necessarily formal, rather than substantive, in character. The substantive interest in sociology centers on the assumptions that give rise to hypotheses about social life; the methodological interest, on the assumptions that make for the clarification and empirical testing of those hypotheses. The one is primarily concerned with the *what* of sociological inquiry; the other, with the *how*.

It is readily agreed, in principle, that substantive and methodological analyses of sociological problems are both indispensable; that they are, indeed, complementary. But this ready agreement is relatively uninstructive unless it results in more clearly defining the distinctive role of each type of analysis and the ways in which the two interlock. How, for example, is substantive sociological analysis clarified by being restated in the formal terms of methodology? What, if anything, is lost in the course of this formal reanalysis of substantive propositions? By dealing with questions such as these in the detailed examination of a case in point, this paper is intended to bring out some of the respects in which substantive and methodological inquiry complement one another. The substantive case in point is that of the social processes involved in the formation, maintenance, and disruption of friendship; the methodological concern is to identify the logical framework of variables presupposed by a substantive analysis of these processes.

Both parts of the paper—the substantive and the methodological—have a direct and considerable relation to some of the recorded intellectual interests of the sociologist Robert M. MacIver. In several of his works, Professor MacIver has evidenced an abiding interest in the analysis of social processes. Not only does he remind us, for example, that "the social sciences are deeply engrossed in the study of social processes," but, in company with other sociologists, he has singled out for special attention the kinds of social process which are involved in "modes of dynamic relationship, particularly the ways in which people become associated or dissociated."[1]

On the substantive side, Professor MacIver has plainly put

the major question with which we are concerned in the special case of the close primary ties involved in intimate friendship. To put it in his own words: "We must . . . consider integration as a social-psychological process operating within the group. How far, under what conditions, and with what limitations does this process actually occur?"[2]

Moreover, Professor MacIver dwells upon the conceptual distinction which is at the heart of the processual analysis of friendship that follows—the distinction between the social and the cultural, between social ties (or interpersonal relations) and a consensus or dissensus of ideas (or values). Among his many statements of this conception, we select one which can serve, almost without the change of a word, to introduce the substantive part of this paper (dealing as it does, with the dynamic interplay of interpersonal attachments and values):

> The principle of integration combines and even confuses two quite different forms of group unity. There is a difference between the subjective harmony of the attitudes of group members toward one another and the harmony of ideas. We can observe in many groups a social unity within which people feel at one though their opinions still differ.[3]

Substantively, then, this paper may be thought of as dealing with these several observations by Professor MacIver; it is an analysis of certain social-psychological *processes* through which *social relations* interact with *cultural values* to produce diverse patterns of friendship.

On the methodological side, too, there is a bridge between conceptions set forth by Professor MacIver and the concerns of this paper. He has recognized that the empirical study of social process—for example, the persisting or changing patterns of interaction between friends—requires examination of the interplay of *specified variables*; that it is not enough to analyze the process in terms which draw upon an unspecified and, therefore, often changing array of implied variables. He has noted, for example, that in the study of social relationships, conceived as social process, the adjustment of interests and attitudes must be "assessed at every stage of the process."[4]

The methodological part of this paper deals with precisely that problem by attempting to specify analytical research operations appropriate for the study of phases in the social process involved in maintaining or disrupting a social relationship.

This paper, then, is conceived as an example of the interlocking use of substantive conceptions (both theoretical and empirical) and of methodological or formal conceptions in the analysis of a particular type of sociological problem. It is intended to explore, through detailed illustration, the nature of that triple alliance between theoretical statements, empirical data, and methodology which, as Professor MacIver's works indicate, is required to advance disciplined knowledge about social processes.

PART ONE—SUBSTANTIVE ANALYSIS

(by R. K. Merton)

This analysis of friendship as social process is drawn from a study, begun some years ago, of social organization and interpersonal relations in two housing communities: Craftown, a project of some seven hundred families in New Jersey, and Hilltown, a biracial, low-rent project of about eight hundred families in western Pennsylvania.[5]

Among other things, we sought to identify the networks of intimate social relationships in these communities. As a first step, Hilltowners and Craftowners were asked to designate their "three closest friends, whether they live in Hilltown (Craftown) or not." In both communities, about 10 percent reported that they did not know as many as three persons whom they could properly describe as really close friends. But the rest had no such difficulty. This resulted in the identification of a cumulative total of almost two thousand friends by Hilltowners and Craftowners, with roughly half of these living in the same community as the informants.[6]

From data of this kind, it was a short further step to search out patterns in the selection of close friends with respect to likeness or difference of attitudes and values or of social status (for example, of sex, race, and age, social class, organizational affiliation, and standing in the local community). Although this is not the place to present these findings in detail, a short general summary is needed as context for our discussion of friendship as social process. Within each community, it was found that the degree of similarity of status attributes of close friends varied greatly for different attributes, running a gamut from the almost complete limitation of intimate friendships among those of the same race and sex,[7] to entirely negligible selectivity in terms of educational status. We found, further, that for some of the *same* social attributes, the degree of selectivity differed widely between the two communities. There was, for example, a relatively high degree of selectivity in terms of religious affiliation in Hilltown, and relatively little in Craftown. The social and cultural context provided by the community went far toward determining both the general extent of selecting status similars as close friends and the particular statuses for which such selectivity was most marked. Thus, the more cohesive community of Craftown consistently exhibited a lower degree of selection of status similars as friends; but when such selectivity did occur, it was as likely to be in terms of *acquired* statuses—those resulting from the individual's own choice or achievement—as in terms of *ascribed* statuses such as nativity and age, which are fixed or predetermined at birth. In Hilltown, on the contrary, selectivity was much more marked in terms of ascribed status, since there was less by way of overarching community purposes to focus the attention of residents on locally achieved or acquired statuses.

From these and comparable findings, it soon became evident that the problem of selection was not adequately formulated by the familiar and egregiously misleading question: When it comes to close friendships, do birds of a feather actually flock together? Rather, it is a more complex problem of determining the degree to which such selectivity varies for different kinds of social attributes, how it varies within different kinds of social structure, and how such selective patterns come about. Our efforts to deal with the first two questions must be left to the complete report of the study; part of the effort to deal with the third question is described in this paper.

Before turning to the analysis of friendship as a social process, however, we must consider a note on terminology.

A Terminological Note

Oddly enough, the English language lacks a word to signify a tendency for friendships to form between people of "the same kind" just as it lacks a word to signify a tendency for friendships to form between those of differing kinds. This is odd because our technical, if not our popular, vocabulary does include words to designate comparable selective tendencies; for example, tendencies for marriage between persons who are alike in one or another respect (this being called *homogamy*) and for the complementary pattern of marriage between persons who are unlike (this being called *heterogamy*).[8] They arrange these matters better among the savage Trobrianders whose native idiom at least distinguishes friendships within one's in-group from friendships outside this social circle.[9] Since our language does not make the appropriate distinction with which we shall be concerned in this paper, terms must be coined for the purpose (since it would probably be unwise to borrow the exotic Trobriand terminology).

Perhaps we shall be allowed, therefore, to summarize the fifteen-word phrase, "a tendency for friendships to form between those who are alike in some designated respect" by the single word *homophily*, and to summarize the complementary phrase, "a tendency for friendships to form between those who differ in some designated respect," by the correlative word *heterophily* (thus following the comparable terminological practice long since established for types of marriage).[10]

These terms offer more advantages than mere economy of language, although this alone might be enough to justify their coinage. They also help us to escape from the practice, encouraged by loose terminology, of assuming that *either* people of like kind "flock together" *or* they do not, rather than seeing this as a matter of degree. We shall find it possible, and useful, to speak of "degrees of homophily," as measured by indices of positive correlation between the attributes of friends, or of "degrees of heterophily," as measured by indices of negative correlation.

This terminological usage will also help us to distinguish readily between *types* of assortative friendship, according to the character of the designated resemblances between friends. For example, we draw a distinction between *status homophily* (observed tendencies for similarity between the group affiliation of friends or between their positions within a group) and *value homophily* (observed tendencies toward correspondence in the values of friends). Following the same terminological principle, we can easily register, with brevity and relative precision, even more specific patterns of selection in friendship: comparing the degree of religious status homophily, say, with the degree of political status homophily. In short, these terms, brought into being by necessity, may have the virtue of facilitating the analysis of friendship behavior by suggesting research problems, some of which, we must report, had escaped our notice until the application of these terms had forced them on our attention.[11]

Selective and Adjustive Processes in Value Homophily

What precedes is by way of prelude. This section will consider selective and adjustive processes in friendship, the discussion being rooted in our empirical materials but branching out to report inferences drawn from these materials.

In this respect, the concern of this discussion differs substantially from that of most empirical studies of patterns of friendship. These deal primarily with the question Who tends to form friendships with whom? But, to the best of my knowledge, empirical studies have not attempted to analyze the processes through which these patterns come about. To be sure, sociologists have never lost sight of the principle that social relations are sustained by social processes, as can be seen, for example, in the "Sociological Analysis of the Dyad" by Howard Becker and Ruth Hill Useem.[12] Nevertheless, the empirical study of friendship has typically been focussed on observed patterns of friendship rather than on the processes which give rise to them. It is clear, however, that the observed patterns can in turn be conceived as the resultants of social interaction, as process rather than product, and it is this conception which is being explored here.

By "selective and adjustive processes in friendship" we mean patterned sequences of social interaction between friends in which each phase generates and regulates the subsequent phase in such manner as to give rise to the observed patterns of friendship between people of designated kinds. In principle, one phase is said to "generate" the next when the conditions obtaining at one time prove to be both necessary and sufficient for the relationship obtaining at the next time of observation. We say that this is so "in principle" because, at the still-primitive stage reached by sociological analyses of social processes, it must be considered adequate if, in actual practice, we can identify the sufficient antecedent conditions without being able to show that they are also necessary.

Throughout our studies of friendship, it has been provisionally assumed that the observed patterns of status homophily—the positive correlation between the statuses of close friends—are, to some significant but unknown extent, the products of an underlying agreement between the values harbored by friends. The dynamic role of similarities and differences of these values in forming, maintaining, or disrupting friendships therefore requires notice in its own right.

Racial Attitudes

As a case in point, we consider the racial attitudes and values of Hilltowners, and their dynamic role in local patterns of friendship. These values are singled out because in Hilltown, with its equal number of Negro and white families, they have great meaning for residents. They may therefore affect patterns of intimate association among those who hold these values (just as our studies have found that political values affect personal association in the intensely political atmosphere of Craftown). These attitudes toward race vary in many, sometimes minute, respects, and no single classification can do justice to their every nuance of detail. For our present purposes, however, it is enough to divide Hilltowners roughly into three types, in terms of their racial values and perceptions.[13]

The first type embraces the Hilltowners who believe that "colored and white people should live together in housing projects" and who support this belief by saying that the two racial groups "get along pretty well" in Hilltown itself. Since their values and their perception of local experience are both consistent with a liberal turn of mind in matters of race relations, these will be called the "liberals." At the other end is the second type, made up of those residents who maintain that the races should be residentially segregated and who justify this view by claiming that, in Hilltown, where the two races do live in the same project, they fail to get along. This kind of consistency between belief and appraisal of the local situation qualifies these residents to be called racial "illiberals." Between these two types is a third, holding an ambivalent position: these residents believe that the races should not be allowed to live in the same project, even though it must be admitted that they have managed to get along in Hilltown. In describing this type as "ambivalent," we mean only that they cannot buttress their opposition to coresidence of Negroes and whites, as the illiberals do, by saying that it inevitably leads to interracial conflict. The logically possible fourth type, comprised by those advocating interracial projects and reporting unsatisfactory race relations in Hilltown, is an empirically empty class and is therefore omitted from further consideration.

With these types before us, we can now ask: Do close friends in Hilltown tend to share the same values and further, what is the bearing of similarity or difference of values upon the formation, maintenance, and disruption of friendship? Is there, in other words, a pattern of value homophily and if so, how does it come about?

To answer these questions, it is obviously necessary to devise appropriate indices of homophily and heterophily. We can develop such indices by tracing out the logic of what is ordinarily meant by saying that particular kinds of people usually choose friends of the same kind in their community. This means, presumably, that the proportion of their friends having the designated similar characteristic (of social status or, in this instance, of racial values) is appreciably greater than the proportion of people with this characteristic in the local population. That is to say, they tend to *overselect* similars as friends and, at the extreme, to confine their friendships to individuals of like kind. Thus, if value homophily does obtain among Hilltowners, then the proportion of friendships involving liberals will be significantly larger than the proportion of liberals in the Hilltown population at large. They will have more liberal friends than "would be expected" under the hypothesis that they choose their friends without regard to their racial values (or without regard to the statuses correlated with those values). Correlatively, if heterophily obtains, they will have fewer liberal friends than would be expected.

By the "expected" proportion, then, we mean nothing other than the proportion of the local population falling in the designated category. To find out if overselection or underselection occurs, this expected proportion needs to be compared with the "observed" proportion of friends in that category. Thus, we can form indices of homophily and heterophily, expressed in terms of percentages, by computing the excess of observed over expected frequencies of designated friendships, divided by the expected frequency, and multiplied by 100. If there is no homophily at all, this percentage will of course equal zero. The higher the *positive* percentage (overselection) of friends of the same kind, the greater the degree of homophily and, correlatively, the higher the *negative* percentage (underselection) of friends of the same kind, the greater the degree of heterophily.[14]

Among the white residents of Hilltown, there are definite patterns of friendship in terms of racial values.[15] What is more, these patterns take the shape to be expected, if the similarity of values does indeed make for the formation and continuance of close friendships. First of all, we find that the residents having consistent racial values—the liberals, at one pole, and the illiberals, at the other—tend to overselect friends among those having the same values. The liberals overselect other liberals by 43 percent; the illiberals, other illiberals, by 30 percent. Correlatively, liberals underselect illiberals as close friends by 53 percent, and illiberals underselect liberals by 39 percent.

But these patterns of value homophily contrast notably with the pattern exhibited by white Hilltowners with *ambivalent* racial attitudes. These residents truly reflect their ambivalence in their interpersonal relations: they manifest neither homophily nor heterophily. They simply do not overselect or underselect, as shown by such entirely negligible departures from zero as 2 and 3 percent. It is as though the ambivalent Hilltowners were expressing their uncertain and inconsistent racial values in a pattern of associating in proportionate measure with all three types of residents: liberals, ambivalents, and illiberals.

These general findings provide a point of departure for discussing the chief problem in hand: What are the dynamic processes through which the similarity or opposition of values shape the formation, maintenance, and disruption of close friendships? On this matter, the very limitations of these data prove instructive. True, we deal here with only one set of values, and, to this extent, we abstract greatly from the many values which find expression in social interaction. But these simplified findings carry further implications: for if some degree of value homophily—as we call the selection of friends on the basis of common values—occurs when even a single set of values is held in common, then it would presumably be all the greater if several sets of values were held in common. In a sense, we are exploring the limiting case and what holds for it should hold, *a fortiori*, for those cases which better approximate the hypothesis that common values promote the formation or maintenance of close friendship. This study is a first approximation and, manifestly, there is need for extension and further empirical testing of the hypothesis.[16]

The Dynamics of Value Homophily*

Whether one or many values are involved, research findings such as these need to be supplemented by data of quite another

---

* Content units of this section of the chapter have been bracketed and coded for purposes of the methodological analysis which follows in part 2. The coding is of two kinds:

1. Each of the content units has been assigned an identifying *letter*. These will be used in our later analysis when we wish to refer to a particular statement in this substantive section.
2. Each of the content units has also been assigned one or more *numbers*. These designate the analytic operations contained or implied in the statement. To anticipate the later discussion, four major analytic operations will be distinguished in part 2. These are:
   (1) the analysis of sequence rules
   (2) the analysis of chains
   (3) the elaboration of variables
   (4) the elaboration of categories

In addition, lines of the text which contain references to the *mechanisms* by which the patterns come about have been marked with an asterisk.

The reader need not pay particular attention to this coding at this point; it will, however, be essential for reexamination of the substantive content in the light of the methodological analysis in part 2.

kind if we are to acquire an understanding of the role of values in the formation of friendships. These statistical indices simply represent the patterns of friendship as they existed *at a particular moment*—in this case, as they were observed at the time of our field interviews. But, of course, these friendships are in fact continually in process of change—some being only in the early stages of formation, others long and firmly established, and still others, for one reason or another, being well along toward dissolution. Static observations, made at a given instant, tempt one to drop this obvious fact from view. Yet we cannot afford to become imprisoned in the framework of fact that happens to be at hand, even if breaking out of this narrow framework means leaving demonstrated fact for acknowledged conjecture. ⌉ A–4

In other words, we must form a picture or a model of the dynamic processes, both social and psychological, of which the observed patterns of friendship are merely the resultants. And since our explorations provide scanty and scattered rather than systematic evidence bearing on such processes, this model must remain, for the time being, largely a matter of supposition. Nevertheless, it may be useful to report our conjectures, growing out of these limited materials, since little enough is known about the dynamic processes that give rise to the observed patterns of an overrepresentation among those with concordant values.[17]

In picturing the processes leading to value homophily, let ⌉ us consider first the early social contacts between people having identical or compatible values. To the extent that these B–1(a), 3 values are given expression, first contacts will be mutually* gratifying and, in some proportion of cases, will motivate per-* sons to seek future contact (or, at the least, not to avoid future⌡ contact). The racial liberals in Hilltown, for example, who ⌉ express their views and find these seconded by like-minded acquaintances have a doubly rewarding experience: they have* C–4 the satisfaction of voicing deep-seated feelings and the further* satisfaction of having these opinions endorsed by others. In*⌡ some proportion of cases, this early series of gratifying ex-⌉ periences will motivate them to seek continued contact and* gradually result in a strong personal attachment. Particularly if propinquity or social organization facilitates further contact, D–3,4

this process of growing interpersonal attachment and of cu-*
mulative reinforcement of values will presumably take place*
in an appreciable proportion of cases.   ⌐

It cannot be supposed, of course, that like-minded persons ⌐
will invariably express a particular value—for example, their
racial values—during their *early* contacts. In cases where this
does not occur, they will not be motivated to seek one another*
out, so far as this one value is concerned. Among these residents, however, some proportion, albeit smaller than in the
cases where they have early discovered their unanimity of
opinion, will meet again and, sooner or later, although perhaps
much later in the history of their relationship, they will have   E-1
occasion to express this particular value. By this time, some
of these will have formed a personal attachment on other
grounds, and the delayed discovery of their common racial
values will serve to reinforce their relationship, through the*
process of mutual gratification, as this has been described for*
the first group of like-minded residents.   ⌐

For those with similar values, then—whether they both be
liberals or illiberals—social contact, because it is rewarding,*
will motivate them to seek further contact. In due course, the*
proportion of these repeated contacts eventuating in close
friendships will be sufficient to produce a pattern of value
homophily along the lines observed in our data on the overselection of like-minded friends. This sketchy picture of the
processes of social interaction between those with antecedent
similar values is consistent with the observed correlation between the values of friends (insofar as these are not owing to
the mutual accommodation of values after the friendship has
matured).

But if this model accounts roughly for the dominant pattern ⌐
of value homophily, can it also account for the further fact
that some close friendships have developed among Hilltowners having diametrically opposed racial values? Is this provisional model of social interaction, personal attachment, and
value reinforcement also consistent with the double fact that   F-1
liberals and illiberals *under*select one another as friends and,
by the same token, that some, though relatively few, friendships between those with differing racial values nevertheless

do occur? How shall we picture the social interaction of persons holding contradictory values, significant to each of them?⌋

Again, let us begin by considering those early contacts in ⌉ which residents express in words or in behavior a value to which the others are radically opposed. In a substantial proportion, perhaps most, of these cases, the fragile beginnings G–1(b) of a social relationship between liberals and illiberals will be broken almost before they have developed. The possible be-* ginnings of friendship are nipped in the bud. Thus, take the*⌋ case of Mrs. Marsh, a white Hilltowner, firmly liberal in her racial attitudes, who believes that "here anyway, Negroes are a lot nicer than the whites. The main thing is that they are friendlier, and want to be nicer to you." She happens to express her views to other white residents, living in her own apartment house.

> When I talk to them about it they just call me an "old nigger-lover." It doesn't bother me. I just say to them, "Well, they're better friends to me than you," and let it go at that. That happened once when I had some Negroes to my house for a supper. Some neighbor said, "What do you mean having niggers in your house?" But I don't care what anyone thinks of me, as long as I know I'm doing right.

Perhaps this exchange of sentiments "doesn't bother" Mrs. Marsh, but the fact remains that she has not formed a close personal relationship with any of her neighbors who harbor illiberal attitudes. This episode might stand almost as a prototype of the consequences that follow the expression of diametrically opposed values by both parties to an incipient social relationship: each individual provides punitive experience for*⌉ the other and, under such circumstances, it is not strange that a warm personal attachment does not develop between them. The expression of conflicting values, even of a single value, motivates both parties to avoid future contact. In short, if a* pair of acquaintances find themselves at sixes and sevens, H–1(a),4 they do not long remain a pair, but become unattached individuals. The incipient friendship is brought to an early halt.* This, then, is one type of process explaining the underselection of liberal friends by illiberals, and correlatively, the underselection of illiberals by liberals. ⌋

However, it is not always the case that *both* parties to an ⌐
incipient relationship will express their opposed values. Not
infrequently, either because of personal timidity, or an in-
grained sense of courtesy or fear of losing status, one party   I–3
may respond to the unpalatable views of the other by pre-⌐
serving an expedient silence. But to inhibit expressions of ⌐
one's values, because their expression would only "irritate"
one's associates, is itself a frustrating experience. Under such *
conditions, further contact with the acquaintance, rather than
being rewarding, becomes an occasion for self-defeat and, at *
times, an occasion for self-contempt. The silent partner is, to *
this degree, motivated to avoid further contact, lest this lead *
to open conflict. The partner who has freely expressed his   J–1(ₐ
views and has no inkling of the punitive experience he has
thus provided for his associate may continue to seek opportunities for further contact which, in an appreciable proportion
of cases, will meet with no success, as his timid but aggrieved
acquaintance sedulously avoids him. This type of interactive
process, generating motivated avoidance, again results in an *
underselection of unlike-minded associates as friends, in the
manner we have found to be the case.   ⌐

There is, however, a third pattern of interaction between
those holding disparate values which does allow close friendships to develop between them. As we noted in the case of
social contact between like-minded individuals, it is not at all
inevitable that a particular value will be expressed, by one or⌐
the other, in the *early* stages of a developing relationship. In ⌐
some proportion of cases, personal attachments will form in
the course of repeated contact long before either partner to   K–1(
the relationship is aware that they are sharply at odds in this
one particular respect—say, with respect to racial values. ⌐
Once the relationship has become firmly established—which ⌐
means only that the partners have experienced separate and *
mutual gratifications from their repeated interaction—it can, *
in some instances, tolerate a larger load of disagreement[18]
over certain values than is possible during the early phases,   L–4
when the relationship is still fragile. The very same kind of
disagreement would threaten or disrupt a developing friendship in its early stages. It would raise doubts about "the kind

of person the other fellow really is," since they had not yet come "to know one another" in the short course of their relationship. ⌟

The implication of this hypothetical pattern for further re-⌝ search is clear: it means that the degree and kind of value conflict between friends must be examined within the distinctly different contexts of firm, established friendships, and of tenuous, early friendships. The same degree and kind of M–1(b),4 divergence in values would, on the average, have very different consequences in the two contexts. In any case, this ⌟ part of our provisional model helps account for the minor statistical pattern of a modicum of close friendships among those holding sharply opposed racial values.

In time, this modicum of intimate personal relations be-⌝ tween those holding opposed values will be further depleted N–1(b),2 after friends make their delayed discovery that they hold these contradictory values. To say that a strong and undisputed ⌟ personal attachment can safely carry the burden of even se-⌝ rious disagreement about certain values is very different from O–1(a) saying that enduring friendships often involve such disagree-⌟ ment. The close attachments which *can* tolerate a conflict of ⌝ values, without acute threat to the relationship, are probably the very ones least subject to such conflict. For the friends, by virtue of their attachment, are strongly motivated to mod-* ify their values in the service of easing strains on the rela-* P–1(a) tionship. In the cumulative give-and-take of the friendship, initial divergences of value tend to be reduced. If the friends ⌟ have an approximately equal emotional stake in the relation-⌝ ship, this is likely to occur through mutual accommodation* of their values. If one is more deeply involved in the rela- Q–4 tionship than the other, his values are more likely to be modified to accord with the values of the less deeply involved. Presumably, if this self-corrective process did not occur, then close friendships would be even harder to come by and to ⌟ maintain than they apparently are. As processes of mutual or ⌝ unilateral accommodations of originally conflicting values run* their course, these cases also contribute to the pattern of value homophily rather than to that of heterophily. This has direct bearing on research, such as ours, which observes patterns

of friendship at a particular instant: for some of the cases of
close friendship between liberals and illiberals which turn up   R-1(a
in our statistical tables will, at a later time, appear as cases
of friendship between like-minded individuals, as one or the
other or both revise their values in the interest of preserving*
the relationship. It is not easy to have a warm personal attachment where there is an opposition of values.[19] This gives
rise to a motivated tendency toward the formation of common*
values among fast friends. Not only does intimate social interaction precipitate a deposit of new common values, but it*
also converts originally disparate values into common values.*
As a result of these two processes, we should expect value
homophily to increase and value heterophily to decrease
among any given aggregate of friendships observed over an
extended period of time.

This conversion of disparate into common values will not,
of course, inevitably take place. The original values may be
so deep-seated that neither individual finds it possible to mod-*
ify or to abandon them. Faced with the dilemma of having to   S-1(a
choose between their close friend and their basic values, and
not wanting to abandon one or the other, the friends may seek
the compromise solution of "agreeing to disagree," of placing
the particular value under dispute in the category of the "not-
to-be discussed." But this would-be solution is essentially
unstable. Although they agree not to argue their opposed values, if these values are significant in the life of the group or
community, their behavior is bound to betray their opposition.
The racial illiberal, for example, joined in friendship with a   T-1(b
racial liberal may set such store by the relationship as to forgo
any effort to convince the other of the error of his ways. But,
at best, he can achieve an uneasy toleration, not a stable
neutrality or indifference. At one time or another in Hilltown,
the liberal-illiberal pair will find themselves in a situation
where Negroes are also present. The issue is then inevitably
joined. The behavior of each will show whether the individual
sides with his friend or with his deep-seated values. Both the
relationship and the values are under strain and, in this un-*
stable condition, one or the other or both tend to be modi-*

fied.[20] When closely interacting persons have strongly op-⌐
posed values, continuance of the relationship involves a series
of reciprocally induced crises, in which the actions of each
often evoke hostility in the other. However, not all such open
conflict of values is destructive of the friendship. The kind of
conflict which clarifies the sources of previously obscure mu- U–1(a),3
tual irritation may actually solidify the relationship, by making*
it clear to both that the relationship means more to them than
their clashing values. In any event, we see once again why
value homophily prevails: for if the close relationship remains
intact, this phase of unstable compromise will in general give
way to accordant, rather than discordant, values.   ⌋

But it is not always the case, of course, that the friendship
does remain intact. When the contradictory values are so⌐
deep-rooted as to be unyielding, the social contacts of friends
are likely to irritate rather than to satisfy. Continued social
interaction then involves progressive alienation from one an-*
other. As the friendship cools, the estranged friends look elsewhere for like-minded companions, and these newfound at- V–1(a),4
tachments hasten the final dissolution of the relationship.
Once more, we see that this model of dynamic interplay between values and friendship anticipates the prevailing pattern
of value homophily among current relationships, because the
opposition of deeply held values tends to disrupt the friendship.⌋

It is now apparent that the static observation of the values⌐
of friends at a particular instant too easily loses sight of one
class of friendships altogether: the class of disrupted or broken
friendships. This oversight is not inherent in the procedure of
cross-sectional interviews and is readily overcome by the use W–2
of panel interviews: it would have been possible, for example,
to ask Craftowners and Hilltowners to designate their recently
broken friendships and to carry on the inquiry from there,
much along the lines we followed for current and still viable⌋
friendships. But if the oversight is not inherent, it is, surely,
prevalent. Few systematic studies of the formation of friendship also incorporate materials on the disruption of friendship.
And candor compels us to insist that such materials do not
appear in our own quantitative data simply because the need

for these materials was not foreseen during our field work. Yet it is the data on broken friendships which may provide the most critical evidence testing this provisional model of the interplay of values and friendship; for these disrupted friendships set a definite analytical task: they should be accounted for by the same model that seeks to account for the prevailing pattern of value homophily among still-current relationships. Future research on friendship, therefore—whether in housing developments or in the "open community"—will have to take explicit and systematic note of these abandoned friendships and have to study the processes leading to their break-up. We pay our own scanty qualitative data no more than the slight respect owing them when we report that they served, at least, to suggest the necessity of studying terminated friendships, if we are to round out our analysis of the role played by common values in the formation and maintenance of friendships.

In spite of these limitations of data, the model we have sketched out does move a certain distance toward a tentative formulation of the processes which give rise to the observed dominant pattern of value homophily and the observed subsidiary pattern of a few friendships among those with opposed values. At bottom, the model represents merely an extended application to the special case of friendship of the hard-won sociological commonplace that, in noncoerced social relations, common values and strong personal attachments act both as cause and effect, modifying and in turn being modified[*] by one another. Common values make social interaction a ⌉ rewarding experience, and the gratifying experience promotes[*] the formation of common values. And just as close association[*] X-1 and common values go hand in hand, so do dissociation and⌋ alienation from one another's values. For when the partners ⌉ to the friendship develop opposed values, their initial close relations are subjected to strain and some may deteriorate to[*] Y-2,4 the final point of dissolution. ⌋

It will be apparent that the conceptions on which this model is based are anything but new, and that they did not originate with any one sociologist.[21] But they take on particular pertinence here by suggesting the dynamic processes which eventuate in the patterns of friendship we have observed statically in Hilltown and Craftown. It may be assumed, finally, that the near future will see the development of a more comprehensive model incorporating, into one scheme of analysis, the processes giving rise both to status homophily—the pattern of friendship prevailing between persons occupying similar statuses—and to value homophily—the pattern of friendship tending to form between persons holding similar values. When this is achieved, sociologists will at long last have met the challenge implicit in Aristotle's doubts about the adequacy of the adage, ancient by his time, that "birds of a feather flock together."

PART TWO—METHODOLOGICAL ANALYSIS

(by P. F. Lazarsfeld)

The foregoing discussion of value homophily affords an occasion for examining, specifically and concretely, the interplay between substantive analysis and methodological formalization.[22]

The substantive analysis begins with the finding that friends in Hilltown tend to hold similar values concerning race relations and proceeds to develop a model of social process which might account for this fact. The logical and other analytical operations in this account remain implicit. We can, however, specify the major "operations"—the logical arrangement of data into categories having specified interrelations—implied in the substantive analysis. That is what is meant by "methodological formalization." This formal analysis has two useful purposes. It will bring out, first of all, a logical scheme for the further analysis of processes involved in the formation of friendship. Secondly, it will bring out the respects in which such a scheme of analysis can apply, not only to friendship, but to other studies of social process.

It will be found that each of the major statements in the substantive section presupposes one or more of four basic operations, soon to be discussed. These operations, moreover, can be stated in terms of an existing formalism, so that no new structure of analysis is required. It turns out, also, that the application of this formal analysis does not call for mathematical procedures, nor does it involve quantitative terms other than statements of "greater than," "less than," and characterizations of relationships between variables as "weak" or "strong."[23]

The data supporting the finding of homophily can be presented in a variety of ways. For our purpose a simple schematic presentation will be best. It does not quite conform to the way the data were originally presented; but it will be seen presently that an adaptation like the one to be introduced is necessary if the interpretations of the main text are to be tested empirically.

Reformulation of the Problem

We will assume that all the members of a community have been classified as liberals or illiberals in terms of their racial attitudes. We will assume, further, that by some kind of chance procedure members of the community have been formed into pairs, which have then been classified as friendship pairs or as nonfriendship pairs.[24] This will carry us along for a considerable number of pages. Later on we shall amply rectify this original simplification; provisions will be made for people being neutral in their attitudes, for the existence of one-sided attachments between pairs and for many other more realistic situations.

Our schematic starting point, then, will be a large number of pairs, each of which has been characterized by the two dimensions of agreement-disagreement, on the one hand, and the presence or absence of friendship, on the other. These pairs can be arranged in a fourfold table, so that the relationship between agreement and friendship can be studied. A set of hypothetical figures which reproduce the finding with which the substantive analysis began might look somewhat like table 9.1.[25] The empirical finding about value homophily is of the type represented in these hypothetical figures. Here, as in the actual data, there is definite relationship between the two variables. Among the pairs characterized by the presence of friendship, a majority are also characterized by agreement of values. But among the pairs which have no friendship, a majority are in disagreement.

Table 9.1

	Friends	Not Friends
Agree	150	50
Disagree	50	150

Table 9.1 represents the type of result which is obtained in a so-called cross-sectional survey taken at one specific period of time. The purpose of the interpretative analysis was to specify, on a hypothetical basis, some of the main processes resulting in an observed correlation between friendship and a similarity of values. But conjectures about processes, of course, require the introduction of a *time dimension*. In order to study the development of a particular pattern one must be able to observe the units of analysis at successive points in time. The first finding is enlarged by the assumption that at some previous period friendship and opinion were not, or not as clearly, related. The static result is replaced by a more complicated one, implying a change; it is this change which then has to be explained. Again we resort to schematic figures. And now an additional element is added to the schematization: in actuality, only one survey was made; but the existence and probable results of an earlier survey are implied in the analysis given in the first part of this paper.

To keep the demonstration as simple as possible, we shall assume that the preceding survey, done at Time I, resulted in the findings of table 9.2(a). Table 9.2(b) repeats the results of the original survey which was carried out at what is now labeled Time II. According to these figures there was no discernible relationship between friendship and agreement at the time of the

Table 9.2

	(a) Time I		(b) Time II	
	Friends	Not Friends	Friends	Not Friends
Agree	100	100	150	50
Disagree	100	100	50	150

first observation, when, say, the residents had been in the community for only a short time. But by the time of the second
observation, after a six months' interval, the relationship between these variables had become marked. This change in the
degree of relationship is exactly of the kind hypothesized in the
substantive section.

We shall find it useful to talk of the contact-value combinations
which are represented in the four cells of each of the tables. The
frequencies of these contact-value combinations have changed
from Time I to Time II. And to add one final bit of terminology:
the "harmonious" combinations have become more frequent.
By "harmonious" we shall mean either pairs who are friends
and agree, or pairs who are not friends and do not hold the same
value. The main issue is now restated in more formal terms: the
increasing number of harmonious contact-value combinations
through time is to be analyzed.

Now such a formal restatement can be useful only if it contains
elements which can be further developed without recourse, at
least at first, to additional ideas or assumptions. This is indeed
possible in the present case because table 9.2 tells only part of
the story which would be available to us as a result of observations made at two periods of time with the same set of pairs.
The reader is invited to study table 9.3, which is sometimes
called a sixteenfold table, with care; it contains all combinations
of friendship and agreement at two time periods. Again we in-

Table 9.3

	Time II				
Time I	FA	FA	FA	FA	
FA	+ +	+ −	− +	− −	
+ +	50	20	10	20	100
+ −	30	20	0	50	100
− +	50	0	40	10	100
− −	20	10	0	70	100
	150	50	50	150	

Note: The first symbol in each designation refers to the presence or
absence of friendship [F] in the pair; the second to agreement or
disagreement [A].

troduce hypothetical figures which, as we shall see, reproduce the substantive discussion we are attempting to analyze.[26] Note that the marginals of this sixteenfold table reproduce the four-fold tables of table 9.2. And they indicate the same fact observed previously, namely, that the relationship between agreement and friendship becomes more marked with the passage of time.

It is the purpose of this discussion to show that the proper analysis of this sixteenfold table, taken in conjunction with other materials which we shall specify, makes it possible to organize profitably all statements about the phenomenon of value homophily and the processes leading to it contained in the substantive section. It is our contention, in other words, that a sixteenfold table of this kind provides a formal scheme for statements of process. In order to demonstrate this we must indicate the various analytic operations which can be carried out through use of a sixteenfold table. We shall then consider whether we have omitted essential parts of the substantive discussion.

The Analysis of Sequence Rules (1)

The analysis of what we shall call sequence rules is perhaps the basic operation in this kind of formalization. We mean by a sequence any particular cell in the sixteenfold table. (We call these cells sequences, because each represents a shift in the state of friendship and agreement from one time to another. Thus, the cell, $[(+ -)$ to $(- -)]$, represents a change, between the first and second times of observation, from the state of friendship-and-disagreement to that of absence-of-friendship-and-disagreement.) And we mean by a sequence rule any statement about the frequency of a single sequence or the comparative size of two or more sequences.

Clearly, sequence rules will be of varying complexity, depending on the number of sequences involved. The simplest ones are those referring to a single cell in the sixteenfold table. There are several statements of this kind in the substantive discussion, and each of these statements has been designated by the symbol 1(a). Thus the substantive account refers to the "fact that some close friendships have developed among Hilltowners having diametrically opposed racial values."[27] This states, in other words, that, perhaps contrary to expectations, some pairs can be found in the cell characterized by the $(- -)$ pattern at the time of the first interview, but by the $(+ -)$ pattern by the time of the second.

Elsewhere we find the following comment:

> To say that a strong and undisputed personal attachment can safely carry the burden of even serious disagreement about certain values is very different from saying that enduring friendships often involve such disagreement.

Restated in the more formal terms which we have introduced here, this statement affirms the relative infrequency of the sequence $[(+ -) \text{ to } (+ -)]$. The analyst says that, while it is possible to observe this pattern, it is not common.

In still another part of the substantive discussion we read that:

> some of the cases of close friendship between liberals and illiberals which turn up in our statistical tables will, at a later time, appear as cases of friendship between like-minded individuals, as one or the other or both revise their values in the interest of preserving the relationship.

A reformulation of part of this statement indicates that the analyst expects to find a number of pairs characterized by the $[(+ -) \text{ to } (+ +)]$ sequence.

In general, then, sequence rules involving single cells in the sixteenfold table are usually concerned with the generality or rarity of particular kinds of shifts. They indicate which patterns of change or stability are expected, and which are unexpected.

A somewhat more complex kind of sequence rule is that involving the comparison of two or more cells in a row of the table. (They are indicated by the symbol 1(b).) The usual purpose of this type of comparison is to show that one kind of shift— one sequence—is more frequent than others. For example, we find the following comment in the substantive section:

> let us begin by considering those early contacts in which residents express in words or in behavior a value to which the others are radically opposed. In a substantial proportion, perhaps most, of these cases, the fragile beginnings of a social relationship between liberals and illiberals will be broken almost before they have developed. The possible beginnings of friendship are nipped in the bud.

Because this is an extended comment, let us analyze it in some detail. The passage starts out by focusing attention on the pairs of friends who were initially in disagreement. In terms of our sixteenfold table these are the pairs characterized by a $(+ -)$ combination of characteristics at the time of the first interview; they will be found in the second row of the table. The analysis then considers the most likely outcome for pairs characterized in this way. It is assumed that "in a substantial proportion, perhaps most, of these cases" the early contacts will not be continued and no firm friendship will develop.[28] It is assumed, in other words, that the sequence $[(+ -)$ to $(- -)]$ is more likely than any other for pairs starting out with this combination of characteristics.

In a later comment, the analyst states a somewhat different sequence rule about the same kinds of pairs. He says that the relationships between friends who are in disagreement is an essentially unstable one, and "both the relationship and the values are under strain and, in this unstable condition, one or the other or both tend to be modified." Again translating this statement into our more formal terms, the analyst assumes that, if one examines the second row in the sixteenfold table, that in which we find pairs who were initially friendly but in disagreement, two sequences will be relatively more frequent than the others. He states that the most likely sequences for the $(+ -)$ cases are the $[(+ -)$ to $(+ +)]$ or the $[(+ -)$ to $(- -)]$. This is a corollary, incidentally, of an assumption which he made earlier, namely, that there will be few cases characterized by the $[(+ -)$ to $(+ -)]$ pattern.

It might be asked at this point what is actually accomplished by this kind of formalization. Seemingly, all that we have done is restate the substantive formulations in terms of the symbols which we introduced.

The Heuristic Value of Schematic Presentation

In order to understand the heuristic value of this formal presentation, let us classify all of the sequence rules found in the text. We shall do this by reproducing the sixteenfold scheme and inserting in each cell the comments which deal with that particular sequence. To make this scheme as manageable as possible each statement or content unit in the substantive text has been assigned a distinctive code letter; it is these which are reproduced in the sixteen cells (table 9.4).

What do we learn from this scheme of reformulation? One fact that becomes immediately evident is that all but one of the eighteen sequence rules which we have classified deal with pairs of individuals characterized by friendship and that thirteen of these seventeen statements[29] concern pairs who, at the outset of observation, were friendly, but disagreed on racial values. The corollary of this is that the substantive section was not concerned with pairs which had not established some degree of social contact. There is, in fact, no sequence rule about pairs having like values, but no contact.[30] This does not mean, of course, that such sequence rules cannot be developed. In accord with other hypotheses in the substantive text, we can state a sequence rule of the 1(b) type, that in which the frequencies of sequences in a particular row are compared. A relatively probable outcome for the pairs characterized by lack of friendship but agreement in values, it might be suggested, is the [(− +) to (+ +)] pattern. That is, even though these pairs may not have become friends at the time when they were first observed, we can assume that, through chance or because they were led by their similar values to take part in the same local organizations, some of them will come into contact with one another. Then, as was suggested in the substantive section, they will find the expression of their compatible values mutually gratifying and will be motivated to seek further contact with one another. The end result is that these will become friends in a larger proportion

Table 9.4

	Time II			
Time I	FA	FA	FA	FA
FA	+ +	+ −	− +	− −
+ +	B,D,E			
+ −	N,P,R,T	K,M,O,S,U		G,H,J,M,N,T,V
− +				
− −		F		

Table 9.5

Time I	Time II	
	+ +	− −
+ −	30	50
− +	50	10

of cases than those with disparate values who are less likely to meet through the same organizations or, if they meet, to establish mutual friendships.

One distinct use of such a formal scheme, then, is that it enables one to bring out specifically and systematically the points which are being stressed in a substantive analysis and, more importantly perhaps, the points which are being disregarded. Another application consists in pointing to alternative options of analysis, to additional ways in which the same material could be analyzed. Our previous distinction between harmonious and disharmonious friendship-value combinations permits us to exemplify such an elaboration.

Looking at table 9.3, we may concentrate on the second and third rows; these contain all the pairs which were disharmonious at the first observation, and indicate what has become of them at the time of the second observation. As a direct consequence of our definition of the process of homophily, we find that 140 of these 200 pairs had become "harmonious," meaning that they either were now friends in agreement (+ +), or people holding different values and not friendly (− −). But how has this progress toward homophily been achieved? Did the value configuration more often determine the fate of friendships, or did friendship more often affect the constancy of attitudes? The theory under analysis is silent on this point, but our formalization has forced us to make some assumptions, if only because the cells of the sixteenfold table, table 9.3, had to be filled in. Its most pertinent part is reproduced as table 9.5. Two kinds of sequences can be distinguished. In [(+ −) to (− −)] and in [(− +) to (+ +)] the second sign, designating the values, remains the same, and the first sign, symbolizing friendship, changes; there are 100 such cases. In the other 40 cases the values at Time II become adjusted to the friendship patterns as they existed at (and persisted from) Time I. In somewhat loose language we can therefore say that the values are "stronger" than the friendships; if there is disharmony between the two, the social system, represented by our hypothetical community, increases homophily by changing the distribution of attitudes.[31] This set of figures is probably more in the spirit of the general theory than a different set implying the opposite assumption. It is important to realize, however, that the homophily result, the shift in marginals, would have remained the same if the entries in table 9.5 had been made to read 60 and 20 in the first line and 20 and 40 in the second. In this case, the implied assumption would have been that friendships are "stronger" than attitudes in their mutual effect.

A second heuristic value of such formalization, then, is to bring out assumptions which have not been made explicit by the original analyst, or those on which he chose not to take a stand. Before pursuing further this relation between general reflections on a topic and its treatment in more systematic forms, we must broaden the whole area under inspection. So far, we have confined ourselves to those rules that can be derived from one sixteenfold table. This is the simplest scheme relating two variables at two times. Various extensions of this notion result in new, and more complicated, rules. With these elaborations we can begin to restore the complexity of the substantive conceptions which our simplification has necessarily eliminated for the time being.

The Analysis of Chains (2)

A first elaboration to be considered is that of the time dimension. So far we have assumed that we have only two observations of the pairs of individuals. We can now study what develops when these observations are increased to three or more. In order to do this, we shall introduce the notion of "chains," sequences which are extended in time. That is, a pair which, in terms of friendship and agreement, is characterized as (− +) at Time I,

$(+ +)$ at Time II, and $(+ -)$ at Time III represents one of the many chains which can be distinguished.

The substantive section of this paper does refer to some of these chains. (They are designated by the number 2.) Perhaps the most clearcut of these references is found in Statement Y:

> when the partners to the friendship develop opposed values, their initial close relations are subjected to strain and some may deteriorate to the final point of dissolution.

This, as we can see, describes the processes accounting for the chain $[(+ +)$ to $(+ -)$ to $(- -)]$.

The special importance of an extended time dimension is that it permits us to explore new problems. Specifically, we can study whether the future shifts of pairs characterized in a particular way depend on their past history. We note in our original sixteenfold table, for example, that at the time of the second interview there are 50 pairs characterized by the $(+ -)$ combination of friendship and agreement. But these 50 pairs have quite different histories: 20 of them were originally friends sharing similar values; another 20 have a past history, as well as a present pattern, of friendship but disagreement; and the final 10 pairs were characterized at Time I both by the absence of friendship and the absence of agreement. The question is how these past histories will influence future courses of development among these 50 pairs. Operationally, what can we expect from a third observation? Will the 20 pairs characterized by the stable sequence, $[(+ -)$ to $(+ -)]$, manifest a different development in the future from those who have shifted to the $(+ -)$ pattern from either the $(+ +)$ or the $(- -)$ states? That is, will disagreeing friends who have exhibited both friendship and disagreement in the past differ, in their future patterns, from disagreeing friends who previously agreed? There is reason to believe that they will.

The importance of this kind of analysis is that it leads to the development of more refined and specific rules of change, which, in turn, permit more accurate predictions of the ways in which particular types of pairs will behave in the future.[32] One aspect of this deserves special attention.

The Idea of Equilibrium

So far we have dealt with two major elements of a process: (a) an initial distribution of the friendship-value combinations, represented by table 9.2(a); (b) a set of sequence rules telling how these combinations change over a designated period of time, represented by table 9.3.[33]

With the help of these two elements we can describe how the system under study changes from a first to a second stage. And table 9.3 tells us what the social theorist has to do: he must make plausible assumptions about the frequencies in each cell; and, in the light of other knowledge, he must state why he makes these assumptions.

But the idea of observations repeated more than twice brings out certain additional matters that have to be considered. One is characteristic for all theory formation: we have to assume that no extraneous factors will disturb the system. Suppose, for example, that as a result of some wave of terror, the community comes to believe that liberal values are dangerous; it might then develop that people who hold liberal values avoid each other in order to deflect suspicion. This would obviously change the sequence rules exemplified in table 9.3, and consequently change the future distribution of the friendship-value combinations.

The present discussion implies, then, that, *ceteris paribus*, the sequence rules remain unaffected by outside influences for a reasonable period of time. But this still leaves two possibilities open: the rules may remain completely constant or may change as a result of intrinsic developments.

Let us first assume that we deal with what is sometimes called a stationary process: the sequence rules controlling the change from one time period to the next remain about the same.

Under these circumstances it is possible to "compute" the equilibrium position of the system. Our scheme showed that in the first time step, the marginal distribution 100-100-100-100 of table 9.2(a) changed to the 150-50-50-150 of table 9.2(b); as a matter of fact, this shift turned out to be the essence of value homophily as a process. We now could predict what would happen in another time step by applying the same sequence rules to this new distribution: without elaborating the arithmetic, we should find a table 9.2(c) (not given here) showing frequencies of 145-55-35-165 for the four friendship-value combinations, respectively.

A somewhat more complicated computation would tell us that the equilibrium distribution would be 133-57-24-186. This distribution can easily be defined in nonmathematical terms: it is the one which does not change if the sequence rules of table 9.3 are applied to it. This kind of equilibrium is well known to social research from many empirical studies. Repeated interviews on such diversified topics as race attitudes, opinions on the role of labor unions, etc., often show the following characteristics: many individual respondents change their positions: but these individual shifts cancel each other out and the so-called marginal distributions for the whole group remain fairly constant over time.

Now let us briefly consider the idea of a process where the sequence rules do not remain constant but are still unaffected by extraneous factors. The sequence rules could depend upon the distribution of friendship-value combinations reached at a certain moment. If, for example, value homophily has become very strong in a community, a countertendency might develop with the view that different kinds of people ought to become associated. The homophily trend described in the text might weaken until a lower degree of correlation between friendship and value has been reached; then the reverse tendency might set in. The result would be an oscillation of the value-friendship distribution around an average. This would be quite different from the introduction of extraneous elements, mentioned above. The whole process would still go on within the system; however, the sequence rules exemplified in table 9.3 would not be constant but would be dependent upon the "marginal" distribution reached at a given moment.

This possibility has been introduced only to show that the formal statement of a process opens up new vistas for substantive speculation. The assumption of a stationary process is probably more in keeping with the spirit of the main analysis than is the assumption of intrinsic oscillations. But even then it can be seen that, for a full understanding of the phenomenon, one more topic needs explication. If one were to apply the notion of homophily loosely, one could ask why the system does not end in complete homogeneity. Why does it not happen that all the people with like values, and only these, are friends? Actually, table 9.3 shows that "countertendencies" are provided for: there are sequences like [(+ +) to (− +)] which tell us that, in spite of agreement, friendships will break off and refill the reservoir of "disharmonious" pairs. At least three kinds of speculations can be attached to these countersequences. One has to do with extraneous elements, often ascribed to chance: accidental feuds, the conversion of one partner, etc. A second possibility is that other values—those not specifically concerned with racial problems—play a part in the formation and dissolution of friendships. The third possibility is perhaps the most interesting: there could be a phenomenon of satiation, a desire for new challenges when agreement has lasted too long. Whether such tendencies actually play a role can only be discovered by empirical research. We shall have occasion later to speculate on the consequences of such a possibility. At this point, our only purpose has been to indicate what problems derive from the notion of equilibrium, which, in turn, derives from formalization of the idea of an explanatory process.

By now we have gone considerably beyond the intent of the text under discussion, not in order to imply a shortcoming, but in order to exemplify the continuity of questions which can be derived from even the simplest set of repeated observations. It is time to return to the text itself, and to do justice to its own complexity; this forces us to introduce further elements into our "translation."

The Elaboration of Variables (3)

So far we have confined ourselves exclusively to the two variables of friendship and agreement. But this represents an oversimplification of the foregoing model of processes leading to value homophily. At numerous points in the discussion, the analyst indicates that other variables need to be considered if the various processes are to be specified adequately. The introduction of these new variables provides another kind of elaboration.[34]

What kinds of additional variables are brought into the discussion? (The statements are identified in the text by the number 3.) The analyst contrasts the situations which exist when members of a pair express or fail to express their values (Statements B, E, and G). He considers the way in which propinquity or social organization affects the processes with which he is dealing (Statement D). He points to timidity,[35] courtesy, or fear of losing status as variables which might explain why some individuals do not express disagreement (Statement I). He indicates that awareness of agreement or disagreement may affect the development of friendship (Statement K). And he suggests that a "conflict [of values] which clarifies the sources of previously obscure mutual irritation may actually solidify the relationship, by making it clear to both that the relationship means more to them than their clashing values" (Statement U).

The introduction of these new variables has the effect, basically, of increasing the number of patterns with which we deal and of adding to the sequence rules which can be specified. Let us consider how this comes about. Suppose that we start with pairs which are friendly, but in disagreement, the (+ −) cases; and suppose that we introduce as our third variable the notion that some of these pairs express their conflicting views while others do not. The first step in analyzing the role of this third variable is to divide the total number of (+ −) pairs into those which express their values and those which do not. By then studying the most likely sequences within these two groups, we can determine the influence of such overt expression on friendship. A hypothetical table (table 9.6) indicates that dissolution of friendship is more likely to take place within pairs which give

Table 9.6

	Time II				
Time I (+ −) cases	FA + +	FA + −	FA − +	FA − −	
Express views	10	5	0	30	45
Do not express views	20	15	0	20	55
	30	20	0	50	

voice to their conflicting values.[36] A sequence rule of the 1(b) type can be derived from these hypothetical figures. The most frequent sequence for those who express their views is $[(+ -)$ to $(- -)]$; 30 out of the 45 pairs made this shift. Among those who do not express their conflicting values, however, no single sequence is numerically outstanding.

There are two further points to be noted in connection with this kind of elaboration. The first is that the same variable may have different consequences with different kinds of pairs. That is, the effect of a third variable will depend, in general, on the configuration of the first two variables. For example, as the analyst suggests, the expression of values will, in all probability, serve to reinforce the friendship of individuals who are in agreement to start with. In other words, we assume that this variable, expression of values, has an effect on the $(+ +)$ pairs different from the one it has on those characterized as $(+ -)$.

A second point is that the substantive contribution made by the introduction of a third variable will depend partly on how that variable is defined. For example, the "expression of values" can mean anything from casual references to those values to incessant discussions of them. Also, the conversations can take place early in the friendship, or at a time when it is well established. The observed effects of these expressions, then, depends partly on how they have been defined and to what stages of the friendship they refer.

The Elaboration of Categories (4)

This last point suggests another type of elaboration, namely, a refinement of the variables so that they are no longer simply dichotomous attributes. Throughout our discussion we have dealt with the dichotomies, agreement-disagreement and friends-not friends. It is clear, however, that both of these variables can be defined differently, as was indeed done in the substantive text. Each might be classified as a trichotomy, for example. In that case, agreement might be divided into complete, partial, and no agreement. Similarly, the attribute of friendship might be converted into a trichotomy. One might then distinguish pairs involving mutual friendship, those in which only one person claims friendly relations with the other, and those in which neither considers the other a friend.[37] Or, different aspects of the variables might be considered. For example, the substantive formulation refers to different phases of friendships—those which are incipient, those which are firmly established, those which are in one stage or another of dissolution (Statement A, for example). (The references to refined categories of the principal variables are indicated by the code number 4 in the text.) There are other comments about the intensity of feeling attached to racial attitudes—those which are deep-rooted, those in which the individual has great emotional involvement, and so on.[38]

These refinements of our variables have the same effect, in general, as the addition of a new one—an increase in the number of patterns to be distinguished and a multiplication of possible sequence rules. If our dichotomies are converted into trichotomies, then our original fourfold tables are transformed into ninefold tables, and the original sixteenfold table, relating the information from two interviews, becomes a somewhat unwieldy table with eighty-one cells.

We have now reviewed the basic operations involved in this kind of analysis. And, except for one type of statement to be considered presently, the substantive part of the text now seems to have been wholly analyzed in formal terms.

"Mechanism" vs. Sequence Rules

We started out with a sixteenfold table reporting personal relations and agreement for all pairs of individuals at two points of time. We then introduced three kinds of elaboration: an extension of the time dimension, an increase in the number of variables considered, and finer subdivisions for some of these variables. This permitted us to classify our pairs in an increasingly discriminating way, or, to put it in different terms, the state in which any pair was at a particular moment became progressively more specific. But the propositions with which we dealt were all of the same kind. They were sequence rules indicating the relative frequencies with which transitions from one state to another took place.

It turned out that a considerable number of the pages under examination could be translated into such "time-series language." An effort was made to show that such translation clarified the interrelation between different parts of a more discursive language, that it brought out assumptions implied in the original analysis, and that it pointed to further problems—not by adding new questions, but by exploiting systematically the operations introduced by the original author.

This does not mean at all that the reflections under scrutiny were obvious to begin with. As a matter of fact, a formalism highlights a substantive contribution. This can be shown in many ways; but two points deserve special mention. It is possible to develop a theory which assumes that people have a tendency to change friends frequently and are eager for varying intellectual experiences; therefore, they prefer their new friends to have different opinions from those their old ones had. Under this assumption we also would find homophily in the sense of increasing correlation of friendship and attitudes from one observation to the next. Appendix 2 gives an example of a sixteenfold table where the two marginal value-friendship distributions are exactly the same as in table 9.3, while the sequence rules within the table are completely different; the reader is invited to study this table in some detail and to see what its behavioral implications are. The formalism, then, only brings out that one aspect of a process analysis is the existence of certain sequence rules and chains; the actual content of the rules is a theoretical contribution, made in the light of general knowledge and susceptible to further empirical test—a test, incidentally, which is often facilitated by a more formal restatement.

The introduction of additional variables points to a second aspect of the substantive contribution. It obviously makes a difference which specifications are introduced. Under some conditions, changes will come about much more rapidly or frequently than under others; some developments will gather momentum over time, whereas others will stimulate counter-tendencies and be arrested. All this can be put into formal language after someone has thought about such alternatives; and some of these hypotheses will later be corroborated by actual findings, while others will remain stillborn speculations. Behind the formal notion of variables is the hidden hope that those variables which alone can make the formalism productive will be selected.

It would be possible to close our discussion on this note. But there is one final matter to be brought to the fore, even if it must remain in the form of an unanswered question. We have now translated almost all the main passages in the pages under scrutiny—but only almost. A careful reader will have noticed that certain terms were not covered by our formalization. The language used in our formalization always took the form: often (or seldom) people move from one kind of state (however specified) to another kind. But at a score of points the document described these movements in a specific kind of language. When pairs moved away from a state it was because of a "frustrating, punitive experience," because the individual was "irritated, subject to strain," etc. Conversely, if pairs maintained a state or moved toward it, this state was described as "mutually gratifying," "rewarding," etc. (Lines of the substantive text, in which words of this kind occur, have been marked with an asterisk.)

There are three ways of looking at these comments. They could be stylistic devices, making the sequence rules more vivid by referring to common experiences and observations; in that case, they would be outside the province of the present endeavor. Or they could be shorthand expressions for the introduction of new variables. Earlier sequence rules regarding friends in disagreement, the $(+-)$ pairs, differed according to whether or not they assumed that the members expressed their conflicting views. Similarly, we might distinguish $(+-)$ pairs according to whether or not they experience irritation as a result of their disagreement. Thus, if these comments about reward-frustration refer to additional specifying conditions or to intermediate steps to be covered in additional observations, then we have dealt with them before and they do not offer a new problem. But it could be, finally, that we are faced with an additional notion: mechanisms which are supposed to account for the observed sequence rules in a way not analyzed before.

If this third alternative is the appropriate one, then a whole new area of formal inquiry opens up. Obviously, the introduction of new variables is itself one form of accounting. How does it differ, then, from these proposed mechanisms? Is it that we are moving here to an underlying psychological level, just as, in the field of thermodynamics, we move from consideration of the heat of bodies to consideration of the velocity of their molecules? Or do we have to introduce new concepts, like Lewin's vectors and barriers, operating in the "field" in which we make our observations?

Within the frame of the task which we set for ourselves, these questions cannot be answered. We meet here residual elements in the text which, in their present form, have not been formalized. If we were told a great deal more about at least some of these mechanisms, it might be possible to explicate the role they play in the total analysis. As it stands, our formalization renders its final service by pointing to a next step in the continuity of inquiry.

APPENDIX 1

The equilibrium is obviously obtained if the contact-value distribution of the 400 pairs satisfies the following condition:

$$A = .5A + .3B + .5C + .2D$$
$$B = .2A + .2B \qquad + .1D$$
$$C = .1A \qquad + .4C$$
$$D = .2A + .5B + .1C + .7D$$

Table 9.7

		Time II			
Time I FA	FA + +	FA + −	FA − +	FA − −	
+ +	66	27	14	26	133
+ −	18	11	0	28	57
− +	12	0	10	2	24
− −	37	19	0	130	186
	133	57	24	186	400

Table 9.8

	Time II				
Time I	FA	FA	FA	FA	
FA	+ +	+ −	− +	− −	
+ +	10	20	10	60	100
+ −	60	5	15	20	100
− +	20	15	5	60	100
− −	60	10	20	10	100
	150	50	50	150	

The coefficients in each of these equations correspond to the columns of table 9.3 in the text. The four frequencies add up to $A + B + C + D = 400$. The terminal turnover is approximately that shown in table 9.7.

For a detailed discussion of the use of transition probabilities in the study of attitude changes, see T. W. Anderson's contribution to the symposium *Mathematical Thinking in the Social Sciences.*[39]

APPENDIX 2

A sixteenfold table which would correspond to the scheme of such a restless and novelty-seeking community is exemplified in table 9.8. The reader should interpret both tables 9.7 and 9.8 in terms of the substantive discussion in the text.

EPILOGUE

(by R. K. Merton)

The methodological part of this paper closes on the note that formal analyses like this one may contribute to the continuity and cumulation of sociological inquiry. It may therefore be helpful for the guinea pig who was subjected to this experiment in continuity to report to the experimenter, and to other observers, what benefits, if any, have been gained from the harrowing experience. This short epilogue is intended as such a report.

The formal restatement of the substantive account, it seems to me, has led to at least seven kinds of clarification, each of which will be briefly described and illustrated.

1. *The formal analysis maps the boundaries of the substantive analysis.* Some of these boundaries were set by design, so that certain problems were deliberately omitted. Others, however, were inadvertent and had escaped my notice entirely until they were highlighted by the formal analysis.

Among the deliberate omissions is any concern with the processes leading to varying rates of social contact between designated kinds of people, as distinct from the processes of subsequent forming of friendships. In other words, the substantive analysis deals only with those cases in which social contact actually has occurred; it does not take such contact to be problematical, as requiring explanation in turn. It advisedly neglects the processes which make for differential probabilities of social contact between persons with similar or discrepant values who live in a sort of enclave (such as a housing development).

Such a problem is considered elsewhere in the study, where it is assumed that persons with similar values, particularly those values salient in the life of the community, will be more often brought into contact, if only because they are more likely to take part in the same organized groups. And this, in turn, would presumably make for value homophily, since at least some of these contacts would eventuate in sustained friendships. For example: although the racial liberals in Hilltown were not formally organized into groups designed to deal with "problems of race relations," they were more likely than illiberals to come into contact through self-selected membership in local organizations which, because of their prevalently interracial composition, were largely boycotted by illiberals. Since this particular problem of forces making for differential social contact happens to be considered in another part of the study from which the substantive section of this paper is drawn, I have all the more reason to appreciate the fact that the formal analysis not only identifies the problem but locates the precise points at which it becomes germane to the study of friendship patterns regarded as social process.

In contrast to such deliberate omissions from the substantive paper, there are other omissions, uncovered by the formal analysis, of which I was wholly unaware. Another way of putting this is that certain analytical problems flow directly from the formal analysis which are not at all evident from the discursive analysis. For example, the "analysis of chains," involving the observation of pairs of categorized people at three or more points in time, brings out with great clarity and with immediate provision for empirical study the problem of the ways in which the past histories of large aggregates of pairs affect the probable future course of their social relationships. It is shown how to distinguish among those who, at a particular time of observation, appear in the same category (for example, as like-minded friends) but who nevertheless differ in terms of their mutual relationships and values at an earlier time of observation. It then becomes possible to connect such past differences to their probable relationship at a third, and still later, time of observation.

Commonplace as this conception would be in the case study of a particular friendship between this or that pair,[40] it is anything but obvious, as the research literature on friendship testifies, in statistical analyses of large numbers of cases designed to uncover regularities in the formation, maintenance, and dissolution of various types of friendship. The formal analysis thus provides an instructive example of a procedure for linking up the historical or genetic approach to the study of large numbers of interpersonal relations (which deals with the development or biography of such relations) and the functional approach (which deals with the consequences of these relations for those directly involved in them and for the larger group at particular times). It shows how to combine what have been called diachronic and synchronic perspectives on interpersonal relations.

2. *The formal analysis brings out and systematizes assumptions hidden in the substantive analysis.* From the formal restatement, it becomes evident that the substantive account deals with friendship-formation as immanent process. In other words, the process resulting in various patterns of friendship is provisionally regarded as taking place in a closed system. But as the formal analysis goes on to show, this immanent process may be either of two kinds. It may be a stationary process in which the sequence rules are comparatively constant, that is, in which the

turnover of cases is such that the distribution of various kinds of interpersonal relations and values remains relatively unchanged. Or it may be an oscillatory process in which the sequence rules depend on the total distribution at each particular time, thus producing successive distributions which vary about an average. Even under the most charitable interpretation, it cannot be said that these types of immanent process were recognized in the substantive account. But once stated, these distinctive types of process suggest further problems, as I shall report later in this epilogue.

3. *The formal analysis clarifies concepts by giving them operational meaning.* In the course of the formal restatement, certain concepts which were loosely embodied in my own account become operationally defined, without loss of meaning, with net gain in clarity, and in terms that enable them to be more readily utilized in empirical study. As an example of this we can take the concept of an "unstable condition" (which I took to characterize cases in which the opposition between deep-seated values of friends put both the relationship and the values under stress so that one or the other or both tend to become modified). In the more exacting symbolism of the formal analysis, this refers to the sequence rule in which the number of cases of friends with conflicting values $(+ -)$ is being depleted at a comparatively rapid rate, losing cases, at each new time of observation, either to the $(- -)$ or the $(+ +)$ category. An unstable condition can be said to obtain, then, for cells in such an analytic tabulation which lose cases at a relatively rapid rate. Although this statement apparently says no more than the statement which it replaces, it says it better—better in the sense that it facilitates analytic operations by the sociologist who would study this process empirically, and better in the further sense that it raises productive questions. Here, for example, the more rigorous formulation directs our attention at once to the circumstances under which this unstable condition is more likely to result in one or in another of the alternative outcomes.

In much the same way, the formal analysis takes a general observation in the substantive analysis and converts it into a problem amenable to further research. Thus, I had suggested at several places that values and personal attachments are *inter-*

dependent, that they "act both as cause and effect, modifying and in turn being modified by one another," and that this tends to result in value homophily. The formal review leads us not to reject this notion of interdependence, but to clarify it. It provides a procedure for discovering which of the interacting elements preponderate; more specifically, for ascertaining whether discrepant values of friends are more often modified to produce accord or whether these values are more often maintained intact at the expense of the relationship. It will be agreed, I suppose, that such provision for discovering which outcomes predominate under specified conditions moves an appreciate step beyond the mere assertion of interdependence. And by providing a means of obtaining empirical findings, the procedure provides a further basis for theoretical elaboration of the problem.

4. *The formal analysis presses for clarification of the logical status of concepts.* In the last part of the methodological analysis, it is observed that one class of terms seems to resist systematic incorporation into the formal framework of analysis. These are the terms that apparently attribute the movement of pairs from one state to another to certain dynamic processes: persons are motivated to seek or to avoid contact, they find the relationship gratifying or punitive, they are subject to strain. Granting that these terms are something more than mere rhetoric, there still remains the troublesome question of their logical status, an obscure question which I am willing to discuss but find myself unable to answer.

It is suggested in the methodological section that these terms may be *either* additional intervening variables of the same order as those already covered by other sequence rules, *or* that they are explanatory mechanisms, possibly requiring a new mode of analysis. Although I am far from clear on the matter, I suspect that the alternatives are overlapping, rather than mutually exclusive. It seems to me that these are interpolated variables which can be formalized by sequence rules but that they are nevertheless mechanisms of an explanatory rather than a depictive character. Such classes of mechanisms are explanatory in the sense that they comprise relationships between variables which have been found, with great regularity, to have observable consequences for designated systems (in principle, the systems may vary greatly: a respiratory system, the organism, the self, partners in a social relationship, a social organization, or a complex of related organizations or institutions). When they are applied to phenomena which are regarded as a special case in point, as another specimen of this regularity, they are said to explain.

In the present case, the mechanisms refer to sequential relationships between variables which are caught up in one or another version of the "law of effect" (a principle which seems to be found in otherwise most varied schools of psychology). By this is meant, in the present context, some version of the principle that patterns of interaction among individuals are sustained or modified by the punitive or gratifying consequences of such interaction.[41] Together with many others, I have assumed that the law of effect is one of the dynamic principles underlying functional and processual analysis in sociology.

From the formal analysis, we can see just where this principle enters into the interpretation. The social and cultural structure, as I shall presently suggest, goes far toward determining what will ordinarily be experienced as punitive or gratifying as well as the circumstances under which such experiences are likely to occur in interpersonal relations; the principle itself provides a basis for anticipating the probable outcomes of this experience. In short, these mechanisms involve sequence rules which, having been found to hold in otherwise diverse situations, are being provisionally applied to see if they "fit" this particular type of situation.

5. *The formal analysis brings out the operational character of the method of successive approximations.* As is well known, successive approximations constitute a procedure through which analysis comes progressively closer to the complexities of actuality by the gradual introduction of more variables. It is also widely recognized that this method is useful and even essential to disciplined analysis. Nevertheless, discursive writing in particular runs the risk of violating this precept in practice although asserting it in principle. Such writing often moves back and forth between first rough approximations, using a few variables, and better approximations, using more variables, without the author's being aware of what is taking place.

It is true that some awareness of all this is expressed in the substantive portion of this paper; the reader is reminded that "we deal here with only one set of values and, to this extent, we abstract greatly from the many values which find expression in social interaction." But this remark is made once and for all, without identifying the precise points at which further approximations to the concrete actuality are being successively introduced.

In the formal analysis, on the other hand, the strategy of successive approximations is under more thorough control because the procedures of analysis require each consecutive step to be specified. Analysis is carried forward a certain distance before it is complicated by new variables, and each of these transitions to further complexity is described in terms of new analytic operations. From the beginning, it is shown how far the analysis of the process can go by considering the interrelations of only two variables at two times of observation, "without recourse to additional ideas or assumptions." Somewhat later (in notes 27 and 28), the reader is informed of certain other variables which are being advisedly neglected for the time being. Still later, it is shown how four additional variables, incorporated in the substantive account, would be systematically utilized in the formal analysis of the process.

Even those who do not deny the necessity for such step-by-step analysis in principle may find it useful to have a procedure which requires this mode of analysis, thus seeing to it that practice conforms to principle. Each consecutive step in the deductive analysis can then be checked with the results of observation before going on to the next. This avoids the danger of constructing shaky though towering edifices of deduction in the shape of long sorites in which each component is a product exclusively of reason rather than of observation organized by reason.

The step-by-step procedure in the formal analysis has the further merit of stipulating the most important restrictions upon the abstract analysis, rather than avoiding this task by assuming "all other possibly relevant things to be equal." By indicating *which* presumably significant variables are being provisionally taken as constant at each stage, the formal analysis provides direction: it points to the next step in the series of approximations.

In this way, the procedure acts as a prophylaxis against the fallacy of misplaced concreteness, in which conclusions are dubious because one has failed to acknowledge what is being left out of account in the analysis and assumes that the conclusions apply to the complex situation as it actually is, rather than to the relations of a few elements within it. In this case, for example, it precludes the fallacy of regarding the degree of homophily in particular groups as the outcome of *nothing but* the few variables here taken into account.

The procedure guards also against a sister fallacy, what might be called the "and-also" fallacy. This is the misconstruction, common among those who are aware of the dangers of misplaced concreteness, which in effect makes an abstract analysis immune to criticism or disproof, by simply attributing all discrepancies between the hypothetical scheme and actual observations to "other factors" in the situation. At times, there are passing allusions to these factors, without serious regard to the complex problems of really incorporating these many additional variables into a disciplined analysis. The nothing-but fallacy is apparently most often exemplified by those who do precise work but implicitly assume that the few factors taken into account tell the whole story; the and-also fallacy by those who allude to a long list of additionally relevant variables without accepting the responsibility of actually incorporating these into the analysis.

It seems to me that the type of formal analysis in this paper goes far toward preventing both kinds of fallacy: it avoids the first, by periodically indicating certain variables which are being eliminated from the analysis for the time being and avoids the second, not by merely listing these additional variables but by showing *how* they can be brought into the analysis.

6. *The formal analysis stimulates the formulation of additional substantive problems.* Not only does the formal analysis serve to clarify problems raised in the substantive account, and to raise new problems of its own, but it leads also to the statement of further problems which neither the substantive nor the formal analysis had stated in so many words.

As we have seen, the formal analysis shows that homophily, provisionally conceived as a self-contained process, may be either a stationary process—in which the distribution of values-and-personal-associations remains fairly constant—or as a process oscillating around an average, in response to self-induced tendencies and countertendencies. Departing from these conceptions of stationary and oscillating processes, the study of friendship can move onto still another conceptual plane, where it deals with the processes through which patterns of homophily and heterophily take on functional significance for the environing social structure. On this plane, the central problem is no longer the familiar one of ascertaining the extent to which friendships are confined to persons of similar social status or with similar values, a problem which, important as it is, tends to be detached from the context of designated variations in social structure.[42] Nor is it the correlative problem, with which this paper has been primarily concerned, of tracing the processes through which such selective patterns come about. Instead, on this plane of functional sociology, it is the problem of discovering the processes through which different degrees of homophily become functionally appropriate or inappropriate for different types of environing social structure. This perspective on interpersonal relations involves questions such as these: Do various types of social structure have distinctive equilibrium positions for homophily? What are the functions and dysfunctions of various kinds and degrees of homophily—how do these consequences affect the workings of the more inclusive social structure? Through which mechanisms do the consequences of homophily for the social structure operate so as to maintain such equilibria? And correlatively, what leads to the failure of such mechanisms to appear, or to operate effectively?

That the degree of homophily varies greatly among social organizations and communities is a matter of common observation; as we have seen in the introductory pages of part 1, for example, it differed materially in the two housing developments under study. Status for status, there was a higher degree of homophily in Hilltown than in Craftown—a far greater proportion of friendships was confined to those of the same age, religion, nativity, occupational status, and so forth. But it now seems that such empirically observed variations in the degree of homophily can be regarded as problematical, as a beginning for further inquiry. Each type of local social structure can be thought of as having its functionally appropriate degree of homophily (corresponding, presumably, to its position of equilibrium). The task then becomes that of discovering whether, in accord with the hypothesis, marked departures from this level of homophily produces dysfunctional consequences for the social structure which tend to return the system of interpersonal relations to the previous level.

Such a conception is not, of course, far removed from what is already known about social organization. It is not difficult to conceive of a type of organization in which "too great" a degree of value homophily would be dysfunctional to the workings of that organization: "excessive" value homophily in a bureaucratic organization, for example, might mean that the recruitment and promotion of personnel are based, in large part, upon friendships of this kind so that major positions become increasingly staffed by men having the same values and outlook. Beyond a certain point, this could result in rigidities and lack of adaptability of the organization which, in due course, lead to marked reactions against such disruptive "cliques." Or again: "too high" a degree of status homophily might reduce the amount of informal communication between subgroups below the point which is functionally required for the organization or the community, with deterioration in its effective operation, and a consequent reaction against homophily.[43]

Analytically distinct from the social structure as a context for homophily is the related context of culture. As the formal analysis in effect states, marked increases of status homophily within a community in which the subculture emphasizes the norm of minimizing status differences (for example, of class, nativity, or occupation) would be expected to precipitate a sense of threat to this norm among members of the community. Local communities disturbed by what is often described as "snobbery" can be taken to exemplify the type of case in which a degree of status homophily culturally defined as "excessive" releases social forces which may affect the frequency and character of friendships. Such counterreactions are often observed in the direct and expressive form of arranging for "get-togethers" among those of differing status. It is in contexts such as these, perhaps, that we can locate the patterns of stationary and oscillatory process to which the formal analysis directs our attention.

In this sense, the formal analysis leads us to strike out in directions of inquiry which supplement, not supplant, studies in which the major problem is characteristically that of identifying the types of people most likely to enter into close friendships. The major concern would be that of tracing the processes through which different degrees of homophily within designated types of social structure and culture produce functional and dysfunctional consequences which in turn react to affect the patterns of friendship.

7. *The formal analysis clearly illustrates the reciprocal relations of methodological and substantive inquiry.* In spite of caveats to the contrary, the foregoing remarks might seem to imply that the analysis of procedure is *preferable* to the analysis of substance. This is of course very far from my intention. As a matter of fact, the formal analysis has shown that the very complexity of social systems puts a special premium on the theoretical basis for selecting significant or appropriate elements for analysis. Thus, far from minimizing the importance of a substantive conceptual scheme, the methodological analysis underscores its importance and does so by focusing attention on the distinctive place of each conceptual element in the total analysis. All this is made quite explicit in the methodological section: "The formalism . . . only brings out that one aspect of a process analysis is the existence of certain sequence rules and chains; the actual content of the rules is a theoretical contribution. . . ." And again: "It obviously makes a difference which specifications are introduced. . . . All this can be put into formal language after someone has thought about such alternatives. . . . Behind the formal notion of variables is the hidden hope that those variables which alone can make the formalism productive will be selected."

In these terms, the entire formal analysis bears out the interlocking and mutually supporting character of methodological and substantive study. This one example suggests that other such reanalyses might usefully take the place of the occasional polemics that would set methodologist and theorist in what must be only mock opposition to one another.

As I now see it in the light of this experience, the formal reanalysis of a substantive interpretation offers a number of devices for thinking through the implications of what has been said, beyond the point which more discursive analysis ordinarily encourages or even permits. It can show that some implications have not been fully drawn, that they lead further than was supposed, and that other implications have not been drawn at all. As an example of the first kind I cite the notion of the interdependence of values and personal relationships which was extended to include the question of preponderating forces in such interdependence under diverse conditions; as an example of the second kind, the range of problems which emerges when homophily is thought of in terms of stationary or dynamic equilibrium.

These few retrospective comments should be seen in context. They are not intended to give credit where credit is due, however laudable such a purpose may be in another connection. They are intended only to single out, as best I can, the various specific uses of this formal reanalysis of a substantive conception, with a view to identifying some of the functions of this reanalysis for social theory and research. If these remarks also imply a tribute to the author of the formal analysis, that cannot be helped.[44]

Notes

Foreword

1. As a result of this research, Lazarsfeld concluded that the Belgian Adolphe Quetelet was the founder of empirical social research. This led his friend Robert K. Merton to suggest to the administrative officers of Columbia University, somewhat after the appearance of this paper, that Lazarsfeld be named Quetelet Professor of Social Science. He bore that title until his retirement from Columbia in 1969.

2. Actually, a precursor of the full elaboration formula appeared in an appendix to a monograph which Lazarsfeld wrote with Samuel A. Stouffer, *The Family in the Depression,* published in 1937 by the Social Science Research Council as one of a series of studies on the effects of the depression. It has since been republished by the Arno Press.

3. Charles Y. Glock, "Survey Design and Analysis in Sociology," in Charles Y. Glock, ed., *Survey Research in the Social Sciences*; Travis Hirschi and Hanan Selvin, *Delinquency Research*; and Morris Rosenberg, *The Logic of Survey Analysis.*

4. Panel studies are longitudinal investigations based on repeated interviews with the same individuals. The name attached to the technique probably had its origins in market research, where panels of consumers were set up to provide easy access to data on preferences for particular products or opinions about different kinds of packaging.

5. For example, Theodore Newcomb, *Personality and Social Change,* which was published in 1942.

6. One of Lazarsfeld's last publications was "Some Episodes in the History of Panel Analysis," a talk that he gave in 1976, shortly before his death. (It was published posthumously in 1978, in Denise Kandel, ed., *Longitudinal Research on Drug Use: Empirical Findings and Methodological Issues.*) This article, too technical for inclusion in this volume, underscores Lazarsfeld's enduring interest in panel studies.

7. This article appeared in 1954 in a volume, *Freedom and Control in Modern Society,* which has long been out of print. In 1963 a fragment of the paper was included in a collection of readings edited by Alvin and Helen Gouldner. In 1970 the entire article was included in a French book on the analysis of social

349

processes, *L'Analyse des processus sociaux*. Thus it has not been readily available to an American audience since its original publication, which is further reason for including it in the present volume.

8. Because the articles included in this volume have not been ordered according to the temporal sequence in which they first appeared, there are sometimes seeming anomalies in references made in one article to another. That is, an article which appears early in the volume may cite another which is found in a later section of the book. Such inconsistencies were unavoidable if the overall structure of the volume was to be maintained.

9. *An Introduction to Applied Sociology* (with Jeffrey G. Reitz and with the collaboration of Ann K. Pasanella); "The Policy Science Movement (An Outsider's View)"; and "The Uses of Sociology by Presidential Commissions" (with Martin Jaeckel).

10. *Latent Structure Analysis* (with Neil Henry), 1968.

11. "The Algebra of Dichotomous Systems" (1961) and "Algebra of Dichotomies" (1972).

Introduction

1. Patricia Kendall and Paul F. Lazarsfeld, "Problems of Survey Analysis."

2. Simon, whose seminal paper on causal ordering with continuous variables paralleled Lazarsfeld's on categorical variables, addresses this problem again in the volume in honor of Lazarsfeld. H. A. Simon, "The Meaning of Causal Ordering," in R. K. Merton, J. S. Coleman, and P. H. Rossi, eds., *Qualitative and Quantitative Social Research: Essays in Honor of Paul F. Lazarsfeld* (New York: Free Press, 1979).

3. D. C. Pelz and F. M. Andrews, "Detecting Causal Priorities in Panel Study Data," *American Sociological Review* (1964), 29:836–48; D. Campbell and K. N. Clayton, "Avoiding Regression Effects in Panel Studies of Communication Impact," *Studies in Publication Communication* (1961), 3:99–118; Leo Goodman, "Causal Analysis of Data from, Panel Studies and Other Kinds of Surveys," *American Journal of Sociology* (1973), 78:1135–91.

4. J. S. Coleman, *Introduction to Mathematical Sociology* (New York: Free Press, 1964), and *Longitudinal Data Analysis* (New York: Basic Books, 1981).

5. The last statement is made in view of the large number of research organizations that have sprung up outside the university in the past ten years. There are many reasons for the growth of such organizations, but their existence outside the constraints of a professional association and academic journal publication means that they lack the self-disciplining qualities that the academic discipline imposes on the work that does take place within the academy. For a discussion of such organizations, see J. S. Coleman, "Sociological Analysis and Social Policy," in T. Bottomore and R. Nisbet, eds., *A History of Sociological Analysis* (New York: Basic Books, 1979).

6. Paul F. Lazarsfeld, Bernard Berelson, and Hazel Gaudet, *The People's Choice*.

7. Bernard Berelson, Paul F. Lazarsfeld, and William McPhee, *Voting: A Study of Opinion Formation in a Presidential Campaign.*
8. Paul F. Lazarsfeld, "The Art of Asking Why" (1934), p. 183.
9. It is true that Lazarsfeld's focus on individual action failed to capture much about social structure. The strain toward dissolution of rigid social structures based on geographic community did not mean that social structure was absent—yet the survey methods had great difficulty in showing the functioning of this social structure. Many at Columbia felt some unease at the individualistic character of analysis made on the basis of survey research. In 1955, after completing graduate work and while still at Columbia, I designed research that reflected my own unease. This was a study of communities of adolescents, who I felt were still enough bound to their environments to make the "adolescent community" a relevant unit to study. Although I did not carry out that research at Columbia, I did so later at Chicago: J. S. Coleman, *The Adolescent Society* (New York: Free Press, 1961).

1. An Episode in the History of Social Research: A Memoir

1. Gordon Allport, *The Use of Personal Documents in Psychological Science*; Louis Gottschalk, Clyde Kluckhohn, and Robert Angell, *The Use of Personal Documents in History, Anthropology, and Sociology.*
2. "Problems in Methodology," in Robert K. Merton, Leonard Broom, and Leonard S. Cottrell, eds., *Sociology Today*, p. 78. (Ed. note: see essay 4.)
3. There was a Viennese branch of the German Sociological Society, but as far as I remember I had no contact with it. I later found some of their members mentioned as discussants in printed reports of the yearly German *Soziologentag*.
4. One of the rare reports in English on the interesting German youth movement of that period is Walter Laqueur's *Young Germany.*
5. My first publication, at the age of twenty-three, was *Gemeinschaftserziehung durch Erziehungsgemeinschaften* (1924) a report on a camp which, together with my late friend Ludwig Wagner, I organized for the development of a socialist spirit in young people.
6. Paul F. Lazarsfeld, "Hinter den Kulissen der Schule," in Sofie Lazarsfeld, ed., *Technik der Erziehung*. (Leipzig: S. Hirzel, 1929). One who has read the introduction to Paul F. Lazarsfeld and Morris S. Rosenberg, eds., *The Language of Social Research* will see the extent to which such intellectual inclinations have endured over a period of forty years.
7. My position as assistant at the Psychological Institute was rather vague and insecure. As a safeguard against possible collapse, I maintained my position in the secondary school system by taking an extended leave of absence. Among our clients was the Frankfurt Institut für Sozialforschung. Its director, Max Horkheimer, had conceived the series of inquiries which were reported finally in *Autorität und Familie*. One of the studies by Erich Fromm required the filling in of questionnaires by young workers, and we were asked

to organize the part of the fieldwork done in Austria. I did not meet any of the Horkheimer group when I was in Europe but got well acquainted with them after they and I came to the United States. As a matter of fact in the United States in 1934 I worked with Fromm on the analysis of the questionnaire we had undertaken in Austria.

8. *Statistisches Praktikum für Psychologen und Lehrer* (1929). Subsequently, in this country, I have worked and published in the field of mathematical sociology. But this has never been an integral part of what has been called the Vienna-Columbia research tradition. I shall therefore not deal with it in this essay.

9. Marie Jahoda, Paul F. Lazarsfeld, and Hans Zeisel, *Die Arbeitslosen von Marienthal*. As part of the activities of my new research center in Vienna, I wanted to do some kind of social survey to balance its market research activities. For reasons I cannot remember, I was interested in doing a leisure-time study, and I discussed it with a leader of the Socialist Party, Otto Bauer. He considered it silly to study leisure problems at a time of severe unemployment, and it was he who suggested the new topic, to which I shall return repeatedly in this essay.

10. The way I received my fellowship has its own interest. The representative of the Rockefeller Foundation gave me an application form. Living in the pessimistic climate of Vienna at the time, I was sure I would not get the fellowship, and did not apply. In November 1932 I got a cable from the Paris Rockefeller office informing me that my application had been misfiled and that they wanted another copy. They had obviously decided to grant me the fellowship on the recommendation of their representative and it had never occurred to them that I had not applied. I mailed a "duplicate," and the fellowship was granted.

11. A condensation of the book in English will soon be published by Random House; its political influence will be traced in a new introduction. It is hard to realize today how neglected the notion of social stratification was at that time.

12. The main conceptual idea was taken over from a psychoanalyst, Siegfried Bernfeld, who had characterized a creative value of middle-class adolescence under the term "extended puberty." American sociologists have recently taken up this notion under the term "deferred gratification." The relation between Bernfeld, Bühler, and myself is described in a monograph by Leopold Rosenmayr, the current professor of sociology at the University of Vienna, on early adolescent research in Austria: *Geschichte der Jugendforschung in Oesterreich, 1914–1931*.

13. Herbert Gans, "Urban Poverty and Social Planning."

14. A similar table was used at the same time by Robert Merton in his dissertation, *Science, Technology and Society in Seventeenth-Century England*. I suppose that both of us got the idea from Max Weber, although I do not remember having known at the time the table on religion and occupational choice that Weber includes in a footnote to the monograph on the Protestant Ethic.

15. Just after I came to this country, I published "The Art of Asking Why"

(1935), which summarizes the resulting interviewing techniques. Though re-printed and widely quoted, I am not sure that it had any great influence on American research. See, however, the extensive entry "Reason Analysis" written by my former student Charles Kadushin in the new *International Encyclopedia of the Social Sciences.*

16. I have traced the importance of the notion of action in a paper read at the Max Weber Centennial, organized by the American Sociological Association: Paul F. Lazarsfeld and A. R. Oberschall, "Max Weber and Empirical Social Research."

17. In France "structural linguistics" is today considered the great glory of modern social science. The founding father is Ferdinand de Saussure, and the second generation is represented by the circle of Prague, with Troubetzkoy and Jakobson as the leaders. The latter corroborates my memory that he and his associates frequently traveled to Vienna to obtain Karl Bühler's wise counsel.

18. Published in the *Harvard Business Review* in October of that year. The Viennese university structure made me classify myself at the time as a psychologist. The fact that six years later I became a member of the Columbia Department of Sociology did not change the character of my work. I am now professor of social science, which resolved for me a terminological embarrassment. Incidentally, the paper cited above was rejected by two psychological journals, which considered the topic not appropriately psychological.

19. This paper, entitled "Principles of Sociography," was submitted in 1934 to the journal of the New School for Social Research. Its graduate faculty had become the exponent of European social sciences, and I thought the editors would be interested in a paper trying to link explicitly empirical work done in both countries. I suppose, however, that "sociography" was at that time not considered a real part of the European tradition. The original paper was refused and was never published. On rereading it for the present purpose, I find it, and especially the examples contained in it, characteristic of the state of affairs in the early 1930s. Incidentally, the term "integrating construct" was originally called *Leitformel* and was first translated as "matrix formula." However, the term "matrix" has become identified with its use in algebra. I therefore prefer the present translation. Sometime later, a more extended treatment of integrating constructs was published in Allen H. Barton and Paul F. Lazarsfeld, "Some Functions of Qualitative Analysis in Social Research." (Ed. note: see essay 7.)

20. Arthur Vidich, Joseph Bensman, and Maurice Stein, eds., *Reflections on Community Studies.*

21. When I was approximately fifteen, I read the memoirs of Lili Braun. She describes an election evening in Germany in the early 1900s, where everyone was waiting for the returns, and then celebrating the Socialist victory. I found this extremely exciting, and in the summer of 1916, when I was living in the custody of Rudolf Hilferding, the Socialist leader, I asked him to explain to me what this election business was all about. He found my attitude rather childish and said I should rather first know what the Socialist program was all about. We made a compromise that I would read a book by Kautsky if, at

the same time, I also got a book on elections. How seriously I read Kautsky at the time I do not know, but as for the little book explaining elections, more than fifty years later I still remember the name of the author: Poensgen.

22. The 1967 meeting of the World Association of Public Opinion Research was held in Vienna, and a day was given to commemorating the fortieth anniversary of the Vienna Center. Hans Zeisel gave a description of its beginning, which is published in the *Revue française de sociologie* (1968), vol. 2.

23. The plan never succeeded, because the very able Kingdon became involved in politics and neglected the institution. Caught between two stools, he ended rather tragically. Today, the building on Rector Street houses a local branch of Rutgers University.

24. The very low salary level may be explained by the economic situation of the time. Still, eight hours a week of teaching for $200 a month was, even then, probably a rather poor way to make one's academic living.

25. Paul F. Lazarsfeld and Rowena Wyant, "Magazines in 90 Cities: Who Reads What?" At one point, I computed the average of all these figures to develop the profile of the typical city; it turned out to be Muncie, Indiana, Lynd's *Middletown*.

26. Included also was my work for the Social Science Research Council on the effects of the depression. Thirteen monographs were planned (and carried out) on various aspects based on the collection and integration of available studies. Stouffer was made research director and asked Lynd to recommend someone for the monograph on the family. On Lynd's suggestion, Stouffer invited me to Chicago, and this first meeting lasted practically the whole day. Within a few hours, we had laid out a joint plan, and from there dates my continuous collaboration with him, to which I will return repeatedly. See Samuel Stouffer and Paul F. Lazarsfeld, *Research Memorandum on the Family in the Depression*.

27. By then, it had become fairly clear that a research director required a new type of skills for which few people had yet been trained. The specifications and preparation for this job have been, for many years, a matter of great concern to me. In my presidential address to the American Sociological Association, "The Sociology of Empirical Social Research" (1962), I discussed the matter in great detail. The problem still seems to me important and as yet unresolved. I am, therefore, adding the corresponding sections of that address as an appendix to this essay.

28. The reader may compare, for example, Adorno's and my reports on the same events. To broaden the view, I want to add a few lines on Kurt Lewin, whom I knew and admired both here and abroad. Lewin had acquired fame in Germany through a series of papers written partly by him and partly by his students. These appeared over the years under the general title of "Psychology of Action." The notion of action, which enjoyed high prestige in Germany, was unacceptable here because of the dominance of behaviorism. When Lewin finally came to this country, he shifted to the topic for which he became famous here, namely "group dynamics." J. L. Moreno claims that it was he who advised Lewin to adopt this term. In 1938, I was visited by a recent

refugee from Vienna, Gustave Bergmann, who asked me for help. I remembered that he was a very good mathematician with great interest in psychology. By then, Lewin was already in Iowa. I phoned him and suggested that he give a job to Bergmann, who could help him to bring his topological ideas in harmony with prevailing procedures in mathematical topology. Lewin did, indeed, invite him, but the venture ended in a disagreement between the two men. Bergmann still teaches logic and philosophy of science in Iowa and has repeatedly published on the nature of psychological theory.

29. Elsewhere, in "Innovation in Higher Education," I have stressed that such a general notion of strategy should be considered more seriously in sociological analysis.

30. My Congress presentation was published in English translation as "An Unemployed Village" (1932).

31. Later the questionnaire served as the model for the Decatur study that resulted in Elihu Katz and Paul F. Lazarsfeld, *Personal Influence.*

32. As far as my own work went, I began a program which was never carried through to completion. Starting from my own ideas on "The Art of Asking Why" and my interest in the German literature on the will, I set out to study the American literature on motivation and to write a monograph on the subject. I still have many folders of extracts and notes on the pertinent publications. I also visited William McDougall in North Carolina to learn more about his theories of sentiments. In retrospect, I believe it was the drift toward American sociologists as a new reference group that accounts for my having let this earlier plan peter out. This drift will become apparent as the story unfolds.

33. This might be a good place to recall an anecdote characteristic of misinterpretations of norms and roles, which obviously do not happen only to Polish peasants. When I came to offer my collaboration to the director of the PSC, he asked me whether I knew how to use a slide rule. Receiving a positive answer, he assigned me to computing percentages on his main study, called the Brand Barometer. It consisted of reports about the brands of food American housewives used, based on a national sample. Understandably, I found it boring to compute percentages for days on end. But I thoroughly "understood" the situation: American culture requires that everyone work his way up from the bottom; I was being put to the test before being admitted to true professional work. After a few days, I timidly asked the director whether I had sufficiently proved my endurance. Only then did he understand what a European Rockefeller Fellow is. He had just taken my work as labor for which he did not have to pay and probably classified me as being supported by WPA. Similarly, on quite a number of my first trips I traveled by coach, even overnight. One day a Rockefeller accountant asked me why I did not use Pullman, to which I was entitled. I had not realized that Pullman cars existed; I had learned in Europe that in the democratic U.S.A. there is nothing like the European distinction between different classes of railroad cars.

34. A paradoxical situation developed during World War II: Likert was then research director of the Department of Agriculture, which conducted morale studies among farmers. I was a consultant to the Office of War Information, which did corresponding studies in urban areas. The research director of OWI

was Elmo Wilson, who favored highly structured interviews. Rather heated battles developed between the OWI and the Likert group. I was asked to study the matter and write a report; it was later published in condensed form under the title "The Controversy over Detailed Interviews—An Offer for Negotiation" (1944).

35. When Hans Zeisel came to the United States in 1958, I suggested that he enlarge this text, and the Columbia Bureau arranged for its first publication. I wanted very much to find a good American title. One day in a flower shop I saw a promotion slogan then much in vogue: "Say It with Flowers." I immediately decided that the title of the book should be *Say It with Figures*, and under that title it appeared in 1947. In social theory, this is called functional equivalence. Zeisel has meantime greatly enlarged the scope of the book; it has been translated into several languages, and is now in its fifth U.S. edition.

36. In the fall of 1933, Gordon Allport invited me to talk to his seminar on the problem of motivation. After a few introductory remarks, I said: "Let me give you a first example from a study of mouthwash." There was a roar of laughter, and I answered: "I don't quite see why 'lifted weights' are so much more dignified than 'mouthwash.' " I think that Edwin Boring's presence that day might have suggested the remark.

37. These and other unpublished studies mentioned in this section are available in mimeographed form at the archives of the History of Psychology, Akron University, Akron, Ohio.

38. In retrospect, I am aware of the costs involved in my style of life. All during the two years I saw hardly anything of the country except for research offices, and I also formed few personal social contacts. At that time, little research was under way on the West Coast, and I am probably the only one of the nine foreign fellows arriving at that time who did not exercise his right to a trip to California.

39. In writing this, I realize that this habit has carried over to the last twenty years, during which I have stayed for considerable time in a variety of European countries. My serious contacts on these occasions have definitely not been with my peers in age and status but with younger people.

40. Volume 23 (1939).

41. One should not overlook the fact that every person has unlikable characteristics and that some of them can feed a stereotype. In the quotation just mentioned, Stouffer says that some people are prejudiced against me. I have a letter from Craig, in which he wants to explain to me why he could not help me more after he left Pittsburgh; he implores me not to come to the United States, because I would have so many personal difficulties. (The letter reached Europe when I had already returned to the States.) Intermingled with his— certainly sincere—expression of friendship, are such sentences as, "People don't feel safe with you. . . . You are too grand at all times and never sufficiently modest. . . . You seem not to have made many fast friends. . . . It is for that I am miserable."

It is obviously impossible for me to judge the extent and concrete basis for this reaction. One thing I am aware of is that, in the first years, I was rather rude to assistants and students, barking at them when they fell down on an assignment. I like to think I changed my behavior as I learned to eat with the fork in the right hand.

42. I described and documented one such abortive effort at the University of Chicago in my presidential address before the American Sociological Association, referred to in note 27.

43. Historians, remembering the *Gueux*, will understand the acceptance of a term which originally had pejorative overtones. Still there is a difference between the organization man and the institution man. The former is supposedly pushed around, while the latter finds in the institution a field for creative self-expression.

44. The sampling design and the questionnaire were very naive, but for years afterward our survey was cited as the first of its kind in Europe. I would not be surprised if it antedated such work in the United States.

45. Herta Herzog, "Stimme und Persönlichkeit."

46. When Robert Merton became my main associate at the Columbia Bureau of Applied Social Research, he approved this philosophy and acted on it. The conditions under which such a strategy makes sense (either on a senior or a junior level) deserve further analysis and discussion. I can do no more here than raise the general problem.

47. The Elias Smith story has a sequel, which deserves mention because of its historical setting. During the McCarthy period I was invited to a UNESCO meeting in Paris. I received the usual questionnaire needed for my clearance, which contained the question as to whether I had ever used a pseudonym. Without thinking, I interpreted the question in a political frame and answered, "No." My clearance was held up; I had to answer a number of specific questions. One of them stated that it was known to the inquiring agency that I had used the pseudonym Elias Smith, and why did I deny it. I sent them the titles of the Elias Smith papers, which satisfied even the clearance agency. The amazing thing about this episode is that some federal agency had found out about this pseudonym in papers on radio research. Incidentally, from time to time we still receive inquiries at Columbia University from people who want to know where Elias Smith is.

48. Similarly, at the time when I turned over the directorship of the Columbia Bureau to my successor, Charles Glock, we had accumulated a moderate deficit, which I, as usual, counted on covering with funds from future studies. The change in directorship was taken as the occasion for a financial review, and the university preferred to cover the deficit from general funds, so that thereafter a stricter accounting system could be set up.

49. One of our early products was a paper by H. M. Beville, then on the research staff of NBC, entitled, "The ABCD's of Radio Audiences."

50. The most accessible summary appears in the entry "Survey Analysis" in the new *International Encyclopedia of the Social Sciences.*

51. It appeared as a special monograph and also in *Radio and the Printed Page* (1940).

52. Herta Herzog, "On Borrowed Experience."

53. The early interviews on the Orson Welles program were summarized by Dr. Herzog in a memorandum to Stanton which was subsequently published

as a contribution to the literature and that was later extended into the book-length study *The Invasion from Mars,* by Hadley Cantril, Hazel Gaudet, and Herta Herzog. Though at the time I had hoped Dr. Herzog would receive a major share of the credit for her imaginative work on that study, there is no doubt that Cantril was responsible for the type of interviews used in this study.

54. Bernard Berelson, *Content Analysis in Communication Research.*

55. Joseph Klapper, *The Effects of Mass Communication.*

56. Paul F. Lazarsfeld, "Some Notes on the Relationships Between Radio and the Press" (1941).

57. The minutes of this conference are still available and might one day deserve more detailed scrutiny.

58. I had assisted Charlotte Bühler when in 1931 she was guest editor on child studies for the main journal on general psychology.

59. This episode, involving the notion of reasonable risk, implies a certain optimistic belief in the malleability of the social environment. A director of the Bureau cannot afford to underestimate or ignore options.

60. Cf. "The Empirical Analysis of Action," in Paul F. Lazarsfeld and Morris S. Rosenberg, eds., *The Language of Social Research* (1955).

61. As director of the Bureau as well as in my teaching, I kept developing and sharpening such formulas over many years; I quote them from accessible publications even though their dates in certain cases lag behind the period in which they originated and in which I place them in this essay.

62. Paul F. Lazarsfeld, "Mass Media of Communication in Modern Society" (1954).

63. Leo Lowenthal, "An Historical Preface to the Popular Culture Debate." The book in which this article appeared is the report of a symposium organized jointly by the Academy of Arts and Sciences and the Tamiment Institute. I was chairman of the sessions and in the introduction to the book I tried again to stress the constructive role of criticism.

64. Paul F. Lazarsfeld, "The Obligations of the 1950 Pollster to the 1984 Historian" (1950). (Ed. note: see essay 2.) For an up-to-date review see Lee Benson, "An Approach to the Scientific Study of Past Public Opinion."

65. Paul F. Lazarsfeld, "Concept Formation and Measurement in the Behavioral Sciences: Some Historical Observations" (1966).

66. Edward Suchman, "Invitation to Music," and Duncan MacDougald, Jr., "The Popular Music Industry."

67. The first formula of which I am aware stems from Max Horkheimer. It can be found in his "Traditional and Critical Theory" and "Philosophy and Critical Theory." Contemporary presentations of the two positions can be found in the following two papers: Hans Albert, "Der Mythos der totalen Vernunft: Dialektische Ansprüche im Lichte undialektischen Kritik," and Jürgen Habermas, "Gegen einen positivistischen halbierten Rationalismus."

68. T. W. Adorno, "Zur gesellschaftlichen Lage der Musik."

69. Paul F. Lazarsfeld, "Administrative and Critical Communications Research" (1941).

70. T. W. Adorno, "The Radio Symphony"; "On Popular Music."

71. Rudolf Arnheim, "The World of the Daytime Serial."

72. This issue appeared only in December 1940 because the regular editor did not want the two radio issues to be published too close together; the papers themselves, however, stem mostly from the Union Square period of the project.

73. I was a member of the magazine audience research program. It was ably guided by Neal DuBois, then research director of *Life*. Most of the major magazines were represented in the group. A summary of the many audience studies done at the time can be found in my paper, "Communications Research and the Social Psychologist" (1948).

74. See, for example, Tore Hollonquist and Edward Suchman, "Listening to the Listener," and Adolf Sturmthal and Alberta Curtis, "Program Analyzer Tests of Two Educational Films."

75. The only exception is a staff paper (1939) by Hazel Gaudet which was later included in Paul F. Lazarsfeld and Morris S. Rosenberg, *The Language of Social Research*.

76. I find in the files a number of memoranda in which I suggested to the associate directors the proper strategy that should be followed and the roles they should play—a fine illustration of the typical behavior of the "worrying director."

77. Samuel Stouffer, *Social Research to Test Ideas*.

78. The question of publication was troublesome because at the time the market that is now provided by the numerous courses on communications research did not exist. Robert Lynd devised the successful strategy: a friend of his wrote a story for the *Readers' Digest* taken from the manuscript. As a result, Duell, Sloan and Pearce published the book. Since then we have had no difficulties in finding outlets for our studies.

79. A year later I was made a permanent member of the Department of Sociology. This made finally effective my change in classification from psychologist to sociologist.

80. Paul F. Lazarsfeld, Bernard Berelson, and Hazel Gaudet, *The People's Choice*.

81. We did not have enough funds for a panel of six hundred respondents and therefore solicited additional contributions. The most important one came from *Life* magazine through the intervention of Elmo Roper. Immediately after the 1940 election, *Life* published two feature stories based on our first tabulations.

82. The Bureau dates its origin properly to the beginning of the radio project and celebrated its twentieth anniversary in 1957.

83. The origin of this collaboration is vividly and correctly reported in a *New Yorker* profile on Merton by M. M. Hunt (January 28, 1961). My collaboration with Merton in the Columbia University Department of Sociology transcends the frame of this essay.

84. Publications resulting from this work include: Paul F. Lazarsfeld and Robert K. Merton, "Studies in Radio and Film Propaganda"; Paul F. Lazarsfeld and Patricia Kendall, "The Listener Talks Back"; Robert K. Merton, Marjorie Fiske, and Patricia L. Kendall, *The Focused Interview*.

85. During the period of the Princeton project, the staff consisted of em-

ployees without academic connections. The problems were simple: they wanted higher salaries, and I wanted to spend more money on research. When the office moved to Columbia University, a shift slowly came about. Increasingly the staff was recruited from graduates of the sociology department for whom status in the academic community was important. Obviously the committee had been informed about this aspect of the relationship between the Bureau and the department. Its report stated that it would be necessary to "frame regulations relating to the appointment of staff members of research agencies and to the responsibilities of the university toward such employees." The matter was not followed up for at least three reasons. The administration was mainly concerned with the contract problem; I fought mainly for recognition and financing by the university; the staff was not too insistent probably because they were a new breed and very much in demand by all major universities. For today's staff, problems of status and tenure are issues of top priority.

86. Cheatham was a hard-working, effective, and insightful chairman. I showed one of his letters, dated February 1, 1945, to Robert Lynd. He returned it with the following penciled annotation: "an altogether admirable letter from a civilized and humane man who carries his own super-ego."

3. Notes on the History of Quantification in Sociology—
Trends, Sources, and Problems

1. In the following notes, foreign titles are given in their original form; in the main text these titles are usually translated and abbreviated so as to support the narrative.

2. For an instructive survey and a new look, see Patrick Dacre Trevor-Roper, "The General Crisis of the Seventeenth Century."

3. Secrecy regarding statistical information collected by government agencies was maintained by some countries well into the nineteenth century. The parallel to contemporary secrecy about atomic physics is obvious. Several revolutionary governments deliberately made statistical data available to the public. I wonder whether the explicit mention of the decennial census in the United States Constitution had partly such ideological implications.

4. This episode is interesting, incidentally, because it shows the efforts which even minor political arithmeticians made to put their work to practical use. The Breslau group wanted to counter the astrologists' contention that certain years in a man's life are especially dangerous. The pertinent historical papers are reviewed by Victor John, *Geschichte der Statistik.*

5. The facts mentioned up to this point can be found in any of the histories of statistics mentioned in the footnotes.

6. E. Strauss, *Sir William Petty.*

7. *Ibid.*, p. 203.

8. *Ibid.*, p. 221.

9. Suessmilch had become interested in demography through reading the

work of William Derham, an English cleric, whose book, *Psycho-Theology; or, A Demonstration of the Being and Attributes of God from His Works of Creation*, had already gone through several editions by the beginning of the eighteenth century.

10. Harald Westergaard, *Contributions to the History of Statistics*.

11. It has often been noted that, in spite of the fact that Suessmilch's was the first serious discussion of the relation between standard of living and population growth, he had no direct intellectual effects or followers. Malthus, whose work did not begin until fifty years later (and who, incidentally, used many of Suessmilch's computations), received all the acclaim. In a later context, I shall try to explain this neglect of the Prussian pastor by his academic contemporaries. I have found only one English summary of Suessmilch's work which goes beyond the conventional histories of statistics, a dissertation by F. S. Crumm, "The Statistical Work of Suessmilch." It is a rather dry but very specific and therefore useful guide through Suessmilch's main writings. In the festschrift for Toennies' eightieth birthday, one contribution by Georg Jahn is entitled "Suessmilch and the Social Sciences of the Eighteenth Century." It is very disappointing. The author gives a brief description of Suessmilch's work and expresses the hope that sociologists will one day pay more attention to it. Jahn's own contributions are some remarks on how Suessmilch fitted in with the rational theology of his period.

12. Herta Jogland, *Ursprünge und Grundlagen der Soziologie bei Adam Ferguson*. The author informs me that the first use of statistical data by a moral philosopher which she could trace is in a book by a George Combe, *Moral Philosophy; or, The Duties of Man*.

13. August Meitzen, *History, Theory, and Technique of Statistics*.

14. George A. Lundberg, "Statistics in Modern Social Thought."

15. George Sarton, "Preface to Vol. 23 of *Isis* (Quetelet)."

16. Nathan Glazer, "The Rise of Social Research in Europe."

17. John, *Geschichte*.

18. John's work grew out of Knapp's broad interest in the history of statistics, to which I shall return in the section on Quetelet. Meitzen himself, who started the original confusion, corrected himself later. He wrote the entry on Conring in the influential German *Encyclopedia of the Social Sciences*.

19. Strauss, *Petty*, p. 196.

20. John, *Geschichte*, p. 58, here translated from the Latin quotation.

21. Anyone who wishes to trace the theory of Conring in English studies will encounter difficulties. Both Frank Hankins and Westergaard agree with John's views that Conring is to be considered the founder of the German tradition, yet both men devote a mere paragraph to Conring and several pages to Achenwall. They might have had difficulties with John's review, which always quotes Conring in Latin and without translation, a tradition, incidentally, which continues in the more recent publications. The original writings of Conring were not available to me. But the German sources give many and often overlapping quotations; thus frequent internal checks were possible.

22. It should be remembered that not long after the death of Conring in

1681, Hanover and Brandenburg were competing for top prestige in Germany. When the Brandenburg elector acquired the title of Prussian king by a legal trick, the Hanoverian tried to balance this success by accepting, somewhat reluctantly, the crown of England.

23. Ernst V. Moeller, *Hermann Conring.*

24. Johann Huizinga, *Men and Ideas.*

25. Paul Felberg, *Hermann Conrings Anteil am politischen Leben seiner Zeit.*

26. It is possible to trace all this in some detail in Guhrauer's biography of Leibnitz, *Gottfried Wilhelm Freiherr V. Leibnitz.* This two-volume book puts great emphasis on Leibnitz' personal contacts and either quotes directly from correspondence or gives at least references indicating where further information can be found. It is, of course, written with Leibnitz as the central figure, and therefore the many allusions to Conring are often brief. It should be worthwhile to follow up Guhrauer's references and to piece the picture together with Conring in mind. Among the monographs on Conring, I have not found one with this emphasis.

27. *Ibid.,* p. 212.

28. *Ibid.,* pp. 213ff.

29. Reinhold Zehrfeld, "Hermann Conring's Staatenkunde."

30. As far as I know, political arithmetic is about the only topic of contemporary knowledge on which Leibnitz himself did not write. It is therefore quite possible that Conring did not even know of the work of his English contemporaries. He was, however, informed on English developments in at least one other field: among his medical writings, I found mention of a treatise on Harvey's discovery of the circulation of blood (in addition to texts on skorbut, fractured skulls, and iatrochemistry).

31. Zehrfeld, "Conring's Staatenkunde," pp. 15ff.

32. *Ibid.,* pp. 46ff.

33. One day the history of universities should be rewritten from a social scientist's point of view. Stephen D'Irsay (*Histoire des universités*) is altogether too superficial, although his footnotes on sources are very valuable. Paulsen's "History of Academic Instruction in Germany" is a fine piece of analytical writing and contains much information on the period after the Thirty Years' War (Friedrich Paulsen, *Geschichte des gelehrten Unterrichts*). His main interest, however, lies in the ups and downs of the classical studies, and he pays less attention to the men and institutions relevant to my narrative.

34. Several princes gave him the title "personal physician and states counselor," which shows how the many facets of his reputation were fused. I do not discuss here the similar positions he held for a while in Denmark and in Sweden. There is evidence that in 1651 he hoped to move to Sweden permanently, but again nothing came of this effort to escape the small town atmosphere of Germany.

35. Achenwall presided over a weekly seminar where transient explorers and diplomats reported on their experiences abroad; it was the task of the

student to subsume this information under the proper categories of "the System."

36. Denifle, in his book on the origin of medieval universities (*Die Entstehung der mittelalterlichen Universität*), raises the question as to why the University of Paris remained intact after the death of Abelard, while preceding foundations disappeared after the death of the charismatic master. He thinks that it is the *methodological* idea of the disputation, the finding of truth by a staged dialectic controversy, which provides the explanation.

37. John, *Geschichte*, pp. 98ff.

38. *Ibid.*, pp. 129ff.

39. Pitirim Sorokin, *Fads and Foibles in Modern Sociology*.

40. John, *Geschichte*, pp. 128–39.

41. One might record the victory of the table statisticians with an ironical smile. Today, they themselves are beginning to be looked upon as mere social bookkeepers. Many a mathematically trained statistician would not deal with the problems the political arithmeticians inaugurated; he would reserve the term "statistics" to an abstract theory of inference.

42. Schloezer promised in one of his books that he would one day present Suessmilch's ideas, but he "never got around to it."

43. John, *Geschichte*, p. 9.

44. The University of Brussels was not created until a decade later.

45. In connection with his work for the observatory, he made a number of other trips, including one to Germany in 1829 when he stayed in Weimar for a week and had several meetings with Goethe, then eighty years old. Goethe was quite fascinated by his young visitor. While Quetelet meant to stay only a few hours, Goethe kept him for a week and corresponded with him for the remaining years of his life. There exist several contemporary reports on this encounter, and Quetelet himself at the age of seventy wrote a reminiscence. The material has been collected in Victor John, "Quetelet bei Goethe," in H. Paesche, ed., *Festgabe für Johannes Conrad*. Goethe discussed with Quetelet repeatedly his favorite notion of "types." John surmises that this might have given Quetelet the idea for his terminology of the "Homme Moyen." Some of John's material has been briefly summarized in a contribution by August Collard to *Isis* ("Goethe et Quételet,").

46. Two years before Quetelet's birth, Belgium was still one of the provinces under the domination of the Austrians. During the Napoleonic wars, it became a part of France, and after the settlement of 1815 it was made a part of the Kingdom of the Netherlands, which combined Belgium and the old Dutch provinces to serve as a buffer state against possible future aggression on the part of the French. The French Revolution of 1830 spread into this new kingdom, however, and led to the separation of Belgium and Holland. Since that time, Belgium has existed as we know it today. The unrest leading to the Belgian insurrection in 1830 intensified Quetelet's interest in social affairs. So far as I can tell, Quetelet was never active in politics in the narrow sense, and this may account for the fact that his emphasis was always on social science

in general, not on the role of the government, which was of such great concern to the political arithmeticians.

47. Quetelet talks often about the "social system" and its "equilibrium." What he means is the fact that the social strata each contribute their own rates, which are constant over time but different from each other.

48. While his early publications on geometrical problems are considered important mathematical contributions, Quetelet did not do any original work in probability theory. He only extended its applications to social phenomena.

49. Adolphe Quetelet, *Physique sociale*.

50. A short book 5 is an extension of book 4. But its introductory pages give a good picture of Quetelet's ideas on the relation of his work with literature and art; he develops a notion which today we would label "national character."

51. Knapp became famous mainly because of his monetary theory. The article about him in the *Encyclopedia of the Social Sciences* is informative, but the appended bibliography does not include any of his numerous publications on Quetelet's moral statistics nor his editions of statistical classics. (A series of pertinent papers by G. F. Knapp appeared in the 1871 volumes of Bruno Hildebrand, *Jahrbücher für Nationalökonomie und Statistik*).

52. Joseph Lottin, *Quetelet, statisticien et sociologue*.

53. Lottin's book also contains valuable material on Quetelet's relation to his contemporaries. Comte, as is well known, complained that Quetelet had stolen the term "social physics" from him and that he had therefore had to invent the word "sociology" to identify his approach. In his review (*Quetelet*, pp. 357–68) Lottin argues that the Belgian probably did not know of the Frenchman's terminological invention. And he adds interesting comments on the very different images of the social sciences held by the two men: Comte was trying to derive from history broad developmental trends which could be projected into the future, while Quetelet was bent on finding precise regularities which would help to explain the contemporary social scene. Quetelet rarely engaged in controversy. His most serious dispute was with the Frenchman Guerry, who invented the term "moral statistics" and who was analyzing crime statistics at the same time that Quetelet was. Lottin provides a detailed analysis of the relevant drafts and publications (*Quetelet*, pp. 128–39). The question of priority is a subtle one, because although their interest in crime statistics developed independently, they were informed of each other's work through a common friend. According to Lottin, Quetelet wins in a photo finish.

54. Frank Hankins, *Adolphe Quetelet as Statistician*.

55. Unless otherwise indicated, page numbers refer to the second volume of Quetelet's *Physique sociale*. Direct quotations from the original are my translations; italics, intended to emphasize points in the present discussion, do not appear in the original.

56. Here Quetelet inserts an elaborate footnote that the measurement of memory might be of the same type if records were made of the length of time different people remembered a text they had learned. He emphasizes that such measures can be used to study variations by age, just as one can study developmental differences in eyesight or acuity of hearing.

57. The most frequently quoted example is the measurement of courage by counting the number of courageous deeds. It is followed by the suggestion of a courage poll (p. 147): "Assume now that society, *in a more perfect state, keeps track of and evaluates all acts of courage and virtue, just as one does today in regard to crime*; would this not make it possible to measure the relative propensity to courage and virtue in different age groups?"

58. Quetelet had previously mentioned (p. 143) that measurement of the productivity of writers would require both counting the number of works and weighing each item according to its literary merits; having elaborated on this and similar examples at some length, he obviously felt that he could deal with the general idea briefly. He therefore proceeded immediately to the question of feasible approximations.

59. It is true that Quetelet repeatedly says that he does not deal with individual measures. This occurs, however, only when he wants to argue for the validity of his rates. As can be seen from our main quotation and from many other passages, he always insisted that in principle quantitative information on individuals could and should be obtained.

60. Maurice Halbwachs, *La théorie de l'homme moyen*.

61. *Ibid.*, p. 146.

62. *Ibid.*, p. 174.

63. Early work on these more complicated distributions was carried out by the German economist and mathematician Wilhelm Lexis. He was a charter member of the Verein für Sozialpolitik in 1872 and taught at Strassburg where, somewhat later, Knapp formed a center for work on Quetelet and the history of statistics in general. Lexis had broad interests, coedited the German *Encyclopedia of the Social Sciences* and himself wrote on moral statistics. Whether the Lexis "distribution with contagion" was developed with reference to Quetelet, I do not know, but the question suggests a good topic for further research.

64. In book 3, Quetelet discusses in great detail the measurement of human strength with the help of dynamometers. These sections give leads to the imagery by which he was probably guided when he tried to explain his ideas on indicators of moral qualities.

65. Readers unfamiliar with recent developments in theory of sociopsychological measurement might find it useful to consult Paul F. Lazarsfeld, "Latent Structure Analysis" (1959), pp. 477–91.

66. This idea has come up all through the period covered by my paper. Thus Petty made this suggestion as "the measure of vice and sin in the nation": "the quantity spent on inebriating liquors, the number of unmarried persons between fifteen and fifty-five years old, the number of corporal sufferings and persons imprisoned for crimes" (Strauss, *Petty*, p. 196). And 250 years later, William James exemplified the pragmatists' notion of a "prudent" man: "that means that he takes out insurance, hedges in betting, looks before he leaps" (Lazarsfeld, "Latent Structure Analysis" [1959], p. 480).

67. In the parlance of modern measurement theory, this is called construct validity.

68. Moritz Wilhelm Drobisch, *Die moralische Statistik und die menschliche Willensfreiheit.*

69. *Ibid.*, p. 52; my translation.

70. Lottin, *Quetelet*, pp. 550ff. Drobisch himself deserves a more detailed study. His exposition of Quetelet is extensive and clear. He was a logician interested in all sorts of statistical applications. I have not had access to a paper of his which seems to be one of the first examples of content analysis: "Statistischer Versuch Über die Formen des lateinischen Hexameters," published by the Saxonian Scientific Society in 1865.

71. Halbwachs, *La théorie*, p. 151.

72. L. L. Thurstone, "Attitudes Can Be Measured."

73. Gordon W. Allport, "Attitudes."

74. Stephan remarks on the same discontinuity in his field: "The foregoing examples suggest that *modern sampling procedure might have developed at least a century sooner than it did if it had received more attention from the scientists of the day.* Only the officials of statistical bureaus . . . were preoccupied with . . . the important problems of trade, finance, industry, agriculture, public health, etc., for which statistical data were needed. Hence they favored complete censuses or the closest approach to them that was feasible." (Frederic Stephan, "History of the Uses of Modern Sampling Procedures.") Quetelet himself is a good example for Stephan's argument. At one point he says that midwives would be a bad source for anyone who wanted to establish the sex ratio at birth; their observations are based on small numbers. He does not argue for a *representative* sample but for a *complete* enumeration.

75. Hildebrand, *Jahrbücher.*

76. Since the appearance of Buckle's *History of English Civilization* (1861), writers mention a Quetelet-Buckle position. A study of Buckle's book shows that he makes only some very inferential references to Quetelet, never seriously uses his material, and does not add any new statistical data. But Buckle mentions Quetelet very early in his long book and uses Quetelet there as a witness for his own social determinism. It is curious that such a completely external coupling has led to a continuously repeated but substantively quite unjustified stereotype which I was able to trace even in books appearing in 1960.

77. Franz Zizek, *Soziologie und Statistik.*

78. Alfredo Niceforo, *La misura della vita.*

79. Niceforo, *Les indices numériques de la civilization et du progrès.*

80. Recently Raymond Cattell has used correlation analysis to develop dimensions relevant for the description of regions and countries. He is obviously not aware of Niceforo's work, another example of the discontinuities previously noted. Niceforo gives in the last two chapters a historical review of early quantifications of cultural phenomena. As one who has done work of this kind, I was embarrassed to find that many techniques considered contemporary inventions had been used many decades ago.

81. It would be worthwhile to follow more in detail the ways in which Quetelet's ideas penetrated into specific subject areas. An interesting example,

accidentally noticed, is the close personal contact he maintained with Florence Nightingale, described in E. W. Kopf, "Florence Nightingale as a Statistician."

82. Frédéric Le Play, *Les ouvriers européens*. [Unless otherwise indicated, translations from this work and addition of italics are by Lazarsfeld.]

83. Another element which accounts for the persuasiveness of the whole work is the skill with which he uses classificatory devices. I have already indicated how each monograph in the six volumes of *The European Workers* is explicitly organized. In turn, the various introductions and appendixes contain a great many cross-references. In the first volume, which has a very complex organization, Le Play repeatedly stops to explain to the reader at what point he finds himself at the moment and where the following sections are supposed to lead him. This classificatory urge obviously relates to his work as a metallurgist and reminds one also of his contributions to the international expositions mentioned above. It is undoubtedly also linked with his grave doubts as to whether writing books is an appropriate means of communication. In a long passage (vol. 1, p. 549), he explains that he has created so many reform organizations because his main reliance is on personal influence. At the same time, he knows that printed empirical descriptions are very important, so he continuously looks for ways of overcoming the obstacle of reader inertia. Characteristically, he places an alphabetic glossary in each volume explaining his main terms as well as pointing out where his factual material can be located in the volume.

I have not drawn upon the long series of monographs in *The Workers of Two Worlds*. Having read a fair sample of them, I agree with the judgment of several French writers that they are inferior. While Le Play was, for the first years, the general secretary of the international society which organized the collection, he seemed to have had relatively little contact with most of the individual contributions. It is, incidentally, worth translating the full title of the international collection: "Studies on the work, the domestic life, and the moral conditions of the workers of various countries and the relations which connect them with other classes."

84. On the following pages references by volume and page refer to *Les ouvriers européens*; the quotations are my translations from the second edition (I had no access to the first); and the emphasis is mine.

85. He refers at one point to Tocqueville's *Democracy in America* as the "most evil book ever written by a man of good will" (vol. 1, p. 193).

86. See *Le Play*.

87. The methodological emphasis of the group is quite remarkable, and a continuous progress toward increased explication and improvement of methods can be traced in *Science sociale* almost from year to year. Nathan Glazer's opinion that Le Play's method was not further developed is obviously based on the fact that he did not have access to the journal (see footnote 16). Special issues summarizing new methodological developments or reassessing the state of affairs will be found in many volumes; see especially November 1912 and October 1913 of *Science sociale*.

88. At the turn of the century, Demolins created a school for young boys,

École des Roches. The school was located in the open country, and the students organized their own work and life. Great emphasis was put on observation of nature as well as on field studies in the local communities and farm regions. The school still exists today. At the time, there was a similar movement in Germany, initiated by Lietz; this later on was important in the history of the German youth movement. Demolins organized exchange visits with other institutions, and there is interesting correspondence between him and W. R. Harper, the first president of the University of Chicago. Demolins' own publications, after he became a Le Play convert, were a combination of his early historical interests and Le Play's insistence on contemporary field studies. In recent bibliographical reviews, Demolins is usually classified as a geographical sociologist. The best source on him is the detailed biography which appeared in *Science sociale* at the time of his death. The journal also published from time to time reports on the activities of the École des Roches. Demolins also published a variety of more popular pamphlets on the research of the Le Play group which I have not examined.

89. Paul Bureau, *Introduction à la méthode sociologique*.

90. Bureau finally broke with the later Le Playistes, accusing them of materialism. He quotes as a witness the French economist Charles Gide to the effect that "in reality the new school has not preserved much from the method of their master" (*Introduction à la méthode*, pp. 116ff.).

91. This is the last volume available in Harvard's Widener Library, and I suppose that World War I brought the publication to an end. Unfortunately, a few earlier volumes are missing, among these, the volume of 1903, which precedes the change of name and the review issue I have just described. I do not know, therefore, whether a special explanation was ever given for the change. The volume of 1904 has an imprint "nineteenth year, second period"; I pass over some other technical changes which the editors made. The content remains otherwise quite unchanged, and Demolins remains editor. The later history can be determined from the retrospective pages of Bureau (*Introduction à la méthode*, Introduction and pp. 115ff).

92. This is strictly true only for Lévi-Strauss's contributions to *Twentieth-Century Sociology*, George D. Gurvich and Wilbert E. Moore, eds. (New York: Philosophical Library, 1945). Stoetzel mentions Le Play several times in passing when he stresses the empirical tradition of French sociologists in his contribution to *Modern Sociological Theory in Continuity and Change*, Howard Becker and Alvin Boskoff, eds. (New York: Dryden Press, 1957). He also refers to Bureau, and so, incidentally, does Merton in his review of French sociology "Recent French Sociology." As far as I can see, Bouglé in his *Bilan de la sociologie française contemporaine* never mentions the Le Playistes.

93. Philip Boardman, *Patrick Geddes, Maker of the Future*.

94. Victor Branford and Patrick Geddes, *The Making of the Future: The Coming Polity*.

95. *Ibid.*, pp. 183ff.

96. S. Branford and A. Farquharson, *An Introduction to Regional Surveys*.

97. The matter is not clarified by a first scrutiny of the *Sociological Review*,

the journal created by Branford. As a matter of fact, a curious episode emerges. One of Geddes' followers was the geographer Herbertson, whose wife, Dorothy, wrote a biography of Le Play about 1900. It was essentially a compilation of statements taken from the first volume of *The European Workers*. She sent the manuscript to Branford, who did not know what to do with it. When Le Play House was created, people became curious about the man after whom it was named. Branford remembered the manuscript of Mrs. Herbertson (she had died in the meantime) and edited and published the first four chapters, which summarized the external data of Le Play's life, in the *Sociological Review*. He never published the rest. I am satisfied that the reason is as follows: when he came to edit further chapters, Branford noticed that they mainly contained a summary of some of Le Play's outmoded anthropological ideas (chapters 5 and 6); lengthy descriptions of the categories used in his budget accounts (chapters 7–9); Le Play's judgment on the contribution of various occupational groups to society, seen from his point of view and based on the situation of fifty years earlier (chapters 11 and 12); and repetitions of Le Play's statement on his own political mission. It was like taking all the ashes from Le Play's altar and leaving the fire behind. Branford obviously found the manuscript too embarrassing. The present editor of the *Review* published the whole manuscript in 1950 as a special issue. His short foreword contains a number of interesting historical remarks; he has a slightly different explanation of why Branford discontinued publication. He mentions incidentally that latter-day Le Playistes were active in the Vichy government during World War II.

98. Charles Booth, *A Memoir*.

99. T. S. Simey and M. B. Simey, *Charles Booth, Social Scientist*.

100. *Ibid.*, p. 190.

101. Frédéric Le Play, "Instruction in the Observation of Social Facts According to the Le Play Method of Monographs on Families."

102. Paul de Rousier, "La science sociale."

103. Pitirim Sorokin, *Contemporary Sociological Theories*.

104. Carl Zimmerman and Merle E. Frampton, *Family and Society*.

105. Let me add that in the eighty pages where the authors of *Family and Society* comment on the importance of what they call "Le Play's theories," none of the actual family monographs is mentioned.

106. Alfons Reuss, *Frederic Le Play in seiner Bedeutung für die Entwicklung der sozialwissenschaftlichen Methode*.

107. In 1960, Thomas D. Eliot, Arthur Hillman et al., *Norway's Families*, studied a Norwegian family to compare it with case 2 in volume 3 of Le Play. They were interested in analyzing change, not in checking on the case Le Play had collected more than 100 years earlier. But from historical records they feel that Le Play painted too rosy a picture of Northern Europe, which is the subject of volume 3. The authors mention in passing that they could not trace the existence of the 1845 family.

108. Philippe Garigue, *Études sur le Canada français*, and Leon Gerin, *Le type économique et social des Canadiens*. I am indebted to Sigmund Diamond, who in the course of his own research on French Canada noticed the great

role of the Le Play tradition among French Canadian sociologists. Some information on Gerin can be found in the 1951 proceedings of the Royal Society of Canada.

109. Engel, himself a mining engineer by training, wanted to combine the Le Play and the Quetelet traditions. He created the term "Quet" for the basic unit in a consumption calculus.

110. Bureau quotes an extensive diatribe by Le Play against statistics (footnote 82, p. 228) without giving the source. In the November 1912 issue of *Science sociale* Descamp compares Le Play's methods with other procedures in social research and again argues against the kind of evidence which today we would call correlation analysis; one of his negative examples is Durkheim's *Suicide*.

111. The Booth survey was repeated later by some of his former assistants. In volume 3 of *The New Survey of London Life and Labour* (London: Orchard House, 1932) one can find a sophisticated discussion of the way Booth tried to translate the notion of poverty into a classificatory instrument. See especially pages 8ff., 70–77, 97–106.

112. On the other hand, they now form important documents for the economic historian. Le Play repeatedly stressed the relevance of his work for the future historian, who due to him would have better information about social conditions during his lifetime than for any other period.

113. In Gabriel Tarde we find a typical remark (condensed translation from his *Lois de l'imitation*, p. 227): "Statistical data are only poor substitutes [for what we really want to know]. Only a psychological statistic, reporting on changes in the specific beliefs of individual people—if this were at all possible—would provide the deeper reasons for the ordinary statistical figures." Just as Tarde considers attitude measurements impossible, so does Zizek feel about the measurement of occupational prestige, which today has become a research routine. He says (*Soziologie*, p. 25, condensed translation): "In the study of social stratification statistics deal with tangible occupational characteristics, while for the sociologist other aspects, like e.g. social prestige might be of importance. The sociologist will therefore often combine statistical data with non-quantitative information." Toennies (Ferdinand Toennies et al., *Sektion Soziographie, siebenter deutscher Soziologentag*), the great believer in "sociography," always added that "of course" many things cannot be quantified; but he was diplomatically vague as to where the limits were.

114. A systematic collection of such global indicators from a variety of community studies has been made by Patricia Kendall ("Qualitative Indicators in Field Work"). The technique is, of course, well known to the historian who often must depend on the interpretation of a single letter or the report on a ceremonial event. Rosenberg has analyzed such procedures in the writings of a number of historians and has recreated the transition from the medieval mind to the spirit of the Renaissance. (George Rosenberg, "Without Polls or Surveys," Ph.D. dissertation, Columbia University, 1960).

115. Lewis Mumford, "Patrick Geddes, Victor Branford, and Applied Sociology in England: The Social Survey, Regionalism, and Urban Planning."

116. Among several biographies of Geddes, Philip Boardman, *Patrick Geddes, Maker of the Future,* is relatively the most sober. Even there Geddes' initiation to Le Play through a lecture by Demolins is described in the following way: "In a flash Geddes saw that in Le Play's travels and his actual observation of society, there lay a method of study which both satisfied him as a scientist and inspired him, as one who often puzzled over mankind's ways and institutions, to follow this lead" (p. 42).

In tracing the charismatic nature of the Le Playist world, one will have to keep the age of the actors in mind. Le Play started his role as a "prophet" at the age of fifty. His most immediate French apostles were thirty to fifty years younger than he was.

117. Mumford, "Patrick Geddes, Victor Branford," p. 684.

118. Mark Abrams, *Social Surveys and Social Action;* O. R. McGregor, "Social Research and Social Policy in the Nineteenth Century."

119. Paul F. Lazarsfeld and Anthony Oberschall, "History of Quantification in Germany."

120. For a sketch of this whole trend, see Marie Jahoda, Paul Lazarsfeld, and Hans Zeisel, *Die Arbeitslosen von Marienthal.*

121. Helen Walker, *Studies in the History of Statistical Methods;* Frederic Stephan, "History of the Uses of Modern Sampling Procedures."

4. Problems in Methodology

1. The studies quoted in the following section are, for the most part, to be found in Paul F. Lazarsfeld and Morris Rosenberg, eds., *The Language of Social Research,* an annotated collection of sixty papers which exemplify various aspects of methodology. The following pages extend at several points the comments made in the original collection.

2. Robert K. Merton, "A Paradigm for the Study of the Sociology of Knowledge."

3. Robert M. MacIver, *Academic Freedom in the United States,* ch. 1.

4. Hans L. Zetterberg, "Compliant Action."

5. Ragnar Rommetveit , *Social Norms and Roles.*

6. For a variety of examples, see Allen H. Barton, "The Concept of Property-Space in Social Research," p. 40.

7. Gardner Lindzey, "Thematic Apperception Test: Interpretive Assumptions and Related Empirical Evidence."

8. John A. Clausen and Melvin L. Kohn, "The Ecological Approach in Social Psychiatry."

9. Allen H. Barton and Paul F. Lazarsfeld, "Some Functions of Qualitative Analysis in Social Research." (Ed. note: see essay 7.)

10. Samuel Stouffer et al., *The American Soldier,* vol. 4, ch. 1.

11. Paul E. Meehl, *Clinical versus Statistical Prediction.*

12. Bernard Berelson, Paul F. Lazarsfeld, and William N. McPhee, *Voting,* ch. 13.

13. Seymour M. Lipset et al., "The Psychology of Voting: An Analysis of Political Behavior," vol. 1, ch. 30.

14. Leon Festinger, "Informal Social Communication,"

15. Leon Festinger, Stanley Schachter, and Kurt Back, "Matrix Analysis of Group Structures." It is interesting to reread Robert R. Sears' earlier study, "Experimental Study of Projection," to see how much clearer his reasoning becomes if his "attribution of traits" is recast in matrix form; he essentially studies the relation between the rows and columns of a matrix, the entries of which are ratings that people made of one another.

16. Herbert A. Simon, *Models of Man,* ch. 7, 8. See p. 142, "Comment on Mathematization," in which possible substantive contributions of formalization are succinctly summarized.

17. In a forthcoming publication on the state of contemporary psychology, edited for the American Psychological Association by Sigmund Koch, my contribution tries to trace historically the various elements which enter into the mathematical approach to the combination of a set of indicators into an index.

18. A parameter in a mathematical learning model can be thought of as a measure of a person's intelligence. The model, together with an appropriate experiment, transforms the concept of intelligence into a measurement. This is not what I have in mind here.

19. See R. Coulborn, ed., *Feudalism in History.*

20. For a recent review, see Robert K. Merton, *Social Theory and Social Structure,* pp. 261ff. Although the correct terminology would be "traits of collectives," we shall use the more colloquial expression, "collective traits." Interestingly enough, similar lists were collected at the beginning of systematic personality research. See Gordon Allport et al., *Trait Names: A Psycholexical Study.*

21. The term has been suggested by Louis Guttman.

22. For a review of the main procedures, see B. Green, "Attitude Measurement," in Lindzey, ed., *Social Psychology,* vol. 1. The procedures there reviewed are characteristic for all the types of indices combining itemized indicators. The restriction of Green's review to "attitudes" is quite irrelevant; the procedures he reviews apply to any of the cases we shall discuss subsequently.

23. T. W. Adorno et al., *The Authoritarian Personality.*

24. The authors facilitate communication by further subdividing each of the two major groups of items. Thus such subgroups as "conventionalism," "projectivity," and "toughness" are introduced. For a first overview, see *ibid.,* p. 328.

25. Clark Kerr and Abraham Siegel, "The Interindustry Propensity to Strike—An International Comparison."

26. Max Horkheimer et al., *Autorität und Familie.*

27. Characteristically, in the United States the opposite to the authoritarian personality became the democratic personality, while in Fromm's programmatic article it is called the revolutionary personality. There are other, more technical, differences between the two studies. The F-scale contains only

4. *Problems in Methodology* 373

explicit statements, while the Frankfurt questionnaire contains more open-ended questions. "Toughness," for example, is derived from the way in which the respondent describes his favorite sport. Comparing the two studies is worthwhile because Max Horkheimer originated both and Theodore Adorno provided the staff link bridging fifteen years of crucial history. Thus the differences will shed light on the role of the originating observation, as well as on the effect of various intellectual environments upon the work of scholars.

28. Neal Gross and W. E. Martin, "On Group Cohesiveness"; Stanley Schachter, "Comment"; Gross and Martin, "Rejoinder," *American Journal of Sociology* (1952), 57:546–64.

29. Emile Durkheim, *Suicide*.

30. For more details, see Philip Hammond, "The Imagery of Durkheim's Concept of Integration in Suicide."

31. Durkheim, *Suicide,* pp. 209 and 170.

32. *Ibid.,* p. 374.

33. *Ibid.,* p. 250.

34. Leon Festinger and Alvin Zander, *Group Dynamics,* sect. 3.

35. Report on the Dartmouth Seminar on Concepts and Indices in the Social Sciences, mimeographed (Hanover, N.H: Dartmouth College, 1953), Sect. 2A, p. 3.

36. Gross and Martin, "Group Cohesiveness."

37. Schachter, "Comment," p. 557.

38. Gross and Martin, "Group Cohesiveness," p. 554.

39. For a recent summary, see Paul F. Lazarsfeld, "Evidence and Inference in Social Research" (1958), sect. 3.

40. Robert K. Merton, *Social Theory and Social Structure,* p. 253.

41. Paul F. Lazarsfeld, "The Interpretation of Statistical Relations as a Research Operation" (1955). (Ed. note: see essay 5.)

42. Paul F. Lazarsfeld and Wagner Thielens, Jr., *The Academic Mind.*

43. Paul F. Lazarsfeld, "Latent Structure Analysis" (1959).

44. Abraham Kaplan, in Lazarsfeld and Rosenberg, eds., *The Language,* pp. 527ff., has clearly shown how, in the early stage of most sciences, this "specification of meaning"—his term—really takes the place of the spurious process of verbal definition. Bo Anderson independently came rather close to this insight in his paper "Operationism and the Concept of Validity."

45. The notion of "general duty" indices was developed by Genevieve Knupfer in "The Measurement of Socio-Economic Status," a review of measures of socioeconomic status current in market research studies.

46. Joseph Kahl and James A. Davis, "A Comparison of Indices of Socio-Economic Status"; James G. March, "Influence Measurement in Experimental and Semi-Experimental Groups."

47. Material on the comparison of two indices with regard to a series of attitude questions can be found in Frederick Mosteller, "Effect of Education and Economic Status on Attitudes"; and Hortense Horwitz and Elias Smith, "The Interchangeability of Indices," pp. 73ff.

48. Many examples are analyzed in H. Menzel, "Specification of Dimensions in Concept Formation."

49. Herbert Blumer, "Sociological Analysis and the 'Variable.'"

50. Donald C. Pelz, "Some Social Factors Related to Performance in a Research Organization."

51. Lazarsfeld and Thielens, *Academic Mind.*

52. There does not yet exist a review, let alone a classification, of pertinent results. However, the interested reader will find many examples in Lazarsfeld and Rosenberg, eds., *The Language,* especially nos. 4 to 7, sect. 11b. The section is introduced by Lazarsfeld, "Interpretation of Statistical Relations as a Research Operation." It shows that conditional relations are only one special case of a more general approach called "elaboration." (Ed. note: see essay 5.)

53. Seymour M. Lipset, Martin Trow, and James Coleman, *Union Democracy.*

54. In principle, ecological data are contextual variates of this kind. But it depends upon the subject matter whether they are used so in fact or are only substitutes for primary information about individuals. This was pointed out by Herbert Menzel, "Comment," in the *American Sociological Review.*

55. Lipset et al., *Union Democracy,* p. 344.

56. Interesting connections between macrosociological writings and contextual propositions are suggested in a paper by Peter M. Blau, "Formal Organizations—Dimensions of Analysis," especially pp. 63–67. John and Matilda Riley and their collaborators at Rutgers University have also worked in this direction. See especially their publication *Sociological Studies in Scale Analysis.*

57. For the modes of panel analysis not discussed here, the reader will find many examples in Lazarsfeld and Rosenberg, eds., *The Language,* sect. 3, and Zeisel, *Say It with Figures,* ch. 10.

58. Paul F. Lazarsfeld and Robert K. Merton, "Friendship as Social Process." (Ed. note: see essay 9.)

59. Horace Miner, "The Folk-Urban Continuum."

60. The number of cases is small because, as we shall see presently, all respondents who did not fit a dichotomy on five questions were excluded in order to sharpen the issue.

61. On this point, an interesting corroboration was found eight years later. In 1940 the Republicans had a businessman as candidate and the Democrats a political figure; in 1948 both candidates had a background of political experience. In 1948 the voters for both parties agreed that politicians were all right, while in 1940 Republicans judged a businessman to be much more desirable.

62. William F. Whyte, *Street Corner Society,* 2nd ed. Edward Shils, "Primordial, Personal, Sacred, and Civil Ties," *British Journal of Sociology* (1957), 8:130–45.

5. The Interpretation of Statistical Relations as a Research Operation

1. To complete our information we still need to know how education is related to listening; or, in other words, we need to know $[ty]$. The data are shown below:

Listen to Discussion Programs				Listen to Classical Music		
	Yes	*No*	*Total*		*Yes*	*No*	*Total*
High Education	460	540	1,000	Low Education	280	1,020	1,300
Low Education	460	840	1,300	High Education	404	596	1,000
(Total)	(920)	(1,380)	(2,300)	(Total)	(684)	(1,616)	(2,300)

6. On the Relation Between Individual and Collective Properties

1. Individuals and collectives made up of individuals do not, of course, exhaust the matters which social scientists describe. Social science propositions may, instead, have various other units for their subjects. Not frequently the subjects are acts, behavior patterns, customs, norms, "items of culture," and the like, as in the assertion that "items of culture that are . . . not much woven into a pattern . . . are least likely to encounter resistance to their diffusion," Ralph Linton, *The Study of Man*, pp. 341–42. "Beliefs and practices have been sorted into four classes according to the pattern of their differential distribution among mobile and nonmobile holders of high and low positions in a stratification system," Peter M. Blau, "Social Mobility and Interpersonal Relations."

2. It is, of course, also possible to make propositions about cities without reference to any members at all, just as it is possible to make propositions about individuals without reference to any collectives. Thus one may, for example, correlate city size with number of churches, or location with building materials used, just as one can correlate individual income and education. In neither case are the distinctions made in the present paper relevant, because the individuals are not treated as "members" and the cities are not treated as "collectives" as here defined (i.e., as composed of "members"— constituent units described by their values on some one set of properties). It is thus clear that the typology of properties here presented is not always pertinent.

3. This procedure can lead to very misleading statistics, as pointed out by William S. Robinson in "Ecological Correlations and the Behavior of Individuals." Sounder methods for inferring individual correlations from ecological data are proposed by Leo A. Goodman, "Ecological Regressions and Behavior of Individuals," and by Otis Dudley Duncan and Beverly Davis, "An Alternate to Ecological Correlation."

4. For details on these and additional examples see Paul F. Lazarsfeld and Morris Rosenberg, eds., *The Language of Social Research*, pp. 302–22. Compare also Herbert Menzel, "Comment."

5. This classification of properties of collectives corresponds closely to the classification presented earlier by Raymond B. Cattell "Types of Group Structures," and by Kendall and Lazarsfeld, "The Relation Between Individual and Group Characteristics in 'The American Soldier,'" and reprinted in Lazarsfeld and Rosenberg, eds., *The Language*, pp. 291–301. Analytical properties are Cattell's population variables and Kendall and Lazarsfeld's Types I, II, and III. Structural properties are Cattell's structural variables and Kendall

and Lazarsfeld's Type IV. Our global properties are Cattell's syntality variables and Kendall and Lazarsfeld's Type V. See also n. 25.

6. It should be understood that the distinctions here proposed do not depend on who performs the operations involved. For example, "average income of a city" would be classified as an analytical property regardless of whether the investigator (a) obtains individual income data from all inhabitants directly and then computes the average, (b) obtains individual income data from the files of the tax collector and then computes the average, or (c) looks up the average income in the published census reports. Compare also n. 17.

7. Phillips Cutright and Peter H. Rossi, "Grass Roots Politicians and the Vote."

8. Melvin L. DeFleur and Otto N. Larsen, *The Flow of Information.*

9. Duncan MacRae, Jr., "Occupations and the Congressional Vote, 1940–1950." For another example, see the evidence used to demonstrate differences in the norms of two housing projects in Leon Festinger, Stanley Schachter, and Kurt Back, "The Operation of Group Standards."

10. See David C. McClelland and G. A. Friedman, "A Cross-Cultural Study of the Relationship Between Child Training Practices and Achievement Motivation Appearing in Folk Tales."

11. See, e.g., Linton C. Freeman and Robert F. Winch, "Societal Complexity: An Empirical Test of a Typology of Societies."

12. Cutright and Rossi, "Grass Roots Politicians."

13. DeFleur and Larsen, *Information.*

14. Robert Redfield, *The Folk Culture of Yucatan;* Margaret J. Hagood, and Daniel O. Price, *Statistics for Sociologists,* pp. 144–152.

15. Although global properties of collectives are not based on information about members, the above examples are, of course, listed here on the assumption that assertions about the members are made somewhere in the same proposition or at least in the same body of work; otherwise the distinction between "global" and "absolute" properties would become pointless (cf. n. 2). It may also bear repeating here that any discussion of a "collective" requires clear specification of what its members are considered to be. The proportion of the buildings of a city which are devoted to cultural activities was given as an example of a "global property" of a city on the assumption that the city is treated as a collective of inhabitants; i.e., that statements involving the inhabitants are made in some connection with this measure of "cultural level." It is, of course, also possible to treat a city as a collective of buildings; then the proportion of buildings devoted to cultural activities would become an analytical property. Which of these two types of property it is can be judged only from the context. (See also the concluding section.)

16. Compare the notion of "counterpart" in Edgar F. Borgotta, Leonard Cottrell, Jr., and Henry J. Meyer, "On the Dimensions of Group Behavior."

17. It may be worth repeating here that the distinctions proposed are independent of who performs the operations involved. Thus, e.g., "sociometric popularity" would be classified as a relational property when measured in any of the following three ways: (a) the investigator counts the number of choices

accorded to a member by his colleagues in answer to a sociometric questionnaire; (b) the investigator observes the frequency of interactions between the member and his colleagues; (c) the member is asked, "How many visits did you receive from colleagues during the last week?" These distinctions are, of course, important in themselves but not relevant to the present typology (cf. n. 6).

18. Some sociometric indices are listed in Hans Zeisel, *Say It with Figures,* pp. 110–14, 148–53. The list includes indices not only of relational properties but of comparative and structural properties as well.

19. Herbert Menzel and Elihu Katz, "Social Relations and Innovation in the Medical Profession: The Epidemiology of a New Drug."

20. See Zeisel, *Say It with Figures,* and Leon Festinger, Stanley Schachter, and Kurt Back, "Matrix Analysis of Group Structures." In both instances matrices are also used to develop indices for structural properties of groups.

21. See, e.g., Robert R. Sears, "Experimental Studies of Projection."

22. Festinger, Schachter, and Back, "Group Standards," pp. 367–81.

23. Samuel Stouffer et al., *The American Soldier,* vol. 1, p. 256.

24. It is sometimes helpful to talk of "collective properties" instead of the cumbersome "properties of collectives"; the same holds for "individual properties." It is important, however, not to be misled by this linguistic condensation.

25. Cattell's classification of population, structural, and syntality variables (cf. n. 5 above), which is closely paralleled in form by our analytical-structural-global distinction, seems to be based on a mixture of measurement criteria and considerations of causality. The latter gain the upper hand in the critique of Cattell's scheme by Borgatta, Cottrell, and Meyer: e.g., "Aggregate measures, to the extent that they cannot be accounted for as population variables (in direct parallel measures), may be considered syntality measures. . . . Further, changes in population variables attributable to social interaction should be regarded as syntality variables," Borgatta, Cottrell, and Meyer, "Dimensions," p. 234. Peter M. Blau's "Formal Organization" contains an analysis in terms of intended underlying concepts which parallels the present discussion of measurement operations in certain respects. In addition, the literature contains, of course, classifications of group properties which are based on quite different criteria. See e.g., John K. Hemphill and Charles M. Westie, "The Measurement of Group Dimensions," and Robert K. Merton, *Social Theory and Social Structure,* "Provisional List of Group Properties," pp. 310–26. The Hemphill-Westie categories are subjected to a factor analysis and compared with certain other schemes in Borgatta, Cottrell, and Meyer, "Dimensions," pp. 223–40.

7. Some Functions of Qualitative Analysis in Social Research

1. Definition of quantitative research given by Daniel Lerner, " 'The American Soldier' and the Public," p. 220.

2. The general idea of codifying existing methods of social research is now being carried out by a special project, Advanced Training in Social Research, at Columbia University. Formalizations of specific pieces of qualitative writing are an essential part of this project. Available in monograph form so far are a formalization by Ernest Nagel of procedures of functional analysis in social research and a formalization by Paul F. Lazarsfeld of certain problems of process analysis, the interaction of social variables through time. The present paper can be considered the typical first step which has to precede a more full-fledged formalization. It is one of the documents developed by the Columbia project.

3. Paul F. Lazarsfeld, *Radio and the Printed Page*, pp. 74ff.

4. Bernard Berelson, "What 'Missing the Newspaper' Means," pp. 122ff.

5. E. H. Sutherland, *The Professional Thief.*

6. A variety of anthropological examples are given in Margaret Mead, "Adolescence in Primitive and in Modern Society," pp. 6ff.

7. A discussion of this point is found in Robert K. Merton, *Social Theory and Social Structure,* ch. 3, "The Bearing of Empirical Research on Sociological Theory."

8. F. J. Roethlisberger and William J. Dickson, *Management and the Worker,* p. 17.

9. Paul F. Lazarsfeld and Patricia L. Kendall, "The Listener Talks Back."

10. Robert K. Merton and Patricia L. Kendall, "The Boomerang Response."

11. Patricia L. Kendall and Katherine M. Wolfe, "The Analysis of Deviant Cases in Communications Research," pp. 158ff. See also E. Cooper and Marie Jahoda, "The Evasion of Propaganda."

12. Robert K. Merton, Marjorie Fiske, and Alberta Curtis, *Mass Persuasion,* pp. 82ff.

13. Wagner Thielens, research in progress, Columbia University, Department of Sociology.

14. Merton, Fiske, and Curtis, *Mass Persuasion,* pp. 188ff.

15. Alfred Adler, *The Neurotic Constitution.*

16. Thorstein Veblen, *The Theory of the Leisure Class.*

17. Edwin H. Sutherland, "White-Collar Criminality;" *White Collar Crime.*

18. Marie Jahoda, Morton Deutsch, and Stuart W. Cook, *Research Methods in Social Relations,* pp. 42ff.

19. For a number of examples, see Paul F. Lazarsfeld, "The Obligations of the 1950 Pollster to the 1984 Historian" (1950). (Ed. note: see essay 2.)

20. E. Franklin Frazier, *The Negro Family in the United States,* pp. 55ff. This and other examples are discussed in Robert Bower, "Training Guide on the Qualitative Use of Documentary Material," mimeographed (New York: Bureau of Applied Social Research, Columbia University, 1950).

21. For example, Barrington Moore, *Soviet Politics: The Dilemma of Power.* See also Alexander Gerschenkron, "A Neglected Source of Economic Information on Soviet Russia."

22. For one example, see Donald V. McGranahan and Ivor Wayne, "German and American Traits Reflected in Popular Drama."

23. Kendall and Wolfe, "Deviant Cases," p. 163.

24. Allison Davis, Burleigh B. Gardner, and Mary R. Gardner, *Deep South*, p. 116.

25. William F. Whyte, *Street Corner Society*, p. 116.

26. Marie Jahoda, Paul Lazarsfeld, and Hans Zeisel, *Marienthal*, quoted in Jahoda, Deutsch and Cook, *Research Methods*, pp. 298ff.

27. Albert Blumenthal, *Small Town Stuff*, pp. 136ff.

28. *Ibid.*, p. 30.

29. Samuel Stouffer et al., *The American Soldier*, vol. 2, p. 99.

30. *Ibid.*, vol. 1, p. 56, fn. 2. This example and others are discussed in Patricia L. Kendall and Paul F. Lazarsfeld, "Problems of Survey Analysis," pp. 183ff.

31. Robert S. and Helen M. Lynd, *Middletown*, p. 118, fn. 2.

32. Louis Wirth, "Some Jewish Types of Personality," p. 106.

33. *Ibid.*, pp. 108ff.

34. *Ibid.*

35. C. Wright Mills, pp. 92ff.

36. *Ibid.*, pp. 144ff.

37. *Ibid.*, pp. 131ff.

38. *Ibid.*, pp. 174ff.

39. *Ibid.*, introduction, p. xv.

40. Katherine M. Wolfe and Marjorie Fiske, "The Children Talk about Comics."

41. For example, Merton, Fiske, and Curtis, *Mass Persuasion*, pp. 50ff.

42. Eduard Spranger, *Types of Men;* for an attempt to develop measuring instruments for Spranger's concepts, see P. E. Vernon and G. W. Allport, "A Test for Personal Values."

43. Leopold von Wiese and Howard Becker, *Systematic Sociology*, pp. 624ff.

44. Robert K. Merton, "Patterns of Influence," p. 218.

45. Kingsley Davis, *Human Society*, ch. 3.

46. Harold D. Lasswell and Abraham Kaplan, *Power and Society* pp. 55ff.

47. Bronislaw Malinowski, "The Group and the Individual in Functional Analysis."

48. Jean Piaget, *The Moral Judgment of the Child.*

49. Max Scheler, *Die Wissensformen und die Gesellschaft*, p. 62. The list given here is adapted from Merton's discussion of Scheler in *Social Theory and Social Structure*, pp. 230ff.

50. David Riesman and Nathan Glazer, "Criteria for Political Apathy," pp. 535ff.

51. Robert K. Merton, "Discrimination and the American Creed." See also Merton's appendix to that paper: "A Note on the Use of Paradigms in Qualitative Analysis."

52. Talcott Parsons and Edward A. Shils, *Toward a General Theory of Action*, part 2.

53. A more detailed discussion will be found in Paul F. Lazarsfeld and Allen H. Barton, "Qualitative Measurement in the Social Sciences," pp. 169ff.

54. Georg Simmel, "The Sociology of Conflict."

55. Werner S. Landecker, "Types of Integration and Their Measurement," p. 332.

56. Mills, *White Collar*, p. 220.

57. Roethlisberger and Dickson, *Management and the Worker*.

58. Elizabeth Zerner (with Robert T. Bower), "German Occupation and Anti-Semitism in France."

59. Kendall and Wolfe, "Deviant Cases," pp. 166ff.

60. Whyte, *Street Corner Society*, pp. 96ff.

61. *Ibid.*, p. 106.

62. Kendall and Wolfe, "Deviant Cases," pp. 163ff.

63. Whyte, *Street Corner Society*, pp. 209ff.

64. Robert K. Merton and Patricia L. Kendall, "The Focused Interview;" Herta Herzog, "Training Guide on the Technique of Qualitative Interviews."

65. Paul F. Lazarsfeld, "The Art of Asking Why" (1935).

66. Mirra Komarovsky, *The Unemployed Man and His Family*, especially pp. 135ff.

67. Bernard Barber, "Participation and Mass Apathy in Associations," pp. 481ff.

68. Arnold Toynbee, *A Study of History*.

69. Max Weber, *Gesammelte Aufsätze zur Religionssoziologie*. A brief outline is presented in Talcott Parsons, *The Structure of Social Action* .

70. Seymour M. Lipset, *Agrarian Socialism: The Cooperative Commonwealth Federation in Saskatchewan*.

71. *Ibid.*, p. 202.

72. *Ibid.*, pp. 303–04.

73. Bronislaw Malinowski, *Magic, Science, and Religion*.

74. Ruth Benedict, *Patterns of Culture*, ch. 4.

75. Jahoda, Lazarsfeld, and Zeisel, *Marienthal*.

76. Merton, "Patterns of Influence," p. 191.

77. Toennies, *Gemeinschaft*. A brief summary is found in Parsons, *Social Action*, pp. 686ff.

78. Merton, Fiske, and Curtis, *Mass Persuasion*, pp. 152ff.

79. Benedict, *Patterns;* see pp. 80, 83, 85, 94, 107, and 112 for instances.

80. Parsons, *Social Action*, pp. 743ff.

81. Merton, *Social Theory and Social Structure*, ch. 2.

82. Emile Durkheim, *Suicide*, bk. 2, ch. 6.

83. Erich Fromm, *Escape from Freedom*, appendix: "Character and the Social Process."

84. *Ibid.*, pp. 185ff.

85. *Ibid.*, pp. 192ff.

86. Mills, *White Collar*, ch. 11, "The Status Panic."

87. Harold Lasswell, "The Garrison State." Reprinted in Lasswell, *The Analysis of Political Behavior*, pp. 146ff.

88. Paul F. Lazarsfeld, "Remarks on Administrative and Critical Communications Research" (1941), gives a number of further examples in the field of mass communications, especially from the work of Max Horkheimer and

T. W. Adorno. In another field, Veblen, *The Theory of the Leisure Class,* offers a classic example of the use of qualitative indicators.

89. The authors are indebted to Professor Merton and the members of his seminar on the sociology of occupation for raising many of these problems in discussing an earlier draft of this paper.

8. The Use of Panels in Social Research

1. Paul F. Lazarsfeld, Bernard Berelson, and Hazel Gaudet, *The People's Choice.*

2. National Opinion Research Center, "Cincinnati Looks Again."

3. A. R. Root and A. C. Welch, "The Continuing Consumer Study: A Basic Method for the Engineering of Advertising."

4. Everett C. Hughes, *French Canada in Transition,* p. 86.

5. Theodore Newcomb, *Personality and Social Change.*

6. Jerome S. Bruner, *Mandate from the People;* Hadley Cantril, *Gauging Public Opinion.*

7. Paul F. Lazarsfeld, "The Change of Opinion During a Political Discussion."

8. Interested readers will find such a discussion and concrete examples in chapter 10, "The Panel," in Hans Zeisel, *Say it with Figures.*

9. An especially rich source for such explanatory variables will be found in a housing study organized by the Lavanburg Foundation under the direction of Robert K. Merton.

10. The interested reader will find a thoroughgoing discussion of important intervening variables in Mutzafer Sherif, *An Outline of Social Psychology.*

9. Friendship as Social Process: A Substantive and Methodological Analysis

1. Robert M. MacIver, *Social Causation,* pp. 130–31; *Society,* pp. 406ff.

2. Robert M. MacIver and Charles H. Page, *Society: An Introductory Analysis,* p. 228; cf. substantially the same passage in an earlier edition: MacIver, *Society,* p. 243.

3. MacIver and Page, *Society: An Introductory Analysis,* p. 229; cf. MacIver, *Society,* p. 243.

4. MacIver, *Social Causation,* p. 133.

5. The subject of this section will be given fuller treatment in a forthcoming book, *Patterns of Social Life: Explorations in the Sociology and Social Psychology of Housing,* by Robert K. Merton, Patricia S. West, and Marie Jahoda of the Columbia University Bureau of Applied Social Research.

6. It should now be plain why we did not adopt the familiar sociometric device of asking residents to designate *only* those intimate friends who happened to live in their own community. Had this been done, we would have had a larger number of "cases for analysis," but these would have included

a substantial proportion of persons who were not regarded, in fact, by Hill-towners and Craftowners as their *most intimate* friends. The category of most intimate friends would thus have been diluted by less significant relationships, making it less likely that actual uniformities underlying the structure of these intimate personal ties would be detected. For this reason, the more inclusive sociometric measure was adopted.

7. It must be emphasized that such extreme concentration of personal ties within each racial group obtains only for the *most intimate* friendships. (It will be remembered that these data refer to the three *closest* friends of residents.) Short of these most intimate attachments, however, there have developed numerous personal relations across race lines in Hilltown, as will be seen in the complete report, *Patterns of Social Life*.

8. This has been recognized usage since the writings of Karl Pearson and Havelock Ellis on assortative mating. For one among many recent examples of this usage, see Ernest W. Burgess and Paul Wallin, "Homogamy in Social Characteristics."

9. As Malinowski reports, "A twofold scheme in the relations between men is clearly defined linguistically by the two words for friend, one meaning 'friend within the barrier,' the other 'friend across the barrier.'" Bronislaw Malinowski, *Sexual Life of Savages*, p. 501.

10. In neither of these phrases, does the word "tendency" refer to some propensity assumed to be rooted in the individual. It refers, rather, to an observed correlation, positive in the one instance, negative in the other, between designated attributes of friends. In other words, homophily and heterophily are descriptive, not interpretative, concepts.

11. Since the popular game of criticizing social scientists for their occasional coinage of technical terms continues unabated, Peirce's observation of half a century ago is still timely. "No study can become scientific . . . until it provides itself with a suitable technical nomenclature, whose every term has a single definite meaning universally accepted among students of the subject, and whose vocables have not such sweetness or charms as might tempt loose writers to abuse them—which is a virtue of scientific nomenclature too little appreciated. It is submitted that the experience of those sciences which have conquered the greatest difficulties of terminology, which are unquestionably the taxonomic sciences, chemistry, mineralogy, botany, zoology, has conclusively shown that the one only way in which the requisite unanimity and requisite ruptures with individual habits and preferences can be brought about is so to shape the canons of terminology that they shall gain the support of moral principle." This is *not* to say that all word coinages necessarily make for scientific advance; each new term must earn its way. But those who are cowed by the indiscriminate charge that every technical term in social science is merely jargon (i.e., gibberish) would do well to study the rest of the discussion by Charles Peirce, in *Pragmatism and Pragmaticism*, pp. 274–76, 428.

12. Howard Becker and Ruth Hill Useem, "Sociological Analysis of the Dyad," *American Sociological Review* (1942), 7:13–26.

13. These types were identified in terms of their answers to two questions

raised during interviews with Hilltowners: "Do you think that colored and white people should live together in housing projects?" and "On the whole, do you think that colored and white people in Hilltown get along pretty well, or not so well?" It was assumed and confirmed in the larger study that intensely held attitudes would affect the perception of relations between the races in the community and, conversely, that perceptions would, in due course, affect attitudes. In other words, the perceptual and attitudinal components of values are here considered interdependent.

14. It is perhaps needless to add the corollaries of this when detailed analysis seeks to identify the particular groups which contribute most to the prevailing patterns of selection: overselection of friends of differing kind indicates heterophily, just as underselection of friends of differing kind may contribute to homophily.

15. We must here confine our inquiry to white residents, since there are too few illiberal and ambivalent Negroes with friends in Hilltown to allow comparative analysis. Further detailed statistics will be found in *Patterns of Social Life;* selected summaries of these statistics are sufficient for present purposes.

16. The great practical difficulties of *empirically* studying the interplay of numerous sets of values and of interpersonal association should not be blinked. The later methodological part of this paper will indicate the complexities that arise as first approximations are followed by successive approximations to the concrete situation under review.

17. We do not, at this point, ask whether the correlation of values among friends may not be the *result* of close association, as well as a basis for the *choice* of friends, so that the correlation is spuriously great if it is taken solely to explain choice. This is probably true and certainly important, and it is considered in due course in the larger study, *Patterns of Social Life*.

18. That such personal attachments are sturdy enough to bear the recognition of disagreement on certain values and of occasional hostility is well attested by studies in clinical psychology. For an application of this hypothesis to quite another context of social behavior, see Robert K. Merton, Marjorie Fiske, and Alberta Curtis, *Mass Persuasion,* pp. 62–63.

19. The capacity to accept disagreement on values among one's friends probably varies from personality to personality and presumably from group to group. Social norms may induce or even prescribe the toleration of opinions at odds with one's own, and in groups where such norms obtain, friendships may more often tolerate a divergence of outlook. But such group variations, which it would be instructive to explore, do not affect the central hypothesis, developed in our provisional model, that *some* agreement in basic values is required to sustain an intimate personal relationship. There is always, so to speak, a breaking point in the relationship, and group differences in the norm of tolerated opposition of outlook only vary the location of this point; they do not abolish it.

20. This process seems to have direct bearing on the modification of values and attitudes among those holding a minority opinion. If lone dissenters enter

into close social relations with groups of other-minded persons, they *tend* to accommodate their values to the majority opinion rather than to disrupt these relations. In this way, the values widely held in a community tend to transform the values of initially dissenting individuals, as long as the latter are motivated to maintain personal relationships with "majority members" of the community. Only if there exist relatively self-contained subgroups, sharing their dissident values, can they continue to maintain acutely opposed values. In either case, there is a structural tendency toward value homophily. Either the dissidents conform to the majority opinion, or if they find subgroups which provide a comfortable "home" for their dissident opinions, they conform to the values held by *these* associates.

21. In their main outlines, for example, they are found in the writings of Georg Simmel, *The Sociology of Georg Simmel,* especially chs. 1 and 2, and in the discussion of "accommodation" in the first modern textbook of sociology by Robert E. Park and Ernest W. Burgess, *Introduction to the Science of Sociology;* cf. Pitirim Sorokin, *Society, Culture, and Personality,* esp. ch. 7. Leopold von Wiese and Howard Becker, *Systematic Sociology,* state some of the germane considerations in part 2 of their book and in ch. 39 on the pair, or dyad. To our mind one of the most insightful diagnoses of the interaction of pairs—in this case, marriage partners rather than friends—is provided by Willard Waller, *The Family,* especially chs. 10 and 11. In more recent years, these conceptions have been taken up and have become a distinct focus of empirical research and sociological theory. See, for example, the excellent discussion by George C. Homans, *The Human Group,* especially chs. 5 and 6; and for a discussion of estrangement of social relations and alienation of values, see Robert K. Merton and Alice S. Kitt, "Contributions to the Theory of Reference Group Behavior," especially pp. 92ff. For the most widely generalized and elaborated formulation of these conceptions, see Talcott Parsons, *The Social System,* esp. ch. 7.

22. This analysis is one of a series of formalizations developed by Columbia University's project for advanced training in social research. The editorial help of Patricia Kendall is warmly acknowledged.

23. In discussing these relationships, we shall use hypothetical figures rather than algebraic or other symbolic terminology.

24. There are a variety of ways in which the pairing of the community members can be accomplished. The exact way in which this is done is irrelevant for the discussion which follows.

25. We repeat that numbers are used only for illustrative purposes to indicate the existence or nonexistence of particular kinds of relationships. We might have used algebraic notation instead, but the numerical examples are probably easier to follow.

26. Other figures might have been invented. With fixed marginals, a sixteenfold table has nine degrees of freedom. But we chose those figures which might have been found had empirical data supporting the several interpretations been available.

27. In this and the remaining examples of the present section, our decision

to consider only the presence or absence of friendship and agreement or disagreement on racial values means, necessarily, a simplification of the substantive content. Here, for example, the analyst talks of "close friendships"; in other instances, as we shall see, he deals with friendships which are "in the early stages of formation," as opposed to others which are "long and firmly established" and still others which are "well along toward dissolution." Further, he sometimes indicates certain substantive conditions which he considers basic to the process under discussion. For example, he contrasts the processes to be expected when the members of a pair express their values and those which are likely when one or both members remain silent.

In later sections we shall see that our formal structure provides ways of dealing with these refinements of the basic variables and with the consideration of conditions. But these complications must come later, when we have made entirely clear the meaning of formalization on the simplest level.

28. Again we oversimplify the substantive implications of the original passage. The sequence rule developed by the analyst is conditional on the expression of conflicting values by the members of a pair. Again, however, we shall delay for later consideration how these conditional statements can be handled in our formal structure.

29. Actually, there are sixteen, rather than fifteen, entries in the second row. This results from the fact that three of the coded comments, Statements M, N, and T, each refer to two sequences, held to obtain at different points in the history of the friendship relation.

30. Otherwise stated, the substantive analysis does not concern itself with the problem of the processes through which social contact is first established. That problem is dealt with in another part of the book from which the analysis is drawn, where the role of propinquity and formal organization in making for social contact is considered at some length. The formalization of the text brings out the self-defined limitations of the analysis and goes on to indicate the additional sequence rules which would be involved if this further problem were considered at this point.

31. For the sake of simplicity, we leave out an additional test which has to be applied to the problem of "mutual effect." Another partial fourfold table would have to be investigated, consisting of the two middle boxes in the first and last rows of table 9.3. This is necessary for numerical reasons and does not affect the general trend of the idea.

32. There is some indication in the substantive section that the analyst was aware of the importance of studying past history in order to develop adequate theories about future developments. The most explicit of these is the observation, in Statement W, that it is of strategic importance to study the "class of disrupted or broken friendships." Implicit in this reference is the supposition that pairs who have broken off their friendship may develop differently from those who have maintained their friendship.

33. To the statistician, these are known as transition probabilities, but we wish to avoid technical language here. Appendix 1 gives a more precise formulation.

34. This form of elaboration is discussed in more general terms, as the procedure of "specification" in Patricia L. Kendall and Paul F. Lazarsfeld, "Problems of Survey Analysis," pp. 154–57 and 163–64.

35. In other parts of the book *Patterns of Social Life,* from which the substantive section of this paper is drawn, some of the conditions making for such "timidity" in social contact—for example, timidity induced by differences in social class background—are, in turn, considered. In other words, these additional variables are not purely ad hoc but are derived from sociological analysis of the local social structure.

36. It will be noted that the introduction of this third variable exactly doubles the number of sequences with which we deal.

37. It is through these elaborations—of variables or of categories—that we are able to deal formally with statements which previously seemed too complex. These operations free us from the restrictions imposed by our initial simplifications, particularly in presenting the notion of sequence rules.

38. This is discussed at length in another part of *Patterns of Social Life.*

39. T. W. Anderson, in Paul F. Lazarsfeld, ed., *Mathematical Thinking in the Social Sciences.*

40. See, for example, Freud's description of the way in which the development of psychoanalysis cost him his friendship with Josef Breuer. Sigmund Freud, *An Autobiographical Study,* ch. 2. And for a perceptively detailed account, surely destined to be a classic, of the process of interaction between ideas and personal relations in the friendship between Freud and Wilhelm Fliess which came to an end over a difference of scientific opinion—a friendship which meant much to Freud and remained unmentioned in his autobiographic fragment—see ch. 13 of Ernest Jones, *Sigmund Freud: Life and Work,* vol. 1. If the Freud-Fliess relationship were one of a large number under observation in a study of processes of friendship formation and disruption, it would be characterized, for immediate purposes, by the sequence chain: $(--)(-+)(++)(+-)(--)$. But, of course, a detailed study, such as Jones', of the dynamics of this friendship in particular would consider much else that was involved in the history of the friendship.

41. This is not a latter-day version of psychological hedonism which, through the years, has been repeatedly found to be an inadequate and unreliable conception. For the principle of the law of effect still leaves open the important question of what makes certain experiences punitive and others gratifying, and it is precisely recognition of this that abandons the naive hedonistic view that diverse social patterns can be *derived* from the same psychological equipment of individuals.

42. Robert M. MacIver called attention, some time ago, to the need for relating processes of interpersonal association to the social structure. As Professor MacIver put it (in his *Social Causation,* pp. 130–31): "The social sciences are deeply engrossed in the study of social processes. . . . One familiar type [of study] is that which centers attention on particular modes of dynamic relationship, particular ways in which people become associated or dissociated, singling each out for characterization either in general or as it manifests

itself in localized instances. In sociology this procedure recalls such names as Simmel and von Wiese and, among Americans, E. A. Ross, R. E. Park, and E. W. Burgess. These writers treat of competition, conflict, domination, submission, assimilation, amalgamation, indoctrination, and so forth, as distinctive forms of social process. . . . One difficulty inherent in the work of all these writers is that social processes, if studied in this manner, are apt to be detached from the social structures that give them definition and specific quality. This detachment sometimes makes the treatment of processes arid or abstract or unconvincing, and from our point of view has the disadvantage that, by its lack of definite reference to structure, it makes causal investigation difficult except in general sociopsychological terms that do not go much beyond mere classification and description."

43. A counterpart to this type of situation was found in Craftown, which had been confronted with a great variety of communitywide stresses: epidemics, "floods," inadequate facilities for schooling, etc. As is observed in another part of *Patterns of Social Life:* "The patterns of inter-status friendships came about, not as the consequence of a planned integration of subgroups within the community, but as the consequence of a series of actions aimed to meet immediate difficulties confronting the community. . . . It is probably true that if differences of nativity, religion, occupation, etc., had been allowed to loom large in Craftown and to preclude or to minimize interpersonal relations between those of different social status, the community would have been relatively ineffectual in meeting its problems. Specific problems would more often have been variously evaluated by the separate subgroups in the community and, to this extent, would probably have intensified group cleavage within the community. . . . A deterioration of community effort and a deterioration of interpersonal relations would have reinforced one another to form a vicious circle of progressive ineffectiveness."

44. For a follow-up study, see "Age, Status, Homophily, and Heterophily," in George S. Rosenberg, *The Worker Grows Old*, pp. 87–107. (Ed. note: this reference was supplied in 1981.)

Selected Bibliography of the Works of Paul F. Lazarsfeld

For a complete bibliography, see Paul M. Neurath "The Writings of Paul F. Lazarsfeld: A Topical Bibliography," in Robert K. Merton, James S. Coleman, and Peter H. Rossi, eds., *Qualitative and Quantitative Social Research: Papers in Honor of Paul F. Lazarsfeld.* New York: The Free Press, 1979.

WORKS OF PAUL F. LAZARSFELD, BY DATE OF PUBLICATION

Gemeinschaftserziehung durch Erziehungsgemeinschaften. Leipzig-Wien: Anzengruber Verlag, 1924.

Statistisches Praktikum für Psychologen und Lehrer. Jena: Gustav Fischer, 1929.

Jugend und Beruf. Jena: Gustav Fischer, 1931.

"An Unemployed Village." *Character and Personality* (1932), 1:147–51.

"The Art of Asking Why." *National Marketing Review* (1935), 1:32–43. (Reprinted in Paul F. Lazarsfeld, *Qualitative Analysis.* Boston: Allyn and Bacon, 1972.)

"The Change of Opinion During a Political Discussion." *Journal of Applied Psychology* (1939), 23:131–47.

Radio and the Printed Page. New York: Duell, Sloan and Pearce, 1940.

"Remarks on Administrative and Critical Communications Research." *Studies in Philosophy and Social Science* (1941), 9:2–16.

"Evaluating the Effectiveness of Advertising by Direct Interviews." *Journal of Consulting Psychology* (1941), 5:170–78.

"Some Notes on the Relationship Between Radio and the Press." *Journalism Quarterly* (1941), 18:10–13.

"The Controversy Over Detailed Interviews—An Offer for Negotiation." *Public Opinion Quarterly* (1944), 8:38–60.

"The Use of Panels in Social Research." *Proceedings of the American Philosophical Society* (1948), 92:405–10.

"Communications Research and the Social Psychologist." In Wayne Dennis, ed., *Current Trends in Social Psychology*. Pittsburgh: University of Pittsburgh Press, 1948.

"The Obligations of the 1950 Pollster to the 1984 Historian." *Public Opinion Quarterly* (1950), 14:618–63.

"Mass Media of Communication in Modern Society." *Borah Foundation Lectures 1954*. Moscow, Idaho: University of Idaho Press, 1954.

Editor. *Mathematical Thinking in the Social Sciences*. Glencoe, Ill.: Free Press, 1954.

"The Interpretation of Statistical Relations as a Research Operation." In Paul F. Lazarsfeld and Morris Rosenberg, eds., *The Language of Social Research*. Glencoe, Ill.: Free Press, 1955.

"Evidence and Inference in Social Research." *Daedalus* (1958), 87:99–130.

"Latent Structure Analysis." In Sigmund Koch, ed., *Psychology: A Study of a Science*, vol. 3. New York: McGraw-Hill, 1959.

"Methodological Problems in Empirical Social Research." *Transactions of the International Congress of Sociology*. Stresa, Italy: 1959.

"Problems in Methodology." In Robert K. Merton, Leonard Broom, and Leonard S. Cottrell, Jr., eds., *Sociology Today*. New York: Basic Books, 1959.

"The Algebra of Dichotomous Systems." In Herbert Solomon, ed., *Studies in Item Analysis and Prediction*. Stanford: Stanford University Press, 1961.

"Notes on the History of Quantification in Sociology." *Isis* (1961), 52(2):277–333.

"The Sociology of Empirical Social Research." *American Sociological Review* (1962), 27:757–67.

"Concept Formation and Measurement in the Behavioral Sciences." In Gordon J. DiRenzo, ed., *Concepts, Theory, and Explanation in the Behavioral Sciences*. New York: Random House, 1966.

"Innovation in Higher Education." *Expanding Horizons of Knowledge about Man*. New York: Ferkauf School of Yeshiva University, 1966.

"An Episode in the History of Social Research: A Memoir." In Donald Fleming and Bernard Bailyn, eds., *The Intellectual Migration: Eu-*

rope and America 1930–1960. Cambridge: Harvard University Press, 1968.

"Survey Analysis." In David Sills, ed., *International Encyclopedia of the Social Sciences*. New York: Macmillan and Free Press, 1968.

"Algebra of Dichotomies." In Henry A. Selby, ed., *Notes of Lectures on Mathematics in the Behavioral Sciences*. Boston: Mathematical Association of America, 1972.

"The Policy Science Movement (An Outsider's View)." *Policy Sciences* (1975), 6:211–222.

"Some Episodes in the History of Panel Analysis." In Denise Kandel, ed., *Longitudinal Research on Drug Use: Some Empirical Findings and Methodological Issues*. New York: Halstead Press, 1978.

WORKS OF PAUL F. LAZARSFELD WITH OTHERS

With Allen H. Barton. "Qualitative Measurement in the Social Sciences." In Daniel Lerner and Harold Lasswell, eds., *The Policy Sciences*. Stanford: Stanford University Press, 1951.

With Bernard Berelson and Hazel Gaudet. *The People's Choice*. New York: Duell, Sloan and Pearce, 1944; 2d and 3d eds., New York: Columbia University Press, 1948 and 1968.

With Neil Henry. *Latent Structure Analysis*. Boston: Houghton Mifflin, 1968.

With Martin Jaeckel. "The Uses of Sociology by Presidential Commissions." In Mirra Komarovsky, ed., *Sociology and Public Policy*. New York: Elsevier, 1975.

With Patricia Kendall. "The Listener Talks Back." In *Radio and Health Education*. New York: Columbia University Press, 1945.

With Herbert Menzel. "On the Relation Between Individual and Collective Properties." In Amitai Etzioni, ed., *Complex Organizations*. New York: Holt, Rinehart and Winston, 1961.

With Robert K. Merton. "Studies in Radio and Film Propaganda." *Transactions of the New York Academy of Sciences* (1943), 6:58–79.

—— "Friendship as Social Process: A Substantive and Methodological Analysis." In Morroe Berger, Theodore Abel, and Charles H. Page, eds., *Freedom and Control in Modern Society*. New York: Van Nostrand, 1954.

With Anthony R. Oberschall. "History of Quantification in Germany." Mimeographed. New York: Bureau of Applied Social Research.

—— "Max Weber and Empirical Social Research." *American Sociological Review* (1965), 30:185–92.

With William S. Robinson. "Quantification of Case Studies." *Journal of Social Psychology* (1940), 24:831–37.

With Wagner Thielens, Jr. *The Academic Mind*. New York: Free Press, 1958.

With Rowena Wyant. "Magazines in 90 Cities: Who Reads What?" *Public Opinion Quarterly* (1937), 1:29–41.

With Morris S. Rosenberg, eds. *The Language of Social Research*. Glencoe, Ill.: Free Press, 1955.

With William H. Sewell and Harold L. Wilensky, eds. *The Uses of Sociology*. New York: Basic Books, 1967.

With Frank N. Stanton, eds. *Radio Research, 1941*. New York: Duell, Sloan and Pearce, 1941.

—— *Radio Research, 1942–43*. New York: Duell, Sloan and Pearce, 1944.

—— *Communications Research, 1948–1949*. New York: Harper and Brothers, 1949. Reprinted in 1979 by Arro Press.

SEE ALSO
Barton and Lazarsfeld
Berelson, Lazarsfeld, and McPhee
Chazel, Boudon, and Lazarsfeld
Jahoda, Lazarsfeld, and Zeisel
Katz and Lazarsfeld
Kendall and Lazarsfeld
Merton and Lazarsfeld, eds.
Stouffer and Lazarsfeld

General Bibliography

Abrams, Mark. *Social Surveys and Social Action*. London: William Heinemann, 1951.

Adler, Alfred, *The Neurotic Constitution*. New York: Dodd, Mead, 1917.

Adorno, T. W. "Zur gesellschaftlichen Lage der Musik." *Zeitschrift für Sozialforschung* (1932), 1:103ff.

—— "On Popular Music." *Studies in Philosophy and Social Science* (1941), 9:17ff.

—— "The Radio Symphony." In Paul F. Lazarsfeld and Frank N. Stanton, (eds.), *Radio Research, 1941*. New York: Duell, Sloan and Pearce, 1941.

Adorno, T. W., Else Frenkel-Brunswick, Daniel J. Levinson, and R. Nevitt Senford, with the collaboration of Betty Aron, Maria Hertz Levinson, and William Morrow. *The Authoritarian Personality*. New York: Harper, 1950.

Albert, Hans. "Der Mythos der totalen Vernunft: Dialektische Ansprüsche im Lichte undialektischen Kritik." *Kölner Zeitschrift* (1954), 16:225–56.

Allport, Gordon. "Attitudes." In Carl Murchison, ed., *Handbook of Social Psychology*. Worcester, Mass.: Clark University Press, 1935.

—— *The Use of Personal Documents in Psychological Science*. New York: Social Science Research Council, 1942.

Allport, Gordon, and H. S. Odbert. *Trait Names: A Psycholexical Study*. New York: Psychological Review, 1936.

Anderson, Bo. "Operationism and the Concept of Validity." *Acta Sociologica* (1957), 2:202ff.

Anderson, T. W. "Probability Models for Analyzing Time Changes in Attitudes." In Paul F. Lazarsfeld, ed., *Mathematical Thinking in the Social Sciences*. Glencoe, Ill.: Free Press, 1954.

Arnheim, Rudolf. "The World of the Daytime Serial." In Paul F. Lazarsfeld and Frank N. Stanton, eds., *Radio Research, 1942–43*. New York: Duel, Sloan and Pearce, 1944.

Barber, Bernard. "Participation and Mass Apathy." In Alvin Gouldner, ed., *Studies in Leadership*. New York: Harper, 1950.

Barnes, Harry E., ed., *An Introduction to the History of Sociology*. Chicago: University of Chicago Press, 1948.

Barnes, Harry E. and Howard S. Becker, eds. *Contemporary Social Theory*. New York: Appleton-Century, 1940.

Barton, Allen H. "The Concept of Property-Space in Social Research." In Paul F. Lazarsfeld and Morris Rosenberg, eds., *The Language of Social Research*. Glencoe, Ill.: Free Press, 1955.

Barton, Allen H. and Paul F. Lazarsfeld. "Some Functions of Qualitative Analysis in Social Research." *Frankfurter Beiträge zur Soziologie*, 1:321–61. Frankfurt: Europaeische Verlagsanstalt, 1955.

Becker, Howard. *Through Values to Social Interpretation*. Durham, N.C.: Duke University Press, 1950.

Benedict, Ruth. *Patterns of Culture*. Boston: Houghton Mifflin, 1934.

Bensen, Lee. "An Approach to the Scientific Study of Past Public Opinion." *Public Opinion Quarterly* (1967), 31:522–68.

Berelson, Bernard. *Content Analysis in Communications Research*. Glencoe, Ill.: Free Press, 1952.

—— "What 'Missing the Newspaper' Means." In Paul F. Lazarsfeld and Frank N. Stanton, eds., *Communications Research, 1948–1949*. New York: Harper, 1949.

Berelson, Bernard, Paul F. Lazarsfeld, and William N. McPhee. *Voting: A Study of Opinion Formation in a Presidential Campaign*. Chicago: University of Chicago Press, 1954.

Beville, H. M. "The ABCD's of Radio Audiences." *Public Opinion Quarterly* (1940), vol. 4.

Black, Max. "Definition, Presupposition, and Assertion." In Sidney Hook, ed., *American Philosophers at Work*. New York: Criterion Books, 1956.

Blau, Peter M. "Social Mobility and Interpersonal Relations." *American Sociological Review* (1956), 21:290–95.

—— "Formal Organization—Dimensions of Analysis." *American Journal of Sociology* (1957), 63:58–69.

Blumenthal, Albert. *Small Town Stuff*. Chicago: University of Chicago Press, 1932.

Blumer, Herbert. "Sociological Analysis and the 'Variable.'" *American Sociological Review* (1956), 21:683–90.

Boardman, Philip. *Patrick Geddes, Maker of the Future*. Chapel Hill: University of North Carolina Press, 1944.

Booth, Charles. *Life and Labour of the People in London*. 17 vols. London: Macmillan, 1902–1903.

————. *A Memoir*. London: Macmillan, 1918.

Borgatta, Edgar F., Leonard Cottrell, Jr., and Henry J. Meyer. "On the Dimensions of Group Behavior." *Sociometry* (1956), 19:233.

Bouglé, Célestin. *Bilan de la sociologie française contemporaine*. Paris: Felix Alcan, 1935.

Branford, S. and A. Farquharson. *An Introduction to Regional Surveys*. Westminster: Le Play House Press, 1924.

Branford, Victor, and Patrick Geddes. *The Making of the Future: The Coming Polity*. London: Williams and Norgate, 1917.

Bruner, Jerome S. *Mandate from the People*. New York: Duell, Sloan and Pearce, 1944.

Bureau, Paul. *Introduction à la méthode sociologique*. Paris: Blond & Gay, 1923.

Burgess, Ernest W., ed. *The Urban Community*. Chicago: University of Chicago Press, 1926.

Burgess, Ernest W. and Paul Wallin. "Homogamy in Social Characteristics." *American Journal of Sociology* (1943), 49:109–24.

Cantril, Hadley. *The Psychology of Social Movements*. New York: Wiley, 1941.

Cantril, Hadley, Hazel Gaudet, and Herta Herzog. *The Invasion from Mars*. Princeton: Princeton University Press, 1940.

————, ed. *Gauging Public Opinion*. Princeton: Princeton University Press, 1944.

Cattell, Raymond B. "Types of Group Structures." In Paul F. Lazarsfeld and Morris Rosenberg, eds., *The Language of Social Research*. Glencoe, Ill.: Free Press, 1955.

———— "Personal Theory Flowing from Multivariate Quantitative Research." In Sigmund Koch, ed., *Psychology*. New York: McGraw-Hill, 1956.

Centers, Richard. *Psychology of Social Classes*. Princeton: Princeton University Press, 1949.

Chazel, F., Raymond Boudon, and Paul F. Lazarsfeld, eds. *L'Analyse des processus sociaux*. The Hague: Mouton, 1970.

Clausen, John A. and Melvin L. Kohn. "The Ecological Approach in Social Psychiatry." *American Journal of Sociology* (1954), 40:140–49.

Coleman, James, Herbert Menzel, and Elihu Katz. "Social Processes in Physicians' Adoption of a New Drug." *Journal of Chronic Diseases* (1959), 9:18.

Collard, Auguste. "Goethe et Quetelet." *Isis* (1933), vol. 20.

Combe, George. *Moral Philosophy; or, The Duties of Man*. New York, 1841.

Cooper, E. and Marie Jahoda. "The Evasion of Propaganda." *Journal of Psychology* (1947), 23:15ff.

Coulborn, R., ed. *Feudalism in History*. Princeton: Princeton University Press, 1956.

Crumm, F. S. "The Statistical Work of Suessmilch." *Quarterly Publication of the American Statistical Association* (1901).

Curti, Merle. *Growth of American Thought*. New York: Harper and Row, 1943.

Cutright, Phillips and Peter H. Rossi. "Grass Roots Politicians and the Vote," *American Sociological Review* (1958), 23:171–79.

Davis, Allison, Burleigh B. Gardner, and Mary R. Gardner. *Deep South*. Chicago: University of Chicago Press, 1943.

Davis, James, Joe L. Spaeth, and Carolyn Husan. "Analyzing Effects of Group Composition." *American Sociological Review* (1961), vol. 26.

Davis, Kingsley. *Human Society*. New York: Macmillan, 1950.

DeFleur, Melvin L. and Otto N. Larsen. *The Flow of Information*. New York: Harper, 1958.

Denifle, Heinrich. *Die Entstehung der mittelalterlichen Universität*. Berlin: Weidmann. 1885.

D'Irsay, Stephen. *Histoire des universités*. Paris: Auguste Picard, 1933.

Drobisch, Moritz Wilhelm. *Die moralische Statistik und die menschliche Willensfreiheit*. Leipzig: Leopold Voss, 1867.

Duncan, Otis Dudley and Beverly Davis. "An Alternate to Ecological Correlation." *American Sociological Review* (1953), 18:665–66.

Durkheim, Emile. *Suicide*. Glencoe, Ill.: Free Press, 1951.

Eliot, Thomas D., Arthur Hillman, et al. *Norway's Families*. Philadelphia: University of Pennsylvania Press, 1960.

Felberg, Paul. *Hermann Conrings Anteil am politischen Leben seiner Zeit*. Trier: Paulinus, 1931.

Festinger, Leon. "Informal Social Communication." *Psychological Review* (1950), 57:271–82.

Festinger, Leon, Stanley Schachter, and Kurt Back. "The Operation of Group Standards." In Paul F. Lazarsfeld and Morris Rosenberg, eds., *The Language of Social Research*. Glencoe, Ill.: Free Press, 1955.

—— "Matrix Analysis of Group Structures." In Paul F. Lazarsfeld and Morris Rosenberg, eds., *The Language of Social Research*. Glencoe, Ill.: Free Press, 1955.

Festinger, Leon and Alvin Zander. *Group Dynamics*. New York: Row-Peterson, 1952.

Frazier, E. Franklin. *The Negro Family in the United States*. Chicago: University of Chicago Press, 1939.

Freeman, Linton C. and Robert F. Winch. "Societal Complexity: An Empirical Test of a Typology of Societies." *American Journal of Sociology* (1957), 62:461–66.

Freud, Sigmund. *An Autobiographical Study*. London: Hogarth Press, 1935.

Fromm, Erich. *Escape from Freedom*. New York: Farrar & Rinehart, 1941.

Gans, Herbert. "Urban Poverty and Social Planning." In Paul F. Lazarsfeld, William H. Sewell, and Harold L. Wilensky, eds., *The Uses of Sociology*. New York: Basic Books, 1967.

Garigue, Philippe. *Etudes sur le Canada français*. Montreal: Université de Montreal, 1958.

Gérin, Léon. *Le type économique et social des Canadiens*. Montreal: Éditions de l'A.C.-F., 1938.

Gerschenkron, Alexander. "A Neglected Source of Economic Information on Soviet Russia." *American Slavic and East European Review* (1950), vol. 9.

Glazer, Nathan. "The Rise of Social Research in Europe." In Daniel Lerner, ed., *The Human Meaning of the Social Sciences*. New York: Meridian Books, 1959.

Glock, Charles Y., ed. *Survey Research in the Social Sciences*. New York: Russell Sage Foundation, 1967.

Goodman, Leo A. "Ecological Regressions and Behavior of Individuals." *American Sociological Review* (1953), 18:663–64.

Gosnell, Harold F. *Getting Out the Vote*. Chicago: University of Chicago Press, 1927.

Gottschalk, Louis, Clyde Kluckhohn, and Robert Angell. *The Use of Personal Documents in History, Anthropology, and Sociology*. New York: Social Science Research Council, 1945.

Gouldner, Alvin W., ed. *Studies in Leadership*. New York: Harper, 1950.

Gross, Neal and W. E. Martin. "On Group Cohesiveness." *American Journal of Sociology* (1952), 57:546–64.

Guhrauer, G. C. *Gottfried Wilhelm Freiherr v. Leibnitz*. Breslau: Ferdinand Hirt, 1846.

Habermas, Jürgen. "Gegen einen positivistischen halbierten Rationalismus." *Kölner Zeitschrift* (1964), 16:635–59.

Hagood, Margaret J. and Daniel O. Price. *Statistics for Sociologists*. Rev. ed. New York: Holt, 1952.

Halbwachs, Maurice. *La théorie de l'homme moyen*. Paris: Felix Alcan, 1912.

Hammond, Philip. "The Imagery of Durkheim's Concept of Integration in Suicide." Mimeographed. New York: Columbia University Project on Advanced Training in Social Research.

Hankins, Frank. *Adolphe Quetelet as Statistician*. New York: Columbia University Press, 1908.

Hempel, Carl, *Science, Language, and Human Rights*. Philadelphia: University of Pennsylvania Press, 1952.

Hempel, Carl and Paul Oppenheim. *Der Typusbegriff im Lichte der neuen Logik*. Leiden: A. W. Sijthoff, 1936.

Hemphill, John K. and Charles M. Westie. "The Measurement of Group Dimensions." In Paul F. Lazarsfeld and Morris Rosenberg, eds., *The Language of Social Research*. Glencoe, Ill.: Free Press, 1955.

Herzog, Herta. "Stimme und Persönlichkeit." *Zeitschrift für Psychologie* (1933), vol. 130.

—— "On Borrowed Experience." *Studies in Philosophy and Social Science* (1941), 9:65–95.

—— "Training Guide on the Technique of Qualitative Interviews." Mimeographed. New York: Bureau of Applied Social Research, 1948.

Hildebrand, Bruno. *Jahrbücher für Nationalökonomie und Statistik*. Jena: Friedrich Mauke, 1871.

Hirschi, Travis and Hanan Selvin. *Delinquency Research: An Appraisal of Analytic Methods*. New York: Free Press, 1967.

Holloquist, Tore and Edward Suchman. "Listening to the Listener." In Paul F. Lazarsfeld and Frank N. Stanton, eds. *Radio Research, 1942–43*. New York: Duell, Sloan and Pearce, 1944.

Homans, George C. *The Human Group*. New York: Harcourt, Brace, 1950.

Horkheimer, Max. "Traditional and Critical Theory." *Zeitschrift für Sozialforschung* (1937), 6:245–95.

—— "Philosophy and Critical Theory." *Zeitschrift für Sozialforschung* (1937), 6:625–31.

Horkheimer, Max et al. *Autorität und Familie*. Paris: Felix Alcan, 1936.

Horwitz, Hortense and Elias Smith. "The Interchangeability of Indices." In Paul F. Lazarsfeld and Morris Rosenberg, eds., *The Language of Social Research*. Glencoe, Ill.: Free Press, 1955.

Hughes, Everett C. *French Canada in Transition*. Chicago: University of Chicago Press, 1943.

Huizinga, Johann. *Men and Ideas*. New York: Meridian Books, 1959.
Jahoda, Marie, Paul Lazarsfeld, and Hans Zeisel. *Die Arbeitslosen von Marienthal*. Leipzig: S. Hirzel, 1933; 2d ed., Allensbach and Bonn: Verlag für Demoskopie, 1960. English ed., *Marienthal*. Chicago: Aldine-Atherton, 1971.
Jahoda, Marie, Morton Deutsch, and Stuart W. Cook. *Research Methods in Social Relations*. New York: Dryden Press, 1951.
Jenkins, John G. *Psychology in Business and Industry*. New York: Wiley, 1935.
Jogland, Herta. *Ursprünge und Grundlagen der Soziologie bei Adam Ferguson*. Berlin: Dunker & Humbolt, 1959.
John, Victor. *Geschichte der Statistik*. Stuttgart: Ferdinand Enke, 1884.
Jones, Ernest. *Sigmund Freud: Life and Work*. London: Hogarth Press, 1953.
Kadushin, Charles. "Reason Analysis." In David Sills, ed., *International Encyclopedia of the Social Sciences*. New York: Macmillan and Free Press, 1968.
Kahl, Joseph and James A. Davis. "A Comparison of Indices of Socio-Economic Status." *American Sociological Review* (1955), 20:317–25.
Kaplan, Abraham. "Definition and Specification of Meaning." In Paul F. Lazarsfeld and Morris Rosenberg, eds., *The Language of Social Research*. Glencoe, Ill.: Free Press, 1955.
Katz, Elihu and Paul F. Lazarsfeld. *Personal Influence*. Glencoe, Ill.: Free Press, 1955.
Kendall, Patricia L. "Qualitative Indicators in Field Work." Mimeographed. New York: Bureau of Applied Social Research.
Kendall, Patricia L. and Paul F. Lazarsfeld. "Problems of Survey Analysis." In Robert K. Merton and Paul F. Lazarsfeld, eds., *Continuities in Social Research*. Glencoe, Ill.: Free Press, 1950.
Kendall, Patricia L. and Katherine M. Wolfe. "The Analysis of Deviant Cases in Communications Research." In Paul F. Lazarsfeld and Frank N. Stanton, eds., *Communications Research, 1948–1949*. New York: Harper, 1949.
Kerr, Clark and Abraham Siegel. "The Interindustry Propensity to Strike—An International Comparison." In Arthur Kornhauser, Robert Dubin, and A. M. Ross, eds., *Industrial Conflict*. New York: McGraw-Hill, 1954.
Klapper, Joseph. *The Effects of Mass Communication*. Glencoe, Ill.: Free Press, 1960.
Knupfer, Genevieve. "The Measurement of Socio-Economic Status." Ph.D. dissertation, Columbia University, 1944.

—— "Portrait of the Underdog." *Public Opinion Quarterly* (1947), 11:103–14.

Koch, Sigmund, ed. *Psychology: A Study of a Science.* New York: McGraw-Hill, 1959.

Komarovsky, Mirra. *The Unemployed Man and His Family.* New York: Social Studies Association, 1940; reprinted in 1971 by Octagon Books.

Kopf, E. W. "Florence Nightingale as a Statistician." *Journal of the American Statistical Association* (December 1916).

Landecker, Werner S. "Types of Integration and Their Measurement." *American Journal of Sociology* (1951), vol. 56.

Laqueur, Walter. *Young Germany: A History of the German Youth Movement.* London: Routledge & Paul, 1962; New York: Basic Books, 1962.

Lasswell, Harold. *Analysis of Political Behavior.* Toronto: Oxford University Press, 1948.

—— "The Garrison State and Specialists on Violence," *American Journal of Sociology* (1941), vol. 46.

Lasswell, Harold D. and Abraham Kaplan. *Power and Society.* New Haven: Yale University Press, 1950.

Lazarsfeld, Sofie, ed. *Technik der Erziehung.* Leipzig: S. Hirzal, 1929.

Le Play, Frédéric. *Les ouvriers européens.* 6 vols. Tours: Alfred Mame, 1879.

—— "Instruction in the Observation of Social Facts According to the Le Play Method of Monographs on Families." Charles A. Ellwood, tr. *American Journal of Sociology* (1896–97), vol. 2.

Le Play. Louis Baudin, ed., Collection des Grands Économistes Series, Paris: Dalloz, 1947.

Lerner, Daniel. "'The American Soldier' and the Public." In Robert K. Merton and Paul F. Lazarsfeld, eds., *Continuities in Social Research* (Glencoe, Ill.: Free Press, 1950.

——, ed. *The Human Meaning of the Social Sciences.* New York: Meridian Books, 1959.

Lerner, Daniel and Harold Lasswell, eds. *The Policy Sciences.* Stanford: Stanford University Press, 1951.

Lewin, Kurt. "Forces Behind Food Habits and Methods of Change." *The Problem of Changing Food Habits.* Bulletin of the National Research Council, no. 108. 1943.

Lindzey, Gardner, "Thematic Apperception Test: Interpretive Assumptions and Related Empirical Evidence." *Psychological Bulletin* (1952), vol. 49.

Link, Henry C. *The New Psychology of Selling and Advertising*. New York: Macmillan, 1932.

—— "An Experiment in Depth Interviewing," *Public Opinion Quarterly* (1943), 7:267–79.

Linton, Ralph. *The Study of Man*. New York: Appleton, 1936.

Lipset, Seymour M. *Agrarian Socialism: The Cooperative Commonwealth Federation in Saskatchewan*. Berkeley: University of California Press, 1950.

Lipset, Seymour M. et al. "The Psychology of Voting: An Analysis of Political Behavior." In Gardner Lindzey, ed., *Handbook of Social Psychology*. Cambridge: Addison-Wesley, 1954.

Lipset, Seymour M., Martin Trow, and James Coleman. *Union Democracy: The Inside Politics of the International Typographical Union*. Glencoe, Ill.: Free Press, 1956.

Lottin, Joseph. *Quetelet, statisticien et sociologue*. Louvain: Bibl. de L'Inst. Sup. de Philosophie, 1912.

Lowenthal, Leo. "An Historical Preface to the Popular Culture Debate." In Norman Jacobs, ed., *Culture for the Millions*. Princeton: Princeton University Press, 1959.

Lundberg, George A. "Statistics in Modern Social Thought." In Harry E. Barnes and Howard S. Becker, eds., *Contemporary Social Theory* (New York: Appleton-Century, 1940.

Lynd, Helen Merrill. *England in the Eighteen-Eighties*. Toronto: Oxford University Press, 1945.

Lynd, Robert S. and Helen M. Lynd. *Middletown*. New York: Harcourt, Brace, 1929.

MacDougald, Duncan. "The Popular Music Industry." In Paul F. Lazarsfeld and Frank N. Stanton, eds., *Radio Research, 1941*. New York: Duell, Sloan and Pearce, 1941.

McClelland, David C. and G. A. Friedman. "A Cross-Cultural Study of the Relationship Between Child Training Practices and Achievement Motivation Appearing in Folk Tales." In Guy E. Swanson, Theodore M. Newcomb, and Eugene L. Hartley, eds., *Readings in Social Psychology*. New York: Holt, Rinehart & Winston, 1952.

McGranahan, Donald V. and Ivor Wayne. "German and American Traits Reflected in Popular Drama." *Human Relations* (1948), 1:429ff.

McGregor, O. R., "Social Research and Social Policy in the Nineteenth Century. *The British Journal of Sociology* (1957), vol. 8.

MacIver, Robert M. *Society*. New York: Rinehart, 1937.

—— *Social Causation*. Boston: Ginn, 1942.

—— *Discrimination and National Welfare.* New York: Harper, 1949.

—— *Academic Freedom in the United States.* New York: Columbia University Press, 1954.

MacIver, Robert M. and Charles H. Page. *Society: An Introductory Analysis.* New York: Rinehart, 1949.

McKinney, John C. "Procedures and Techniques in Sociology." In Howard Becker and Alvin Boskoff, eds., *Modern Sociological Theory in Continuity and Change.* New York: Dryden Press, 1957.

MacRae, Duncan, Jr. "Occupations and the Congressional Vote, 1940–1950." *American Sociological Review* (1955), 20:332–40.

Malinowski, Bronislaw. *Sexual Life of Savages.* New York: Harcourt, Brace, 1929.

—— "The Group and the Individual in Functional Analysis." *American Journal of Sociology* (1939), 44:938ff.

—— *Magic, Science, and Religion and Other Essays.* Boston: Beacon Press, 1948.

March, James G. "Influence Measurement in Experimental and Semi-Experimental Groups." *Sociometry* (1956), 19:260–71.

Marsh, C. Paul and A. Lee Coleman. "Group Influences and Agricultural Innovations: Some Tentative Findings and Hypotheses." *American Journal of Sociology* (1956), 61:588–94.

Mead, Margaret. "Adolescence in Primitive and in Modern Society." In Theodore Newcomb and Eugene L. Hartley, eds., *Readings in Social Psychology* New York: Holt, 1947.

Meehl, Paul E. *Clinical versus Statistical Prediction.* Minneapolis: University of Minnesota Press, 1954.

Meitzen, August. *History, Theory, and Technique of Statistics.* Philadelphia: American Academy of Political and Social Science, 1891.

Menzel, Herbert. "Comment." *American Sociological Review* (1950), 15:674.

—— "Specification of Dimensions in Concept Formation." Mimeographed. New York: Columbia University Project on Advanced Training in Social Research.

Menzel, Herbert and Elihu Katz. "Social Relations and Innovation in the Medical Profession: The Epidemiology of a New Drug." *Public Opinion Quarterly* (1956), 19:337–52.

Merton, Robert K. "Recent French Sociology." *Social Forces* (1934), 12:537–45.

—— *Social Theory and Social Structure.* Glencoe, Ill.: Free Press, 1949; 2d ed., 1957; 3d ed., 1968.

—— *Science, Technology, and Society in Seventeenth-Century England.* Bruges, Belgium: St. Catherine Press, 1938.

—— "Discrimination and the American Creed." In Robert M.

MacIver, *Discrimination and National Welfare*. New York: Harper, 1949.

—— "Patterns of Influence." In Paul F. Lazarsfeld and Frank N. Stanton, eds., *Communications Research, 1948–1949*. New York: Harper, 1949.

—— "A Paradigm for the Study of the Sociology of Knowledge." In Paul F. Lazarsfeld and Morris Rosenberg, eds., *The Language of Social Research*. Glencoe, Ill.: Free Press, 1955.

Merton, Robert K., Marjorie Fiske, and Alberta Curtis. *Mass Persuasion*. New York: Harper, 1946.

Merton, Robert K., Marjorie Fiske, and Patricia L. Kendall. *The Focused Interview*. Glencoe, Ill.: Free Press, 1956.

Merton, Robert K. and Patricia L. Kendall. "The Boomerang Response." *Channels* (1944), vol. 21.

—— "The Focused Interview." *American Journal of Sociology* (1946), 51:541–57.

Merton, Robert K. and Alice S. Kitt. "Contributions to the Theory of Reference Group Behavior." In Robert K. Merton and Paul F. Lazarsfeld, eds., *Continuities in Social Research*. Glencoe, Ill.: Free Press, 1950.

Merton, Robert K., Patricia S. West, and Marie Jahoda. *Patterns of Social Life: Explorations in the Sociology and Social Psychology of Housing*. New York: Columbia Bureau of Applied Social Research, 1948.

Merton, Robert K., Leonard Broom, and Leonard S. Cottrell, Jr., eds. *Sociology Today*. New York: Basic Books, 1959.

Merton, Robert K. and Paul F. Lazarsfeld, eds. *Continuities in Social Research*. Glencoe, Ill.: Free Press, 1950.

Metraux, Rhoda. "Qualitative Attitude Analysis—A Technique for the Study of Verbal Behavior." *The Problem of Changing Food Habits*. Bulletin of the National Research Council, no. 108. 1943.

Mills, C. Wright. *White Collar*. New York: Oxford University Press, 1951.

Miner, Horace. "The Folk-Urban Continuum." In Paul F. Lazarsfeld and Morris Rosenberg, eds., *The Language of Social Research* (Glencoe, Ill.: Free Press, 1955.

Moeller, Ernst V. *Hermann Conring*. Hanover: Ernst Geibel, 1915.

Moore, Barrington. *Soviet Politics: The Dilemma of Power*. Cambridge: Harvard University Press, 1950.

Mosteller, Frederick. "Effect of Education and Economic Status on Attitudes." In Hadley Cantril, ed., *Gauging Public Opinion*. Princeton: Princeton University Press, 1944.

Mumford, Lewis. "Patrick Geddes, Victor Branford, and Applied Sociology in England: The Social Survey, Regionalism, and Urban Planning." In Harry E. Barnes, ed., *An Introduction to the History of Sociology*. Chicago: University of Chicago Press, 1948.

Murchison, Carl, ed. *Handbook of Social Psychology*. Worcester, Mass.: Clark University Press, 1935.

Nagel, Ernest. "A Formalization of Functionalism." In *Logic Without Metaphysics*. Glencoe, Ill.: Free Press, 1956.

—— *The Structure of Science*. New York: Harcourt, Brace & World, 1961.

National Opinion Research Center. "Cincinnati Looks Again," Report No. 37a. Denver: University of Denver, 1948.

Newcomb, Theodore. *Personality and Social Change*. New York: Dryden Press, 1942.

Newcomb, Theodore and Eugene L. Hartley, eds. *Readings in Social Psychology*. New York: Holt, 1947.

Niceforo, Alfredo. *La misura della vita*. Turin: Fratelli Bocca, 1919.

—— *Les indices numériques de la civilization et du progrès*. Paris: Ernst Flammarion, 1921.

Paesche, H., ed. *Festgabe für Johannes Conrad*. Jena: Gustav Fischer, 1898.

Park, Robert E. and Ernest W. Burgess. *Introduction to the Science of Sociology*. Chicago: University of Chicago Press, 1921.

Parsons, Talcott. *The Social System*. Glencoe, Ill.: Free Press, 1951.

—— *The Structure of Social Action*. New York: McGraw-Hill, 1937.

Parsons, Talcott and Edward A. Shils. *Toward a General Theory of Action*. Cambridge: Harvard University Press, 1951.

Paulsen, Friedrich. *Geschichte des gelehrten Unterrichts*. Leipzig: Veit, 1919.

Peirce, Charles S. *Pragmatism and Pragmaticism*, vol. 5, *Collected Papers*. Cambridge: Harvard University Press, 1934.

Pelz, Donald C. "Some Social Factors Related to Performance in a Research Organization." *Administrative Science Quarterly* (1956), 1:310–25.

Piaget, Jean. *The Moral Judgment of the Child*. New York: Harcourt, Brace, 1932.

Poffenberger, A. T. *Psychology of Advertising*. New York: McGraw-Hill, 1932.

Polanyi, Karl. *Origins of Our Time: The Great Transformation*. Toronto: Oxford University Press, 1944.

Quetelet, Adolphe. *Physique sociale*. Brussels: C. Muquardt, 1869.

Redfield, Robert. *The Folk Culture of Yucatan*. Chicago: University of Chicago Press, 1941; Cambridge: Cambridge University Press, 1941.

Reilly, W. J. *Marketing Investigation*. New York: Ronald Press, 1929.

Reuss, Alfons. *Frédéric Le Play in seiner Bedeutung für die Entwicklung der sozialwissenschaftlichen Methode*. Jena: Gustav Fischer, 1913.

Riesman, David, Nathan Glazer, and Ruel Denney. *The Lonely Crowd*. New Haven: Yale University Press, 1950.

Riesman, David and Nathan Glazer. "Criteria for Political Apathy." In Alvin W. Gouldner, ed., *Studies in Leadership*. New York: Harper, 1950.

Riley, John et al. *Sociological Studies in Scale Analysis*. New Brunswick, N.J.: Rutgers University Press, 1954.

Robinson, William S. "Ecological Correlations and the Behavior of Individuals." *American Sociological Review* (1950), 15:351–57.

Roethlisberger, F. J. and William J. Dickson. *Management and the Worker*. Cambridge: Harvard University Press, 1939.

Rommetveit, Ragnar. *Social Norms and Roles*. Minneapolis: University of Minnesota Press, 1955.

Root, A. R. and A. C. Welch. "The Continuing Consumer Study: A Basic Method for the Engineering of Advertising." *Journal of Marketing* (1942), vol. 7.

Rosenberg, George. *The Worker Grows Old*. San Francisco: Jossey-Bass, 1970.

Rosenberg, Morris. *The Logic of Survey Analysis*. New York: Basic Books, 1968.

Rosenmayr, Leopold. *Geschichte der Jugendforschung in Oesterreich, 1914–1931*. Vienna: Oesterreichisches Institut für Jugendkunde, 1962.

de Rousier, Paul. "La science sociale." In *Annals of the American Academy of Political and Social Sciences* (1894).

Sarton, George. "Preface to Vol. 23 of *Isis* (Quetelet)." *Isis*. (1935), 65:6–24.

Schachter, Stanley. "Comment." *American Journal of Sociology* (1952), vol. 57.

Scheler, Max. *Die Wissensformen und die Gesellschaft*. Leipzig: Neuer-Geist, 1926.

Sears, Robert R. "Experimental Studies of Projection." *Journal of Social Psychology* (1936), 7:151–63.

Sherif, Mutzafer. *An Outline of Social Psychology*. New York: Harper, 1948.

Simey, T. S. and M. B. Simey. *Charles Booth, Social Scientist.* London: Oxford University Press, 1960.

Simmel, Georg. "The Sociology of Conflict." *American Journal of Sociology* (1904), 9:521ff.

—— *The Sociology of Georg Simmel.* Kurt H. Wolff, tr. and ed. Glencoe, Ill.: Free Press, 1950.

Simon, Herbert. *Models of Man.* New York: Wiley, 1957.

Skott, Hans E. "Attitude Research in the Department of Agriculture." *Public Opinion Quarterly* (1943), 7:280–92.

Smith, Elias and Edward Suchman. "Do People Know Why They Buy?" *Journal of Applied Psychology* (1940), 24:673–84.

Sorokin, Pitirim. *Contemporary Sociological Theories.* New York: Harper, 1928.

—— *Society, Culture, and Personality.* New York: Harper, 1947.

—— *Fads and Foibles in Modern Sociology.* Chicago: Regnery, 1956.

Spranger, Eduard. *Types of Man.* Halle: M. Niemeyer, 1928; New York: Stechert, 1928.

Stephan, Frederic. "History of the Uses of Modern Sampling Procedures." *Journal of the American Statistical Association* (March 1948).

Stoetzel, Jean. In Howard Becker and Alvin Boskoff, eds., *Modern Sociological Theory in Continuity and Change.* New York: Dryden Press, 1957.

Stouffer, Samuel. *Social Research to Test Ideas.* New York: Free Press, 1962.

Stouffer, Samuel et al. *The American Soldier.* 4 vols. Princeton: Princeton University Press, 1949.

Stouffer, Samuel and Paul Lazarsfeld. *Research Memorandum on the Family in the Depression.* New York: Social Science Research Council, 1937; reprinted by the Arno Press, 1972.

Strauss, E. *Sir William Petty.* Glencoe Ill.: Free Press, 1954.

Studenski, Paul. "How Polls Can Mislead." *Harpers Magazine* (December 1939).

Sturmthal, Adolf and Alberta Curtis. "Program Analyzer Tests of Two Educational Films." In Paul F. Lazarsfeld and Frank N. Stanton, eds., *Radio Research, 1942–43.* New York: Duell, Sloan and Pearce, 1944.

Suchman, Edward. "Invitation to Music." In Paul F. Lazarsfeld and Frank N. Stanton, eds., *Radio Research, 1941.* New York: Duell, Sloan and Pearce, 1941.

Sutherland, Edwin H. *The Professional Thief.* Chicago: University of Chicago Press, 1937.

—— "White-Collar Criminality." *American Sociological Review* (1940), 5:1ff.

—— *White Collar Crime*. New York: Dryden Press, 1949.

Symonds, P. and W. Samuel. "Projective Methods in the Study of Personality," *Review of Educational Research* (1941), 11:80–93.

Tarde, Gabriel. *Lois de l'imitation*. 5th ed. Paris: F. Alcan, 1907.

Thurstone, L. L. "Attitudes Can Be Measured." *American Journal of Sociology* (1928).

Tocqueville, Alexis de. *De la démocratie en Amérique*. Brussels: L. Hauman, 1835.

Toennies, Ferdinand. *Gemeinschaft und Gesellschaft*. Leipzig, 1887.

Toennies, Ferdinand et al. *Sektion Soziographie, siebenter duetscher Soziologentag*. Tübingen: Mohr, 1931.

Toynbee, Arnold. *A Study of History*. Abridged edition by D. C. Somerville. New York: Oxford University Press, 1947.

Trevor-Roper, Patrick Dacre. "The General Crisis of the Seventeenth Century." In *Past and Present* (1959), vol. 16.

Tyron, Robert. "Identification of Social Areas by Cluster Analysis." *University of California Publications in Psychology* (1955), vol. 8.

Veblen, Thorstein. *The Theory of the Leisure Class*. New York: Modern Library, 1934.

Vernon, P. E. and G. W. Allport. "A Test for Personal Values." *Journal of Abnormal and Social Psychology* (1931), 26:231ff.

Vidich, Arthur, Joseph Bensman, and Maurice Stein, eds. *Reflections on Community Studies*. New York: Wiley, 1964.

Von Wiese, Leopold and Howard Becker. *Systematic Sociology*. New York: Wiley, 1932.

Walker, Helen. *Studies in the History of Statistical Methods*. Baltimore: Williams & Wilkins, 1929.

Wallas, Graham. *Human Nature in Politics*. New York: Knopf, 1921.

Waller, Willard. *The Family*. New York: Cordon, 1938.

Wallin, Paul. In Paul Horst, ed., *Case Study Methods in the Prediction of Personal Adjustment*. New York: Social Science Research Council, 1941.

Weber, Max. *Gesammelte Aufsätze zur Religionssoziologie*. 3 vols. Tübingen: Mohr, 1920–21.

—— *The Protestant Ethic and the Spirit of Capitalism*. Talcott Parsons, tr. New York: Scribners, 1930.

Wecter, Dixon. *Age of the Great Depression, 1929–1941*. New York: Macmillan, 1948.

Westergaard, Harald. *Contributions to the History of Statistics*. London: P. S. King, 1932.

White, Percival. *Market Analysis*. New York: McGraw-Hill, 1921.

Whyte, William F. *Street Corner Society*. Chicago: University of Chicago Press, 1943; 2nd ed., 1956.

Wirth, Louis. "Some Jewish Types of Personality." In Ernest W. Burgess, ed., *The Urban Community*. Chicago: University of Chicago Press, 1926.

Wolfe, Katherine M. and Marjorie Fiske. "The Children Talk About Comics." In Paul F. Lazarsfeld and Frank N. Stanton, eds., *Communications Research, 1948–1949*. New York: Harper, 1949.

Wyant, Rowena and Herta Herzog. "Voting Via the Senate Mailbag." *Public Opinion Quarterly* (1941), 5:590–624.

Zehrfeld, Reinold. "Hermann Conring's Staatenkunde." *Sozialwissenschaftliche Forschungen* (1925), 5:79ff.

Zeisel, Hans. *Say It with Figures*. New York: Harper, 1946.

Zerner, Elizabeth, with Robert T. Bower. "German Occupation and Anti-Semitism in France." *Public Opinion Quarterly* (1948), 11:258ff.

Zetterberg, Hans L. "Compliant Action," *Acta Sociological* (1957), 2:179ff.

Zimmerman, Carl and Merle E. Framptom, *Family and Society*. New York: Van Nostrand, 1935.

Zizek, Franz. *Soziologie und Statistik*. Leipzig: Duncker & Humbolt, 1912.

Name Index

Subject Index

Algebra of dichotomies, xii, 350n11

American Association for Public Opinion Research, 51, 74, 92

American Sociological Association, 29, 197, 353n16, 354n27, 357n42

American Soldier, The, 81, 89, 95, 249, 371n10, 377n23, 379n29

Analysis of chains, 265–66, 326–27, 334, 339; as an explanatory process, 265–66

Applied sociology, xii

Booth tradition: British social survey, 166; measurement of poverty, 154

Collectives, x, 197–98, 203, 225–36, 376n15

Collectives traits of, 229–32, 372n20; analytical, 189, 229–31, 375n5, 376nn6, 15, 377n25; global, 189, 229–31, 235, 376nn6, 15, 377n25; structural, 189, 229–31, 233, 375n5, 377nn18, 25

Concepts, 176–77, 179, 190, 382n10; classificatory, 177–79, 181–84, 188–89; formation of, x, 178, 373n48; originating observation, 179, 186–87, 189–90, 373n27

Conring school and system, 115–18, 165–66

Content analysis, 49

Controlled experiment, 215, 240, 261, 270, 279

Deviant cases, 263, 378n23, 380nn59, 62

Deviant individuals, 269

Dispositions, 137, 173, 177, 220, 295–96

Durkheim school, 129, 131

Elaboration paradigm, x, 209–24, 330–33; causal relations, 2, 224, 266; conditional relations, x, 188–89, 202; interpretation, 2, 12, 222, 295–96, 341, 381n10; partial associations, 210–11, 213–16, 221–22, 385n31; specification, 220–21, 386n34; spurious relations, 2, 221, 266; test factors, 209–13, 216; time order among variables, 217–19

Empirical study of action, 4, 7, 21, 54, 353n16

Explication of research techniques, x, 14, 29, 173–75, 177

Federal Communications Commission, 52–53

Folk-urban continuum, 204–5, 207

Formalization: propositional theories, 175; systematic inventory, 175–76

Frankfurt Institute for Social Research, 28, 49, 58, 60, 351n7; *The Authoritarian Personality*, 180, 184–86, 196, 372n27; the F-scale, 61, 180, 185, 372–73n27

Functionalism, 104, 138, 342, 345–47, 378n2, 379n47

Graduate Faculty of Political Science, Columbia University, 68; Cheatham Committee, 68–69

Group, 185, 187–88, 196, 373nn28, 36, 38

Group dynamics, 187–88, 196

Heterophily, 303, 306–7, 313–14, 345, 382n10, 387n44

Homophily, 303, 306–7, 325–26, 329–30, 334, 344–45, 348, 382n10, 387n44; appropriate degree of, 307–8, 345–47;

Properties of members, x, 177–78;
absolute, 232–33, 235–36, 376*n*15;
comparative, 233–34, 377*nn*18, 20;
contextual, 200–1, 234, 374*n*54;
relational, 233
Psychological Corporation (P.S.C.),
33–34, 355*n*33
Psychological Institute (University of
Vienna), 15, 19–20, 26, 31–33, 38,
354*n*22

Qualitative analysis, xi, 239–85;
functions of qualitative data, xi; matrix
formula, 240, 274–79, 284; qualitative
classifications, 251–5, 279; qualitative
indicators, 242, 246–50, 381*n*88;
support of theory, 240, 279–85;
systematic analysis, 240, 270–74;
systematic typologies, attribute space,
251, 255–58, 260–61
Quantification, 97–167, 176; causal
relations, 108; history of quantification
in the social sciences, 119, 162,
371*n*119; Le Play's technique, 159–66
Quasi-statistics, 267–70; quasi-
distributions, 268; Quasi-experimental
data, 268, 273

Reason analysis, 5, 266, 353*n*15; reason
questions, 266; discerning, 266
Rockefeller Foundation, 16, 29, 31,
39–40, 42, 52, 56, 64, 352*n*10

Sampling, 167, 173, 239, 268–69, 271, 280
Scales, 173, 239, Guttman, 174
Sequences rules, 321–24, 326, 328–29,
331–34, 339–42, 386*n*37
Socialist Student Movement, 13, 25;
Young Socialist Workers Movement,
23
Social-psychological processes, 300,
304–5, 309, 314, 317, 321, 329, 334,
338, 342, 344–45, 347, 387*n*42
Social Science Research Council, 12
Social stratification, 17, 47, 271–73, 290,
370*n*113, 375*n*1; effective scope, 17;
occupational choice, 15, 19; proletarian
youth, 17
"Statistique Morale," 119–40; life cycle,
121; multivariate tabulations, 121
Survey research, 1, 5, 22, 94–95, 239,
270, 357*n*50, 371*n*118; market research,
1, 2; secondary analysis, 47, 62, 70,
254, 270–71

University of Newark, viii, 16, 26–27, 29
University statistics, 105–6, 108–17, 165,
363*n*41
Uses of social research, 1

Variates, 176–97, 199–200, 203;
generalized variates, 184–85; traits,
177, 180–81, 183, 188–89, 205